A Reader for Developing Writers

A Reader for Developing Writers

Santi V. Buscemi

Middlesex County College

McGraw-Hill Publishing Company
New York St. Louis San Francisco Auckland Bogotá
Caracas Hamburg Lisbon London Madrid Mexico
Milan Montreal New Delhi Oklahoma City Paris
San Juan São Paulo Singapore Sydney Tokyo Toronto

This book was set in Plantin by the College Composition Unit
in cooperation with General Graphic Services, Inc.
The editors were Emiiy Barrosse, Susan D. Hurtt, Lesley Denton,
and Bernadette Boylan; the production supervisor was Louise Karam.
The cover was designed by Fern Logan.
R. R. Donnelley & Sons Company was printer and binder.

A READER FOR DEVELOPING WRITERS

2 3 4 5 6 7 8 9 0 D O C D O C   9 4 3 2 1 0

ISBN 0-07-009312-1

Library of Congress Cataloging-in-Publication Data
Buscemi, Santi.
   A reader for developing writers/Santi Buscemi.
     p.   cm.
   Includes index.
   ISBN 0-07-009312-1
   1. College readers.   2. English language—Rhetoric.   I. Title.
PE1417.B855 1990
808'.0427—dc19   89-2387

For Joseph and Theresa Buscemi
and for all the other Sicilian heroes
who came to this country to make a better
life for their children

ABOUT THE AUTHOR

Santi V. Buscemi chairs the English Department
and teaches reading and writing at
Middlesex County College in Edison, NJ.

Contents

Preface

Research in the teaching of composition has long pointed to the clear and obvious connection between reading and writing skills, and many composition theorists argue that no basic-skills program in English makes sense without the integration of these skills in classroom instruction. More and more teachers of developmental writing see the need to increase the emphasis on effective reading in order to reinforce the teaching of basic rhetorical principles important to the student's development as a writer, to provide sources of inspiration for the student's own writing, and, in general, to improve the student's perception and appreciation of language.

The primary purpose of *A Reader for Developing Writers* is to encourage students to read carefully, to react to what they have read, and, most important, to use these reactions as creative springboards for their own writing. Each selection in this text has been chosen with an eye toward motivating students to use their own experiences and opinions as sources of information and insight through which to explore and to write about topics inspired by if not drawn directly from the reading.

A secondary purpose of the text is to provide developmental students access to reading materials that will help them begin to appreciate the kind, variety, and sophistication of written discourse they will encounter in college. As such, I have tried to make the text eclectic by offering both student and professional writing, by including poetry and fiction as well as the essay, and by drawing upon a variety of academic disciplines to reflect a wide range of social, political, economic, and scientific concerns. Finally, while I have limited the table of contents to selections that are appropriate to the reading abilities of developmental students, I have not hesitated to include pieces that may require some healthy intellectual stretching. Nevertheless, the text is replete with easy-to-follow aids designed to foster comprehension.

Behind the design of *A Reader for Developing Writers* is a belief—cultivated during twenty years as a teacher of composition—that there should be a natural and clear connection between what students are asked to read and what they are asked to write, especially in developmental writing classes. That is not to say that reading selections should serve as models for the students' own writing. However, they should illustrate important, albeit basic rhetorical principles and techniques clearly and emphatically. More important, they should inspire students to use writing as a way to understand and to explain ideas, emotions, and issues that they find interesting and important. This essential connection between the function of the reading selections and the students' own writing is fostered by the text's instructional apparatus. Section and chapter introductions discuss fundamental principles of composition and rhetoric illustrated in the reading selections that follow. In addition, each selection is accompanied by apparatus designed to help students practice important principles and techniques explained in the section and chapter introductions and illustrated by the selection itself. Apparatus for each selection includes: Looking Ahead (comments to help students preview the material), Vocabulary, Questions for Discussion, and Suggestions for Journal Entries. In addition, a list of suggestions for sustained writing appears at the end of each chapter.

The apparatus is planned to help students explore topics of their own choosing through a systematic and careful application of the writing process. Special attention is given to the early stages of the process since developmental writers often find collecting detail difficult. As such, perhaps the most useful piece of instructional apparatus is Getting Started. This brief introduction to the text discusses several prewriting strategies that are often recommended in the Suggestions for Journal Entries at the end of each selection and that will help students gather information with which to begin longer projects described in the Suggestions for Writing at the end of each chapter.

An important feature of the text is that its instructional apparatus is integrated. Items in the Looking Ahead and Vocabulary sections help students preview the contents and structure of the paragraph, essay, poem, or short story they are about to read. At the same time, these materials prepare them for the Questions for Discussion, which follow. Finally, there is a very obvious connection between the Suggestions for Journal Entries and the Suggestions for Writing. The latter provide detailed instructions to help students choose, approach, and develop topics they find interesting. Many make direct reference to the details, insights, and ideas students have recorded in their journals during prewriting so as to encourage the use of such materials as the basis and inspiration for longer projects.

Though *A Reader for Developing Writers* carries a single byline, it would not have been written without the help of several good friends and colleagues. First, I would like to thank Robin Browder, Tidewater Community College; Jim Creel, Alvin Community College; Marilyn Eanet, Rhode Island College; Ann Fields, West Kentucky University; Steven Lynn, University of South Carolina; Mary McGann, Rhode Island College; Marilyn Maxwell, Massasoit Community College; Denny May, Northern Virginia Community College; Alfred Nicolai, Middlesex County College; Jeff Schiff, Columbia College; Suzanne St. Laurent, Broward Community College; Wanda Van Goor, Prince Georges Community College; and Carolyn West, Daytona Beach Community College for their careful reviews of the manuscript and their helpful suggestions for revision. Among my colleagues and friends at Middlesex County College, I want to extend my heartfelt gratitude to RoseAnn Morgan, Richard Strugala, Emanual diPasquale, Patt Stuart, and James Keller for their support and advice. Special thanks must go to Albert Nicolai, a fine teacher and even better friend, without whose advice, prodding, and encouragement I simply could not have completed this project. I also want to express sincere appreciation to my good friends at McGraw-Hill, especially Bob Redling and Emily Barrosse, who believed in me and in this book from the very start, and Sue Hurtt, Lesley Denton, Charlotte Smith, and Bernadette Boylan. I am also grateful to the fine student writers who allowed me to use their work in this text. Finally, I want to thank my wife, Elaine, for her patience and support through the many months in which she had to vie with our word processor for my time and affection.

Santi V. Buscemi

Getting Started

The reading selections in this book illustrate principles and strategies that you will want to learn as you develop your skills as a writer. Some of them will even serve as models for the kinds of writing you will complete in other college courses. More important, because of the interesting topics they discuss, these essays, poems, and short stories might very well inspire you to use writing as a way to explore, understand, and communicate your ideas on a variety of subjects important to you.

Ideally, then, everything you read in this book should serve as a springboard to help you get started on your own writing projects. Some selections will supply you with useful facts and ideas that you may want to include and make reference to in your own work. Others will motivate you to write paragraphs and essays about similar themes, questions, and concerns by drawing details from what you know best—your own experiences, your own observations, and your prior reading. In short, *A Reader for Developing Writers* has been designed to help you recognize and use the important connection between reading and writing, and it will help you strengthen your skills in both areas.

INSTRUCTIONAL MATERIALS

At the heart of this book are the reading selections—sixty-nine essays, poems, and short stories by students and professional writers. In addition, *A Reader for Developing Writers* contains a complete set of instructional materials to assist you in making the most of what you read and in beginning your own writing projects. The book is organized as follows:

1. Each of its five sections and fifteen chapters is introduced by an explanation of the principles and techniques illustrated by the reading selections and important to your development as a writer.

2. Every chapter contains four to six reading selections. Each of these is prefaced by a short biography of the author and by a list of vocabulary words designed to help you increase your understanding of the selection and to strengthen your command of language.
3. Following each selection are questions for discussion, and following these are suggestions for writing notes in your journal (a record of your personal responses to the readings).
4. At the end of each chapter are suggestions for writing paragraphs and full-length essays.
5. Important terms used throughout the chapters are gathered in a glossary at the end of the book.

SUGGESTIONS FOR JOURNAL ENTRIES

Keeping a journal of your responses to this book's essays, poems, and short stories is one of the most important things you can do to improve your reading and writing skills. Making regular journal entries will help you increase your understanding and appreciation of what you have read. Even more important, it is an easy way to gather details and ideas for the paragraphs and essays that you will be developing as you respond to the Suggestions for Writing at the end of each chapter. In fact, most of the Suggestions for Writing refer to the Suggestions for Journal Entries earlier in the chapter, and they discuss ways to use journal material as the starting point for longer projects.

Keeping a journal is not difficult. First, buy a notebook in which to record your journal entries; ask your instructor about the type that is best for your class. Next, carefully read the essay, poem, or short story that your instructor has assigned, and answer all the Questions for Discussion (you might even want to write your answers in your journal). Finally, write in your journal responses to one or more of the Suggestions for Journal Entries that follow the assigned reading selection.

PREWRITING TECHNIQUES

Prewriting, also called invention, is an important part of the writing process. For professional and student writers alike, prewriting techniques are especially useful during the early stages of developing a long project's ideas and details, and many writers rely on them for short projects as well. Five of these techniques are described below, and in many cases the Suggestions for Journal Entries will direct you to use one or more of them. Because these techniques are so useful, you will want to master them; the best way to do so is to use as many as you can in your journal.

Listing

You can use your journal to make a list of details by recording what you think is most important, most startling, or most obvious about your topic. Sometimes, in fact, you can compile a useful list of details simply by putting down whatever comes to mind about your topic. Here's a list that student-writer Aggie Canino made when she was asked to describe a recent storm and its effects on her community:

Cloged rain sewers overflowing
Giant tree limbs acros the road
Flooding
Strong winds
Birch trees bent duble in the wind
Cracked utility poles
Downed power lines
Loss of electric
Lasted only one hour
Dog hidding under bed
Flooded basements
Thunder/lightening
Loss of power
Frightning sounds—howling of the wind, crash of thunder
Complete darkness in the middle of the day
Old oak on corner struck by lightening—bark ripped off

This list is repetitious and has many spelling errors, but don't worry about such problems at first; you can correct them later. Just concentrate on your topic and record the details as fast as they pop into your head.

Make sure to read your list after—but only *after*—you run out of things to say. Doing so will allow you to eliminate repetition and correct obvious errors. More important, it will help you make various items more specific and even come up with a few new details. For instance, Aggie expanded her mention of "cracked utility poles" by describing the "white sparks that flew from downed power lines" and by detailing the terror she felt as she heard the splintering of a utility pole struck by lightning.

Brainstorming

This method of gathering details is much like making a list and, in fact, might even result in the creation of a list. You can begin brainstorming by asking yourself a series of questions about your topic. The most common are those used by journalists to develop news stories: What happened? Who was involved? When did it occur? Where did it happen? How and why did it occur?

Such questions are especially important for recalling particular events. In addition, various kinds of questions can be used to generate details. Let's say that you want to describe your Uncle Charlie. You might ask: What does he look like? What kind of clothes does he wear? What does his car look like? How old is he? What details best describe his personality? What kind of friends does he have? Where does he work? Of course, not all of these questions will yield appropriate details—the kind that will help you create an accurate picture of Uncle Charlie—but your responses to only one or two might provide enough information to begin a more complete description. In any case, remember that prewriting is called invention, so feel free to invent as many different kinds of questions as you like.

Brainstorming is the kind of activity that you can and should share with other writers. Often you will be able to help each other come up with the number and kinds of questions and answers that might not have been possible if you had worked separately. Indeed, don't be surprised if your instructor asks your entire class to brainstorm a particular subject.

Focused Freewriting

Freewriting is a very common technique to help overcome *writer's block,* a problem that results in staring at a blank piece of paper while trying unsuccessfully to come up with something to say. *Freewriting* involves writing nonstop for five or ten minutes, simply recording ideas that come into your mind at random. *Focused freewriting* is similar, but it involves concentrating on a predetermined topic.

Let's say that you want to do some focused freewriting on a storm. The results might look like this:

> The clogged rain sewers were overflowing, and there was a lot of
> flooding with strong winds knocking down power lines. Thunder
> crashed, and lightning flashed. Giant tree limbs fell across the road
> and a birch was bent double, and there were lots of flooded
> basements. Even though the storm lasted only one hour. Several
> downed power lines threw threatening sparks and flashes across the
> road. My street was blocked; a large oak had fallen across it. We lost
> our electricity. The crash of thunder shook me to my bones. My dog
> hid under the bed. We were terrified.

Again, don't worry about grammar and other such errors at this point in the process. Simply try to focus on your topic and record your ideas quickly and completely.

As always, read your journal entry as soon as possible after you've recorded your ideas. Doing so will help you cut out repetition, rework parts that require clarification, and add more details that come to mind in the process.

Interviewing

Asking appropriate questions of people who know as much or even more about your topic than you do is an excellent way to gather detail. It gives you at least one other perspective from which to view your topic and might yield information that you otherwise would not have learned.

Just make sure that the person you plan to interview is knowledgeable about your subject, and come prepared with several questions (you can list them in your journal ahead of time) that will help you get the information you need. The kinds of questions you ask during an interview can be similar to those you use during a brainstorming session.

Summarizing

This prewriting method involves condensing another writer's ideas and putting them into your own words. It is especially effective if you want to combine information found in your reading with details you have gathered from your own experiences or from other sources. Just be sure to use your own language *throughout* the summary. In addition, if you plan to use any of this information in an essay, make certain to tell your readers that it comes from the work of another writer by mentioning the writer's name. For instance, if you decide to paraphrase the introduction to Rachel Carson's *Silent Spring*, a selection in Chapter 13, you might begin: "As Carson explains in her study of the effects of pesticides on our environment ..."

Using one or more of these five prewriting techniques should help you write effective journal entries. Remember to label each of the entries in your journal by mentioning the title of the reading selection and the number of the journal suggestion to which you are responding. Most important, work hard at each journal entry. Generate as much detail as you can, and then reread the essay, poem, or short story in order to gather even more material. Remember that what you put into your journal might serve as the start of a longer writing project. Therefore, the more complete your journal, the easier it will be to begin the paragraph and essay assignments described in the Suggestions for Writing at the end of each chapter.

Enjoy the reading selections in the fifteen chapters that follow. Along with the instructional materials that accompany them, they will give you a great start in becoming an effective writer. Best of luck!

Section I

Organization and Development

In Getting Started you learned several ways to gather facts, ideas, and opinions about the subjects you choose to write about. Collecting sufficient information about your subject—making sure that you know as much about it as you need to—is an important first step in the writing process.

Next, you will need to determine what it is about your subject that you wish to communicate and how to use your information to get your point across clearly and effectively. Learning how to make such decisions is what the four chapters of Section I are all about.

In Chapter 1 you will learn that two of the most crucial steps early in the writing process are *focusing* and *limiting* the information you've collected so that you can begin to decide upon a *central idea*. Sometimes referred to as the "main" or "controlling" idea, the central idea of a paragraph or essay expresses the main point its writer wishes to develop.

The process of determining your central idea begins with carefully reviewing the information recorded in your journal (information collected through brainstorming, freewriting, or the other prewriting activities explained in Getting Started). You must then evaluate these details in order to determine not only what they say about your subject but also exactly what you want to tell your reader about it. Therefore, always keep your journal handy, because the more information you collect about a subject, the easier it will be to find an interesting central idea to write about. And once you have found it, this central idea will help you choose the kinds and amounts of detail needed to develop your main point most effectively.

Chapter 2 introduces you to *unity* and *coherence*, two key principles to observe in organizing your information. The section on unity explains how to choose details which best accomplish your purpose and which relate most directly to your central idea. The section on coherence shows you how to create connections in and between paragraphs in order to maintain your reader's interest and to make your writing easy to follow.

Chapter 3, Development, explains how to determine the amount of detail a paragraph or essay should contain. It also describes several ways to arrange these details and to develop the ideas you wish to communicate.

Finally, the last chapter in this section, Introductions and Conclusions, explains the importance of introductory and concluding paragraphs, and it will offer suggestions to help you write these units of composition more effectively. In short, Chapter 4 will explain a number of ways to start and to end an essay.

The reading selections in Section I contain examples of the important principles of organization and development explained in the chapter introductions. They are also a rich source of interesting topics you might want to develop in your own writing. However, like the other selections in *A Reader for Developing Writers,* each has an intrinsic value—a value all its own—which goes far beyond its usefulness to any textbook. Whether written by professionals or by college students like you, these paragraphs and essays discuss people, places, or ideas that you are sure to find interesting, informative, humorous, and even touching. Here's hoping they will inspire you to continue reading and writing about a variety of subjects, especially about those you care about most!

Chapter 1

The Central Idea

An important concern for any writer is the ability to organize information in a form that is easy to follow. The best way to do this is to arrange, or focus, the details you've collected around a central idea.

IDENTIFYING THE CENTRAL IDEA

The central idea is often called the "main idea" because it conveys the writer's main point. It is also called the "controlling idea," for it controls (or determines) the kinds and amounts of detail that a paragraph or essay contains.

You might think of the central idea of a paragraph or essay in the same way that you think of the foundation of a building. It is the major idea upon which all other ideas and details are based; it holds the entire piece of writing together, just as a foundation keeps the rest of the building standing. To be more accurate, the central idea of an essay or paragraph is the focal point to which every detail must relate and which every bit of information must develop.

Notice how the central ideas (shown in italics) let us know from the very start exactly what the student authors of the following paragraphs have in mind:

America is as diverse as its weather. You can bask in 85° Fahrenheit sun and fly off to ski at −17° Fahrenheit in the same day. You can wander through lush, tropical vegetation or walk in a hot, almost barren desert. You can even climb snow-capped mountains.   (Kitty Jentis, "America.")

Upon reaching mid-life, many people feel a sense of panic, but I am only getting my second wind. I often feel like Janus, the two-faced Roman god who greeted each new year by looking both forward and behind at the same time. Although it is a time for reflection, it is not a time for idle moments because the future is now just as long as the past. A

person without a future is not someone of advanced age, but someone
who has no vision. Each day brings a future, every yesterday a
tomorrow, and each step brings a new view of the horizon.   (Donna
Becker, "Second Wind.")

In most cases the central idea of a paragraph is expressed in a *topic sentence*, and the central idea of an essay is expressed in a *thesis statement*. In some pieces of writing, however, the central idea is so obvious that the author might not feel the need to state it explicitly in a formal topic sentence or thesis statement; this often happens in narration and description, the kinds of writing you'll read in Sections III and IV. Nonetheless, as a general practice you should try to express the central idea outright, either in a *topic sentence* when you are writing a paragraph or in a *thesis statement* when you are tying several paragraphs together to form a well-organized essay.

Very often, authors state the central idea early, placing the topic sentence or thesis statement at the very beginning of a paragraph or essay. However, this is not always appropriate. Sometimes it is necessary to provide the reader with explanatory details or background material before revealing the central idea; in such cases you will want to place your topic sentence or thesis somewhere in the middle or even at the end of a paragraph or essay. Another good reason for not revealing the central idea right away is to fill your writing with a sense of expectation or suspense. Finally, waiting until the end of a paragraph or essay to reveal your central idea is a good way to avoid offending or antagonizing a reader who may not at first be in favor of the idea or opinion you are presenting.

WRITING A PRELIMINARY TOPIC SENTENCE OR THESIS STATEMENT

As a developing writer, make sure that you have a good grasp of the central ideas that will control the paragraphs and essays you write. You can do this early in the writing process by jotting down a working version of your central idea on a piece of scratch paper or in your journal. This will be your preliminary topic sentence or thesis statement. It is called *preliminary* because you can and often should make significant changes in this version of your topic sentence or thesis statement after you've begun to write your paragraph or essay.

Of course, before you draft a preliminary topic sentence or thesis, you must choose a subject to write about. Keep in mind that by its very nature a subject represents a kind of thinking that is abstract, general, and incomplete. A central idea, on the other hand, is a concrete, specific, and complete expression of thought. For example, notice how much more meaningful the subject "waterskiing" becomes when you turn it into a central idea: "Waterskiing can be *dangerous*."

In order to turn any subject into a central idea, whether it winds up as the topic sentence of a paragraph or the thesis of an essay, you will have to *focus* and *limit* your discussion of a subject by saying something concrete and specific about it. Focusing and limiting are important thinking processes that will help you begin to organize the information you've collected about your subject. Here's how they work:

Focusing Your Discussion

A good time to think about focusing on a central idea and drafting a working thesis or topic sentence is immediately after you have reviewed your journal for facts, ideas, and opinions that you gathered through one or more of the various prewriting activities discussed in Getting Started. While these important details are still fresh in your mind, ask yourself three questions:

1. *Purpose:* What do I want this piece of writing to accomplish?
2. *Main point:* What is the main point I wish to communicate about my subject?
3. *Details:* What details can I use to develop this main point?

Purpose   As well as you can at this stage in the writing process, determine your purpose—what you want your essay or paragraph to do. For instance, it may be to entertain the reader with a humorous event from your childhood, to describe a beautiful forest, to explain an interesting idea, or to compare two automobiles.

Once you've determined this purpose, it will become easy to decide what the main point of your writing should be, for you will already have begun determining which of the details you've gathered will be useful to you and which will not.

Let's say that your purpose is to describe the forest you hiked through last autumn. You begin by reviewing your notes, and you decide that it makes sense to include details about the symphony of colors—the brilliant reds, the burnt oranges, the subtle yellows—against which you saw a family of deer prance through the wilderness. It might also be appropriate to describe the old truck tire someone had dumped by the side of the path or the party of hunters you saw as you entered the woods. On the other hand, it might not be appropriate to explain that you traveled three hours in an old pickup to get there, that you bumped into a high school friend in a clearing, or that one of the forest rangers you met once dated your great-aunt Matilda. These last three details would not likely help you describe the forest.

Main Point The next step is to determine exactly what you want to say about your walk through the woods. Ask yourself what for *you* is the most interesting or important aspect of the subject. This will be your *main point,* the point that will help you tie all the details together logically.

In short, you can turn a subject into a central idea by making a main point about the subject. If you decide that the most interesting or important aspect of your walk in the forest is that it was *inspiring,* your central idea might read; "The forest I hiked through this autumn was inspiring."

As you learned earlier, focusing lets the writer turn an abstract, general, incomplete subject into the central idea for a paragraph or essay. Notice how much clearer, more specific, and more complete the central ideas on the right are than the abstract subjects on the left:

Subject	Central Idea
The forest I hiked through this autumn	The forest I hiked through this autumn was inspiring.
Cross-country skiing	Cross-country skiing is good exercise.
The Battle of Gettysburg	The Battle of Gettysburg was the turning point in the Civil War.
My great-grandmother	My great-grandmother was very resourceful.

As you can see, focusing on a main point helps change an abstract idea into something specific and concrete—into a central idea.

Details Finally, focusing also provides a starting point for a first draft of an essay because it guides you in selecting the kinds of details that you should and should not include. If you decide to focus on the inspirational aspects of the forest, for example, you certainly ought to include a lengthy description of the changing leaves and of the family of deer that crossed your path. But should you also mention the old tire and the party of hunters? These details are certainly a part of the experience, but do they relate to the idea that your hike through the forest was inspirational? Probably not.

Limiting Your Discussion to a Manageable Length

Typically, students are asked to write short essays, usually ranging between 250 and 750 words, with paragraphs seldom longer than 75 words. That's why one of the most important things to remember when writing a thesis statement or topic sentence is to limit your central idea as much as you can. Otherwise, you won't be able to develop it in as much detail as will be necessary to make your point clearly, effectively, and completely.

Let's say that you are about to buy a new car and want to compare two popular makes that you know a great deal about. In a short essay it would be foolish to try to compare these automobiles in more than two or three different ways. Therefore, you might limit yourself to cost, appearance, and comfort, rather than discuss their performance, handling, and sound systems as well. You might even want to limit your central idea to only one of these aspects—cost, for instance. You can then divide "cost" into more specific subsections, which will be easier to organize when it comes time to write your first draft. The thesis for such an essay might read:

> I chose the 1988 Whizbang over the 1988 Dream Machine because it costs less to buy, to operate, and to repair.

CONTROLLING UNITY AND DEVELOPMENT

At the beginning of the chapter, you read that the central idea can be called the controlling idea because it helps the writer determine the kinds and amounts of detail that a paragraph or essay should contain. This is explained further in Chapters 2 and 3.

For now, you should know that the kinds of details that a piece of writing contains determine whether it is unified. A paragraph is unified if each of its ideas relates directly and ummistakably to its central idea, whether or not this central idea is expressed in a formal topic sentence. Similarly, an essay is unified if each of its paragraphs relates directly and unmistakably to its central idea, whether or not this central idea is expressed in a formal thesis statement.

The amount of detail that a piece of writing contains determines whether it is well-developed. A paragraph or essay is well developed if it contains all the detail it needs to prove, illustrate, or otherwise support its central idea.

REVISING THE CENTRAL IDEA

One last and very important bit of advice. As mentioned earlier, always remember that you can and often should revise the working, or preliminary, versions of your thesis statements and topic sentences during the writing process. Like taking notes or writing a first draft of a paper, writing a preliminary version of a thesis statement or topic sentence is intended only to give you a starting point and to provide you with a sense of direction. Don't be afraid to reword, edit, or completely rewrite your central idea at any point. Like all processes, writing involves a series of steps or tasks to be completed. However, there is no rule that prevents you from stopping at any point along the way, looking back upon what you've already accomplished, and changing it as thoroughly and as often as you like. What's more, the process of writing always includes discovery. And the more you discover about your subject, the more likely you are to understand it better and to revise what you *thought* you had wanted to say about it.

The reading selections that follow illustrate the important organizational principles discussed in this chapter. Read them carefully, and take some time to respond to the Questions for Discussion and the Suggestions for Journal Entries that accompany them. Doing so will help you develop a more complete understanding of the central idea and its importance to organization.

From *The Sea Around Us*

Rachel Carson

Rachel Carson (1907–1964) was one of the founders of the American environmental movement and one of its most eloquent spokespersons. It was she, more than anyone else, who helped convince people of the terrible effects of chemical pollution. In 1951 she won the National Book Award for *The Sea Around Us*, from which this paragraph is taken. You will learn more about Carson when you read a selection from her most famous work, *Silent Spring*, in Chapter 13.

Looking Ahead

1. Carson begins with a statement of her central idea. As you read this paragraph, ask yourself what main point she is making about the sea in her topic sentence.
2. You've learned that before deciding on a central idea you must ask yourself what you want to accomplish. Try to determine Carson's purpose when she wrote this paragraph from *The Sea Around Us*.

Vocabulary

accounts   Reports, stories.
cosmic   Of the world, of the universe.
testimony   Written or spoken evidence.

Beginnings are apt to be shadowy, and so it is with the beginnings of that great mother of life, the sea. Many people have debated how and when the earth got its ocean, and it is not surprising that their explanations do not always agree. For the plain and inescapable truth is that no one was there to see, and in the absence of eyewitness accounts there is bound to be a certain amount of disagreement. So if I tell here the story of how the young planet Earth acquired an ocean, it must be a story pieced together from many sources and containing whole chapters the details of which we can only imagine. The story is founded on the testimony of the earth's most ancient rocks, which were young when the earth was young; on other evidence written on the face of the earth's satellite, the moon; and on hints contained in the history of the sun and the whole universe of star-filled space. For although no man was there to witness this cosmic birth, the stars and the moon and the rocks were there, and, indeed, had much to do with the fact that there is an ocean.

Questions for Discussion

1. What is the paragraph's subject? What is the author's purpose?
2. Reread Carson's topic sentence. What one word in that sentence establishes her focus and reveals her main point about "Beginnings"?
3. What details does she use to develop or explain her main point later in the paragraph?

Suggestions for Journal Entries

1. Review your answers to the Questions for Discussion above. In your own words, explain Carson's purpose and central idea. Then list the details and ideas that she uses to develop this central idea.
2. Think about a familiar subject. Then list some of the reasons why this subject is interesting or important to you. Use each of the items in your list as the main point of a topic sentence in what could later become a complete paragraph. Write as many topic sentences as you have items in your list; for instance, if "Thanksgiving" were your subject, you might end up with the following topic sentences:
   Thanksgiving is a time for overeating.
   Thanksgiving at my grandmother's house was a day filled with love and laughter.
   Watching football on TV is a Thanksgiving ritual at my house.
   Preparing a Thanksgiving dinner takes a lot of work.

Three Paragraphs for Analysis

The following three selections show how important the central idea is to a piece of writing. They were written by different authors and discuss three very different subjects, but they all focus clearly on a main point that is developed through detail.

Gilbert Muller and Harvey Wiener are college English professors and scholars. The paragraph from "On Writing" first appeared in *The Short Prose Reader,* one of several textbooks they have written.

Milton Cross is an authority on symphonic and operatic music. His *Encyclopedia of the Great Composers and Their Music,* from which the paragraph about composer Jean Sibelius is taken, is a standard reference work for students of classical music.

A teacher, journalist, and auto mechanic, Don Sharp has written a great deal about his love for cars. His paragraph is from "Under the Hood," an essay he published in *Harper's* magazine in 1980.

Looking Ahead

1. You've learned that one of the ways a writer decides on a main idea is to focus on a main point—the one aspect of the subject that the writer believes is most worth discussing. Look for the topic sentence in each of the following paragraphs, and identify each author's main point.
2. Each paragraph contains a clear and distinct central idea expressed in a formal topic sentence, but as you've learned the central idea does not have to appear at the beginning of a selection. In some cases the author will provide a few sentences of background or explanatory detail first or might even wait until the end of a paragraph to reveal the central idea so as to create suspense or to achieve another important purpose. Depending on the author's purpose, therefore, a topic sentence might be placed anywhere in a paragraph.

Vocabulary

abominable   Despicable, hateful.

colleagues   People engaged in the same profession.

contraption   Gadget, device, invention.

desist   Stop.

diamond jubilee   Seventy-fifth birthday.

random   By chance.

reverence   Deep respect.

rifle through   Search through vigorously.

unprecedented   Never done before.

ON WRITING by Gilbert Muller and Harvey Wiener

Few writers begin without some warmup activity. Generally called prewriting, the steps they take before producing a draft almost always start with thinking about their topic. They talk to friends and colleagues; they browse in libraries and rifle through reference books; they read newspaper and magazine articles. Sometimes they jot down notes and lists in order to put on paper some of their thoughts in very rough form. Some writers use free-association: they record as thoroughly as possible their random, unedited ideas about the topic. Using the raw, often disorganized materials produced in this preliminary stage, many writers try to group related thoughts with a scratch outline or some other effort to bring order to their written notes.

JEAN SIBELIUS by Milton Cross

America recognizes Sibelius as a great composer, one of the greatest of our time. But in his native Finland he was much more than that. He was a national hero. The Finnish government issued stamps bearing the picture of Sibelius, an unprecedented honor for a living composer. In 1940 a campaign was launched in Finland to erect a statue of him for his diamond jubilee; the project was dropped only when Sibelius wrote to a newspaper urging his friends to desist. Rarely before has a composer meant so much to his country as Sibelius does. He is the voice of Finland, its symbol. Those who have visited Finland know what a unique position he occupied. The children in the streets know his name and sing his melodies; they speak of him with the awe which, in other lands, is usually reserved for athletes or military heroes. The older people (not necessarily music lovers) honor his name and speak it with reverence.

UNDER THE HOOD by Don Sharp

Time was when most men knew how to replace their own distributor points, repair a flat tire, and install a battery. Women weren't assumed to know as much, but they were expected to know how to put a gear lever in neutral, set a choke and throttle, and crank a car by hand if the battery was dead. Now, odds are that 75 percent of men and a higher percentage of women don't even know how to work the jacks that come with their cars. To be sure, a bumper jack is an abominable contraption—the triumph of production economies over good sense—but it will do what it is supposed to do, and the fact that most drivers cannot make one work says much about the way motorists have changed over the past forty years.

Questions for Discussion

1. Identify each paragraph's topic sentence. What is each paragraph's subject? What is each topic sentence's main point about its subject?
2. Would the selection from "On Writing" have been as effective and as easy to read if Muller and Wiener had placed the topic sentence in the middle or at the end of the paragraph?
3. What important information does Cross provide before he introduces the topic sentence in "Jean Sibelius"?
4. What is Don Sharp's main point about motorists? Why does he wait until the last line to reveal it?
5. Sharp doesn't come right out and say exactly what he thinks of the lack of

mechanical ability in today's typical motorist. Does he need to? Why, or why not?

Suggestions for Journal Entries

1. In your own words, write down what you believe to be the central idea and the purpose of each paragraph.
2. Pick a subject you know a great deal about, and ask yourself what you believe to be its most important or interesting aspect. Make this aspect the main point of a central idea, and write this central idea down in the form of a formal topic sentence for a paragraph you might want to write later on. Do the same for three or four other subjects you know a great deal about. Remember to focus and limit your topic sentences as much as you can.

Three Passions I Have Lived For

Bertrand Russell

One of the most widely read philosophers and mathematicians of the twentieth century, Bertrand Russell (1872–1970) is even better remembered as a social and political activist. For many years, he was considered an extremely unorthodox thinker because of his liberal opinions on sex, marriage, and homosexuality. Politically, Russell was a socialist and pacifist. In the 1950s and 1960s he became one of the leaders of the "ban the bomb" movement in Europe, and later he helped organize opposition to U.S. involvement in Vietnam.

Among his most famous works are *Principles of Mathematics* (1903), *A History of Western Philosophy* (1945), and a three-volume autobiography (1967–1969) in which the selection that follows first appeared. Russell won the Nobel Prize for literature in 1950.

Looking Ahead

1. The first paragraph contains Russell's thesis. Read it carefully; it will give you clues about the topic sentences on which he develops three of the paragraphs that follow.
2. The word "passions" should be understood as deep, personal concerns which Russell developed over the course of his life and which had a significant influence on the way he lived.

Vocabulary

abyss   Deep hole.
alleviate   Lessen, soften, make less harsh or painful.
anguish   Grief, sorrow, pain.
consciousness   Mind, intelligence.
mockery   Ridicule, scorn.
prefiguring   Predicting, forecasting.
reverberate   Resound, repeatedly echo.
unfathomable   Unmeasurable.
verge   Edge.

Three passions, simple but overwhelmingly strong, have governed my   1
life: the longing for love, the search for knowledge, and unbearable pity for
the suffering of mankind. These passions, like great winds, have blown me
hither and thither, in a wayward course over a deep ocean of anguish, reaching to the very verge of despair.

I have sought love, first, because it brings ecstasy—ecstasy so great that   2
I would often have sacrificed all the rest of my life for a few hours of this joy.
I have sought it, next, because it relieves loneliness—that terrible loneliness
in which one shivering consciousness looks over the rim of the world into the
cold unfathomable lifeless abyss. I have sought it, finally, because in the union
of love I have seen, in a mystic miniature, the prefiguring vision of the heaven
that saints and poets have imagined. This is what I sought, and though it
might seem too good for human life, this is what—at last—I have found.

With equal passion I have sought knowledge. I have wished to under-   3
stand the hearts of men. I have wished to know why the stars shine....A little
of this, but not much, I have achieved.

Love and knowledge, so far as they were possible, led upward toward   4
the heavens. But always pity brought me back to earth. Echoes of cries of pain
reverberate in my heart. Children in famine, victims tortured by oppressors,
helpless old people a hated burden to their sons, and the whole world of loneliness, poverty, and pain make a mockery of what human life should be. I long
to alleviate the evil, but I cannot, and I too suffer.

This has been my life. I have found it worth living, and would gladly   5
live it again if the chance were offered me.

Questions for Discussion

1. The title gives us a clue about why Russell wrote this selection. What was
   his purpose?
2. Russell expresses the central idea—the thesis—in paragraph 1. What is his
   thesis?
3. In your own words, explain each of the central ideas—topic sentences—in

paragraphs 2, 3, and 4. In other words, what three passions did Russell live for?

4. How do these three passions relate to the thesis?
5. What details does Russell use to develop the topic sentence in paragraph 2? In paragraph 3? In paragraph 4? Explain how these details relate to their topic sentences in each case.
6. You've learned in this chapter how to limit your discussion to a manageable length. In what ways did Russell make sure to limit his essay's length?

Suggestions for Journal Entries

1. In your own words, summarize the three reasons why Russell has "sought love."
2. In Looking Ahead you read that Russell used the word "passions" to describe the deep, personal concerns that determined the way he lived. Using Russell's essay as a model, write a series of topic sentences for paragraphs that describe the passions—at least three of them—that *you* live for. The kinds of passions you mention should be personal and real. Remember to limit each topic sentence to one and only one passion. If you're embarrassed to write about yourself, write about someone else's passions. Here are some examples:

> One of the most important concerns in my life is getting a good education.
> My religion is the cornerstone of my existence.
> My brother lives to eat.
> My grandmother's most important concern was her children.
> Mother Theresa's sole purpose in life is to serve the poor.

Echoes

Maria Cirilli

Maria Cirilli was born in a very small town near Campobasso, in southern Italy, and immigrated to the United States in 1971. In 1983 she decided to take courses in nurse education at a local community college, from which she earned an associate's degree. She is now a registered nurse at The Robert Wood Johnson Hospital in New Brunswick, New Jersey.

"Echoes" is a recollection of her beloved grandfather, who had visited America and from whom Cirilli got her first knowledge of what was to become her new homeland. She wrote this essay as an assignment in a college composition class.

Looking Ahead

1. Cirilli chose not to reveal the central idea of this essay—her thesis statement—in paragraph 1. However, the first paragraph is important because it contains information that we can contrast with what we read in paragraph 2.
2. All the paragraphs in this essay, except the first, make an important point about the author's grandfather or about the way in which he affected her life. As you would expect, each of these main points is expressed in its paragraph's topic sentence.
3. Paragraph 2 mentions the "graciously sculptured seventeenth-century church" in Cirilli's home town. The reference to the seventeenth century means that the church was built about 300 years ago, between 1600 and 1699.

Vocabulary

distinguished   Made different from.

exuberance   Joy, enthusiasm.

I hardly remember my grandmother except for the fact that she used to   1
bounce me on her knees by the old-fashioned brick fireplace and sing old songs. I was only four years old when she died. Her face is a faded image in the back of my mind.

In contrast, I remember my grandfather very well. He was 6' 4" tall, a   2
towering man with broad shoulders and a pair of mustaches that I watched

turn from black to gray over the years. He also possessed a deep voice, which distinguished him from others whether he was in the streets of our small picture-perfect town in southern Italy or in our graciously sculptured seventeenth-century church. He appeared to be strong and powerful. In fact, he used to scare all my girlfriends away when they came over to play or do homework, yet he was the most gentle man I have ever known.

He was always available to help people. They used to seek his advice, 3 whether it was about land they had to purchase or a home. People usually stopped by the house on Sunday mornings after the 9 a.m. mass. There was always a tray of fresh, homemade cookies and a pot of coffee on our oversized, oval kitchen table ready for our Sunday visitors.

I also vividly remember the hours we children spent listening to our 4 grandfather's stories. He would sit by the fireplace in his wooden rocking chair and tell us about the time he had spent in America. Each one of us kids would aim for the chair closest to him. We didn't want to miss anything he said. He would tell us about a huge tunnel, the Lincoln Tunnel, that was built under water. He would also talk about the legendary Statue of Liberty. We were fascinated by his stories of that big, industrialized land called America.

As I grew up and became a teenager, I dreamt of immigrating to Amer- 5 ica and seeing all the places that my grandfather had talked about. His exuberance about this land had a definite influence on my decision to come to America.

A few months before I arrived here, my grandfather died. I still miss 6 him very much, but each time I visit a place that he knew I feel his presence close to me. The sound of his voice echoes in my mind.

Questions for Discussion

1. What important information does Cirilli give us in paragraph 1?
2. What is her thesis? Why does she wait until paragraph 2 to reveal it?
3. Paragraphs 3, 4, 5, and 6 contain very clear topic sentences. Identify each of them.
4. What do these topic sentences tell us about Cirilli's grandfather?
5. Why is "Echoes" a good title for this essay?

Suggestions for Journal Entries

1. Each of Cirilli's paragraphs reveals a different aspect of her grandfather or explains how he affected her life. Reread the topic sentences in paragraphs 2 to 6, and summarize their central ideas in your journal.
2. Think of someone special in your life, and write down a wealth of preliminary details about this person; use brainstorming, interviewing, or any of the other information-gathering techniques discussed in Getting Started.

Then tell the reader about this special person in three or four well-written sentences. Like the topic sentences in "Echoes," those that you write should focus on a single aspect or characteristic of this individual. In other words, make sure that your topic sentences contain only one *main idea*.

SUGGESTIONS FOR WRITING

1. If you remember some of the prewriting exercises discussed in Getting Started (pp. 1–6), begin freewriting or brainstorming about a subject you know well. List as many details about this subject as you can in your journal.

   Then, in preparation for the writing of a well-focused paragraph, reread this list of details and try to answer the three questions discussed earlier in this chapter to help you focus your writing:
   a. Purpose: What do I want this piece of writing to accomplish?
   b. Main point: What is the main point I want to communicate about my subject? Why is it important or interesting to me?
   c. Details: What details can I use to develop this main point?

   After you've determined your main point, write a topic sentence for your paragraph. Finally, choose details from your list that relate directly to your topic sentence, and organize them into a well-developed paragraph that is based on your topic sentence.

2. You may have responded to item 2 of the Suggestions for Journal Entries after the paragraph from Carson's *The Sea Around Us*. If so, you may recall that you were asked to write several topic sentences on a particular subject, each of which was to explain a reason you found that subject interesting or important.

   Write one paragraph each for at least three of these topic sentences. Make sure that the details you include support or explain the central idea expressed in the paragraph's topic sentence.

3. In "Three Passions I Have Lived For," Bertrand Russell explains three deep, personal concerns that have "governed" his life. If you responded to item 2 in the Suggestions for Journal Entries following this essay, you have probably written a few topic sentences about the passions you or someone you know well lives for.

   Use each of your topic sentences as the basis or beginning of a fully developed paragraph about each of these passions. Next, take the main points expressed in your topic sentences and combine them into a sentence that might serve as the thesis statement to an essay made up of the paragraphs you have just written.

   Refer to Russell's essay as a model. Remember that his thesis statement mentions three passions: "the longing for love, the search for knowledge, and unbearable pity for the suffering of mankind." These three passions are used individually as the main points in each of the topic sentences of the paragraphs that follow and develop his thesis.

4. Write a short essay in which you explain three reasons that you are doing something important in your life. Include these three reasons in a central idea that you will use as your thesis statement. Let's say that you decide to explain three of your reasons for going to college. You might write "I decided to attend Metropolitan College to prepare for a rewarding career, to meet interesting people, and to a learn more about music and literature." Put this thesis somewhere in your introductory paragraph.

   Next, use *each* of the reasons in your thesis as the main point in the topic sentences of the three paragraphs that follow. In keeping with the example above, you might use the following as topic sentences for paragraphs 2, 3, and 4. The main point in each topic sentence is shown here in italics:

   Paragraph 2: The most important reason I decided to attend Metropolitan College was *to prepare myself for a rewarding career.*
   Paragraph 3: The opportunity to meet interesting people was another reason I thought that going to college would be a good idea.
   Paragraph 4: My decision to continue my schooling also had a lot to do with my desire *to learn more about literature and music.*

   Finally, try to develop each of these in a paragraph of three or four sentences that will help you explain the main point of your topic sentence completely and effectively.

5. In item 2 of the Suggestions for Journal Entries that appeared after Maria Cirilli's "Echoes," you were asked to write three or four sentences, each of which was to focus on a single aspect or characteristic of someone special in your life. Make each of these the topic sentence to a paragraph that describes or explains that aspect or characteristic. If necessary, reread "Echoes." Many of the paragraphs in the body of this essay will serve as excellent models for your writing.

   Next, write an appropriate thesis statement for an essay containing the three or four paragraphs you've just written. Make sure that your thesis statement somehow reflects the main points found in the topic sentences to the three or four paragraphs in your essay. Make this thesis part of your essay's first or introductory paragraph.

Chapter 2

Unity and Coherence

Chapter 1 explained the importance of focusing on a central idea. As you learned, the central idea is also referred to as the controlling idea because it controls, or determines, which information a writer uses to develop a paragraph or essay.

Deciding how much information to include in a piece of writing has to do with development, a principle discussed in the next chapter. Deciding what kinds of information to include and making sure that all such information fits together logically have to do with the two important principles of organization discussed in this chapter: unity and coherence.

CREATING UNITY

A piece of writing is unified if it contains only those details that help develop (explain and/or support) the central idea. In the following paragraph by student Craig Pennypacker, notice that every detail relates to either "love" or "infatuation," the two feelings he contrasts in his topic sentence:

> *Many people feel that they are in love when they are really only infatuated, but love and infatuation are quite different.* First, infatuation leaps into being, while love takes root and grows one day at a time. Second, infatuation is accompanied by a sense of uncertainty; one is stimulated and thrilled but not really happy. Love, on the other hand, begins with a feeling of security; the lover is warmed by a sense of nearness even when the beloved is away. Third, infatuation tells us to "get married right away." Meanwhile, love advises: "Don't rush into anything; learn to trust each other." These are important differences. Unfortunately, too many people overlook them and wind up getting hurt in the end.

In contrast to what you read in Craig's paragraph, beginning writers sometimes mistakenly include information that is irrelevant—information that does not help explain or support the central idea. Guard against this problem. Including irrelevant material only sidetracks the reader, drawing attention away from your main point and toward details unimportant to your central idea. With such unrelated material, your writing will lack unity, and your reader will thus have difficulty determining exactly what it is you want to say.

The following paragraph about seventeenth-century Moscow is taken from Robert K. Massey's biography of the famous Russian czar, Peter the Great. However, it has been modified, so you will notice that it contains many details unrelated to its central idea. This material was added to the paragraph (as were the bracketed sentence numbers) just to prove the point that irrelevant details and ideas can destroy the focus of a piece of writing and make it difficult to follow.

> [1]Not unnaturally in a city built of wood, fire was the scourge [devastation] of Moscow. [2]In winter, when primitive stoves were blazing in every house, and in summer when the heat made wood tinder-dry, a spark could create a holocaust. [3]Some of the homes had beautiful carved porches, windows, and gables, which were unknown in other parts of Europe, where buildings were made of stone. [4]Caught by the wind, flames leaped from one roof to the next, reducing entire streets to ashes. [5]Moscow was also subject to terrible Russian winters, which often caused severe damage to the city's wooden structures. [6]In 1571, 1611, 1626, and 1671, great fires destroyed whole quarters of Moscow, leaving vast empty spaces in the middle of the city. [7]These disasters were exceptional, but to Muscovites the sight of a burning house...was a part of daily life. [8]So were the heavy wooden planks that covered the streets, which had become filled with mud after the heavy autumn rains.

Massey establishes his focus—states his central idea—in a topic sentence at the very beginning of this paragraph. His main point in this sentence, that "fire was the scourge of Moscow," is what he sets out to develop in the paragraph; therefore each detail *should* relate directly to that idea. With the added material, however, this is *not* the case.

Let's analyze the paragraph to determine which details belong and which do not:

- Sentence 1, the topic sentence, expresses the central idea.
- Sentence 2 details the causes of fire in winter and summer, so it relates directly to the topic sentence.
- Sentence 3 explains that some wooden homes in Moscow displayed beautiful carvings seen nowhere else in Europe. This sentence tells us something about Moscow, but is doesn't help explain the topic sentence's main point that "fire was the scourge of Moscow." Therefore, sentence 3 should be removed.

- Sentence 4 shows how fire spread in the city. Like sentence 2, it relates directly to the topic sentence.
- Sentence 5 explains how severe the Russian winters were, but it doesn't relate to the point that "fire was the scourge of Moscow." Sentence 5 is thus extraneous and should be removed.
- Sentences 6 and 7 show how often and to what extent fire endangered the city. Therefore, like sentences 2 and 4, they contribute relevant information and thus help develop the topic sentence.
- Sentence 8 discusses another aspect of daily life in Moscow, but it makes no mention of the threat of fire. Since it is thus unrelated to the central idea, sentence 8 should be removed in order to keep the paragraph unified.

This analysis demonstrates that the details added to Massey's original paragraph are irrelevant. Compare the disunified version above with his original version below. Notice how much more focused and easy to read the paragraph becomes with the extraneous material removed:

> Not unnaturally in a city built of wood, fire was the scourge of Moscow. In winter, when primitive stoves were blazing in every house, and in summer when the heat made wood tinder-dry, a spark could create a holocaust. Caught by the wind, flames leaped from one roof to the next, reducing entire streets to ashes. In 1571, 1611, 1626, and 1671, great fires destroyed whole quarters of Moscow, leaving vast empty spaces in the middle of the city. These disasters were exceptional, but to Muscovites the sight of a burning house...was a part of daily life.

MAINTAINING COHERENCE

The second principle important to organization is coherence. A paragraph is coherent if the sentences it contains are connected clearly and logically in a sequence (or order) that is easy to follow. An essay is coherent if the writer has made sure to create logical connections between paragraphs. The thought expressed in one sentence or paragraph should lead directly—without a break—to the thought in the following sentence or paragraph.

Logical connections between sentences and between paragraphs can be created in two ways: (1) by using transitional devices and (2) by making reference to words, ideas, and other details that the writer has mentioned earlier.

Maintaining Coherence by Using Transitional Devices

Transitional devices, also called "transitions" or "connectives," are words, phrases, and even whole sentences that establish or show definite relationships in and between sentences and paragraphs. As seen in the following, transitional devices can be used for many different purposes.

To Indicate Time You would be describing the passage of time if you wrote: "Henry left home just before dawn. *After a short while,* sunlight burst over the green hills." Other connectives that relate to time include:

Afterward	In the meantime
After a few minutes	Meanwhile
All the while	Prior to
As soon as	Since
Before	Then
Before that time	Thereafter
During	When
In a few hours	Whenever
	While

To Indicate Similarities or Differences You can also use transitions to show that things are similar or different: "Philip seems to be following in his sister's footsteps. *Like* her, he has decided to major in engineering. *Unlike* her, he doesn't do very well in math." Other transitions that indicate similarities and differences include:

Similarities	**Differences**
Similarly	Although
In the same way	Even though
Like	On the other hand
Likewise	However
As	Otherwise
As if	Nevertheless
As though	In contrast

To Introduce Examples, Repeat Information, or Emphasize a Point You would be using a transition to introduce an example if you wrote: "Mozart displayed his genius early. *For example,* he composed his first symphony when he was only a boy."

You would be using a transition to repeat information if you wrote: "At the age of 21, Mozart was appointed court composer for the emperor of Austria. This event was *another* indication of how quickly the young man rose to fame."

You would be using a transition to emphasize a point if you wrote: "The end of Mozart's career was hardly as spectacular as its beginnings. *In fact,* he died in poverty at age 35."

Other transitional devices useful for these purposes include:

Introducing Examples	Repeating Information	Emphasizing a Point
As an example	Again	As a matter of fact
For instance	Once again	Indeed
Specifically	Once more	More important
Such as		To be sure

In fact

To Add Information If you wanted to add information by using a transition, you might write: "When Ulysses S. Grant and Robert E. Lee met at Appomattox Courthouse in 1865, they brought the Civil War to an end. *What's more,* they opened a whole new chapter in U.S. political history." Here are some other connectives you will find useful when adding information:

Also	Furthermore
As well	In addition
Besides	Moreover
Further	Too

To Show Cause and Effect If you wanted to explain that an action or idea led to or was the cause of another, you could indicate this relationship by using a transitional device like "consequently," the word that draws a connection between the two thoughts in the sentences that follow: "During the early days of the Revolution, General George Washington was unable to defend New York City. *Consequently,* he was forced to retreat to Pennsylvania." Other transitional devices that show cause-effect relationships are:

As a result *–E*	So that *–E*
Because *– C*	Then
Hence *–E*	Therefore *E*
Since *–C*	Thus *E*

Consequently E

To Show Condition If you need to explain that one action, idea, or fact depends on another, you might create a relationship based on condition by using words like "if," as in the sentences that follow: "Professor Jones should arrive in a few minutes. *If* she doesn't, we will have to go on without her." Some other transitions that show condition include:

As long as	Provided that
As soon as	Unless
In case	When
In order to	

Maintaining Coherence by Making Reference to Material That Has Come Before

Two common and very effective ways to connect details and ideas in one sentence or paragraph with what you have discussed in earlier sentences or paragraphs are (1) to use pronouns to link details and ideas and (2) to restate important details and ideas.

Using Pronouns to Link Details and Ideas   One of the best ways to make reference to material that has come before is to use *linking pronouns*, pronouns that point clearly and directly to specific names, ideas, or details you've mentioned earlier. Such pronouns direct the reader's attention to nouns in earlier sentences or even in earlier paragraphs; these nouns are called "antecedents." Relying on pronouns to maintain coherence also helps you avoid mentioning the same noun over and over, a habit that might make your writing repetitious and boring.

The most important thing to remember about using linking pronouns is to make sure that they refer directly and unmistakably to the nouns you want them to. In other words, all pronouns of reference should have antecedents that the reader will be able to identify easily and without question.

Notice how well freshman Helen Giannos uses pronouns (shown in italics) to establish coherence in the opening paragraph of "Aids: An Epidemic?":

> In the winter of 1981, Dr. Michael Gottlieb, an immunologist at the
> Harbor-UCLA Medical Center near Los Angeles, was among the first
> physicians...to notice that something strange was going on. In just
> three months, *he* treated four patients with an unusual lung infection.
> Each of *these* men was approximately 30 years old, and *they* were
> avowed [admitted] homosexuals. *Their* immune systems were
> extremely depressed, although *they* had previously enjoyed excellent
> health. "I knew that I was witnessing medical history, but I had no
> comprehension of what this illness would become," commented Dr.
> Gottlieb. *He* was talking about a new virus, *which* was later named
> AIDS (Acquired Immune Deficiency Syndrome).

Helen's paragraph includes only a few of the pronouns you might want to use to make your writing more coherent. Here are some others.

Personal Pronouns   These are pronouns that refer to people and things:

I (me, my, mine)
He, she, it (him, his; her, hers; its)

We (us, our, ours)
You (your, yours)
They (them, their, theirs)

Relative Pronouns   These are pronouns that help describe nouns by connecting them with clauses (groups of words that contain nouns and verbs):

Who (whose, whom)	Whatever
That	Which
What	Whichever

Demonstrative Pronouns These are pronouns that precede and stand for the nouns they refer to. Sentences like *"Those* are the best seats in the house" or *"That* is my worst subject" make use of demonstrative pronouns. The most common demonstrative pronouns are:

| This | These |
| That | Those |

Indefinite Pronouns These are pronouns used for general rather than specific reference. You can make good use of these pronouns as long as you are sure that the reader can identify their antecedents easily. For instance: "Both Sylvia and Andrew were released from the hospital. *Neither* was seriously injured." In this case, the antecedents of "neither" are Sylvia and Andrew. Here are other indefinite pronouns:

All	Neither
Another	Nobody
Both	None
Each	No one
Either	Several
Everybody	Some
Everyone	Someone

Restating Important Details and Ideas The second way to make reference to material that has come before is to restate important details and ideas by repeating words and phrases or by using easily recognizable *synonyms*, terms that have the same (or nearly the same) meaning as those words or phrases.

A good example of outright repetition is the introduction of Patricia Volk's "A Family of Firsts" (a selection in Chapter 3):

> In my family, success is weighed by a single standard: The ability to be *first*. It does not matter what you are *first* at as long as you are *first* at something.

In the following paragraph from "How the Superwoman Myth Puts Women Down," Sylvia Rabiner repeats the word "women" three times but also uses easily recognizable synonyms for the sake of variety:

> *Women* are self-critical creatures. We can always find reasons to hate ourselves. Single *women* believe they are failing if they don't have a loving, permanent relationship; *working mothers* are conflicted about

leaving their children; divorced *women* experience guilt over the break-up of their marriages; *housewives* feel inadequate because they don't have careers; *career women* are wretched if they aren't advancing, and *everyone* is convinced she is too fat!

Both of these paragraphs hold together quite well because their authors were conscious of the need to maintain coherence through the careful repetition of words and ideas.

This chapter has introduced you to two very important principles of organization: unity and coherence. A paragraph or essay is *unified* if all its ideas and details relate to and contribute to the central idea. A paragraph or essay is *coherent* if the reader can move from sentence to sentence and paragraph to paragraph easily because the writer has connected the ideas clearly and logically.

Look for signs of unity and coherence as you read the following selections. More important, apply these principles in your own writing as you respond to the Suggestions for Journal Entries and the Suggestions for Writing.

From "Pain Is Not the Ultimate Enemy"

Norman Cousins

Norman Cousins was the editor of *Saturday Review*, an important literary magazine, for four decades. In the early 1960s he became stricken with an illness that left him almost totally paralyzed. His doctors told him he would never recover, but Cousins refused to believe them and prescribed his own cure. Above all, he remained steadfastly optimistic, believing that a strong will was the surest way to recovery.

"Pain Is Not the Ultimate Enemy" first appeared in *The Anatomy of an Illness*, a book about his successful struggle to regain his health.

Looking Ahead

1. Look up the word "ultimate" in the dictionary. Try to determine what Cousins is driving at in the title.
2. Using what you learned in Chapter 1 about the central idea, identify Cousins' topic sentence, which contains the central idea of this paragraph.
3. After reviewing the transitional devices and other ways to maintain coherence discussed in this chapter, identify the methods that Cousins uses to maintain coherence throughout his paragraph.

Vocabulary

overzealous   Too eager, too enthusiastic.

pain suppressants   Pain killers, drugs used to relieve or diminish pain.

sustained   Over a long period.

Professional athletes are sometimes severely disadvantaged by trainers whose job it is to keep them in action. The more famous the athlete, the greater the risk that he or she may be subjected to extreme medical measures when injury strikes. The star baseball pitcher whose arm is sore because of a torn muscle or tissue damage may need sustained rest more than anything else. But his team is battling for a place in the World Series; so the trainer or team doctor, called upon to work his magic, reaches for a strong dose of butazolidine or other powerful pain suppressants. Presto, the pain disappears! The pitcher takes his place on the mound and does superbly. That could be the last game, however, in which he is able to throw a ball with full strength. The drugs didn't repair the torn muscle or cause the damaged tissue to heal. What they did was to mask the pain, enabling the pitcher to throw hard, further damaging the torn muscle. Little wonder that so many star athletes are cut down in their prime, more the victims of overzealous treatment of their injuries than of the injuries themselves.

Questions for Discussion

1. What is Cousins' topic sentence? What is his main point?
2. You've learned that a paragraph is unified if all its details relate to and contribute to the central idea. For instance, when Cousins talks in the third sentence about "The star baseball pitcher whose arm is sore," he is making a direct reference to the term "professional athletes" in the topic sentence. Examine each of his other sentences, and make sure you understand how it relates to or supports the central idea.
3. As you know, a good way to maintain coherence is to use transitional devices or "connectives." Reread pages in this chapter that explain how to use such words and phrases. Then, identify a few of them in Cousins' paragraphs.
4. Another good way to keep your writing coherent is to use linking pronouns. Reread the pages in this chapter that discuss such pronouns; then identify a few of these pronouns in Cousins' paragraph.
5. Still another way to maintain coherence is to restate important details and ideas. Which ones does Cousins repeat in order to make his writing coherent?

Suggestions for Journal Entries

1. In any of your other textbooks, look for a paragraph of about 75 to 100 words. Write this paragraph's topic sentence in your journal. If the paragraph's central idea is not expressed in a topic sentence but is only implied, put the central idea into your own words. Then explain if and how each of the other sentences in this paragraph relates to the central idea.
2. Find another paragraph like the one mentioned in item 1. What has the author done to maintain coherence within this paragraph? What linking pronouns has he or she used? What transitional devices do you find? What words or ideas are repeated?

From "The Search for Adam and Eve"

Newsweek

On January 11, 1988, the cover story of *Newsweek* magazine proclaimed that a group of anthropologists (scientists who study the origins of the human race) may have found our "common ancestor—a woman who lived over 200,000 years ago" and whose genes are "carried by all of mankind." Having examined a large number of living women around the world, the anthropologists found that every one of the women carries this ancient woman's DNA (the material that determines heredity). Thus, it is possible that among our many and varied ancestors, everyone's family tree includes this woman as one of its members. If this is indeed the case, it means that all peoples of the Earth are related.

The selection that follows is the introductory paragraph of the *Newsweek* story.

Looking Ahead

1. Scientists have decided to call the woman whom they believe to be our common ancestor "Eve," after the woman who appears in Genesis, the first book of the Old Testament. The Bible tells us that after eating of the "tree of knowledge," Adam and Eve were cast out of the Garden of Eden and later became the father and mother of the human race.
2. Many Renaissance painters used the story of Adam and Eve as the subject of their works. The Renaissance was a period of great intellectual and artistic achievement in Europe during the fifteenth, sixteenth, and seventeenth centuries. Milton's *Paradise Lost* (1667), an epic poem written at the end of the Renaissance, tells the story of the angel Lucifer's rebellion against God and of Adam and Eve's loss of innocence.
3. Martina Navratilova, whom this paragraph mentions, is a professional tennis player.

Vocabulary

evokes   Suggests.

fruitful   Productive, fertile, bearing many offspring.

genes   The biological units that carry the characteristics that offspring inherit from their parents. Genes are composed of DNA (deoxyribonucleic acid).

maternal   Motherly.

propagating   Producing, breeding, generating.

provocative   Suggestive, fascinating.

reluctantly   Hesitantly, unwillingly.

savanna   Flat grassland.

tresses   Hair.

voluptuary   Pleasure seeker.

Scientists are calling her Eve, but reluctantly. The name evokes too many wrong images—the weak-willed figure in Genesis, the milk-skinned beauty in

Renaissance art, the voluptuary gardener in "Paradise Lost" who was all "softness" and "meek surrender" and waist-length "gold tresses." The scientists' Eve—subject of one of the most provocative anthropological theories in a decade—was more likely a dark-haired, black-skinned woman, roaming a hot savanna in search of food. She was as muscular as Martina Navratilova, maybe stronger; she might have torn animals apart with her hands, although she probably preferred to use stone tools. She was not the only woman on earth, nor necessarily the most attractive or maternal. She was simply the most fruitful, if that is measured by success in propagating a certain set of genes. Hers seem to be in all humans living today: 5 billion blood relatives. She was, by one rough estimate, your 10,000th great-grandmother.

Questions for Discussion

1. Is the central idea of this paragraph expressed in a formal topic sentence, or is it simply left up to the reader to determine? What is the central idea communicated in this paragraph? Put it into your own words.
2. The information in this paragraph is developed and organized quite well; each sentence relates clearly to one central idea. Explain how each of these sentences helps develop the central idea.
3. What linking pronouns do you find in the paragraph?

Suggestion for a Journal Entry

Check your library or local newsstand for the current issue of a magazine you read often or have wanted to read. Read two or three of the major stories in this issue. Then analyze each of their introductory paragraphs by responding to the following:

- What is the central idea of the paragraph?
- Is the central idea expressed in a formal topic sentence, or is it implied?
- Do all of the other ideas and details in the paragraph relate directly and clearly to this central idea? In other words, is the paragraph unified?
- What ideas and details does the author use to create coherence between sentences? What synonyms does he or she use?
- What linking pronouns can you find in the paragraph?
- What transitional words and phrases (connectives) does the author use to maintain coherence?

"Real" Men and Women

Charles Osgood

Charles Osgood is a noted TV commentator who appears on CBS. Recalling his start as a radio journalist, Osgood ends each installment of his television news spot, *The Osgood File,* with the somewhat odd closing: "See you on the radio." He often delivers his commentaries as poems, complete with rhyme and rhythm. Whatever his likable eccentricities, Osgood never fails to provide insight into the important human problems of our day. " 'Real' Men and Women" first appeared in *Nothing Could Be Finer Than a Crisis That Is Minor in the Morning,* 1979.

Looking Ahead

1. Chapter 1 noted that writers sometimes don't put their ideas in the first sentence of a paragraph or in the first paragraph of an essay. Remember this as you read Osgood's essay.
2. As you've learned, writers create coherence within and between paragraphs by using transitional devices, by repeating words and ideas, and by using linking pronouns. Look for these devices in "'Real' Men and Women."

Vocabulary

affiliation   Connection, loyalty.
assumption   An idea that is presumed, upon which other ideas are based.
idealized   Wished for, hoped for.
proclivities   Inclinations, preferences.

Helene, a young friend of mine, has been assigned a theme in English 1 composition class. She can take her choice: "What is a *real* man?" or if she wishes, "What is a *real* woman?" Seems the instructor has some strong ideas on these subjects. Helene says she doesn't know which choice to make. "I could go the women's-lib route," she says, "but I don't think he'd like that. I started in on that one once in a class, and it didn't go over too well." So, what is a real man and what is a real woman?

"As opposed to what?" I asked. 2

"I don't know, as opposed to unreal men and women, I suppose. Got 3 any ideas?"

Yes, it just so happens I do. Let's start with the assumption that reality 4 is that which is, as opposed to that which somebody would like, or something that is imagined or idealized. Let's assume that all human beings who are alive, therefore, are real human beings, who can be divided into two categories: real men and real women. A man who exists is a real man. His reality is in no way lessened by his race, his nationality, political affiliation, financial status, religious persuasion, or personal proclivities. All men are real men. All women are real women.

The first thing you do if you want to destroy somebody is rob him of his 5 humanity. If you can persuade yourself that someone is a gook and therefore not a real person, you can kill him rather more easily, burn down his home, separate him from his family. If you can persuade yourself that someone is not really a person but a spade, a Wasp, a kike, a wop, a mick, a fag, a dike, and therefore not a real man or woman, you can more easily hate and hurt him.

People who go around making rules, setting standards that other people 6 are supposed to meet in order to qualify as real, are real pains in the neck— and worse, they are real threats to the rest of us. They use their own definitions of real and unreal to filter out unpleasant facts. To them, things like crime, drugs, decay, pollution, slums, et cetera, are not the real America. In the same way, they can look at a man and say he is not a real man because he doesn't give a hang about pro football and would rather chase butterflies than a golfball; or they can look at a woman and say she is not a real woman because she drives a cab or would rather change the world than change diapers.

To say that someone is not a real man or woman is to say that they are 7 something less than, and therefore not entitled to the same consideration as, real people. Therefore, Helene, contained within the questions "What is a real man?" and "What is a real woman?" are the seeds of discrimination and of murders, big and little. Each of us has his own reality, and nobody has the right to limit or qualify that—not even English composition instructors.

Questions for Discussion

1. In your own words, explain Osgood's thesis. In what paragraph is this thesis stated?
2. Why does Osgood begin his essay by describing Helene's essay assignment?
3. What is the topic sentence of paragraph 5? What does it have to do with Osgood's thesis? What about the topic sentences in paragraphs 6 and 7?
4. What do you think the author means in the first sentence of paragraph 6? In what other parts of this essay does he discuss the same idea?
5. In paragraph 5, Osgood uses repetition to maintain coherence. Identify the repetitions, and explain how they build coherence.
6. What linking pronouns does Osgood use to keep paragraph 6 coherent?
7. What transitional word can be found in paragraph 7?
8. Paragraph 4 uses a number of different techniques for maintaining coherence. What are they?

Suggestions for Journal Entries

1. Think of a close friend or relative who is different from other people in many ways but whom you admire nonetheless; write down the reasons you admire this person. Then, make sure each reason is expressed in a complete sentence that could serve as the central idea of a paragraph or essay about this individual.
2. In his conclusion, Osgood writes that "contained within the questions 'What is a real man?' and 'What is a real woman?' are the seeds of discrimination and of murders, big and little." Put this curious sentence into your own words. Then use this as the topic sentence of a paragraph in which you explain Osgood's meaning more fully. To keep your paragraph unified, make sure that each sentence in the paragraph relates to your topic sentence directly. To maintain coherence, use connectives, repeat ideas, and use linking pronouns whenever you can.

Gambling

Michael Witt

Michael Witt graduated from Middlesex County College in Edison, New Jersey, with an associate of arts degree in journalism. "Gambling" was written in response to an assignment in an advanced composition class. When the instructor asked members of the class to interview someone with a unique personality or problem and write a character sketch, Witt knew just whom to call. "Richie Martin," an alias the author assigned one of his closest friends, provided him with all the material he needed to put together a touching, penetrating portrait of a young man in agony. Witt's essay is a record of Richie Martin's battle with an evil as strong and as destructive as drug addiction or alcoholism.

Looking Ahead

1. Witt's thesis statement, the first sentence in his essay, contains two parts, each of which helps define his idea of gambling. Read it carefully.
2. One of the reasons for Witt's success is that he did a thorough job of gathering important facts in his interview with "Richie Martin." Another is that he organized the material about his subject in unified and coherent

paragraphs, each of which is introduced with a clear, distinct, well-written topic sentence. Examine these topic sentences carefully.

3. Still another reason this essay is so successful is that each of the topic sentences in the body (paragraphs 2 to 7) relates directly to the thesis, keeping the essay unified.

Vocabulary

affliction   Disease, illness, misfortune.
attest   Bear witness to.
doldrums   Depression.
exhilarating   Exciting.
profound   Deep, significant.
rehabilitate   Make healthy, make sound.
suppress   Control.
transcend   Go beyond.

Though most people don't seem to realize it, it's a disease, akin to alcoholism and drug addiction, and it has ruined more families and more relationships than statistics can accurately define. It's gambling—and it's one of the most underrated problems in America today.   1

Richie Martin can attest to this fact. As he speaks, his eyes tell the story   2
as they transcend the excitement of a racetrack photo finish and the disappointment of losing this month's rent on a solitary basketball game. He's excited, then subtle. His mood changes reflect a man whose very life goes from ecstatic highs to severe doldrums—depending on Sunday's games.

Richie bets on anything, from the World Series to the presidential elec-   3
tion. Hours before his sister delivered her first child, he attempted to bet his brother-in-law thirty dollars it would be a boy. But mainly he gambles on sports and, when playoff time arrives, Richie's money usually departs. "Over the last five years, I've lost at least twenty-five thousand dollars," he admitted, "and even though it hasn't really broke me, I feel like I'm always chasing what I've lost."

His obsession with gambling has also had a profound effect on several   4
relationships. "I used to bring my ex-girlfriend to the racetrack and Atlantic City all the time," he remembered, "but when I'd lose I'd snap at her all the way home. She couldn't take it any more." His gambling habits started early when, as a young boy, he'd bet nickels with his father on TV bowling tournaments. "We'd bet on every ball that went down the alley," he recalled. "It was just for fun." Though it seemed harmless at the time, it led to a more serious and distressing involvement in gambling. And this, he feels, has thrust upon his father strong feelings of guilt. "I've never blamed him for my problem and he knows it, but I don't think he'll ever be satisfied until I quit."

He freely admits his affliction, which he feels is an important step to- 5
wards recovery, but the exhilarating world of taking chances is not an easy
place to leave. "When I win, it's like everything I touch turns to gold, but
when I lose, I wanna dig a hole and crawl right in it," he said. It's these
sensations, these extremes of emotion, that give his life a sense of meaning and
keep him in constant touch with his bookie.

At times, the stench of losing becomes so unbearable he vows to reha- 6
bilitate himself. Every Monday morning, after a weekend of gambling away
half of Friday's paycheck, he takes an oath to change his destructive ways—so
far without success. "Every time I'm ready to quit, I win a good buck. Then
I'm right back where I started."

Lately, however, he has taken some drastic steps towards rehabilitation. 7
He has quit his day job and taken a night one in the hope of isolating himself
from the world of racetracks and ballparks, which operate primarily at night.
"What I don't know won't hurt me," he says with a sad smile. He also hopes
the change in "work friends" will influence his habits.

"It's a no-win situation, just like alcohol and drugs," he concludes. "And 8
I'm tired of it." The world of sports will never go away, nor will the excitement of winning and losing, but with a little luck and a lot of self-control he
may suppress his disease—but don't bet on it.

Questions for Discussion

1. In his thesis statement, Witt tells us that gambling is "a disease" and that it has
   "ruined more families and relationships than statistics can accurately define."
   In which of the paragraphs that follow does the author seem to describe gambling as a disease? In which does he talk about the relationships it has destroyed?
2. What is the topic sentence in each of the paragraphs that follows Witt's
   introductory paragraph?
3. In Looking Ahead you learned that this essay is unified so well because the
   topic sentences in paragraphs 2 to 7 relate directly to the thesis. Explain
   how each topic sentence contributes to the reader's understanding of Witt's
   central idea.
4. What transitional devices and linking pronouns does the author use to
   create coherence between paragraphs? Does he ever repeat words or ideas
   to accomplish this? Explain how the use of these techniques makes the
   essay coherent.
5. Review paragraphs 2 to 7 carefully. Make a list of the transitional devices,
   linking pronouns, and repeated words and ideas that Witt uses in each.

Suggestions for Journal Entries

1. If you know someone who is suffering from an addiction, write a paragraph that discusses the addiction and its effect on this individual. Start

with a topic sentence that names the addiction (such as alcoholism, drug abuse, gambling, or even an addiction to money), and make sure that the topic sentence also explains how the addiction has affected this person's life.

Both the topic sentence and the paragraph's development must be specific. Limit your discussion to one aspect (or part) of your subject's life; for instance, you might say that "Martha's drinking problem is affecting her performance on the job." Then provide details that support (or prove) your topic sentence: explain that Martha has been late three mornings this week because of severe hangovers, that she didn't make it to work the day after a holiday party, and that she never returns to the office if she has a drink with lunch.

In addition, be sure that your paragraph is unified. Check to see that each detail helps explain how the addiction has affected your subject's life. Finally, maintain coherence throughout the paragraph. Include transitional expressions, repeat words and ideas, and use synonyms and linking pronouns whenever you can to connect one sentence with the next.

2. If you know a person who is suffering from a serious illness, write a paragraph in which you identify the illness and describe one and *only* one of the effects it is having on this individual. For instance, your topic sentence might read, "Aunt Clara's diabetes has caused her to make radical changes in her diet." Develop and organize your paragraph by following the advice in item 1.

Vegetable Gardens Are for the Birds

Howard Scott

Home vegetable gardens have become increasingly popular recently, perhaps because so many of us have the need to "get back to nature." But Howard Scott feels otherwise. In this well-developed, well-organized essay, he humorously explains why he prefers store-bought veggies to those you can grow in the backyard.

"Vegetable Gardens Are for the Birds" first appeared in *The New York Times*.

Looking Ahead

1. The thesis of this essay is not contained in a single sentence. To understand Scott's central idea, combine the main points in paragraphs 1 and 2.
2. Scott tells us in his opening sentence that in admitting he hates vegetable

gardens he runs "the risk of committing heresy." "Heresy" involves advocating ideas that are in opposition to accepted religious beliefs. His use of this word is facetious, of course, designed to make his readers chuckle.

3. The "Crockett" mentioned in paragraph 4 is *Crockett's Victory Garden*, a book on home gardening.

4. In paragraph 3, the "Second Coming" is the Second Coming of Christ predicted in the New Testament.

Vocabulary

consistency Regularity.

gluttony Sin of eating to excess.

horrendous Atrocious, dreadful.

illusion Fantasy, deception.

induces Causes, produces.

optimum Very best.

paraphernalia Equipment, gear.

tiller A tool for turning the soil.

At the risk of committing heresy, I want to state my biggest summer gripe: I hate vegetable gardens. 1

Worse, I scorn gardeners....Even more horrendous, I prefer to eat store-bought veggies instead of newly plucked offerings. 2

Here are my complaints. Growing plants doesn't take much skill. Every gardener pridefully displays a ripe tomato or a giant cucumber as though she's personally carved it out of the earth. "Look at this," she'll say, expecting your face to look as if it were witnessing the Second Coming. The plain fact is that any halfwit can grow things. All it takes is doing dumb repetitive tasks with the plodding consistency of a workhorse. 3

A garden takes time. Not only is there readying the soil, planting, watering, weeding, debugging, pruning and harvesting, but also there is the research. A gardener is constantly checking into Crockett's about snails, reading up on herbs at the library and phoning fellow planters to arrive at optimum plant dates. So much so, many of us spouses become earth widows(ers). 4

A garden costs. First there are the tools. Then the seeds and flats. Next comes the renting of the tiller. After that comes mulch, manure and prep medication. Next, water followed by insect spraying. Then the experiments with new irrigation systems and updated equipment. Finally, jars, labels and canning paraphernalia. 5

A garden creates waste. At harvest time, 15 heads of lettuce must be picked within two weeks' time or they'll rot. So you eat three salads a day and bring bags full to all your friends (most of whom have their own oversupply 6 problems). Needless to say, buying a head or two at the supermarket each week avoids such cycles of gluttony and famine.

Home-grown vegetables aren't as clean as store-bought produce. You 7 risk chomping on worms or slugs, breaking a tooth on a pebble, grinding into dirt and smelling the manure through which the thing prospered. The cellophane wrapping, the official-looking label and the pale, dry coloring of packaged goods eliminate those possibilities.

Garden vegetables don't taste as mellow as shelved stock. The carrots 8 are too crispy, the peppers too tangy, the scallions too potent, the celery too stringy. I prefer my veggies to blend in like a symphony beneath heaping tablespoons of dressing.

A garden ties its owner down. Taking a week's vacation is impossible 9 because, what if—God forbid—it doesn't rain. Even a long weekend is tough. And anybody who lives with a gardener knows the fanaticism of the daily watering.

A gardener's needs tend to expand. This year it's a 10 by 12 foot plot. 10 Next year, it's a 15 by 20 space and a compost bin. The year after, it's the larger plot, an experimental patch out front and a shed. The year after, it's a greenhouse.

Gardens make boring conversations. After the umpteenth walk to see 11 little buds popping up, you run out of things to say. Then, as the summer progresses, it's, "Oh, isn't this salad fresh," and, "I can't get over how succulent these cantaloupes are." On top of all that, you have to listen to shop talk among gardeners. Early on, you might make discreet jokes, but after seeing that nobody's listening you just stand around bored.

Gardens offer the illusion of accomplishment. Seeds are planted, and 12 two months later a lush bounty of vegetables emerges from the ground. Amazing, says the grower. Amazing, nothing. For years, the Government has been paying farmers billions of dollars for not planting their lands. Warehouses are bursting with excess crops. Face it. The success of this nation is based more on perfect climate and fertile soil than any other condition.

A garden induces contentment. Cultivating the earth makes its owner 13 feel at peace with the world. Fine—but, as with cocaine, medication and booze, it reduces ambition to attempt other challenges. And as inwardly satisfying as the routine might be, there are some things growing vegetables can't solve. But try to tell a gardener that.

Questions for Discussion

1. Scott's thesis is composed of three main points expressed in three different sentences. What are these main points?
2. Identify the topic sentences in paragraphs 3 to 13.

3. A sentence in paragraph 3 makes it easy for the reader to draw a connection between Scott's thesis and the topic sentences in each of the paragraphs that follow. What is this transitional sentence?
4. In which of the paragraphs after Scott's introduction is the topic sentence *not* the first sentence of the paragraph?
5. Paragraph 5 is filled with transitional words that make it easy to follow. What other connectives do you find in the essay's other paragraphs?

Suggestions for Journal Entries

1. Write a paragraph in which you explain why you like or dislike a certain food. In the topic sentence, state one and only one reason for liking or disliking the food. For instance, you might write, "I hate corn on the cob because it is hard to eat" or "I enjoy munching on raw carrots because I know they're very nutritious."

   Next provide ideas and details that support your topic sentence. Make sure your paragraph is unified by including only details that relate clearly to your topic sentence. For instance, if you hate corn on the cob because it is difficult to eat, you might mention that bits of corn often get caught between your teeth or that the melted butter has a way of dripping all over your clean clothes. However, you probably won't mention that your parents forced you to eat corn on the cob all summer long when you were a child, a piece of information that has nothing do with the fact that the corn is hard to eat.

   Finally, maintain coherence within the paragraph by using transitional devices, linking pronouns, and so forth.
2. Following the advice in item 1, write a paragraph in which you explain why you like or dislike a certain activity. For example, discuss why you enjoy or despise gardening, mowing the lawn, walking the dog, flossing your teeth, going bowling, visiting relatives, or getting up to go to class on a cold morning.

SUGGESTIONS FOR WRITING

1. Reread two or three of the selections in this chapter, and find a paragraph of about 75 or 100 words that you particularly like. If the paragraph has a formal topic sentence, rewrite that topic sentence in your own words. If the paragraph's central idea is not stated outright but is only implied, create your own topic sentence.

   Next, rewrite the rest of the paragraph in your own words. Make sure that your new paragraph is unified by including only those details that relate directly to your topic sentence. Finally, maintain coherence between sentences by supplying your own transitional devices and linking pronouns and by repeating words and ideas as necessary.

2. Look over the journal notes you made after reading Norman Cousins' "Pain Is Not the Ultimate Enemy." Then, reread the paragraph that you found in one of your other textbooks and that you chose to write about in your journal.

   Rewrite that paragraph in your own words, complete with a topic sentence and all the supportive details and ideas that relate to that topic sentence. In addition, make sure that your version of this paragraph is coherent. Use transitional devices and linking pronouns, or repeat words and ideas whenever you need to.

3. If you responded to item 1 of the Suggestions for Journal Entries after Charles Osgood's "'Real' Men and Women," you've probably begun explaining the reasons that you admire a close friend or relative whom others might find "different." Make sure that each of these reasons is expressed in a topic sentence.

   Use each topic sentence as the beginning of a paragraph that fully explains the reasons you admire this individual. After you have written three or four paragraphs, try to think of a central idea to which each of the topic sentences can relate. In other words, write a thesis statement that will help you join these separate paragraphs into a unified essay. For instance, let's say your topic sentences read:

   Paragraph 1: Mike gives a big part of his weekly salary to charity.
   Paragraph 2: Mike frequently offers to help people in need.
   Paragraph 3: Mike is always considerate of others' feelings.
   Your thesis might read: Mike is one of the most unselfish persons I've ever met.

   Use this thesis as an introduction to an essay you construct from these paragraphs. Make sure you have maintained coherence in and between paragraphs by using techniques discussed in this chapter.

4. The Suggestions for Journal Entries following Michael Witt's "Gambling" involve writing about a person who is suffering from an addiction or serious illness. If you responded to either suggestion, you have probably written a unified and coherent paragraph that discusses one of the ways the addiction or illness has affected his or her life.

   Review this paragraph carefully. Then, write several more well-organized paragraphs, each of which explains another way in which the person's life has been changed by this addiction or illness. Next, turn these separate paragraphs into a unified essay by providing an appropriate thesis statement that will appear at the beginning of your essay and serve as its introduction. Finally, check to see that you have maintained coherence in and between paragraphs by using techniques explained in the introduction to this chapter.

5. Howard Scott's "Vegetable Gardens Are for the Birds" may have inspired you to discuss your feelings (negative or positive) about a certain food or activity. Reread the journal entry you made after reading this selection.

   Then, expand your discussion. Write at least two other paragraphs, *each of which* contains yet another reason you "like walking the dog" or "despise eating cauliflower." Once again, be careful. For the sake of unity, make sure that each paragraph you write explains *one and only one reason*. Tie these paragraphs together into an essay with a thesis statement to which each of the topic sentences you've written can relate clearly and logically. Finally, be certain that you maintain coherence in and between paragraphs.

Chapter 3
Development

By now you know from practice that you use the central idea to focus your writing on a main point and to keep it unified. You do so by making sure that all the information in your paragraphs and essays relates clearly to the central idea. This chapter explains how the central idea also controls *development—* how much information a piece of writing contains and how this information is organized.

A paragraph or essay is said to be well developed if if contains all the details it needs to prove, illustrate, or otherwise support its central idea. You should provide enough details to establish your point clearly and convincingly. You should also arrange these details in a way that is appropriate to your purpose and that will help your readers follow your train of thought easily.

DETERMINING HOW MUCH A PARAGRAPH OR ESSAY SHOULD CONTAIN

It is not always easy to determine how much detail is enough to develop a particular point, and there is no simple rule for determining how long a paragraph or essay should be. It all depends on what you judge your readers need to understand your central idea. At times you will need to write a great many paragraphs to develop your essays.

In some of these paragraphs, extensive development will be required; in others, you might be able to make your point clearly with only one or two supportive details; and in a *few* you might find that one sentence is all you need to achieve your purpose.

In any event, it is always a good idea to rely on your central idea, as well as the purpose behind it, as a guide for development. After all, the central idea contains the main point you want to make. Therefore, it should give you a good clue about the kinds and amounts of detail you will need to make this point.

49

Let's say you want to explain that there are *several* career opportunities for people majoring in biology. To develop your paragraph adequately, you might start by discussing teaching and medicine. But you will also have to include other fields (such as laboratory research, environmental management, and forestry) if you want your reader to understand all of what you meant when, in your topic sentence or thesis, you wrote, "Majoring in biology can provide a good foundation for *several* careers."

You already know that in order to come up with a good central idea, you need to focus on the main point you want to make about your subject. The subject in the sentence above is "Majoring in biology." The main point you want to make about this subject is that it can lead to "*several* careers." In order to write a paragraph or essay that develops this point fully, therefore, you will have to discuss *several*—at least three—careers.

In short, you can think of the central idea as a promise you make to your readers at the beginning of a paragraph or essay—a promise to discuss your main point in as much detail as is appropriate. If you start off by writing that "Three types of birds visit your backyard regularly during the winter," make sure to discuss all *three* birds. If you set out to explain that "There are many ways to decrease cholesterol in the blood stream," discuss *many* ways, not just one or two. If you want to prove that your brother is not very neat, don't be content to describe his closet and leave it at that. Talk about the mess of papers and books he often leaves scattered across the floor, and mention the jumble of sporting equipment and dirty clothes on the back seat of his car.

At times, of course, you might find it difficult to decide how many details are enough to develop a paragraph or essay fully. But the more experienced you become as a writer, the easier it will be to determine how much to include. For now, remember that developing your central idea in too much detail is preferable to providing too little detail. Including too much information might bore your readers a bit, but including too little might leave them unconvinced or even confused. The first of these sins is forgivable. The second is not.

CHOOSING THE BEST METHOD OF DEVELOPMENT

Information can be developed in any number of ways. The choice of method depends on your purpose—on what point you are making and what impact you want it to have on your readers. This purpose can be description, narration, explanation, persuasion, or a combination of these.

Description

If your purpose is to introduce your reader to a person, place, or thing, you will probably want to *describe* your subject in concrete detail. The easiest way to gather details for this kind of paragraph or essay is to rely on your physical senses. Sight, smell, hearing, taste, and touch will give you the concrete, specific details to make your writing vivid and effective. Description is also discussed in Chapters 8 and 9.

Narration

If your purpose is to tell a story—to explain what happened—you will most likely *narrate* a series of events as they occurred in time, explaining each event or part of an event according to the order in which it actually took place. Narration is also discussed in Chapters 10, 11, and 12.

Explanation and Persuasion

If your purpose is *to explain* an idea (expository writing) or *to persuade* your reader that an opinion or belief you hold is correct (persuasive writing), you can choose from several methods to develop your ideas. Among these, of course, are narration and description, as well as the very simple method called conclusion and support, which will enable you to explain an idea or defend an opinion by using concrete and specific details that relate to it directly. However, you might also want *to explain* or *to persuade* by choosing from the following seven methods, each of which can be found in this chapter's reading selections:

- Illustration (using details to develop examples)
- Definition (using details to explain a term or concept)
- Classification (using details to distinguish between different types or classes)
- Comparison and contrast (using details to point out similarities and differences)
- Cause and effect (using details to explain why something happens)
- Conclusion and support (using details to clarify or prove an idea or opinion)
- Process analysis (using details to explain how to do something or how something is done)

Deciding which of these methods of development will be most effective for your purposes depends a great deal on the idea you are trying to explain or the point you are trying to make. If, for instance, you want to persuade your readers that the way to clean up the rivers in your town is to impose stiff fines on polluters, you might use the cause-and-effect method. If you are trying to explain that the salary offered by your employer is not as fair as what other employers offer for similar work, you might choose contrast as a way to develop your ideas.

All of the methods mentioned above appear in the reading selections found in this chapter. You will also learn more about illustration, comparison/contrast, and process analysis later in this book. For now, it is important to remember that methods of development can be used alone or in combination with one another to develop paragraphs and essays that explain or persuade.

DECIDING HOW TO ARRANGE THE IDEAS AND DETAILS IN A PARAGRAPH

Often, the best way to organize description or narration is simply to recall the details naturally—just as the writer saw or experienced them. When *describing*, you can arrange your concrete details in a spatial pattern; that is, you might describe a person from head to toe or from forehead to chin, a place from east to west or from left to right, and an object from top to bottom or from inside to outside. When narrating, you can arrange your details or events according to the same order in which they actually happened; this is called chronological order, or order of time.

Once again, however, more choices are available when you are trying your hand at exposition—writing that explains—and at persuasion—writing that proves a point or defends an opinion. Here are just a few patterns of organization you might want to use.

From General to Specific

Starting with a general statement and supporting it with specific details and ideas is one of the most popular and effective ways to organize a paragraph. Each of the following paragraphs has a different purpose and uses a different method of development, but each begins with a general statement (the topic sentence) that is followed and developed by specific information:

Illustration: Providing Examples

When the most massive stars die, they explode, releasing as much light as a galaxy of stars. The explosion, called a supernova, can catapult [hurl] a star from obscurity into spectacular prominence in the night sky. One supernova in 1006 shone so brightly that objects could be seen by its light for weeks. Another in 1054 was visible during the day. Astronomers believe that one in 1,000 stars becomes a supernova; a star probably blows up in the Milky Way every 100 years or so.   (Ellen Fried, "The Ungentle Death of a Giant Star.")

Comparison and Contrast: Showing Similarities and Differences

Grant and Lee were in complete contrast, representing two diametrically opposed elements in American life. Grant was the modern man emerging: behind him, ready to come on the stage, was the great age of steel and machinery, of crowded cities and a restless, burgeoning [blossoming] vitality. Lee might have ridden down from the old age of chivalry, lance in hand, silken banner fluttering over his head. Each man was the perfect champion of his cause, drawing both his strengths and his weaknesses from the people he led.   (Bruce Catton, "Grant and Lee: A Study in Contrasts.")

Classification: Listing or Explaining Types

In general, there are seven basic signals that get communicated from the [baseball] manager...to the players. The batter may be ordered to take a pitch on a three-and-zero count, or to hit away. He may be asked to protect a base runner on a hit-and-run by trying to slug the ball on the ground. On a run-and-hit, the batter is ordered to swing at a pitch only if it is in the strike zone; however, on the bunt-and-run, the batter must try to bunt to protect the breaking runner....The batter can be told to sacrifice bunt, which means he should try for the ball only if it is in the strike zone. There are signs for squeeze bunts, and finally, there is the sign to steal a base.   (Rockwell Stenrud, "Who's on Third.")

Cause and Effect: Explaining Why Something Happens

Many lower-income families of the barrio manage to maintain a comfortable standard of living through the communal action of family members who contribute their wages to the head of the family. Economic need creates interdependence and closeness. Small barefoot boys sell papers on cool, dark Sunday mornings, deny themselves pleasantries, and give their earnings to *mamá*. The older the child, the greater the responsibility to help the head of the household provide for the rest of the family.   (Robert Ramirez, "The Woolen Sarape.")

Definition: Explaining a Term or Concept

Nicotine is a familiar and widely recognized drug, a stimulant to the central nervous system. It is addictive. The toxic effects of nicotine have been detailed at great length by the Surgeon General. Americans smoke 600 billion cigarettes a year.   (Adam Smith, "A Very Short History of Some American Drugs Familiar to Everybody.")

From Specific to General

Beginning from specific details or ideas and moving toward a general conclusion (the topic sentence) about them is another common way to build a
paragraph. Although using different methods of development, all of the following paragraphs are organized from specific to general:

Conclusion and Support: Using Details That Explain or Prove

A New York taxi driver...is licensed to operate, and thereby earn his
living, by the city. One of the rules in the taxi code stipulates that the
cabdriver must take his customer to any point within the city limits
that the rider requests. Never mind that the driver makes more money
operating in Manhattan; is lost when he enters the precincts of
Brooklyn; is frightened by the prospect of a trip to Harlem at night.
The rules are clear. He must go where the customer asks.   (Willard
Gaylin, *The Rage Within.*)

Comparison and Contrast: Showing Similarities and Differences

...writing is hard work. One has to sit down on that chair and think
and transform thought into readable, conservative, interesting
sentences that both make sense and make the reader turn the page. It
is laborious, slow, often painful, sometimes agony. It means
rearrangement, revision, adding, cutting, rewriting. But it brings a
sense of excitement, almost of rapture; a moment on Olympus [home
of the gods of ancient Greece]. In short, it is an act of
creation.   (Barbara Tuchman, "In Search of History.")

Cause and Effect: Explaining Why Something Happens

More than three-quarters of all the ice in the world is in the southern
polar continent of Antarctica, a conveniently distant place. Most of the
rest of the world's ice lies in Greenland, also a remote place. So we are
accustomed to thinking of the heavily populated lands of the Earth as
being ice-free, except for the minute smears of the stuff we encounter
in winter.   (Sir Frederick Hoyle, "The Next Ice Age.")

From Question to Answer

Another good way to develop a paragraph is to attract the reader's attention
with an interesting question and then to answer this question in detail. If you
choose this pattern of organization, you will probably want to place the question as close to the beginning of the paragraph as possible. You can then
devote the rest of your paragraph to details that develop an effective answer.

Cause and Effect: Explaining Why Something Happens

Why should you examine your writing style with the idea of improving it? Do so as a mark of respect for your readers, whatever you're writing. If you scribble your thoughts any which way, your readers will surely feel that you care nothing about them. They will mark you down as an egomaniac or a chowderhead—or worse, they will stop reading you.   (Kurt Vonnegut, "How to Write with Style.")

Definition: Explaining a Term or Concept

"What is a kike?" Disraeli once asked a small group of fellow politicians. Then, as his audience shifted nervously, Queen Victoria's great Jewish Prime Minister supplied the answer himself. "A kike" he observed, "is a Jewish gentleman who has just left the room."   (Charles F. Berlitz, "The Etymology of the International Insult.")

From Problem to Solution

Stating a problem in the first sentence and explaining its solution in the rest of the paragraph is much like asking a question and answering it. It is especially effective when you are analyzing a process—explaining how to do something, how something works, or how something happens.

Process Analysis: Explaining How to Do Something

If you are tempted to do something that you know is academically dishonest—such as copy another student's results or lift an idea for a paper without crediting the source or, worse, cheat on an exam—then you are already in the clutches of grade frenzy. Take a break; discuss your situation with an adviser or a friend. Relax.   (Thomas C. Hayden, *Handbook for College Admissions.*)

By Order of Importance

Writers of fiction often place the most important bit of information last. This makes their work suspenseful and thus creates a more effective climax. By using this pattern in a paragraph, you can guide your readers to the details and ideas you believe are most important. Notice that Anthony Lewis waits until the end of the paragraph to mention the most important of all rights—the right to vote—which had been denied blacks in the south before 1954:

Illustration: Providing Examples

It is hard to remember, now, what this country was like before May 17, 1954 [the day the U.S. Supreme Court outlawed racial segregation in public schools]. More than a third of America's public schools were segregated by law. And not just schools: In the Southern and Border states, black men and women and children were kept out of "white" hospitals, and parks, and beaches, and restaurants. Interracial marriage was forbidden. In the deep South, law and brutal force kept blacks from voting.   (Anthony Lewis, "The System Worked.")

As you read the following selections, remember what you've just learned about (1) the various methods that writers use to develop their ideas and (2) the various patterns they use to organize their paragraphs. Approach each selection carefully, and devote as much effort to determining *how* the author has organized and developed the material as you do to understanding what the essay means. Doing so will help you develop your own writing more effectively.

The Hibernation of the Woodchuck

Alan Devoe

Alan Devoe (1909–1955) was a naturalist who wrote several delightful books and hundreds of articles about the animals he observed on his 100-acre wildlife sanctuary in New York State. He was a staff writer for *The American Mercury, The Audubon Magazine, The Atlantic Monthly,* and *Nature.*

According to Devoe, the best way to learn about animals is to live near them. He could often be seen walking the grounds of his estate as he observed, talked to, and even fed the many creatures who made it their home. "The Hibernation of the Woodchuck" appeared in *Lives Around Us,* a book on animal behavior that was based on such experiences.

Looking Ahead

1. In some of Devoe's paragraphs, the central idea is stated clearly and explicitly in a topic sentence; in others, it is only implied. Where the central idea is stated, identify it. In paragraphs where it is not stated, explain in your own words what central idea the paragraph develops. (The central idea was discussed in Chapter 1.)
2. To reinforce what you learned in Chapter 2, explain the ways in which Devoe maintains coherence in and between his paragraphs. Look for linking pronouns, for transitional devices, and for the repetition of key words or ideas.
3. Although Devoe's main purpose is to explain a process (how something happens), he uses other methods of development as well. These include comparison and contrast, cause and effect, and conclusion and support. Watch for them as you read "The Hibernation of the Woodchuck."

Vocabulary

ascends Rises.
axils Places at which the legs are joined to the body.
dormancy Unstable, fluctuating.
foraging Searching for food.
gait Walk.
lethargic Sluggish.
oblivion Unconsciousness.

The woodchuck's hibernation usually starts about the middle of September. For weeks he has been foraging with increased appetite among the 1

clover blossoms and has grown heavy and slow-moving. Now, with the coming of mid-September, apples and corn and yarrow tops have become less
plentiful, and the nights are cool. The woodchuck moves with slower gait,
and emerges less and less frequently for feeding trips. Layers of fat have accumulated around his chest and shoulders, and there is thick fat in the axils
of his legs. He has extended his summer burrow to a length of nearly thirty
feet, and has fashioned a deep nest-chamber at the end of it, far below the
level of frost. He has carried in, usually, a little hay. He is ready for the Long
Sleep.

When the temperature of the September days falls below 50 degrees or 2
so, the woodchuck becomes too drowsy to come forth from his burrow in the
chilly dusk to forage. He remains in the deep nest-chamber, lethargic, hardly
moving. Gradually, with the passing of hours or days, his coarse-furred body
curls into a semicircle, like a foetus, nose-tip touching tail. The small legs are
tucked in, the handlike clawed forefeet folded. The woodchuck has become
a compact ball. Presently the temperature of his body begins to fall.

In normal life the woodchuck's temperature, though fluctuant, averages 3
about 97 degrees. Now, as he lies tight-curled in a ball with the winter sleep
stealing over him, his body heat drops ten degrees, twenty degrees, thirty.
Finally, by the time the snow is on the ground and the woodchuck's winter
dormancy has become complete, his temperature is only 38 or 40. With the
falling of the body heat there is a slowing of his heartbeat and his respiration.
In normal life he breathes thirty or forty times each minute; when he is excited, as many as a hundred times. Now he breathes slow and slower—ten
times a minute, once a minute, and at last only ten or twelve times in an hour.
His heartbeat is a twentieth of normal. He has entered fully into the oblivion
of hibernation.

The Long Sleep lasts, on an average, about six months. For half a year 4
the woodchuck remains unmoving, hardly breathing. His pituitary gland is
inactive; his blood is so sluggishly circulated that there is an unequal distri-
bution in the chilled body; his sensory awareness has wholly ceased. It is
almost true to say that he has altered from a warm-blooded to a cold-blooded
animal.

Then, in the middle of March, he wakes. The waking is not a slow and 5
gradual thing, as was the drifting into sleep, but takes place quickly, often in
an hour. The body temperature ascends to normal, or rather higher for a
while; glandular functions instantly resume: the respiration quickens and stead-
ies at a normal rate. The woodchuck has become himself again, save only that
he is a little thinner, and is ready at once to fare forth into the pale spring
sunlight and look for grass and berries.

Such is the performance each fall and winter, with varying detail, of bats 6
and worms and bears, and a hundred other kinds of creature. It is a marvel

less spectacular than the migration flight of hummingbirds or the flash of shooting stars, but it is not much less remarkable.

Questions for Discussion

1. What are the individual central ideas—stated or implied—that you found in Devoe's paragraphs?
2. In paragraph 2, Devoe uses the cause-and-effect method to tell us what happens to the woodchuck when the temperature falls below 50 degrees. Identify the cause and the effects in this paragraph.
3. The pattern of organization used in paragraph 2 takes the reader from a general statement to specific details. This same organizational pattern is used in paragraphs 4 and 5. What methods of development are used in these paragraphs?
4. Paragraph 3 uses details to contrast (point out differences between) the ways in which the woodchuck's body functions during hibernation and during consciousness. What details does Devoe use to develop this contrast?
5. Is paragraph 3 developed well? Does it provide enough information to help you understand the essential differences between hibernation and consciousness?
6. Paragraph 6 also contains details that contrast. Identify them.
7. Paragraphs 3 and 5 are developed through process analysis. Explain how they work.
8. What methods does Devoe use to maintain coherence in and between his paragraphs? Pick out transitions, linking pronouns, and words or ideas that have been repeated.

Suggestions for Journal Entries

1. Think about an animal you know well—your Siamese cat, the neighbor's German shepherd, a bird that visits your backyard feeder often, or the woodchuck that's been eating up your vegetable garden. List important things you know about this creature—anything that would provide clues about its behavior, lifestyle, character, or personality.

   Then ask yourself what this information tells you. Draw three or more general conclusions about this animal from the details you've listed, and write out these conclusions in the form of topic sentences for paragraphs that you might later develop about the animal.
2. Devoe uses comparison and contrast to help us understand the woodchuck's hibernation. This is especially true in paragraph 3, in which he contrasts

the animal's "normal life" with his "winter dormancy." But animals aren't the only creatures that need to adapt to different conditions.

Think about the way you dress for a date and the way you dress for work or school, the way you act with friends and the way you act among strangers, the schedule you keep during the week and the schedule you follow on weekends, or the foods you eat when you're on a diet and when you're not. Then list as many details as you can to show how your behavior changes under different circumstances.

The Thick and Thin of It

Blythe Hamer

"The Thick and Thin of It" first appeared as a column in *Science,* a magazine that published a variety of informative scientific articles and studies. In this essay Hamer probes the reasons that some areas of the world are so crowded while others are sparsely populated.

Looking Ahead

1. Hamer doesn't express her central idea in a formal thesis statement, so don't look for one. Instead, draw your own conclusion about her main point in "The Thick and Thin of It."
2. In addition to being well developed, her essay is both unified and coherent. Look for signs of unity and coherence as you read it.
3. Hamer develops this expository (or explanatory) essay in several ways. Comparison and contrast is the primary method of development in at least two paragraphs, while illustration, cause and effect, and conclusion and support are used in others. Look for these.
4. However, the author begins with an *analogy,* which is a type of comparison. An analogy can help clarify complex ideas by pointing out similarities between things that may not at first seem to have anything in common. Writers use analogies to explain abstract concepts by making reference to concrete objects with which their readers are familiar. Hamer does this in paragraph 1 when she writes that if everyone in Macau were given the same amount of land, "each would live in a space a quarter the size of a tennis court." Look for other analogies in this essay.
5. The Falkland Islands, mentioned in paragraph 2, are a colony of Great Britain located in the South Atlantic Ocean off Argentina. Several years

ago these countries fought a brief war over the Falklands, which Britain retained.

Vocabulary

arable   Usable for farming.

compensate   Make up for.

demographer   Expert on population trends.

hinterlands   Wilderness, back country.

impenetrable   Not capable of being penetrated or broken through.

perceptions   Opinions, beliefs.

socioeconomic   Having to do with the kind of society that people live in and/or the economic conditions in which they earn their livings.

subsistence   The bare minimum required to live.

If every person in Macau were given equal portions of land, each would   1
live in a space a quarter the size of a tennis court. If you take into account the room necessary for streets, stores, and offices, people living in Macau (like people living in Manhattan) are more likely to end up with an apartment the size of a Ping-Pong table. With more than 63,000 people per square mile, Macau, a tiny city-state off the coast of China, is the most densely populated place in the world.

Every Falkland Islander, by contrast, could roam over two and a half   2
square miles without ever seeing another human. But he'd better watch where he steps; sheep outnumber people by more than 300 to one.

No single cause explains why some areas of the world are so much more   3
thickly settled than others. But high population density can be an accident of political history, as it is in city-states such as Macau. And it is often the result of geography: the three most densely populated countries in the world—Macau, Hong Kong and Singapore—are all islands. Many larger island countries, such as Malta, Taiwan, and Barbados, also rank among the most densely settled parts of the world.

Density can also be the result of the economy of an area. "The Falkland   4
Islands are so thinly settled because they have no resources other than sheep," says Tom Merrick of the Population Reference Bureau in Washington, D.C. "The population doesn't grow because so many people emigrate."

The countries that are least densely populated often have obvious cli-   5
matic or geographical flaws, like Mongolia (three people per square mile). Australia has a population density of five per square mile, and Canada has only seven, demonstrating the effect of huge hinterlands. The United States is not very crowded, despite perceptions to the contrary, with 65 people per square mile. "A lot of our land is uninhabitable," says Ken Hill, a demographer at the National Academy of Sciences in Washington, D.C. "The Rock-

ies, the desert, and the rangeland are not places people want to live, so they crowd together in pleasanter surroundings."

If high population density were a measure of pleasantness, then Bang-   6
ladesh would be pleasant indeed. With 1,800 people per square mile, it the most densely settled nonisland nation in the world. Nearly 100 million people live in an area the size of Arkansas. All of Bangladesh is arable, and that explains its density. "There are no deserts, mountains, or impenetrable forests," says Hill. "There's plenty of rainfall, so most fields yield two crops a year."

Socioeconomic factors also influence population density. In Bangladesh,   7
mothers and fathers see additional children as contributing to the family labor force, not detracting from the family food supply. Children often work 10-hour days on their families' subsistence-level farr s. Women usually have seven or eight children, partly to compensate for the high infant mortality rate. Falkland Islanders, in comparison, have only two children per family. "They have a European attitude toward children," says Hill. "They don't see the need for more, even though for years emigration has been causing the country's population to decline."

When is a place too empty or too crowded? That's a judgement everyone   8
has to make for himself. In Manhattan people press together in subways and on street corners without batting an eye. But in America a hundred years ago, the sound of an axe in the next clearing signalled that it was time to move on.

Questions for Discussion

1. What is the essay's central idea? What main point is Hamer explaining?
2. What methods of development does she use in paragraphs 2 through 8?
3. Paragraph 2 is much shorter than the others. Does this mean that it is not well developed? Explain why or why not.
4. Every paragraph but one uses the general-to-specific pattern of organization. Which one is the exception? What pattern does it follow?
5. In Looking Ahead you learnc d about an analogy Hamer used to help develop paragraph 1. Is there a second analogy in that paragraph? What other analogy did you find later on?
6. Is this essay unified? How do you know?
7. At the beginning of paragraph 4, Hamer uses a transitional word to create coherence between this and the preceding paragraph. What is it? What other words, phrases, and techniques does Hamer use to maintain coherence in and between her paragraphs?

Suggestions for Journal Entries

1. While Hamer's eight paragraphs show various methods of development, all but one follow the general-to-specific pattern of organization. Choose

one of these seven paragraphs, and reorganize it by using the specific-to-general pattern.

2. How densely or sparsely populated is your campus, home town, or county? List details in your journal that show how crowded or uncrowded your environment is. Like Hamer, you might list statistics along with illustrations and analogies, or you might simply begin describing your surroundings.

3. Using Hamer's fine analogies as models, think of an analogy that reveals something important about a subject you know well (such as a friend or relative, a place you visit often, your education, or your lifestyle). Then put this analogy into a well-written topic sentence. Here are some sample topic sentences that contain analogies:

> After I stay up all night cramming for a big test, my mind becomes an intellectual garbage heap.
> Trying to make good grades in Professor Jones's class is like running an obstacle course.
> Eating at Mel's Diner is as close as I've come to playing Russian roulette.
> The content of some game shows, soap operas, and situation comedies helps support the opinion that television has become a moral wasteland.

Finally, think about the kinds of details that will develop your topic sentence clearly, and list these details in your journal.

A Family of Firsts

Patricia Volk

Members of Patricia Volk's family, many of them immigrants to a growing America, prided themselves on their inventiveness and their ability to succeed. "A Family of Firsts" is the author's humorous, touching, and intensely personal portrayal of some of her most interesting and colorful relatives. In it, you will encounter a delightful parade of fascinating characters who measured their success "by a single standard: The ability to be first."

"A Family of Firsts" was originally published in *The New York Times Magazine.*

Looking Ahead

1. Volk expresses her central idea in a formal thesis statement early in the essay. Look for it as you begin reading.

2. This essay is extremely well developed. It contains numerous examples (or illustrations) of what Volk means when she claims that she comes from "a family of firsts." But illustration is not the only method of development in this selection; Volk also uses narration, classification, and definition.

3. The author does an excellent job of maintaining coherence within and between her paragraphs. Look for the elements—transitional words and expressions, linking pronouns, and repetition—that she uses to keep her essay flowing smoothly and logically.

4. The eighteen paragraphs in "A Family of Firsts" are arranged in several different patterns of organization. Among those which you will recognize are general to specific, specific to general, order of importance, and question and answer.

5. In paragraph 9, Volk tells us that James Thurber (an important American writer) called her Uncle Jake a "housewrecker out of 'Herculean mythology.'" In Greek mythology, Hercules was a hero of tremendous strength and courage.

First Lady Eleanor Roosevelt, mentioned in paragraph 12, was the wife of Franklin Delano Roosevelt, President of the United States through the great depression and most of World War II.

Poland, Lithuania, and Rumania, from which many of Volk's ancestors came, are countries in eastern Europe.

Vocabulary

bon mots   Clever sayings.

dollop   Large drop, lump, or helping.

eulogized   Honored by praising in a speech at a funeral.

hydraulic   Operated through the use of fluid, usually water, that is under pressure.

inverted   Reversed.

retractable   Able to be drawn or pulled back.

weighed   Measured.

In my family, success is weighed by a single standard: The ability to be first. It does not matter what you are first at as long as you are first at something. 1

My relatives came from Europe at the height of the Machine Age. Every day, something else in America was new and first. The first flush toilet, the first emery board, the first air-conditioned hat. My family got first fever. Recipes, bon mots and good ideas all counted. Styles, inventions, slogans, too. The sole criterion for being first at something was simply not having heard that someone else had done it. Then you earned the right to say the magic words: "I did it first!" 2

My great-grandfather on my mother's mother's side invented the toodle. The toodle is a little square of waxed paper rolled into a cone with a dollop 3 of mustard in it. You could take a toodle to work in the morning with a piece of cold meat and squeeze a squiggle of fresh mustard on it at lunch.

This great-grandfather, the toodle inventor, had three daughters: Ruthie, 4 the first girl who ever made a lace curtain into a shawl; Gertie, the first girl who ever made a lace shawl into a curtain; and Polly, my grandmother, who perfected a brush to clean the inside of a faucet. "Just because you can't see it doesn't mean it isn't dirty," she was fond of saying.

Polly was proud of the fact that every inch of her apartment was 5 touched by human hand at least twice a year. She even dusted the tops of doors, using a top-of-the-door duster made of old stockings with runs in them, stuffed with old stockings with runs in them. Old stockings with runs in them have always been perceived as a challenge by my family. My mother uses hers as an onion bag, an idea she says she invented. She also takes credit for being the first person to use pantyhose simultaneously, one leg for onions, one leg for potatoes or garlic. But I am getting ahead of myself.

Perhaps my most famous relative of all, the one who really left his im- 6 print on America, was Reb Sussel, my great-grandfather on my father's father's side. According to family folklore, he brought the pastrami sandwich to the New World. In 1879, Reb Sussel left his native Lithuania to find fame and fortune on the streets of New York. He had been a miller in Vilna, but, finding the wheat business too much of a grind, became a tinker, selling pots and pans off his back. He had no home and would sleep in the stables or basements of the people he sold pots to. While praying one morning he was kicked by a horse, which made him tear his hair and shout, "My life lacks dignity!"

Being a religious man, Reb Sussel knew how to butcher meat, so he 7 opened a small butcher shop on Delancey Street. The first week, a Rumanian friend stopped by and asked if he could store a trunk in the back of the shop. "I'm just going back to Rumania for a few years," he said. "If you store my trunk, I'll give you the recipe for pastrami." As the story goes, Great-Grandpa took the trunk and the recipe and began selling hunks of pastrami over the counter. Soon he was selling it by the slice. Then, between two pieces of rye. He met up with my great-grandfather on my mother's side, who introduced him to the toodle, and before long, people were coming to Sussman Volk's for sandwiches more than they were coming for meat.

Legend has it that about this time my Great-Great-Uncle Albert, work- 8 ing independently, became the first man to stir scallions into cream cheese.

My paternal grandfather, Jacob Volk, took credit for the wrecking ball. 9 According to James Thurber, who eulogized him in *The New Yorker* in March 1929, Jake was a housewrecker out of "Herculean mythology." (In our family, Jake is also famous for inventing the caviar sandwich eaten on a soda cracker. Until then, everyone ate caviar on pumpernickel with a little chopped egg and onion.)

Jake took his wrecking ball all over lower Manhattan. His slogan, painted 10 on the sides of all his trucks, was "The Most Destructive Force on Wall Street." He married Granny Ethel, who was such a knockout she did not have to be first at anything. She was, though—the first calendar girl in Princeton, N.J. In the early 1900's her picture was used by a bank there for its first calendar. That's where Grandpa met her, in the bank. She was so beautiful, she once received a letter addressed:

> Postman, Postman
> Do your duty
> Deliver this letter
> To the Princeton beauty.

It was dropped off right at her front door.

The union between Jake and the prettiest girl in Princeton produced my 11 father, the 1938 shag-dancing champion at the University of West Virginia. He invented the six-color retractable pen and pencil set, but was sold out by his partner, the mention of whose name in our family is still followed by spitting. My father did receive patents for the hydraulic-powered garbage-can brush and the two-sided lighter so you never have to worry about which side is up when you go to light. But perhaps most impressive, my father made the first illuminated Lucite single-shaft fender guide, which clamped on to your car and facilitated nighttime parking by showing you where your fender ended.

My mother invented the Pinch Code, a series of pinches that had clear 12 interpretations: Don't stare! Don't say that! Be quiet! How do you know? She's lying! Clean your plate! Watch that tone of voice! No, you may not! I heard that! We'll talk about it later! A dresser of local renown, my mother went around in Great-Aunt Bertha's blouses. Bertha claimed to have invented the reverse tuck, a sewing technique that created parallel rows of inverted pleats. The style was favored by First Lady Eleanor Roosevelt, who, according to Aunt Bertha, once said she felt she could go anywhere in a Bertha Brecher blouse.

My maternal grandmother invented the shoe pocket. It was her belief 13 that if you always kept a nickel in your shoe, nothing bad would happen to you. You could always make a phone call. You could always buy something. You would never be broke. But the nickel could slide around. And if it could slide around, it could slide out. So she constructed a small pocket that fit under the arch and fastened to the inner sole. That way, any pair of shoes could have its own bankroll. Her nephew, Cousin Wally, is said to have been the first soldier to have had a sponge left in his back during surgery after World War II. He was fine as long as he didn't sit. This forced him to look for work he could do standing up. That's how he found his second first:

Cousin Wally was the first cameraman for the first live cooking show on television.

When Wally's uncle, my Grandpa Herman, came to this country in the 14
1800's at the age of 12, he made a promise to himself. Leaning over the railing
of his ship, watching the Statue of Liberty fade in and out of the mist, he
swore he would never speak German or Polish again, that the little town he
came from in the Tatra Mountains that was sometimes German and sometimes Polish would no longer be a part of his life. He would never go back,
never see his parents again, never climb the mountains of Nowy Targ. Herman Morgen would be American now. He would bathe every day. He would
chew gum. He would invent something.

Herman got a job sweeping the floor of a restaurant, then he became a 15
busboy, then a waiter, then a manager, then the owner, and then he found his
first: He was the first man to carve meat in a window. It brought the customers in. It began a restaurant business that lasted for 60 years.

Me, I have yet to make my mark. I am still waiting to find a first. Some- 16
times I think my life is too cozy. Why should I mother an invention if all my
necessities are met? But then something nudges me. How hard it is to start
a roll of toilet paper! How annoying it is when dental floss gets stuck between
the teeth! What a waste it is throwing out old light bulbs, egg shells and
typewriter ribbons! Should bobby pins be used only in the hair? Why isn't
there anything on the wheels of the bed frame to stop you from stubbing your
toe? If Saran Wrap has a longer life expectancy than I do, why is it thrown
out after using just once? Could dust balls really have been put on this earth
for no reason?

When you come from a family of firsts, whether you like it or not, you're 17
thinking all the time.

When you come from a family of firsts, you never forget the burden and 18
the inspiration of your past.

Questions for Discussion

1. What is Volk's thesis?
2. Is her essay unified? In other words, does each of the paragraphs that
   follow the introduction relate directly to the thesis?
3. In paragraph 3, Volk defines the term *toodle*. In what other paragraphs
   does she use definition as the method of development?
4. Which parts of this essay are developed through narration?
5. Paragraph 2 uses illustration. What are some of the examples Volk provides to explain that her relatives came to America at "the height of the
   Machine Age"? What do you think she means by "Machine Age"?
6. Which other paragraphs does Volk develop with examples?

7. Paragraph 4 begins, "This great-grandfather...had three daughters." What method does Volk use to develop this paragraph?
8. What phrase in paragraph 11 makes it clear that this paragraph is arranged according to order of importance?
9. What other paragraph in this essay uses order of importance as an organizational pattern? Which paragraph uses the question-to-answer pattern? Which begin with a general statement that is then developed with specifics?
10. Paragraphs 7 and 15 contain a number of elements that show how well Volk can maintain coherence within a paragraph. What are they?

Suggestions for Journal Entries

1. Some of the events in the history of Volk's family are preposterous, too strange to be believed; take the fact that her father invented a two-sided lighter, for example. What other parts of this essay do you find preposterous? In a short paragraph or two, explain why these parts seem so far-fetched. You might want to use the cause-and-effect method to develop your ideas.
2. What is your family famous for? Pick a colorful relative, deceased or living, whom you know a great deal about. Write a paragraph in which you explain one thing that this person did to become famous (or at least to become highly interesting in some way); you might want to develop this paragraph by using narration, just as Volk frequently does. A good way to begin is with a statement like "Uncle Mort was the only man in Tucson to climb a greased flagpole in front of city hall while eating a beef taco!" Thereafter, you can provide specifics about how it all happened.

A Brother's Dreams

Paul Aronowitz

Paul Aronowitz was a medical student at Case Western Reserve University when he wrote this very sensitive essay comparing his dreams, hopes, and ambitions with those of his schizophrenic brother. Schizophrenia is a mental illness characterized by withdrawals from reality.

Aronowitz's love, compassion, and understanding come across clearly as he unfolds the story of how he learned to deal with the fact that his brother's strange, sometimes violent behavior was the symptom of an illness and not a defect in character. This essay is also Aronowitz's admission and unselfish affirmation that, however "elusive" and "trivial," his brother's dreams might be even more meaningful than his own.

"A Brother's Dreams" first appeared in "About Men," a weekly column in *The New York Times Magazine*.

Looking Ahead

1. Aronowitz's central idea concerns how he came to understand his brother's illness and to accept the fact that his brother's dreams were meaningful and important. However, the author does not begin to reveal this central idea until well near the end of this essay, and he never puts the idea into a formal thesis statement.
2. Many of the paragraphs in this selection are developed through narration and description, but Aronowitz also makes good use of cause and effect, comparison and contrast, illustration, and conclusion and support.
3. Josef Mengele, whom Aronowitz mentions in paragraph 5, was a Nazi medical researcher who conducted unspeakable experiments in which he tortured and maimed or killed thousands of human beings.

Vocabulary

acrid Bitter, harsh, sharp.
aimlessly Without purpose.
alienate Make enemies of, isolate oneself from.
delusions Misconceptions, fantasies.
depravity Immorality, corruption.
elusive Hard to grasp, intangible.
paranoid Showing unreasonable or unwarranted suspicion.
prognosis Prediction about the course or outcome of an illness.
resilient Able to bounce back.
siblings Sisters and brothers.

Each time I go home to see my parents at their house near Poughkeepsie, N.Y., my brother, a schizophrenic for almost nine years now, comes to visit from the halfway house where he lives nearby. He owns a car that my parents help him to maintain, and his food and washing are taken care of by the halfway house. Somewhere, somehow along the way, with the support of a good physician, a social worker and my ever-resilient parents, he has managed to carve a niche for himself, to bite off some independence and, with it, elusive dreams that, to any healthy person, might seem trivial. 1

My brother sits in a chair across from me, chain-smoking cigarettes, trying to take the edge off the medications he'll be on for the rest of his life. 2

Sometimes his tongue hangs loosely from his mouth when he's listening or pops out of his mouth as he speaks—a sign of tardive dyskinesia, an often-irreversible side effect of his medication.

He draws deeply on his cigarette and tells me he can feel his mind heal- 3 ing—cells being replaced, tissue being restored, thought processes returning. He knows this is happening because he dreams of snakes, and hot, acrid places in which he suffocates if he moves too fast. When he wakes, the birds are singing in the trees outside his bedroom window. They imitate people in his halfway house, mocking them and calling their names. The birds are so smart, he tells me, so much smarter than we are.

His face, still handsome despite its puffiness (another side effect of the 4 medications that allow him to function outside the hospital), and warm brown eyes are serious. When I look into his eyes I imagine I can see some of the suffering he has been through. I think of crossed wires, of receptors and neurotransmitters, deficits and surpluses, progress and relapse, and I wonder, once again, what has happened to my brother.

My compassion for him is recent. For many years, holidays, once happy 5 occasions for our family of seven to gather together, were emotional torture sessions. My brother would pace back and forth in the dining room, lecturing us, his voice loud, dominating, crushing all sound but his own, about the end of the world, the depravity of our existences. His speeches were salted with paranoid delusions: our house was bugged by the F.B.I.; my father was Josef Mengele; my mother was selling government secrets to the Russians.

His life was decaying before my eyes, and I couldn't stand to listen to 6 him. My resentment of him grew as his behavior became more disruptive and aggressive. I saw him as being ultimately responsible for his behavior. As my anger increased, I withdrew from him, avoiding him when I came home to visit from college, refusing to discuss the bizarre ideas he brought up over the dinner table. When I talked with my sister or other two brothers about him, our voices always shadowed in whispers, I talked of him as of a young man who had chosen to spend six months of every year in a pleasant, private hospital on the banks of the Hudson River, chosen to alienate his family with threats, chosen to withdraw from the stresses of the world. I hated what he had become. In all those years, I never asked what his diagnosis was.

Around the fifth year of his illness, things finally changed. One hot 7 summer night, he attacked my father. When I came to my father's aid, my brother broke three of my ribs and nearly strangled me. The State Police came and took him away. My father's insurance coverage had run out on my brother, so this time he was taken to a locked ward at the state hospital where heavily sedated patients wandered aimlessly in stockinged feet up and down long hallways. Like awakening from a bad dream, we gradually began talking about his illness. Slowly and painfully, I realized that he wasn't responsible for his disease any more than a cancer patient is for his pain.

As much as I've learned to confront my brother's illness, it frightens me   8
to think that one day, my parents gone from the scene, my siblings and I will
be responsible for portions of my brother's emotional and financial support.
This element of the future is one we still avoid discussing, much the way we
avoided thinking about the nature of his disease and his prognosis. I'm still
not capable of thinking about it.

Now I come home and listen to him, trying not to react, trying not to   9
show disapproval. His delusions are harmless and he is, at the very least,
communicating. When he asks me about medical school, I answer with a
sentence or two—no elaboration, no revelations about the dreams I cradle in
my heart.

He talks of his own dreams. He hopes to finish his associate's degree—   10
the same one he has been working on between hospitalizations for almost
eight years now—at the local community college. Next spring, with luck, he'll
get a job. His boss will be understanding, he tells me, cutting him a little slack
when he has his "bad days," letting him have a day off here or there when
things aren't going well. He puts out his cigarette and lights another one.

Time stands still. This could be last year, or the year before, or the year   11
before that. I'm within range of becoming a physician, of realizing something
I've been working toward for almost five years, while my brother still dreams
of having a small job, living in his own apartment and of being well. As the
smoke flows from his nose and mouth, I recall an evening some time ago when
I drove upstate from Manhattan to tell my parents and my brother that I was
getting married (an engagement later severed). My brother's eyes lit up at the
news, and then a darkness fell over them.

"What's wrong?" I asked him.   12

"It's funny," he answered matter-of-factly, "You're getting married,   13
and I've never even had a girlfriend." My mother's eyes filled with tears, and
she turned away. She was trying her best to be happy for me, for the dreams
I had—for the dreams so many of us take for granted.

"You still have us," I stammered, reaching toward him and touching his   14
arm. All of a sudden my dreams meant nothing; I didn't deserve them and
they weren't worth talking about. My brother shrugged his shoulders, smiled
and shook my hand, his large, tobacco-stained fingers wrapping around my
hand, dwarfing my hand.

Questions for Discussion

1. If you wanted to write a formal thesis statement for this essay, what would
   it be?
2. "A Brother's Dreams" contains at least two paragraphs that are developed
   through description. Identify one of them. What important idea does this
   paragraph communicate?

3. The purpose of paragraph 6 is to explain a cause and an effect. What is the paragraph's topic sentence (cause)? What details (effect) does Aronowitz provide to develop the paragraph fully?
4. Which paragraphs use narration?
5. Aronowitz gets specific about his brother's dreams in paragraph 10, which he develops by stating a conclusion and then supporting this conclusion with details. Identify these details.
6. Paragraph 11 contrasts some of Aronowitz's dreams to some of his brother's. In what other paragraph do we see their dreams contrasted?
7. Most paragraphs in this essay are organized in the general-to-specific pattern. However, paragraphs 11 and 13 are organized according to order of importance. What is the most important idea in each of these paragraphs?
8. This is a powerful essay. Which paragraph affects you most strongly? What do the details in this paragraph tell you about the author or his brother or both?

Suggestions for Journal Entries

1. Aronowitz writes about a person whose lifestyle and dreams are very different from those of most other people. Do you know someone like this? If so, write a paragraph showing how this person's lifestyle or dreams differ from those of most others. Use one major method of development; for instance, you might *describe* what this individual looks like (much in the way Aronowitz describes his brother in paragraphs 2 and 4), or you might use *narration* to tell a story about the kind of behavior you have come to expect from the person (as Aronowitz does in paragraphs 3, 5, and 7). You might even want to try your hand at the cause-and-effect method by telling your reader how you normally react to or deal with this person and then explaining what causes you to react in this way.
2. Aronowitz's essay contrasts his brother's dreams to his own. Write a paragraph in which you show how different you are from your brother, sister, or other close relative by contrasting a major goal in your life to one of his or hers.

    Clearly identify the two different goals in your topic sentence, and fill the rest of your paragraph with details showing how different they are; that is, develop the paragraph by contrast. Your topic sentence might go something like this: "My sister Janet intends to move to the city and find a high-paying job, even if she hates every minute of it; I'll be happy earning the modest income that comes with managing our family farm."

SUGGESTIONS FOR WRITING

1. If you responded to the first of the Suggestions for Journal Entries after Devoe's "The Hibernation of the Woodchuck," you have already begun

to gather details and to draw some general conclusions about an animal with which you are quite familiar. Your list should include a number of specific details, as well as more general ideas or conclusions, that may provide important clues about this animal's habits, lifestyle, behavior, character, or "personality."

Use one of the conclusions you've come up with as the topic sentence of a paragraph that will tell your reader something important about the animal you've chosen to discuss. Develop your paragraph with details from your journal, but make sure that the details you use relate directly to your topic sentence. If you need to, try to recall additional *appropriate* details to develop your paragraph more fully. In any case, make sure your paragraph is unified!

Incidentally, you can use a variety of patterns to organize this paragraph including the question and answer approach. For instance, you might start off with a sentence like, "Are domestic cats as intelligent as they seem?" "Do beavers really work as hard as everyone thinks?" or "Are German shepherds as ferocious as they look?"

2. Using the cause-and-effect method, write a paragraph explaining why you do something habitually. For instance, explain why you're late for work every day, why you always take the same road home, why you frequent a particular restaurant, or why you study in the same place night after night. Arrange the paragraph in a general-to-specific or specific-to-general pattern, provide enough details to develop your central idea clearly and convincingly, and check for unity and coherence. You'll find good examples of cause-and-effect paragraphs in "The Hibernation of the Woodchuck," "The Thick and Thin of It," and "A Brother's Dreams."

3. Look over the notes you made in your journal after reading Blythe Hamer's "The Thick and Thin of It." If you responded to item 2 in the Suggestions for Journal Entries, turn your notes into a paragraph that explains how densely or sparsely populated your campus, your home town, or your county is. Use either illustration or conclusion and support as a method of development.

If you need to review other paragraphs that use these methods, turn back to the introduction, or reread paragraphs 4 and 5 in Hamer's essay. Make sure that you have a clearly identifiable topic sentence and that you develop your central idea in as much detail as you can. Also, make sure that your paragraph is unified and coherent.

4. In "A Family of Firsts," Patricia Volk discusses a number of colorful relatives who became "famous." If you responded to this essay in your journal, you too might have begun writing about an interesting relative. Expand your discussion of this person; write at least three paragraphs, plus an introduction containing your thesis.

Make sure each of the topic sentences relates directly to your thesis.

Also make sure to maintain coherence in and between paragraphs by using techniques explained in Chapter 2. Here are three different ways from which you might choose to proceed:

a. In addition to what you've written in your journal, think of other interesting things your subject did to become famous. Develop each of these "accomplishments" in a paragraph of its own.

b. Limit your essay to your subject's most famous accomplishment; use narration to tell the story of this accomplishment. Develop each paragraph in as much specific detail as you can.

c. In your thesis, mention a habit or personal characteristic for which your subject became famous. Provide a well-developed illustration of this habit or characteristic in each of the paragraphs that follow. Say your Uncle Mort was known as the biggest spender in Tucson. In one paragraph, you might describe his lavish wardrobe. In another, you could recall a huge banquet he hosted at an expensive restaurant. In still another, you might provide details to show how generous a gift-giver he was.

5. After completing Paul Aronowitz's "A Brother's Dreams," you might have written a paragraph in your journal explaining how different your goal in life is from that of your brother, sister, or other close relative. If so, the method by which you developed this paragraph was contrast.

Reread this paragraph. What does it tell you about your subject's character? What kind of person is he or she? Turn your answer into the central idea (thesis statement) of an essay in which you continue to discuss this relative. In fact, make the paragraph you've already written the introduction to your essay.

As you plan this essay, consider writing a paragraph or two in which you describe this individual—the way he walks, the way she dresses, etc. You might also want to include a narrative paragraph, one in which you tell a story that helps support what you say about him or her in your thesis. Finally, think about using additional methods of development—illustration and conclusion–and–support, for example—in other paragraphs to develop your thesis further.

Chapter 4

Introductions and Conclusions

In the previous chapters you learned a number of important principles to help you focus on the central idea of a paragraph or essay and to express this central idea in a topic sentence or thesis statement. You also learned how to develop paragraphs adequately and to make sure that each paragraph in an essay clearly develops the essay's thesis.

Most effective essays begin with an interesting and informative introduction—a paragraph or a series of paragraphs that reveals the essay's thesis and captures the reader's attention. Similarly, most successful essays end with a paragraph or a series of paragraphs that brings the writer's discussion of the subject to a timely and logical conclusion. Effective conclusions always leave the reader satisfied that everything the writer set out to discuss from the very beginning has been discussed.

Clearly, then, introductions and conclusions have special uses and are important to the success of an essay. That's why this entire chapter is devoted to explaining how to write them.

WRITING INTRODUCTIONS

Before deciding exactly what to include in an introduction, how to organize it, or even how to begin it, ask yourself whether the essay you're writing actually calls for a formal introduction. If you're writing a narrative, for instance, you might simply want to start with the very first event in your story. Of course, you can always begin with colorful details, exciting vocabulary, or intriguing ideas that will spark your reader's interest. But you need not provide a thesis statement, background information, explanatory details, or other introductory material before getting into the story proper. If you feel the need to express your central idea in a formal thesis statement, you can do so later, at a convenient point in the body of your essay or even at its conclusion.

75

On the other hand, you might decide that a formal introduction is important to your essay and that your readers will benefit from the information it provides. If this is the case, remember that, *in general*, a formal introduction accomplishes the following:

- It reveals the essay's central idea as expressed in the thesis.
- It guides the readers to important considerations in the body of the essay.
- It provides background information or explanatory detail important to understanding the writer's purpose and thesis.
- Most important of all, it captures the readers' attention and makes them want to read on.

Consider these important objectives when you plan your introduction. But if you find yourself unable to decide how to begin, simply write out what you think your thesis should be (the preliminary thesis) and go directly on to the body of your essay. You can always return to and revise your introduction later in the writing process.

However you choose to get started, remember that an exciting part of the writing process is discovering exactly what you want to say about your subject. You usually won't make this discovery until after you've completed at least one draft—and often more than one draft—of the middle or body paragraphs of your essay. But once you've accomplished that much, your chances of being able to go back and draft a clearer, more direct, and more substantial thesis will have been greatly improved. So will your chances of writing an effective and interesting introduction.

Of course, the simplest way to structure an introductory paragraph is to place your thesis at the very beginning and to follow it with explanatory or supportive detail. However, depending on your purpose, your thesis, and your audience, this may not be the best course to follow. In Chapter 3 you learned that you can use a number of methods to organize and develop an essay's middle paragraphs. Similarly, there are many methods for organizing and developing its introductory paragraph or series of paragraphs. Here are eight:

1. Use a startling remark or statistic.
2. Ask a question.
3. Challenge a widely held assumption or opinion.
4. Use a comparison, contrast, or analogy.
5. Use an anecdote.
6. Use a quotation.
7. Define an important term or concept.
8. Address your readers.

These eight methods are described below, and each is illustrated by one or more sample paragraphs. In some of these sample paragraphs the idea is expressed in a formal thesis statement (shown in italics); in others the central idea is only implied, and no formal thesis can be identified.

Use a Startling Remark or Statistic

Quite often, professional writers begin with a statement or statistic that, while true to their intent, has an effective shock value—one sure to make the reader want to continue. Such is the case in the following lead paragraph from a recent column in a well-known newspaper:

> Last winter, a company that makes a machine for quickly measuring how much cholesterol people have in their blood offered tests for $3 in downtown Indianapolis and at four suburban shopping centers. To the company's surprise, as many as 30,000 customers showed up.   (Gina Kolata, "Advice about Cholesterol Is Finding an Eager Market.")

You might find this technique particularly effective if you have to take an unpopular stand on a well-known subject, as did former Philadelphia Phillies pitcher Robin Roberts in the opening of "Strike Out Little League":

> In 1939, Little League baseball was organized by Bert and George Bebble and Carl Stotz of Williamsport, Pa. What they had in mind in organizing this kids' baseball program, I'll never know. But *I'm sure they never visualized the monster it would grow into.*

A startling statement or statistic is often followed by details that explain the writer's point. Such is the case in the introduction to Fred Powledge's powerful essay "Let's Bulldoze the Suburbs":

> *For almost 30 years now, America has been systematically destroying the centers of her cities.* In the name of urban renewal, we have declared choice parcels of downtown real estate to be slums and then forced their rightful owners—often stable but poor families and small businesses—to move away. We have sent bulldozers in at taxpayers' expense to flatten the old housing, and then we have given the cleared land away at bargain prices to the operators of parking garages, overpriced hospitals, and chain hotels, to the developers of high-rise bank buildings and luxury housing.

Ask a Question

Most writers who use this approach begin with the kind of question to which the rest of the essay will provide the answer or answers. In "I Want a Wife," for example, Judy Syfers concludes her two-paragraph introduction with a question that the rest of her essay addresses:

> I belong to that classification of people known as wives. I am A Wife. And, not altogether incidentally, I am a mother.

Not too long ago a male friend of mine appeared on the scene fresh
from a recent divorce. He had one child, who is, of course, with his
ex-wife. He is obviously looking for another wife. As I thought about
him while I was ironing one evening, it suddenly occurred to me that
I, too, would like to have a wife. Why do I want a wife?

Challenge a Widely Held Assumption or Opinion

This can be a quick, direct way to state your thesis and stir the reader's interest. In most cases it will take only a few sentences for you to deny the
assumption or opinion and to state your own views. Notice how smoothly
Roger D. McGrath does this in the introduction to "The Myth of Frontier
Violence":

> It is commonly assumed that violence is part of our frontier heritage.
> But *the historical record shows that frontier violence was very different
> from violence today.* Robbery and burglary, two of our most common
> crimes, were of no great significance in the frontier towns of the Old
> West, and rape was seemingly nonexistent.

Use a Comparison, Contrast, or Analogy

Comparing or contrasting a new idea to one with which your readers are already familiar can be an excellent way to introduce a concept that they may
at first find new, unfamiliar, or difficult to understand.

For example, in a chapter from *The Enchanted Loom*, Robert Jastrow
uses an effective and startling comparison between human and electronic brains
to explain the complex logic with which computers operate:

> Circuits, wires and computing are strange terms to use for a biological
> organ like the brain, made largely of water, and without electronic
> parts. Nonetheless, they are accurate terms because brains work in
> very much the same way as computers. Brains think; computers add
> and subtract; but *both devices seem to work on the basis of the same
> fundamental steps in logical reasoning.*

Donald Murray achieves a similar purpose by using contrast to develop
the first paragraph of "The Maker's Eye":

> When students complete a first draft, they consider the job of writing
> done—and their teachers too often agree. *When professional writers
> complete a first draft, they usually feel that they are at the start of the
> writing process.* When a draft is completed, the job of writing can
> begin.

Using an analogy can serve the same purpose. An analogy draws similarities between two ideas or subjects that, on the surface, are quite different.
For example, one of the chapters of *On Writing Well*, William Zinsser's

famous study of contemporary writing, begins with an analogy between problems associated with writing and a serious illness:

> *Clutter is the disease of American writing.* We are a society strangling in unnecessary words, circular constructions, pompous frills and meaningless jargon.

Use an Anecdote

Everyone loves a good story, and writers use anecdotes (brief, interesting narratives) to prove or illustrate a point. Using an anecdote in an opening paragraph can clearly indicate the issues or problems you will be discussing later in the essay without your having to state the thesis directly. In the first paragraph of "The Ambivalence of Abortion," for example, Linda Bird Francke explains by means of an anecdote how she broke the news of her fourth pregnancy to her husband, and this anecdote provides the introduction to her discussion of abortion in the rest of the essay:

> We were sitting in a bar on Lexington Avenue when I told my husband I was pregnant. It is not a memory I like to dwell on. Instead of the champagne and hope which had heralded [announced] the impending [coming] births of the first, second and third child, the news of this one was greeted with shocked silence and Scotch. "Jesus," my husband kept saying to himself, stirring the ice cubes around and around "Oh Jesus."

Use a Quotation

Quoting an expert or simply using an accurate, interesting, informative statement from another writer, from someone you've interviewed formally, or even from someone with whom you've only been chatting can lend interest and authority to your introduction. If you use this method, however, remember to quote your source accurately. Also be sure that the quotation relates to the other ideas in your paragraph clearly and logically.

Notice how Philip Shabecoff uses a quotation from world-famous scientist and writer Rachel Carson to lead us to his thesis in the introduction to his essay on pesticides:

> "The most alarming of all man's assaults upon the environment is the contamination of air, earth, rivers, and sea with dangerous and even lethal materials," Rachel Carson wrote a quarter of a century ago in her celebrated book, *Silent Spring.* Today there is little disagreement with her warnings in regard to such broad-spectrum pesticides as DDT, then widely used, now banned. *But there is still hot debate over how to apply modern pesticides—which are designed to kill specific types of weeds or insects—in ways that do not harm people and their*

environment. ("Congress Again Confronts Hazards of Killer Chemicals.")

Define an Important Term or Concept

Defining a term somewhere in the first paragraph can sometimes be a very natural and effective way to explain important aspects of your subject that support your central idea. If possible, however, avoid quoting dictionary definitions; they can be limited and rigid, and they make for uninteresting reading when they appear at the beginning of an essay. Instead, rely on your own knowledge and ingenuity to create a definition that will be informative, interesting, and, most important of all, appropriate to your purpose. This is what Carl Sagan has done in the introduction to "In Defense of Robots":

> The word "robot," first introduced by the Czech writer Karel Capek, is derived [originates] from the Slavic root for "worker." But it signifies a machine rather than a human worker. Robots, especially robots in space, have received derogatory notices [negative comments] in the press. We read that a human being was necessary to make the terminal landing adjustments on Apollo 11, without which the first manned lunar landing would have ended in disaster...and that machines could never have repaired, as men did, the Skylab sunshade....

> But all these comparisons turn out, naturally enough, to be written by humans. I wonder if a small self-congratulatory element...has not crept into these judgments.

Address Your Readers

Speaking to your readers directly and mentioning something that is important to them is an excellent way to get their attention. Notice how effectively Carrie Tuhy uses this technique in "So Who Needs College?" which first appeared in *Money* magazine in 1982:

> Career seekers, the want ads are trying to tell you something. Despite the highest unemployment rate since 1941, Sunday papers...are thick with job postings for specialized skills. Employers seem unable to find enough qualified people for such positions as bank teller, commercial artist, computer programmer, data processor, electronics technician, medical technologist, nurse, office manager, salesperson and secretary. *Fewer and fewer classified ads stipulate college as a requirement.*

Another effective way to address your readers is to invite them—or even direct them—to place themselves in the setting or situation you are discussing so that they can understand and appreciate your point better. For example, Rockwell Stenrud draws us into the action of his first paragraph of "Who's on Third?" by asking us to put ourselves mentally into the ballpark grand-stands:

> During the next baseball game you see, watch the man standing in the coach's box behind third base. He rubs his stomach, crosses his chest first with his left arm, then with his right. He touches the top of his cap, holds his right elbow with his left hand, then repeats the motion. A second later, he reverses the motion....This all may appear as a random symptom of nervousness, but in fact, *the third base coach is signaling to his team what he wants them to do.*

In "What Is Poverty," Jo Goodwin Parker has also chosen to address the reader directly, but she begins with a question. Notice how much more urgent and emphatic her introduction is than Stenrud's:

> You ask me what is poverty? Listen to me. Here I am, dirty, smelly, and with no "proper" underwear on and with the stench of my rotting teeth near you. I will tell you. Listen to me. Listen without pity. I cannot use your pity. Listen with understanding. Put yourself in my dirty, worn out, ill-fitting shoes, and hear me.

WRITING CONCLUSIONS

Make sure that your essay has an effective conclusion. Not only may it be the most memorable part of your essay, it may also be on the basis of your conclusion alone that your readers judge and act upon your essay's content.

The conclusion's length depends on the essay's length and purpose. For a very short essay, you can simply end the last paragraph with a concluding sentence, which might itself contain details important to developing your thesis. Such is the case in Kenneth Jon Rose's "2001 Space Shuttle." Rose's last paragraph, a description of the shuttle's landing on its return to Earth, also contains his conclusion (shown in italics):

> ...the sky turns lighter and layers of clouds pass you like cars on a highway. Minutes later, still sitting upright, you will see the gray runway in the distance. Then the shuttle slows to 300 mph and drops its landing gear. Finally, with its nose slightly up like the Concorde SST and at a speed of about 225 mph, the shuttle will land on the asphalt runway and slowly come to a halt. *The trip into space will be over.*

Although a one-sentence conclusion is fine for a very short essay, you will usually find it appropriate to devote at least one full paragraph to your conclusion. In any event, a conclusion should bring your discussion of the thesis to a timely and logical end. Never end abruptly, without some kind of signal to your reader that you are about to wrap things up, and never use your conclusion to introduce new ideas for which you did not prepare the reader earlier in the essay. Rather, use it to indicate that you have developed your thesis in full and that your essay is about to end.

As you might expect, there are several ways to write formal conclusions to an essay. Here are seven:

1. Rephrase or make reference to your thesis.
2. Summarize or rephrase your main points.
3. Make a call to action.
4. Look to the future.
5. Explain how a problem was resolved.
6. Use a rhetorical question.
7. Close with an anecdote.

Rephrase or Make Reference to Your Thesis

In Chapter 1 you learned that it can be appropriate to place the thesis statement not in the introduction, but in a later paragraph or even in the conclusion. As a beginning writer, however, you might want to use the more traditional pattern of organization, which is to place your thesis at the beginning of the essay. Of course, this doesn't mean that you shouldn't rephrase or refer to the thesis in your conclusion. Doing so can be an excellent way to emphasize your central idea.

Notice how well the conclusion to Donald M. Murray's "The Maker's Eye" recalls the central idea in this essay's introduction (see page 78):

> A piece of writing is never finished. It is delivered to a deadline, torn out of typewriter on demand, sent off with a sense of accomplishment and shame and pride and frustration. If only there were a couple of more days, time for just another run at it, perhaps then....

Summarize or Rephrase Your Main Points

For long essays, restating your thesis can be combined with summarizing or rephrasing each of the main points you have made in the body paragraphs. Doing so will help you write an effective summary of the entire essay and emphasize important ideas. This is exactly what Robin Roberts has done in his two concluding paragraphs of "Strike Out Little League" (see his introduction on page 77):

> I still don't know what those three gentlemen in Williamsport had in mind when they organized Little League baseball. I'm sure they didn't want parents arguing with their children about kids' games. I'm sure they didn't want young athletes hurting their arms pitching under pressure....I'm sure they didn't want young boys...made to feel that something is wrong with them because they can't play baseball. I'm sure they didn't want a group of coaches drafting the players each year

for different teams. I'm sure they didn't want unqualified men
working with the young players. I'm sure they didn't realize how
normal it is for an 8-year-old boy to be scared of a thrown or batted
baseball. For the life of me, I can't figure out what they had in mind.

Make a Call to Action

A very common and effective way to conclude is to suggest that something be
done about a problem you've discussed in the essay. A good example appears
in the last two paragraphs of "The Nuclear Winter," an essay in which Carl
Sagan explains that nuclear arms threaten to destroy humanity:

> It is now almost 40 years since the invention of nuclear weapons. We
> have not yet experienced thermonuclear war—although... we have
> come tremulously [fearfully] close. I do not think our luck can hold on
> forever. Men and machines are fallible.... Fools and madmen do exist
> and sometimes rise to power. Concentrating on the near future, we
> have ignored the long-term consequences of our actions. We have
> placed our civilization and our species in jeopardy [danger].
> Fortunately, it is not yet too late. We can safeguard civilization and
> the human family if we so choose. There is no more important or
> more urgent issue.

Jo Goodwin Parker accomplishes the same purpose in her conclusion
to "What Is Poverty?" (see her introduction on page 81):

> I have come out of my despair to tell you this. Remember I did not
> come from another place to another time. Others like me are all
> around you. Look at us with an angry heart, anger that will help you
> help me. Anger that will let you tell of me. The poor are always silent.
> Can you be silent too?

Look to the Future

If you believe that the subject you are discussing might someday undergo
significant changes, a good way to end your discussion is to explain what you
believe these changes will be. Notice how well Gina Kolata accomplishes this
at the end of her essay about cholesterol tests (see her introduction on page
77):

> [Doctors] believe that [new] guidelines [regarding cholesterol
> problems]—combined with better diagnostic devices and ever more
> effective drugs—may mark the beginning of a new era in public
> health. The hope... is that cholesterol will become like high blood
> pressure—easily and frequently measured, and usually controlled.

Explain How a Problem Was Resolved

If you began your essay by discussing a problem, you might end it by explaining how the problem was or was not resolved. In "The Ambivalence of Abortion" (see page 79), Linda Bird Francke wrote about the difficulty she and her husband had in deciding whether to have or to abort their fourth child. Francke's conclusion clearly indicates how they resolved the situation, and like many effective conclusions of this kind it also reveals the author's feelings about that decision:

> My husband and I are back to planning our summer vacation and his
> career switch. And it certainly does make sense not to be having a
> baby right now—we say to each other all the time. But I have this
> ghost now. A very little ghost that only appears when I'm seeing
> something beautiful, like the full moon on the ocean last weekend.
> And the baby waves to me. And I wave at the baby. "Of course, we
> have room," I cry to the ghost. "Of course, we do."

Use a Rhetorical Question

A rhetorical question (a question whose answer is obvious) asks your readers to participate in your essay's conclusion by answering the question. If you judge that the essay has made the answer so obvious that all readers will indeed respond to the question as you want them to, ending with a rhetorical question can be a fine way to make your essay memorable. As a reader, it's hard to forget an essay when you've answered its question in your own words.

For example, Judy Syfers ends "I Want a Wife" by asking, "Who wouldn't want a wife?" Because her essay showed numerous important ways in which wives contribute to their husbands' comfort, security, and happiness, the question's answer is obvious: "No one." Furthermore, note that the question circles back to the one she asked at the end of her introduction (see page 78), giving her essay a strong sense of unity and emphasis.

Not all rhetorical questions need be as snappy as Syfers', of course. The philosopher Eric Fromm ends the essay "Is Love an Art?" with a profoundly thoughtful question:

> Could it be that only those things are considered worthy of being
> learned with which one can earn money..., and that love, which
> "only" profits the soul, but is profitless in the modern sense, is a
> luxury we have no right to spend much energy on?

Close with an Anecdote

Brief stories that show the essence of the central idea can be used to conclude an essay as well as to introduce it. Using an anecdote to conclude will help you summarize or highlight important points you've made earlier. A good example of such an anecdote appears at the end of Suzanne Britt Jordan's "Fun, Oh Boy. Fun. You Could Die from It," the first reading selection in this chapter.

Read the introductions and conclusions to the following four essays carefully, and take some time to respond to the Questions for Discussion and the Suggestions for Journal Entries that follow each selection. As always, you will want to try your hand at the Suggestions for Writing at the end of the chapter. Doing so will help you develop the skills needed to write good introductions and conclusions of your own—the kinds that will capture your readers' attention and make them look forward to more and more of your writing.

Fun, Oh Boy. Fun. You Could Die from It.

Suzanne Britt Jordan

Jordan's introduction and conclusion play with definitions of "fun," nicely catching the reader's attention and highlighting her purpose throughout the essay, which is to define and humorously evaluate the "fun" side of American culture. Her essay first appeared in *The New York Times*.

Looking Ahead

1. In her five-paragraph introduction, Jordan states her thesis in two short sentences at the very beginning. Spreading the thesis over two sentences is unusual, but here it works well.
2. As you read paragraphs 3 to 5, try to identify one or more of the other techniques discussed earlier in this chapter that you find Jordan using in her introduction.
3. You've learned that an anecdote is a brief story that can be used in the beginning, middle, or end of an essay to illustrate or summarize a particular point. Pay special attention to the anecdote that Jordan uses to conclude her essay.

Vocabulary

blaspheme   Speak disrespectfully of.

by Jove   An exclamation or expression used to emphasize a point. Jove was the king of the gods in Roman mythology.

epitome   Ultimate form of or embodiment of.

fetish   An unreasonable preoccupation with or regard for something.

licentiousness   Sexual immorality.

mirth   Fun, gaiety.

puritans   Followers of a strict moral code who regarded many types of pleasure as sinful.

reverently   Devoutly, religiously, respectfully.

Fun is hard to have.   1

Fun is a rare jewel.   2

Somewhere along the line people got the modern idea that fun was there   3
for the asking, that people deserved fun, that if we didn't have a little fun
every day we would turn into (sakes alive!) puritans.

"Was it fun?" became the question that overshadowed all other ques-   4
tions: good questions like: Was it moral? Was it kind? Was it honest? Was it

beneficial? Was it generous? Was it necessary? And (my favorite) was it self-less?

When the pleasure got to be the main thing, the fun fetish was sure to 5 follow. Everything was supposed to be fun. If it wasn't fun, then by Jove, we were going to make it fun, or else.

Think of all the things that got the reputation of being fun. Family 6 outings were supposed to be fun. Sex was supposed to be fun. Education was supposed to be fun. Work was supposed to be fun. Walt Disney was supposed to be fun. Church was supposed to be fun. Staying fit was supposed to be fun.

Just to make sure that everybody knew how much fun we were having, 7 we put happy faces on flunking test papers, dirty bumpers, sticky refrigerator doors, bathroom mirrors.

If a kid, looking at his very happy parents traipsing through that very 8 happy Disney World, said, "This ain't fun, ma," his ma's heart sank. She wondered where she had gone wrong. Everybody told her what fun family outings to Disney World would be. Golly gee, what was the matter?

Fun got to be such a big thing that everybody started to look for more 9 and more thrilling ways to supply it. One way was to step up the level of danger or licentiousness or alcohol or drug consumption so that you could be sure that, no matter what, you would manage to have a little fun.

Television commercials brought a lot of fun and fun-loving folks into 10 the picture. Everything that people in those commercials did looked like fun: taking Polaroid snapshots, swilling beer, buying insurance, mopping the floor, bowling, taking aspirin. We all wished, I'm sure, that we could have half as much fun as those rough-and-ready guys around the locker room, flicking each other with towels and pouring champagne. The more commercials people watched, the more they wondered when the fun would start in their own lives. It was pretty depressing.

Big occasions were supposed to be fun. Christmas, Thanksgiving and 11 Easter were obviously supposed to be fun. Your wedding day was supposed to be fun. Your wedding night was supposed to be a whole lot of fun. Your honeymoon was supposed to be the epitome of fundom. And so we ended up going through every Big Event we ever celebrated, waiting for the fun to start.

It occurred to me, while I was sitting around waiting for the fun to start, 12 that not much is, and that I should tell you just in case you're worried about your fun capacity.

I don't mean to put a damper on things. I just mean we ought to treat 13 fun reverently. It is a mystery. It cannot be caught like a virus. It cannot be trapped like an animal. The god of mirth is paying us back for all those years of thinking fun was everywhere by refusing to come to our party. I don't want to blaspheme fun anymore. When fun comes in on little dancing feet, you probably won't be expecting it. In fact, I bet it comes when you're doing your duty, your job, or your work. It may even come on a Tuesday.

I remember one day, long ago, on which I had an especially good time. 14
Pam Davis and I walked to the College Village drug store one Saturday morning to buy some candy. We were about 12 years old (fun ages). She got her
Bit-O-Honey. I got my malted milk balls, chocolate stars, Chunkys, and a
small bag of M & M's. We started back to her house. I was going to spend
the night. We had the whole day to look forward to. We had plenty of candy.
It was a long way to Pam's house but every time we got weary Pam would put
her hand over her eyes, scan the horizon like a sailor and say, "Oughta reach
home by nightfall," at which point the two of us would laugh until we thought
we couldn't stand it another minute. Then after we got calm, she'd say it
again. You should have been there. It was the kind of day and friendship and
occasion that made me deeply regretful that I had to grow up.

It was fun.   15

Questions for Discussion

1. Explain the essay's thesis in your own words.
2. Which of the techniques for writing introductions discussed earlier in this
   chapter does Jordan use in the first two sentences of her essay? Among
   those you might choose from are anecdote, comparison and contrast, and
   definition.
3. Jordan makes use of a startling remark and a series of questions in other
   parts of her introduction. In which paragraphs do we find these techniques?
4. In which paragraph of the essay does Jordan address the reader directly?
5. In which paragraphs does she use illustration to develop the topic sentence? For a review of illustration as a method of development, see
   Chapter 3.
6. In paragraph 13, Jordan tells us that fun "is a mystery," that "It cannot
   be caught like a virus," and that "It cannot be trapped like an animal."
   What method of development is she using in this paragraph? For a review
   of paragraph development, see Chapter 3.
7. Jordan concludes her essay with an anecdote. Summarize this anecdote in
   your own words. Does it make for a good conclusion? Does it support the
   idea that "fun is a rare jewel"?

Suggestions for Journal Entries

1. Jordan's purpose is to define and evaluate fun. What do *you* think fun is?
   Write a short introductory paragraph or series of introductory paragraphs
   in which you explain your definition. Use one or more of the techniques
   discussed earlier in this chapter; for instance, try an analogy, a comparison
   or contrast, a definition, a startling fact or opinion, or a question.
2. Write an introductory paragraph or series of introductory paragraphs that

you might use to explain your notion of friendship, pain, courage, devotion, honesty, unselfishness, poverty, wealth, comfort, health, or any other idea that is as abstract as Jordan's fun. Use one or more of the techniques for writing introductions discussed in this chapter.

How to Keep Air Clean

Sydney Harris

Sydney Harris was born in London in 1917 and began writing as a regular columnist for the *Chicago Daily News* in 1941. Models of interesting and effective prose, Harris's newspaper columns, like "How to Keep Air Clean," have proven him to be an important American essayist and earned him thousands of devoted readers over the years. Many of these columns have been used in college textbooks and gathered in book-length collections of his work.

Looking Ahead

1. The essay's introduction consists of the first three paragraphs. Read these paragraphs carefully, and try to determine what technique Harris relies on most to open this essay.
2. Harris uses two terms from meteorology, the study of the Earth's atmosphere. The *troposphere* (paragraph 4) is the bottom layer of the atmosphere, where clouds, rain, snow, and other weather phenomena occur. Directly above the troposphere is the *stratosphere* (paragraph 2), which extends to about 30 miles up.
3. In his conclusion (paragraph 9), Harris calls our attention to the industrial revolution, which occurred in the eighteenth and nineteenth centuries in Europe and North America. Not an armed conflict, the industrial revolution was a series of technological developments that led to the modern factory system, mass production, and automation.

Vocabulary

infinitely   Without end.
irreversible   Not reversible or repairable.
noxious   Toxic, dangerous, harmful.
particulates   Small particles.

Some months ago, while doing research on the general subject of pol- 1
lution, I learned how dumb I had been all my life about something as common
and familiar—and essential—as air.

In my ignorance, I had always thought that "fresh air" was infinitely 2
available to us. I had imagined that the dirty air around us somehow escaped
into the stratosphere, and that new air kept coming in—much as it does when
we open a window after a party.

This, of course, is not true, and you would imagine that a grown man 3
with a decent education would know this as a matter of course. What is true
is that we live in a kind of spaceship called the earth, and only a limited
amount of air is *forever* available to us.

The "walls" of our spaceship enclose what is called the "troposphere," 4
which extends about seven miles up. This is all the air that is available to us.
We must use it over and over again for infinity, just as if we were in a sealed
room for the lifetime of the earth.

No fresh air comes in, and no polluted air escapes. Moreover, no dirt 5
or poisons are ever "destroyed"—they remain in the air, in different forms,
or settle on the earth as "particulates." And the more we burn, the more we
replace good air with bad.

Once contaminated, this thin layer of air surrounding the earth cannot 6
be cleansed again. We can clean materials, we can even clean water, but we
cannot clean the air. There is nowhere else for the dirt and poisons to go—we
cannot open a window in the troposphere and clear out the stale and noxious
atmosphere we are creating.

Perhaps every child in sixth grade and above knows this, but I doubt 7
that one adult in a hundred is aware of this basic physical fact. Most of us
imagine, as I did, that winds sweep away the gases and debris in the air, taking
them far out into the solar system and replacing them with new air.

The United States alone is discharging *130 million tons of pollutants a year* 8
into the atmosphere, from factories, heating systems, incinerators, automobiles and airplanes, power plants and public buildings. What is frightening is
not so much the death and illness, corrosion and decay they are responsible
for—as the fact that this is an *irreversible process*. The air will never be cleaner
than it is now.

And this is why *prevention*—immediate, drastic and far-reaching—is our 9
only hope for the future. We cannot undo what we have done. We cannot
restore the atmosphere to the purity it had before the Industrial Revolution.
But we can, and must, halt the contamination before our spaceship suffocates
from its own foul discharges.

Questions for Discussion

1. What technique discussed earlier in this chapter does Harris rely upon
   most to open his essay?

2. In paragraph three, Harris also makes use of an analogy, another of the techniques for beginning an essay discussed earlier. What is this interesting analogy? In what other paragraph does Harris make reference to it?
3. Reread paragraph three of "How to Keep Air Clean." What is Harris's thesis?
4. What techniques does Harris use to conclude his essay?
5. The title suggests that Harris has used process analysis to develop his ideas. Identify one paragraph in which he uses this method of development. (Process analysis was discussed in Chapter 3.)
6. The essay is very well developed and organized. What techniques does Harris use to maintain coherence in and between his paragraphs? (For ways to maintain coherence, see Chapter 2.)

Suggestions for Journal Entries

1. Summarize in a paragraph of your own the three paragraphs Harris uses to introduce his essay. Make sure to use your own words throughout.
2. To introduce his essay, Harris challenges a widely held opinion or assumption. Think of a widely held opinion or assumption that you believe is incorrect. In a sentence or two, write this idea in your journal. Then, using one of the prewriting techniques described in Getting Started, write down your major reasons for disagreeing. Here are a few examples of the kinds of opinions or assumptions you might want to correct:

> Someone who has had only one or two drinks shouldn't be prevented from driving a car.
> Breaking an alcohol or drug addiction is relatively easy.
> Women have no aptitude for math.
> Reading poetry, listening to opera, and going to the ballet aren't things that "real" men do.

The New Enemies of Journalism

Charles Kuralt

A native of North Carolina, Charles Kuralt has long been one of this country's most respected journalists and has won almost every major award for television journalism. He is currently the host of CBS's "Sunday Morning," a television magazine that has earned national acclaim.

In "The New Enemies of Journalism," Kuralt denies the notion that the American people want only the kind of quick and superficial coverage of im-

portant events that the television networks usually provide. He makes it clear
that viewers need, want, and deserve more serious and more complete reporting of the news. Anything less, he insists, is an insult to their intelligence.

Looking Ahead

1. Kuralt's introduction spans the first three paragraphs. In these three, look
   for some of the techniques for writing introductions that you learned earlier in this chapter.
2. As he tells us in paragraph 9, Kuralt wrote this essay at a time when unemployment in the United States was higher than at any time since the
   great depression. This depression was an economic one that began after
   the stock market crash in 1929 and lasted through the 1930s.
3. In paragraph 10, Kuralt mentions the American involvement in Central
   America. He is referring most specifically to the U.S. support for the government in El Salvador and for the Contras, a group trying to overthrow
   the Sandinista government in Nicaragua.

Vocabulary

inevitably   Unavoidably, eventually.

prevailing   Current, widespread.

reflective   Thoughtful.

sensational   Given to reporting events through details that are exaggerated, racy, or
otherwise inaccurate simply to arouse the viewer's interest.

serendipity   The ability to come upon good luck by accident.

spontaneity   The quality by which things are accomplished without apparent cause
or planning.

On the television news programs now, bells ring, pictures flip and tum- 1
ble, and everybody seems to be shouting at me. This may be the way to do
it, but I don't think so.

The news is bad enough without added jingle and flash. I think it would 2
be better to tell it calmly, with as many of the details as possible, and not to
try to make it more exciting than it is. I even think viewers would appreciate
that, and tune in.

This runs contrary to the prevailing opinion at the networks. One of my 3
bosses said of a program I used to work on, "We want to keep it a news
broadcast, but one that is more interesting, rapidly paced, with more spontaneity and serendipity, almost like all-news radio....We want a news program that better serves the needs of people who don't have time to watch
television for long periods...and need to get information quickly."

I respect this man, but I respectfully disagree with his judgement. I 4
don't see how a news broadcast can be quick without also being cheap and

shallow. Almost any story worth mentioning is worth an additional word of explanation. The story told in a few seconds is almost always misleading. It would be better not to mention it at all. And all those electronic beeps and bells and flashy graphics designed to "grab" the viewer and speed the pace along only subtract a few more seconds that could be used to explain the events of the day in the English language.

The "quick news" idea has been preached for years by the shabby news   5 consultants who have gone about peddling their bad advice to small television stations. They have never given a thought to the needs of the viewer, or to the reason the news is on the air in the first place—namely that this kind of country cannot work without an informed citizenry. The ninety-second news story does not serve the people; neither do the thirty- and twenty-second stories, and that's where we're headed. Fast. With bells and graphics.

In this sort of journalism there is something insulting to the viewer, the   6 man or woman who sits down in front of the television set in the wistful hope of being informed. We are saying to this person, "You are a simpleton with a very short attention span," or, "You are too much in a hurry to care about the news anyway." Sooner or later, this viewer, who is *not* a simpleton and *not* too much in a hurry to care, will get the message and turn the dial. The networks are in a news-ratings race. The one that wins it will be the one that stays calm and intelligent and reliable—the most responsible, not the most excitable.

(I offer an analogy from the newspaper world: When I first came to   7 work in New York, such sensational newspapers as the *Journal-American*, the *Mirror*, the *News*, and the *Post* nipped at the heels of the solid reflective *New York Times*. The *News* is on its uppers, the *Post* is a joke, and the others are memories. The *Times* may be the only one of them all to survive.)

Even if I am wrong, even if it turns out that a network news department   8 *can* achieve high ratings by putting red slashes on the screen and shouting out the headlines and jangling people's nerves, does that mean it *should*?

Right now, more Americans are out of work than at any time since the   9 Great Depression. The President is asking that the country spend more dollars on military hardware than the government possesses. Meanwhile, many dollars for the unemployed, the poor, the blind, and the disabled, may be taken away. How can any discussion of these matters be carried out in short, loud bursts on television?

In Geneva, negotiators for the United States and the Soviet Union are   10 meeting to seek some way out of the terrible nuclear confrontation. Our country seems to be sliding into a bog of Central American quicksand. The Congress has on its agenda a sweeping revision of the federal criminal law. These subjects also call for much explanation and public debate.

They will inevitably slow the pace of any news program that takes them   11 up. But they are the stuff of our national life. The people expect us to inform them about these things, and if we don't, who will? If the people are given baby food when they are hungry for a meal of information, they will be undernourished and weakened—and then what will become of the country that is the last, best hope of man?

The best minds in television news are thinking more about packaging and 12 promotion and pace and image and blinking electronics than about thoughtful coverage of the news. I have worked in the field for twenty-five years, and every year I thought we were getting better. Suddenly, I think we're getting worse.

Questions for Discussion

1. What is Kuralt's thesis, and in what paragraph does this thesis appear?
2. Which one of the techniques discussed earlier in this chapter does Kuralt use in the first paragraph?
3. In what way does paragraph 3 help him introduce his arguments against "quick news"? What technique for writing introductions does he use in this paragraph?
4. Kuralt uses the essay's conclusion to rephrase his thesis and to restate many of the essay's major points. What are some of the points that he includes in the essay's last two paragraphs?
5. Kuralt also includes rhetorical questions in his conclusion. What are they, and how would you answer them?
6. In paragraph 5, he explains that our "country cannot work without an informed citizenry." What does he mean by this statement, and how does it relate to his thesis?
7. Why does Kuralt believe, as he tells us in paragraph 6, that the way networks now broadcast the news is insulting to viewers?
8. Discuss the analogy in paragraph 7. Why is it an analogy? What does it tell us? How does this information help Kuralt develop his thesis?
9. Explain how his comments about the way in which the networks cover such important topics as unemployment, the negotiations in Geneva, and the U.S. involvement in Central America (paragraphs 9 and 10) help him develop his thesis.
10. What techniques does Kuralt use to maintain coherence in this very well organized essay?

Suggestions for Journal Entries

1. Do you agree with Kuralt that television news has too much "jingle and flash"? If so, list details about a recent television news story that serve to illustrate this point. Then turn these details into an anecdote (a brief, illustrative story) that you could use as the introduction to an essay on this topic.

2. Reread the essay's introduction carefully. Then write a paragraph of your own in which you begin with a quote from Kuralt, tell the reader whether you agree or disagree with the idea expressed in the quote, and explain why you agree or disagree with it. For example, you might begin with something like this: "In 'The New Enemies of Journalism,' Charles Kuralt explains that 'On the television news programs now, bells ring' and 'pictures flip and tumble.'"

The Decline and Fall of Teaching History

Diane Ravitch

Diane Ravitch is a professor of the history of education at Columbia University's Teachers College and coauthor of *What Do Our 17-Year-Olds Know?* According to Ravitch, there is a significant need for improvement in the teaching of literature and history in high school. One of the suggestions that she and her coauthor, Chester E. Finn, made to revise the curriculum is that high school students be required to complete at least two years of world history.

In "The Decline and Fall of Teaching History," Ravitch argues that unless we study history we will find it harder and harder to make the kinds of educated and "independent judgments on current issues" that will keep our democracy strong.

Looking Ahead

1. Ravitch takes two full paragraphs to introduce her essay. Read them carefully, and identify some of the methods she uses for writing good introductions.
2. The essay's title is interesting because it suggests the title of Edward Gibbon's *The History of the Decline and Fall of the Roman Empire*.
3. Ravitch uses a great many anecdotes and quotations to develop the body paragraphs of her essay. Look for these techniques as you read the essay.

Vocabulary

abysmal Terribly low and empty (like a huge pit or cavern).
assessment Evaluation.
causation The relationship between causes and effects, the study of why events happen.

chronology   A history, a series of events in time.

civics   The study of how government works.

collaboration   Cooperation, joint effort.

derives   Issues or originates from.

eminent   Famous, important, distinguished.

evolved   Developed, grew.

indifference   Lack of interest.

perspective   Point of view, way of looking at something.

premise   A principle or assumption upon which actions, ideas, or other principles are based.

sequenced   In an order, in a continuous series.

subjective   Based on personal opinion, preference, or reaction.

vocational   Occupational.

During the past generation, the amount of time devoted to historical 1 studies in American public schools has steadily decreased. About 25 years ago, most public high-school youths studied one year of world history and one of American history, but today, most study only one year of ours. In contrast, the state schools of many other Western nations require the subject to be studied almost every year. In France, for example, all students, not just the college-bound, follow a carefully sequenced program of history, civics and geography every year from the seventh grade through the twelfth grade.

Does it matter if Americans are ignorant of their past? Does it matter 2 if the general public knows little of the individuals, the events and the movements that shaped our nation? The fundamental premise of our democratic form of government is that political power derives from the informed consent of the people. Informed consent requires a citizenry that is rational and knowledgeable. If our system is to remain free and democratic, citizens should know not only how to judge candidates and their competing claims but how our institutions evolved. An understanding of history does not lead everyone to the same conclusions, but it does equip people with the knowledge to reach independent judgments on current issues. Without historical perspective, voters are more likely to be swayed by emotional appeals, by stirring commercials, or by little more than a candidate's good looks or charisma.

Because of my interest as a historian of education in the condition of the 3 study of history, I have been involved during the last year, in collaboration with the National Assessment of Educational Progress, in planning a countrywide study of what 17-year-olds know about American history. In addition, my contacts with college students during the last year and discussions with other historians have led me to believe that there is cause for concern.

On the college lecture circuit this past year, I visited some 30 campuses, 4 ranging from large public universities to small private liberal-arts colleges.

Repeatedly, I was astonished by questions from able students about the most elementary facts of American history. At one urban Minnesota university, none of the 30 students in a course on ethnic relations had ever heard of the Supreme Court's Brown v. Board of Education decision of 1954, which held racial segregation in public schools unconstitutional. At a university in the Pacific Northwest, a professor of education publicly insisted that high-school students should concentrate on vocational preparation and athletics, since they had the rest of their lives to learn subjects like history "on their own time."

The shock of encountering college students who did not recognize the   5
names of eminent figures like Jane Addams or W.E.B. Du Bois led me to conduct an informal, unscientific survey of professors who teach history to undergraduates. "My students are not stupid, but they have an abysmal background in American, or any other kind of, history," said Thomas Kessner, who teaches American history at Kingsborough Community College in Brooklyn. "They never heard of Daniel Webster; don't understand the Constitution; don't know the difference between the Republican and Democratic parties."

This gloomy assessment was echoed by Naomi Miller, chairman of the   6
history department at Hunter College in New York. "My students have no historical knowledge on which to draw when they enter college," she said. "They have no point of reference for understanding World War I, the Treaty of Versailles or the Holocaust." More than ignorance of the past, however, she finds an indifference to dates and chronology or causation. "They think that everything is subjective. They have plenty of attitudes and opinions, but they lack the knowledge to analyze a problem." Professor Miller believes that "we are in danger of bringing up a generation without historical memory. This is a dangerous situation."

Questions for Discussion

1. What techniques does Ravitch use in paragraphs 1 and 2 to introduce her essay?
2. The essay's thesis is found at the end of paragraph 2. Put this thesis into your own words.
3. In paragraph 4, Ravitch quotes a professor of education at a university in the Northwest. What does this passage tell us about how some people, even some educators, view the teaching of history?
4. Ravitch quotes another teacher in paragraph 5. What information or insights does this paragraph contribute?
5. Ravitch concludes her essay with a quotation from yet another educator. What does this individual tell us about the "decline and fall of teaching

history" in the high schools? Do her remarks make for an effective conclusion?

6. In which of the six paragraphs of this essay does the author use an anecdote? What details does she use to develop this anecdote?

7. What transitional devices and techniques does Ravitch use to maintain coherence within paragraphs 1, 3, 4, 5, and 6? What does she do to maintain coherence between paragraphs 4 and 5? Between 5 and 6?

Suggestions for Journal Entries

1. In the middle of paragraph 2, Ravitch tells us that "The fundamental premise of our democratic form of government is that political power derives from the informed consent of the people." Reread the whole paragraph carefully, and then explain in your own words what she is driving at in this sentence. Make sure you understand exactly what she means by "informed consent." Define this term in your journal.

2. What other subjects do you think high school students should be learning more about? Rely on your own experiences to a make list of important subject areas, skills, or topics of concern with which young people should become more familiar.

3. In paragraph 6, we learn that many students have no "point of reference" for understanding such important historical developments as "World War I, the Treaty of Versailles or the Holocaust." If you need to learn more about these or any of the other events Ravitch mentions in this essay, look them up in an encyclopedia in your college library or in any world-history textbook used at your school. Record your findings in your journal.

SUGGESTIONS FOR WRITING

1. Reread any one of the college papers you've written this semester. Try to pick the one you or your instructor liked best, but don't limit your choice to papers you've completed for English class. Then, rewrite the beginning and ending to that essay by using any of the techniques for writing effective introductions and conclusions discussed in this chapter.

2. If you responded to any of the Suggestions for Journal Entries that followed Suzanne Britt Jordan's "Fun, Oh Boy. Fun...," you may have made a start in defining *fun, friendship, pain, courage, devotion* or some other abstract idea of your choice. Add details to this journal entry, and then expand it into a short essay that explains your notion of this abstract idea.

   Before you begin, however, read the following suggestions. You may find them useful in planning or writing your essay:

   a. Try to open by using one or more of the techniques for writing introductions discussed earlier in this chapter.

b. Make sure your introduction includes a thesis statement.

c. Use the principles of unity and coherence you learned about in Chapter 2. In short, make sure each of the paragraphs in the body of your essay relates to and develops your thesis, and provide clear connections between paragraphs.

d. Finally, try to conclude with an anecdote as Jordan does. However, if you find that an anecdote would be inappropriate for your essay, try to use one of the other effective methods for concluding essays that was explained earlier.

3. In one of the Suggestions for Journal Entries that follows Sydney J. Harris's "How to Keep Air Clean," you were asked to write down a number of reasons that have led you to disagree with a widely held assumption or opinion. If you responded to this item, read over what you recorded in your journal. Then, do the following:

a. Turn your notes into an introductory paragraph—complete with a formal thesis statement—that challenges this assumption and briefly explains your reasons for disagreeing.

b. Make each of your reasons for disagreeing the topic of a well-developed paragraph. Use these paragraphs to develop the body of your essay.

c. Finally, write a concluding paragraph that:

Rephrases your thesis and summarizes your major points;
Uses an anecdote to illustrate those ideas;
Makes a call to action, as Harris does at the end of his essay;
or
Uses one of the other methods for writing effective conclusions discussed in this chapter.

Incidentally, although you may want to follow the steps in this Suggestion for Writing, remember that you need not complete them according to the order in which they are listed. For instance, writing the body paragraphs and the conclusion before you write the introduction might be a far more effective way for you to proceed than following the order described above.

Remember that writing is a process of discovery and that, often, you should revise one paragraph in light of what you've written in another. Therefore, if you begin by writing your introduction, don't be afraid to rewrite it later if you believe that what you've included in the body of your essay calls for a change—major or minor—in your thesis or in other parts of your introduction.

4. Do you agree with Charles Kuralt that television news has too much "jingle and flash"? If you do, perhaps you responded to one of the Suggestions for Journal Entries after "The New Enemies of Journalism"

and have written about a recent television news story that illustrates his point.

Review this journal entry and use it as an introduction for an essay in which you provide other examples of the "jingle and flash" that Kuralt wants taken out of television news broadcasting.

Incidentally, a good way to end your essay is by making a call to action or by restating your thesis and major points as Kuralt does at the end of his essay.

5. In one of the Suggestions for Journal Entries that followed Diane Ravitch's "The Decline and Fall of Teaching History," you were asked to think about subjects in addition to history that high-school students should be learning more about. Reread the list you made in your journal and focus on the *one* subject about which you have the strongest feelings.

   Then, write a short essay in which you explain why spending more time studying this subject in high school would have been advantageous for you. Before you begin planning your essay, however, here are a few words of advice:

   a. Get your reader's attention by beginning with:

   A startling fact or statement,
   An appropriate anecdote,
   A definition of your subject, or
   One of the other methods for beginning an essay discussed earlier.

   b. Make sure your introduction contains a thesis statement that briefly mentions each of the reasons you believe more time should be spent on the subject in question.

   c. Develop each of these reasons in the body paragraphs of your essay. You can organize these paragraphs easily and effectively by stating each of your reasons in a topic sentence.

   d. End your essay by:

   Making a call to action,
   Using another anecdote,
   Looking to the future, or
   Using any of the other techniques for writing conclusions that you have learned about.

Section II

Word Choice and Sentence Patterns

In Section I you learned how to approach a subject, to focus on a purpose and central idea, and to organize and develop the information you collected. The three chapters in Section II explain how to use language and sentence structure to make your writing clearer, more interesting, and more emphatic.

What you will learn in Section II is just as important as what you learned earlier. In most cases, however, the techniques discussed in this section—refining word choice, creating figures of speech, and reworking sentence structure for emphasis and variety—are things you will turn your attention to after having written at least one version of a paper, not while you are focusing on a central idea, organizing details, or writing your very first rough draft.

Keep this in mind as you read the next three chapters. Chapter 5 explains how to choose vocabulary that is concrete, specific, and vivid. You will learn even more about using words effectively in Chapter 6, which explains three types of figurative language: metaphor, simile, and personification. Finally, Chapter 7 will increase your ability to create variety and emphasis through sentence structure.

Enjoy the selections that follow. Reading them carefully and completing the Questions for Discussion, the Suggestions for Journal Entries, and the Suggestions for Writing will not only help you learn more about the writing process but should also inspire you to continue developing as a writer.

Chapter 5

Word Choice: Using Concrete, Specific, and Vivid Language

A writer has three ways to communicate a message: by (1) implying it, (2) telling it, or (3) showing it. Of course, all three types of writing serve specific and important purposes. Usually, however, writing that is the clearest and has the greatest impact uses language that shows what you wish to communicate. Words that show are always more concrete, specific, and usually more interesting than those which simply tell the reader what you want to say, and they are always more direct than language which only implies or suggests what you mean.

Although the following two paragraphs discuss the same subject, they contain very different kinds of language. Which of the two will have the greatest impact on the reader?

Writing that tells

Smith's old car is the joke of the neighborhood. He should have gotten rid of it years ago, but he insists on keeping this "antique" despite protests from his family and friends. The car is noisy and unsafe. What's more, it pollutes the environment, causes a real disturbance whenever he drives by, and is a real eyesore.

Writing that shows

Whenever Smith drives his 1957 Dodge down our street, dogs howl, children scream, and old people head inside and shut their windows. Originally, the car was painted emerald green, but the exterior is so covered with scrapes, dents, and patches of rust that it is hard to tell what it looked like when new. His wife, children, and close friends

103

have begged him to junk this corroded patchwork of steel, rubber,
and chicken wire, but Smith insists that he can restore his "antique"
to its former glory. It does no good to point out that its cracked
windshield and bald tires qualify it as a road hazard. Nor does it help
to complain about the roar and rattle of its cracked muffler, the
screech of its well-worn brakes, and the stench of the thick, black
smoke that billows from its rusty tail pipe.

As you will learn in the chapters on narration and description, language
that shows makes for effective and interesting writing, especially when your
purpose is to describe a person or place or to tell a story. But such language
is important to many kinds of writing, and learning how to use it is essential
to your development as a writer.

There are three important things to remember about language that shows:
It is concrete, it is specific, and it is vivid.

MAKING YOUR WRITING CONCRETE

Concrete language points to (or identifies) something that the reader can experience or has experienced in some way. Things that are concrete are usually
material; they can be seen, heard, smelled, felt, or tasted. The opposite of
concrete is *abstract*, a term that refers to ideas, emotions, or other intangibles
that, while very real, exist in our minds and hearts.

Compare the nouns in the following list. The ones on the left represent
abstract ideas. The ones on the right stand for concrete embodiments of those
ideas; that is, they are physical representations, showing us what such ideas
as "affection" and "hatred" really are.

Abstract	Concrete
Affection	Kiss, embrace
Hatred	Sneer, curse
Violence	Punch, shove
Anger	Shout
Fear	Scream, gasp
Joy	Laugh, smile

The following are three ways to make your writing concrete.

Use Your Five Senses to Re-create an Experience

Giving your readers a straightforward, realistic account of how things look, smell,
sound, taste, or feel is one of the most effective ways to make your writing concrete. There are several examples in this book of how authors appeal to the five

senses, especially in the chapters on description. For now, read the following passage from "Once More to the Lake," in which E. B. White recalls concrete, sensory details about arriving at the camp in Maine where he spent his summer vacations as a boy. The only sense that White does not refer to is taste; see if you can identify details in this paragraph that appeal to the other four:

> The arriving...had been so big a business in itself, at the railway station the farm wagon drawn up, the first smell of the pine-laden air, the first glimpse of the smiling farmer...and the feel of the wagon under you for the long ten-mile haul, and at the top of the last long hill catching the first view of the lake after eleven months of not seeing this cherished body of water. The shouts and cries of the other campers when they saw you, and the trunks to be unpacked, to give up their rich burden.

Use Your Five Senses to Create a Concrete Image

An *image* is a mental picture that will help your readers understand the abstract idea you're explaining. One of the best ways to create a clear image is to pack your writing with details, usually in the form of nouns and adjectives, that show the reader what you've seen, heard, touched, smelled, or tasted.

This is exactly what James Joyce has done in his famous description of hell from *A Portrait of the Artist as a Young Man*, an autobiographical novel. Like White, Joyce relies on the senses. Notice how many effective nouns and adjectives he uses to create an image of what it must be like to suffer eternal damnation, an idea that would otherwise have remained very abstract indeed:

> Hell is a strait [narrow] and dark and foulsmelling prison, an abode [home] of demons and lost souls, filled with fire and smoke. The straitness of this prisonhouse is expressly designed by God to punish those who refused to be bound by His laws. In earthly prisons the poor captive [prisoner] has at least some liberty of movement, [if] only within the four walls of his cell or in the gloomy yard of his prison. Not so in hell. There, by reason of the great number of the damned, the prisoners are heaped together in their awful prison, the walls of which are said to be four thousand miles thick: and the damned are so utterly bound and helpless that...they are not even able to remove from the eye a worm that gnaws it.

White's and Joyce's paragraphs communicate abstract ideas in such concrete detail that we clearly understand what each writer is explaining. In White's passage, concrete details allow us to experience the excitement and anticipation that the author felt as he began his vacation at that camp in Maine, feelings with which we could never identify without such details. Concrete details are even more important to Joyce's description of hell. Unlike the earthly camp in Maine, hell is only an abstraction; we have nothing in our world with which to compare it. Therefore, in order to *show* us his notion of hell clearly, Joyce must rely on concrete details that appeal to our senses.

Use Examples

Using easily recognizable examples is a very effective way to help your readers grasp abstract ideas, which might otherwise seem vague or unclear. For instance, if you want to explain that your uncle Wendell is eccentric, you can write that "he has several quirks," that "he is odd," or that "he is strange." But such synonyms are as abstract and as hard to grasp as "eccentric." Instead, why not provide examples that your readers are sure to understand? In other words, *show* them what "eccentric" means by explaining that Uncle Wendell never wears the same color socks, that he often cuts his own hair, that he refuses to speak for days at a time, and that he sometimes eats chocolate-covered seaweed for dessert.

In "Less Work for Mother?" Ruth Schwartz Cowan uses a number of examples we are certain to recognize and understand as she explains the idea that technology has transformed the American household:

> During the first half of the twentieth century, the average American household was transformed by the introduction of a group of machines that profoundly altered the daily lives of housewives.... Where once there had been a wood- or coal-burning stove there now was a gas or electric range. Clothes that had once been scrubbed on a metal washboard were now tossed into a tub and cleansed by an electrically driven agitator. The dryer replaced the clothesline; the vacuum cleaner replaced the broom; the refrigerator replaced the ice box and the root cellar.... No one had to chop or haul wood any more. No one had to shovel out ashes or beat rugs or carry water; no one even had to toss egg whites with a fork for an hour to make an angel food cake.

MAKING YOUR WRITING SPECIFIC

As you've learned, writing that shows uses details that are both specific and concrete. Writing that lacks specificity often contains language that is general, which makes it difficult for the writer to communicate clearly and completely. One of the best ways to make your language more specific is to use carefully chosen nouns and adjectives. As you probably know, nouns represent persons, places, and things; adjectives modify (or help describe) nouns, thereby making them more exact and distinct. In the following list, compare the words and phrases in each column; notice how much more meaningful the items become as you move from left to right:

General	More Specific	Most Specific
Automobile	Sports coupe	Fuel-injected Ford Mustang
Residence	House	Large three-bedroom ranch
Fruit	Melon	Juicy cantaloupe
School	College	The University of Kentucky
Tree	Evergreen	Young Douglas fir
Baked goods	Pastries	Chocolate-filled cream puffs
Airplane	Jetliner	Brand-new Boeing 747
Beverage	Soft drink	Caffeine-free diet cola

At first, you might have to train yourself to use specifics. After a while, though, you will become skilled at eliminating flat, empty generalizations from your writing and filling it with details that clarify and focus your ideas.

Notice the differences between the following two paragraphs. The first uses vague, general language; the second uses specific details—nouns and adjectives—that make its meaning sharper and clearer and hold the reader's interest better.

General

The island prison is covered with flowers now. A large sign that is visible from a long way off warns visitors away. But since the early 1960s, when they took the last prisoners to other institutions, the sign has really served no purpose, for the prison has been abandoned. The place is not unpleasant; in fact, one might enjoy the romance and solitude out there.

Specific

Alcatraz Island is covered with flowers now: orange and yellow nasturtiums, geraniums, sweet grass, blue iris, black-eyed Susans. Candytuft springs up through the cracked concrete in the exercise yard. Ice plant carpets the rusting catwalks. "WARNING! KEEP OFF! U.S. PROPERTY," the sign still reads, big and yellow and visible for perhaps a quarter of a mile, but since March 21, 1963, the day they took the last thirty or so men off the island..., the warning has been only *pro forma* [serving no real purpose]. It is not an unpleasant place to be, out there on Alcatraz with only the flowers and the wind and the bell buoy moaning and the tide surging through the Golden Gate. (Joan Didion, "Rock of Ages.")

The differences between these two paragraphs can be summed up as follows:

- The first calls the place an "island prison." The second gives it a name, "Alcatraz."
- The first claims that the prison is covered with flowers. The second shows us that this is true by naming them: "nasturtiums, geraniums," etc. It also explains exactly where they grow: "through the cracked concrete" and on "rusting catwalks."
- The first tells us about a sign that can be seen "from a long way off." The second explains that the sign is "visible for perhaps a quarter of a mile" and shows us exactly what it says.
- The first mentions that the last prisoners were removed from Alcatraz in the 1960s. The second explains that they numbered "thirty or so" and that the exact date of their departure was March 21, 1963.
- The first tells us that we might find "romance and solitude" on Alcatraz Island. The second describes the romance and solitude by calling our attention to "the flowers and the wind and the bell buoy moaning and the tide surging through the Golden Gate."

MAKING YOUR WRITING VIVID

Besides using figurative language (the subject of the next chapter), you can make your writing vivid by choosing verbs, adjectives, and adverbs carefully.

1. Verbs express action, condition, or state of being. If you wrote that "Jan *leaped* over the hurdles," you would be using an action verb. If you explained that "Roberta *did not feel* well" or that "Mario *was* delirious," you would be describing a condition or a state of being.
2. Adjectives are words that help describe nouns. You would be using adjectives if you wrote that "the *large, two-story white* house that the *young Canadian* couple bought was *old* and *weather-beaten*."
3. Adverbs modify (or tell the reader something about) verbs, adjectives, or other adverbs. You would be using adverbs if you wrote that "the *extremely* large oak swayed *gently* over the *beautifully* designed front porch, which *very nearly* had been crushed during the last hurricane."

Choosing effective verbs, adjectives, and adverbs can turn dull writing into writing that keeps the readers' interest and communicates ideas with greater emphasis and clarity. Notice how much more effective the rewritten version of each of the following sentences becomes when the right verbs, adjectives, and adverbs are used:

1. The old church needed repair.

   The pre-Civil War Baptist church cried out for repairs to its tottering steeple, its crumbling stone foundation, and its cracked stained-glass windows.

2. The kitchen table was a mess. It was covered with the remains of peanut-butter-and-jelly sandwiches.

   The kitchen table was littered with the half-eaten remains of very stale peanut-butter sandwiches and thickly smeared with the crusty residue of strawberry jelly.

3. Her fellow students showed their approval and their support as the old woman graduated.

   Her fellow graduates applauded warmly and enthusiastically as the eighty-six-year-old chemistry major rose proudly and strutted across the auditorium stage to accept her college diploma.

Word choice is extremely important to anyone who wants to become an effective writer. Using the right kind of language marks the difference between writing that is flat, vague, and uninteresting and writing that makes a real impact on its readers. The following selections present the work of one poet and three essayists who have written clear and effective explanations of very abstract ideas, ideas they would have been unable to explain without language that is concrete, specific, and vivid.

Those Winter Sundays

Robert Hayden

Robert Hayden (1913–1980) taught English at Fisk University and at the University of Michigan. For years, the work of this talented black writer received far less recognition than it deserved, and too few people read his poetry. Recently, however, his reputation has grown, especially since the publication of his complete poems in 1985.

"Those Winter Sundays" uses the author's vivid memories of his father to show us the depth and quality of love that the man had for his family. Unlike much of Hayden's other work, this poem does not deal with the black experience as such, but it demonstrates the same care and skill in choosing effective language that Hayden used in all his poetry.

If you want to read more by Hayden, look for these poetry collections in your college library: *A Ballad of Remembrance*, *Words in Mourning Time*, *Angle of Ascent*, and *American Journal*.

Looking Ahead

1. As you read this poem, look for details that appeal to the senses and make Hayden's writing concrete. Also, pick out nouns and adjectives that make his writing both specific and vivid.
2. Hayden's primary purpose is to explain the love his father felt for his family. Find details that show us signs or physical representations of this emotion.
3. In lines 4 and 5, Hayden tells us that his father "made / banked fires blaze." Wood and coal fires were "banked" by covering them with ashes so as to make them burn slowly through the night and continue to give off heat. In the mornings, someone would have to add more fuel and stir up the ashes in order to make the fire "blaze."
4. Hayden doesn't use the word "offices" in its usual sense. Here, it means important services or ceremonies.

Vocabulary

austere   Severe, harsh, difficult, without comfort.
chronic   Persistent, unending, constant.
indifferently   Insensitively, without care or concern.

Sundays too my father got up early
and put his clothes on in the blueblack cold,
then with cracked hands that ached

from labor in the weekday weather made
banked fires blaze. No one ever thanked him.

I'd wake and hear the cold splintering, breaking.
When the rooms were warm, he'd call,
and slowly I would rise and dress,
fearing the chronic angers of that house,

Speaking indifferently to him,
who had driven out the cold
and polished my good shoes as well.
What did I know, what did I know
of love's austere and lonely offices?

Questions for Discussion

1. What details in this poem appeal to our senses?
2. In line 2, Hayden uses "blueblack" to describe the cold in his house on Sunday mornings. What other effective adjectives do you find in this poem?
3. Hayden shows us his father in action. What were some of the things this good man did to show his love for his family?
4. What was Hayden's reaction to his father's "austere and lonely offices" when he was a boy? How did he feel about his father when he wrote this poem?

Suggestions for Journal Entries

1. In Looking Ahead, you read that Hayden describes his father's love by using language that is concrete, specific, and vivid. In your own words, discuss the kind of love that Hayden's father showed his family.
2. Do you know someone who demonstrates love for other people day in and day out, as Hayden's father did? In your journal, list the "offices" (services, tasks, or activities) that he or she performs to show this love. Include as many concrete and specific terms as you can. Then expand each item in your list to a few short sentences, showing that these activities are clearly signs of love.

The Station

Robert J. Hastings

Robert Hastings is an ordained Baptist minister and has taught at numerous colleges and seminaries in the United States, Great Britain, and South America. Hastings' short fiction, much of it set in a mythical American village called Tinyburg, has become quite popular. However, his reputation rests on his work as a syndicated religious columnist in Kentucky and Illinois.

"The Station" was originally published in Ann Landers' nationally syndicated newspaper column.

Looking Ahead

1. In comparing our journey through life with a long trip by train across the continent, Hastings uses analogy as a primary method of development. (To review what you've learned about analogy, see the Glossary near the end of this book.)
2. The abstract idea Hastings explains so well is that, in spending too much time planning for the future or dwelling on the past, we often forget that the true joy of life exists in the present. In other words, the only way to be happy is to make the most of every day. Look for places in this essay where Hastings has used concrete, specific, and vivid language to bring this message home.

Vocabulary

idyllic   Lovely, picturesque, charming, romantic.
relish   Enjoy.
vision   Idea, mental picture.

Tucked away in our subconscious minds is an idyllic vision in which we   1
see ourselves on a long journey that spans an entire continent. We're traveling
by train and, from the windows, we drink in the passing scenes of cars on nearby
highways, of children waving at crossings, of cattle grazing in distant
pastures, of smoke pouring from power plants, of row upon row of cotton
and corn and wheat, of flatlands and valleys, of city skylines and village halls.

But uppermost in our minds is our final destination—for at a certain   2
hour and on a given day, our train will finally pull into the station with bells
ringing, flags waving, and bands playing. And once that day comes, so many

wonderful dreams will come true. So restlessly, we pace the aisles and count the miles, peering ahead, waiting, waiting, waiting for the station.

"Yes, when we reach the station, that will be it!" we promise ourselves. 3 "When we're eighteen...win that promotion...put the last kid through college...buy that 450 SL Mercedes Benz...pay off the mortgage...have a nest egg for retirement."

From that day on we will all live happily every after. 4

Sooner or later, however, we must realize there is no station in this life, 5 no one earthly place to arrive at once and for all. The journey is the joy. The station is an illusion—it constantly outdistances us. Yesterday's a memory, tomorrow's a dream. Yesterday belongs to history, tomorrow belongs to God. Yesterday's a fading sunset, tomorrow's a faint sunrise. Only today is there light enough to love and live.

So, gently close the door on yesterday and throw the key away. It isn't 6 the burdens of today that drive men mad, but rather the regret over yesterday and the fear of tomorrow.

"Relish the moment" is a good motto, especially when coupled with 7 Psalm 118:24, "This is the day which the Lord hath made; we will rejoice and be glad in it."

So stop pacing the aisles and counting the miles. Instead, swim more 8 rivers, climb more mountains, kiss more babies, count more stars. Laugh more and cry less. Go barefoot oftener. Eat more ice cream. Ride more merry-go-rounds. Watch more sunsets. Life must be lived as we go along.

Questions for Discussion

1. What is Hastings' central idea, and in what paragraph is it most clearly stated?
2. In paragraphs 1 and 2, Hastings creates an image to describe the journey of our lives. Identify a few of the concrete details he uses to create this image. Which of the five senses does he rely on?
3. In paragraph 2, we read that "so many wonderful dreams will come true" when we get to our life's destination. What examples in paragraph 3 explain this abstract idea?
4. In paragraph 7, Hastings advises us to "Relish the moment." What does he mean by this? What examples does he use later in the essay to make this idea more concrete?
5. This selection contains a number of effective verbs and adjectives. In paragraph 1, for instance, Hastings writes that "we *drink* in the passing scenes" and see "smoke *pouring* from power plants." What other verbs and adjectives does he use to make his writing vivid?

Suggestions for Journal Entries

1. Reread the essay's conclusion. Do you agree that going barefoot, swimming rivers, and watching sunsets are good ways to "relish the moment"? List other ways to get more out of life every day.
2. Hastings provides a number of examples to explain what many people see as the "destination" of their life's journey. List a few details and examples that will help to explain your life's goals.

The San Francisco Earthquake

Jack London

One of the world's best-loved adventure writers, Jack London (1876–1916) held a number of colorful jobs that took him around the world and supplied him with materials for his exciting stories. He left his native San Francisco when only a boy and shipped out on a commercial steamer for Japan. A few years and several adventures later, London traveled to the Klondike to prospect for gold. He went to Japan and Korea in 1904 to report on the Russo-Japanese War and to Mexico in 1914 to cover the Mexican Revolution. Among his best-known novels are *The Call of the Wild*, *White Fang*, and *The Sea Wolf*.

London's report of the San Francisco earthquake contains many examples of his careful choice of language, showing his ability to portray events accurately and vividly.

Looking Ahead

1. London makes his writing concrete and specific by choosing nouns carefully. In paragraph 1, he calls the blaze that followed the earthquake a "conflagration," not simply a fire. In paragraph 2, he tells us about the "hotels and palaces of the nabobs" when he could simply have mentioned their "houses."
2. In paragraph 3, London uses the adjective "lurid" to describe the tower of smoke from the burning city. In paragraph 6, he makes use of an interesting adverb when he explains that dynamite was used "lavishly." Pick out other effective adjectives and adverbs as you read this selection.
3. London was a master at creating concrete visual imagery. One of his best can be found in paragraph 3, but there are others in this essay. Identify them.

Vocabulary

colossal   Gigantic.
conflagration   Large and very destructive fire.
contrivances   Inventions.
cunning   Skillful.
debris   Fragments, remains.
enumeration   Listing.
lavishly   Generously, in great amounts.
lurid   Glaring, shocking.
nabobs   People of wealth and power.
vestiges   Traces.
wrought   Caused.

The earthquake shook down in San Francisco hundreds of thousands of   1
dollars worth of walls and chimneys. But the conflagration that followed burned
up hundreds of millions of dollars worth of property. There is no estimating
within hundreds of millions the actual damage wrought.

Not in history has a modern imperial city been so completely destroyed.   2
San Francisco is gone. Nothing remains of it but memories and a fringe of
dwelling houses on its outskirts. Its industrial section is wiped out. Its social
and residential section is wiped out. The factories and warehouses, the great
stores and newspaper buildings, the hotels and palaces of the nabobs, all are
gone. Remains only the fringe of dwelling houses on the outskirts of what was
once San Francisco.

Within an hour after the earthquake shock, the smoke of San Fran-   3
cisco's burning was a lurid tower visible a hundred miles away. And for three
days and nights this lurid tower swayed in the sky, reddening the sun, dark-
ening the day, and filling the land with smoke.

On Wednesday morning at quarter past five came the earthquake. A minute   4
later the flames were leaping upward. In a dozen different quarters south of Market Street, in the working class ghetto and in the factories, fires started. There
was no opposing the flames. There was no organization, no communication. All
the cunning adjustments of a twentieth century city had been smashed by the
earthquake. The streets were humped into ridges and depressions, and piled with
the debris of fallen walls. The steel rails were twisted into perpendicular and
horizontal angles. The telephone and telegraph systems were disrupted. And the
great water mains had burst. All the shrewd contrivances and safeguards of man
had been thrown out of gear by thirty seconds' twitching of the earth-crust.

By Wednesday afternoon, inside of twelve hours, half the heart of the   5
city was gone. At that time I watched the vast conflagration from out on the
bay. It was dead calm. Not a flicker of wind stirred. Yet from every side wind

was pouring in upon the city. East, west, north, and south, strong winds were blowing upon the doomed city. The heated air rising made an enormous suck. Thus did the fire of itself build its own colossal chimney through the atmosphere. Day and night this dead calm continued, and yet, near to the flames, the wind was often half a gale, so mighty was the suck.

Wednesday night saw the destruction of the very heart of the city. Dynamite was lavishly used, and many of San Francisco's proudest structures were crumbled by man himself into ruins, but there was no withstanding the onrush of the flames. Time and again successful stands were made by the firefighters, and every time the flames flanked around on either side, or came up from the rear, and turned to defeat the hard won victory.   6

An enumeration of the buildings destroyed would be a directory of San Francisco. An enumeration of the buildings undestroyed would be a line and several addresses. An enumeration of the deeds of heroism would stock a library and bankrupt the Carnegie medal fund. An enumeration of the dead—will never be made. All vestiges of them were destroyed by the flames. The number of the victims of the earthquake will never be known.   7

Questions for Discussion

1. In Looking Ahead, you read that London made his writing specific by choosing nouns carefully. Pick out a few examples of nouns. Which ones made the greatest impact on you?
2. One reason that London's essays and novels are still popular is that they are filled with adjectives that make them interesting and lively. Identify a few that you found especially vivid in this selection.
3. London is famous for having created brilliant visual images like the one in paragraph 3. What other effective images did you find?
4. In paragraph 4, London says that "All the cunning adjustments of a twentieth century city had been smashed by the earthquake." What examples does he use to explain this idea?
5. Reread paragraphs 1 and 2. What is London's thesis statement?
6. This is an extremely well organized essay. Pick out a few of London's techniques for maintaining coherence in and between paragraphs. (Techniques for maintaining coherence were discussed in Chapter 2.)

Suggestions for Journal Entries

1. Have you ever seen the results of a great natural disaster (a flood, earthquake, forest fire, tornado, or hurricane)? If so, write down as many concrete, specific, and vivid details about the scene as you remember. Use the focused-freewriting method, discussed in Getting Started, to generate details.
2. Take your journal with you as you walk along one of the main streets of a town or city near your college or your home. Spend a half hour or so gathering

details about what you see, hear, feel, smell, and even taste. Don't bother listing these sensory details in any specific order; just jot them down as you walk along, journal in hand. When you complete your short outing, find a quiet place to read your notes. Then write a paragraph or two explaining your impression of and reaction to what you just experienced.

Sinnit Cave

Henry Stickell

Henry Stickell grew up in the Baltimore area, not a great distance from the mountains of West Virginia, where his fascinating story of spelunking (cave exploration) takes place. Actually, the essay uses details from several expeditions that Stickell and his wife, Betty, have made to Sinnit Cave.

Stickell is now head of circulation at the Ledy Library of Mt. Sinai Medical Center in New York City. He wrote "Sinnit Cave" for a college writing course he recently completed.

Looking Ahead

1. One of Stickell's greatest strengths is his ability to choose verbs. In paragraph 4, he writes that "the miles slid by as we sped over the well-paved expressways." Find other examples of verbs that make this essay lively and interesting.
2. Stickell is careful to use nouns that are concrete and specific. To make his writing even more realistic, he tells us about the geologic formations he observed, and he makes mention of such special equipment as "carbine lamps" and "belay lines."
3. Finally, "Sinnit Cave" demonstrates Stickell's talent for creating visual images. Look for them throughout the essay.

Vocabulary

dumb Speechless.
inventory List.
negotiated Dealt with successfully.
precipice Cliff, top of a steep hill.
predicament Problem, emergency.
rappelled Descended with the aid of a rope.
welled up Rose up

We were struck dumb as we gazed upward from the bottom of the pit.   1
Eighty feet above, we could see debris clogging the entrance that we had used
only eight hours earlier to enter the cave. With the light from our carbide
lamps and flashlights, we probed every crack and crevasse of the shaft in
search of an opening we could squeeze through, that is if one of us could climb
the sheer walls of the shaft to lower a rope for the rest of us to climb up on.
The rappelling rope that we had left in place had been washed to the bottom
of the pit along with the tree it was attached to. My gut tightened into a
painful knot, and panic welled up inside of me as the realization of our predicament struck home. Why was I here? It all started several days ago when
a close friend, Dick, telephoned.

"I'm going cave crawling this weekend. Are you and Betty interested?"   2
He continued to tell us, "There's a cave in Pendleton County, West Virginia,
called Sinnit Cave. I've been there once before and want to return to explore
a different section."

I sealed our fate with an enthusiastic, "When do we leave?" Friday   3
evening we loaded the car and drove to Dick's house. As we pulled up in
front, we spotted Roger, Beverly, and Larry waiting in an overloaded blue
1959 Chevy station wagon. We shifted the load in our vehicle to accommodate
Dick and his mountain of equipment and pulled out of the driveway as the
sun was disappearing over the horizon.

The drive from the Baltimore/Washington area started easily, and the   4
miles slid by as we sped over the well-paved expressways. However, once into
central Virginia, the highway pinched down to two lanes and eventually changed
into a narrow country road winding up and down the lush mountains of West
Virginia.

It was nearly midnight when we pulled off the road. There was a steep   5
mountain on one side and a stream with an old rickety bridge on the other.
We got out of our cars and paused to savor the cool mountain solitude. The
stars were blazing above, and the Milky Way, usually obscure in the sky over
Baltimore, was plainly visible. We soon had our tents pitched and sleeping
bags unfurled on a level, grassy area near the stream. Larry gathered kindling
and fallen branches while Betty and Beverly broke out the coffee and ham
sandwiches. Soon, we were huddled around a roaring campfire making plans
for the next day's assault on Sinnit Cave.

After supper, Betty and I crawled into our sleeping bags, zipped up the   6
tent, and passed out. In what seemed like only a few moments, however, I
heard Larry saying, "Rise and shine, you all. It's 7:00 a.m. Let's move it!"

The early morning sun bathed the campsite in a hazy glow as we gulped   7
down a hasty breakfast of rolls and coffee. We assembled our gear and, before
long, began the long trek up the steep mountainside in search of the cave's
entrance. By 9:30, we found the entrance shaft in a meadow near the summit.
We rigged a rappelling rope and a belay line, checked our harnesses, and lit
the carbide lamps.

"I'll go first," Dick said. He clipped his carbiners to the rappelling 8
rope, stood on the brink of the precipice, and disappeared over the edge,
glancing over his shoulder to see his way down. I controlled the belay line as
he descended.

Soon the downward tug on the line ceased and I heard Dick holler, "I'm 9
at the bottom! Let up on the belay!"

The rest of us quickly rappelled down the entrance shaft. The world of 10
light disappeared as we penetrated into the dark, damp underground. The
next seven hours flowed easily as we explored deeper and deeper into the
cavern. There was a variety of speleothemes throughout the cave—beautiful
stalactites, stalagmites, and walls of quartz crystal. We even discovered col-
onies of bats suspended upside down waiting for night to fall in the world
above before venturing out in search of supper.

For a time, it seemed as if we were climbing through a fantasy world. 11
Eventually, however, diminishing carbide in the lamps, fatigue, and a rav-
enous desire for hot food drew us back toward the entrance. That's when we
made the frightening discovery that a small avalanche had sealed the cave
entrance with earth and rock. Betty squeezed my arm tightly, and suddenly
I was jolted from my daydream and into the reality of our predicament.

"Is there another way out?" I asked.   12

Dick answered, "I remember that there was an article in the latest *Grotto* 13
News about a group from Washington, D.C., who found a connection between the upper and lower cave."

He pulled out his map and we all gathered around. With a muddy finger, 14
he poked at the approximate location on the map. We took an inventory of our
equipment and supplies, and we decided to continue to use up our carbide to the
bitter end. We would then rely on candles as our major light source and save the
flashlights for illuminating the more difficult sections of the cave.

We searched frantically for more than an hour for the entrance to the 15
connection. It was Beverly who finally found the small squeeze hole under a
low ledge. We were sure this was the way. The limestone of the squeeze hole
was worn smooth, and there were scratched areas where equipment attached
to belts could have scraped the walls of the opening. After two hours of squirm-
ing on our bellies through mud, we realized that the squeeze hole was starting
to expand. The connection gradually became larger and finally opened into a
long chamber with a high ceiling.

"I know this room," Dick exclaimed. "It's called the Big Room on the 16
map. I was in here on my last trip."

Beverly asked, "Do you know the way out?"   17

"Yes. We'll need about another hour or two," Dick answered.   18

As we set out on the last leg of our adventure, our carbide lamps sput- 19
tered out one by one. As our lamps failed we lit candles and kept moving. On
the way out we negotiated a steep area, called the Silo, that dropped down into
the mountain. Then came a long, deep crevasse in the last section of the cave.

Up ahead I could see several small points of light. Suddenly, I realized I was looking out the cave entrance at the stars.

The closer I came to the entrance, the more the tension eased from my 20 body. We soon stumbled into the safety of our campsite. The lower cave entrance was only a short distance away. We collapsed into our sleeping bags, and some of us said prayers of thanks before slipping into unconsciousness. I know I did.

Questions for Discussion

1. In Looking Ahead, you learned that Stickell's writing is vivid because of the verbs he chooses. Identify several verbs that make his writing lively and interesting.
2. Do you agree that the language in this essay is concrete and specific? Pick out two or three paragraphs that you find especially well written, and underline the words that make them so effective. Concentrate on nouns, but also look for well-chosen adjectives and adverbs.
3. What visual images does Stickell create to show us the seriousness of his predicament?
4. What techniques does he use to maintain coherence?
5. "Sinnit Cave" begins in the middle of things, with Stickell's party returning to the cave entrance only to find that it has been blocked. Does starting at this point help the author capture the reader's interest better than starting with Dick's invitation to go spelunking? Explain why it does or doesn't.

Suggestions for Journal Entries

1. Recall a dangerous, exciting, or frightening experience. Use focused freewriting, as explained in Getting Started, to record concrete details about this experience in your journal. List as many concrete nouns as possible; like Stickell, also include proper nouns—names of specific persons, places, or things. Whenever possible, use details from one or more of your senses. Finally, choose effective adjectives to help describe what you saw, heard, felt, etc.
2. As noted earlier, Stickell uses visual images to show us his experiences in Sinnit Cave. Use details to write a short visual description (in a paragraph or two) of a natural setting you have visited recently and remember well, such as a meadow, a mountain, a beach, a river, or even a cave.
3. Like Stickell, recall a special or memorable outing. List all the details you'll need for showing your readers how special or memorable a trip it really was.

SUGGESTIONS FOR WRITING

1. One of the Suggestions for Journal Entries after "Those Winter Sundays" asks you to discuss someone in your life who demonstrates his or her love for others. If you responded to this item, you have probably made a list of the "offices" (activities, tasks, or services) he or she performs to show that love.

Focus on at least three "offices" that mean the most to you, and expand your discussion into a full-length essay that shows how much this individual does for others. Give your essay an interesting introduction (complete with thesis) and an effective conclusion, as explained in Chapter 4. Limit each of the body paragraphs to only one of the "offices" in your list. Most important, like Hayden, use concrete and specific details to develop the main idea in each of these paragraphs.

2. After reading Hastings' "The Station," you may have used your journal to list several things you do to get more out of life. From your list, select the three that are most important, and use them as the basis of a letter advising a friend to "relish the moment." Make your writing concrete by using examples and by appealing to the senses; make it specific by using effective nouns and adjectives; and make it vivid by choosing verbs, adjectives, and adverbs carefully.

3. In item 2 of the Suggestions for Journal Entries after "The Station," you were asked to list some of your goals. If you responded to this item, expand your discussion of at least three of these goals into a well-developed essay. Use language that is concrete, specific, and vivid.

   Begin and end your essay by using one of the techniques for writing introductions and conclusions discussed in Chapter 4. Limit each of the body paragraphs to a discussion of only one goal.

4. If you responded to the first of the Suggestions for Journal Entries after Jack London's "The San Francisco Earthquake," you have already begun gathering details to describe the results of a natural disaster you witnessed recently. Use your notes as the starting point of an essay about the effects of this fire, tornado, earthquake, flood, etc. Like London, rely on your senses to create effective images, and use verbs and adjectives to make the experience come alive for your readers!

   Add excitement to your writing by beginning and ending with specific details about the event. Be sure that your introduction identifies *what* the disaster was and *where* and *when* it occurred, and fit your thesis into your first or second paragraph as London does.

5. You might have always wanted to write about a dangerous, exciting, or frightening experience like the one in "Sinnit Cave." If you have recorded concrete and specific details about such an experience in your journal, turn your notes into a well-developed essay.

   In addition to the concrete and specific nouns and adjectives in your journal, try to use lively verbs, adjectives, and adverbs that will help your readers react to the experience as you did. Like Stickell, use a dramatic introduction to capture your readers' attention, and remember to explain *where* and *when* the event took place. Check for unity and coherence, and write a short conclusion that brings the experience to an end.

Chapter 6

Word Choice: Using Figurative Language

In Chapter 5 you learned that you can clarify abstract ideas by using concrete language. One way to do this is to fill your writing with specific details or to create verbal images (pictures in words) that appeal to the reader's senses. You also learned that using effective verbs, adjectives, and adverbs can help make your writing vivid. All of these techniques will help you *show*—and not simply tell—your reader what you mean.

Another way to make your writing clearer, more vivid, and more effective is to use figures of speech. Explaining an idea through the use of figurative language is different from relying only on language that communicates literally and directly. Figures of speech help you explain abstract ideas by creating comparisons or other relationships between the abstraction and those concrete realities which readers easily recognize.

Notice how much more effective your description of a friend becomes when you compare him to a "bull in a China shop" rather than merely state that he is "clumsy." The concrete picture of a "bull in a China shop"—the shattered bowls, plates, and glassware—is sharper and more meaningful than an abstract idea like "clumsy" could ever be. In other words, it *shows* the reader something.

All figures of speech work by creating or pointing out relationships between things. Sometimes these relationships take the form of comparisons—as with simile, metaphor, and personification, the three very common types of figurative language discussed in this chapter.

SIMILE

A simile creates a comparison between two things by using the word "like" or "as." For example, say that you're writing your sweetheart a letter in which you want to explain how much you need him or her. You could xpress your feelings literally and directly by writing "I need you very much." Then again, you could *show* how strongly you feel by writing that you need him or her "as a great oak needs sunlight," "as an eagle needs the open sky," or "as the dry earth needs spring rain."

Read the following list carefully. Notice how much more concrete, exciting, and rich the ideas on the left become when they are expressed in similes:

Literal Expression	Simile
Harry has gained a lot of weight.	Harry has gotten as heavy as a horse.
Eugene is a fancy dresser.	Eugene dresses like a peacock.
The children's bedroom was a mess.	The children's bedroom looked like a pigsty.
Jonathan is patient.	Jonathan is as patient as a saint.

Finally, look at a passage from "Java Jive," an essay in which Al Young recalls a hot Mississippi afternoon from his childhood. Pick out the two effective similes Young uses in this passage:

> The sun—like a hot, luminous magnet—happened to be shining powerfully that antique afternoon. My father was busy being his auto mechanic self, and I could see him through the dusty window screen out there in the grass and dirt and clay of the sideyard driveway, fixing on our dark blue Chevy coupe, grease all over his face and forearms; black on black. Pious as a minister or metaphysician [philosopher], he was bent on fixing that car.

METAPHOR

A metaphor also uses comparison to show the relationship between things in order to make the explanation of one of these things clearer and livelier. In fact, a metaphor works just like a simile except that it does not make use of "like" or "as." For instance, you can turn the simile "Eugene dresses like a peacock" into a metaphor by writing "Eugene is a peacock." In each case, of course, you don't actually mean that Eugene is a bird; you're simply pointing out similarities between the way he dresses and the showiness we associate with a peacock.

The important thing to remember is that, like all figures of speech, similes and metaphors turn abstract ideas (like "Eugene is a fancy dresser") into vivid, concrete images. In other words, they communicate more emphatically and clearly than if the writer had used literal language alone. Study the following list of similes and metaphors carefully. What effect do they have on you, especially when compared with the literal expressions on the left?

Literal Expression	Simile	Metaphor
The two young men battled through the night.	The two young men battled like gladiators through the night.	The two young gladiators battled through the night.
In spring, the meadow is beautiful.	In spring, the meadow looks like a painting by Renoir.	In spring, the meadow is a painting by Renoir.
My old car is hard to drive.	My old car drives like a tank.	My old car is a tank!
During holidays, shopping malls are crowded and noisy.	During holidays, shopping malls are so crowded and noisy that they seem like madhouses.	During holidays, shopping malls are so crowded and noisy that they become madhouses.

Finally, read the following excerpt from Martin Luther King's "I Have a Dream," a speech he delivered at the Lincoln Memorial during the 1963 march on Washington. Identify the metaphors and similes that Dr. King used to captivate the thousands in his audience and to make his message more concrete, vivid, and effective:

> Five score years ago, a great American, in whose symbolic shadow we stand today, signed the Emancipation Proclamation. This momentous decree came as a great beacon light of hope to millions of Negro slaves who had been seared in the flames of withering injustice. It came as a joyous daybreak to end the long night of their captivity.
>
> But one hundred years later, the Negro still is not free. One hundred years later, the life of the Negro is still sadly crippled by the manacles of segregation and the chains of discrimination.

PERSONIFICATION

Personification is the description of animals, plants, or inanimate objects by using terms ordinarily associated with human beings. Like metaphor and simile, personification is an effective way to turn abstract ideas into vivid and concrete realities that readers will grasp easily and quickly.

One common example of personification is Father Time, the figure of an old man trailing a white beard and carrying a scythe and hourglass. Another is the Grim Reaper, the representation of death pictured as a skeleton holding a scythe. Shakespeare often used personification to enrich the language of his poems and plays. In "Sonnet 18," for example, he described the sun as "the eye of heaven." William Least Heat Moon does something similar when, in *Blue Highways,* he describes the saguaro cactus of the American Southwest:

> Standing on the friable slopes..., saguaros mimic men as they salute,
> bow, dance, raise arms to wave, and grin with faces carved in by
> woodpeckers. Older plants, having survived odds against their
> reaching maturity of sixty million to one, have every right to smile.

The following poems and essays demonstrate very careful uses of language, both literal and figurative. As you read them, identify their similes, metaphors, and personifications and ask yourself if these figures of speech have made the selections clearer, more vivid, and more effective than if their authors had relied on literal language alone.

"Joy of an Immigrant, a Thanksgiving" and "Old Man Timochenko"

Emanuel di Pasquale

Emanuel di Pasquale immigrated to the United States from Ragusa, Sicily, when he was fourteen. An accomplished poet and a teacher of composition, creative writing, and children's literature, di Pasquale has published in several important periodicals, including *The Nation* and *The Sawanee Review*. His work has been anthologized in college textbooks and in several collections of children's poems. *Genesis*, a full-length collection of his poetry, was published in 1988.

"Joy of an Immigrant, a Thanksgiving" and "Old Man Timochenko" reveal di Pasquale's intense love of nature and his talent for creating powerful figures of speech that make his writing clear and captivating.

Looking Ahead

1. Di Pasquale is a master at showing rather than telling the reader what he means. Both of these poems contain similes and metaphors that help the poet explain his ideas through the creation of vivid and concrete images, or verbal pictures
2. "Joy of an Immigrant, a Thanksgiving" contains an extended metaphor in which di Pasquale compares himself to a wandering bird. It is an "extended" metaphor because the writer develops the comparison *throughout* the poem.
3. "Old Man Timochenko" is a brilliant portrait of an old man the poet spotted regularly during drives along a country road in eastern Pennsylvania. Identify the many similes and metaphors that di Pasquale uses to reveal important things about Timochenko's character.

Vocabulary

lineaments   Lines.

Joy of an Immigrant, a Thanksgiving

Like a bird grown weak in a land
where it always rains

and where all the trees have died,
I have flown long and long
to find sunlight pouring over branches
and leaves. I have journeyed, oh God,   5
to find a land where I can build a dry nest,
a land where my song can echo.

Old Man Timochenko

Winds scratch his hands
and his sharp bones
deeply assert
their lineaments.
He stands like a   5
trembling leaf
on the branch
of an evergreen,
and will not fall.

Careful,   10
by the road's edge,
silent as a sunray,
he waves
as I drive by.
Like birds' wings,   15
loose as they coast
in the high air,
his eyes
soften and expand.

He moves in slow waves,   20
like an ancient snake,
knowing the end can wait.

Questions for Discussion

1. In "Joy of an Immigrant," di Pasquale compares himself to a bird through
   an extended metaphor. What details does he use to develop this comparison fully?
2. What is "Joy of an Immigrant" about? Why does di Pasquale subtitle it "a
   Thanksgiving"?

3. What do the metaphors "where I can build a dry nest" and "where my song can echo" show us about the poet's feelings for his new "land"?
4. What is your emotional reaction to the words in the first three lines of "Joy of an Immigrant"? What do they tell you about the place the poet has left?
5. What do the metaphors and similes in "Old Man Timochenko" show us about the old man? What is the poet's attitude toward his subject?
6. In Looking Ahead you learned that di Pasquale uses figures of speech to create vivid and effective images. Describe the verbal pictures you see in his poems.
7. Recall what you learned about concrete details in Chapter 5. What concrete details, other than those which appear in the similes and metaphors you have identified, does di Pasquale include in "Old Man Timochenko"?

Suggestions for Journal Entries

1. In your own words, explain di Pasquale's opinion of the land he has come to. Use any of the prewriting techniques explained in Getting Started to speculate (wonder out loud) about what he means when he explains that he has found "sunlight pouring over branches and leaves."
2. Have you ever experienced a change—any change—in your life that was as dramatic or as important as the one di Pasquale describes in "Joy of an Immigrant"? It need not involve moving from one country or even from one town to another, but it should be something that has had an effect on the person you have become. Describe how this change affected you by listing as many concrete details about it as you can. Try to create similes and/or metaphors that will help you describe its effects more vividly.
3. Is there some interesting person in your life who, like Timochenko, would make a good subject for a short descriptive paragraph or poem? Begin gathering details that will help show your reader how you feel about this individual.

The Death of Benny Paret

Norman Mailer

Norman Mailer established his reputation in 1948, when he published *The Naked and the Dead*, a popular and influential novel about World War II. Since then, he has produced a number of important works, both fiction and nonfiction, many of which have been critical of modern American society.

Mailer has won Pulitzer prizes for *Armies of the Night* (1968), his account of
the 1967 peace march on Washington, D.C., and for *The Executioner's Song*
(1979), the story of convicted murderer Gary Gilmore.

Looking Ahead

1. Mailer was at ringside on the night of March 25, 1962, when Emile Griffith
   knocked out Benny Paret in the twelfth round of a welterweight championship bout in New York City's Madison Square Garden. The beating
   that Paret took that night led to his death a week later. He was twenty-
   four.
2. "The Death of Benny Paret" contains good examples of all three of the
   figures of speech discussed earlier in this chapter. Look for places in which
   Mailer uses simile, metaphor, and personification throughout this frank
   and vivid account of one of the most brutal episodes in sports history.
3. Another important aspect of this essay has to do with the way Mailer uses
   concrete and specific details to make his reporting of this horrible event
   vivid and realistic. Recall what you learned about using details in Chapter
   5 as you read "The Death of Benny Paret."

Vocabulary

irrevocably   Irreversibly.
maulings   Beatings.
psychic   Mental, spiritual.

On the afternoon of the night Emile Griffith and Benny Paret were to   1
fight a third time for the welterweight championship, there was murder in
both camps. "I hate that kind of guy," Paret had said earlier to Pete Hamill
about Griffith. "A fighter's got to look and talk and act like a man." One of
the Broadway gossip columnists had run an item about Griffith a few days
before. His girl friend saw it and said to Griffith, "Emile, I didn't know about
you being that way." So Griffith hit her. So he said. Now at the weigh-in that
morning, Paret had insulted Griffith irrevocably, touching him on the but-
tocks, while making a few more remarks about his manhood. They almost had
their fight on the scales.

The rage in Emile Griffith was extreme. I was at the fight that night, I   2
had never seen a fight like it. It was scheduled for fifteen rounds, but they
fought without stopping from the bell which began the round to the bell which
ended it, and then they fought after the bell, sometimes for as much as fifteen
seconds before the referee could force them apart.

Paret was a Cuban, a proud club fighter who had become welterweight   3
champion because of his unusual ability to take a punch. His style of fighting
was to take three punches to the head in order to give back two. At the end

of ten rounds, he would still be bouncing, his opponent would have a head-
ache. But in the last two years, over the fifteen-round fights, he had started
to take some bad maulings.

This fight had its turns. Griffith won most of the early rounds, but   4
Paret knocked Griffith down in the sixth. Griffith had trouble getting up,
but made it, came alive and was dominating Paret again before the round
was over. Then Paret began to wilt. In the middle of the eighth round,
after a clubbing punch had turned his back to Griffith, Paret walked three
disgusted steps away, showing his hindquarters. For a champion, he took
much too long to turn back around. It was the first hint of weakness Paret
had ever shown, and it must have inspired a particular shame, because he
fought the rest of the fight as if he were seeking to demonstrate that he
could take more punishment than any man alive. In the twelfth, Griffith
caught him. Paret got trapped in a corner. Trying to duck away, his left
arm and his head became tangled on the wrong side of the top rope. Griffith was in like a cat ready to rip the life out of a huge boxed rat. He hit
him eighteen right hands in a row, an act which took perhaps three or four
seconds, Griffith making a pent-up whimpering sound all the while he
attacked, the right hand whipping like a piston rod which has broken
through the crankcase, or like a baseball bat demolishing a pumpkin. I was
sitting in the second row of that corner—they were not ten feet away from
me, and like everybody else, I was hypnotized. I had never seen one man
hit another so hard and so many times. Over the referee's face came a look
of woe as if some spasm had passed its way through him, and then he
leaped on Griffith to pull him away. It was the act of a brave man. Griffith
was uncontrollable. His trainer leaped into the ring, his manager, his cut
man, there were four people holding Griffith, but he was off on an orgy,
he had left the Garden, he was back on a hoodlum's street. If he had been
able to break loose from his handlers and the referee, he would have jumped
Paret to the floor and whaled on him there.

And Paret? Paret died on his feet. As he took those eighteen punches   5
something happened to everyone who was in psychic range of the event. Some
part of his death reached out to us. One felt it hover in the air. He was still
standing in the ropes, trapped as he had been before, he gave some little
half-smile of regret, as if he were saying, "I didn't know I was going to die
just yet," and then, his head leaning back but still erect, his death came to
breathe about him. He began to pass away. As he passed, so his limbs descended beneath him, and he sank slowly to the floor. He went down more
slowly than any fighter had ever gone down, he went down like a large ship
which turns on end and slides second by second into its grave. As he went
down, the sound of Griffith's punches echoed in the mind like a heavy ax in
the distance chopping into a wet log.

Questions for Discussion

1. Some of Mailer's most powerful similes appear in paragraph 4 when he describes Griffith's attack on Paret in round twelve. What are these similes?
2. Where in paragraph 4 does Mailer use metaphors? Where else in the essay does he use them?
3. The conclusion of this essay contains an excellent example of personification. What is it? What similes can you find in this paragraph?
4. In paragraph 5, Mailer combines specific detail, simile, and personification in one sentence, which begins "He was still standing in the ropes...." Analyze this sentence carefully, and explain where these three techniques appear.
5. Mailer's use of concrete and specific detail is especially evident in paragraph 4. Which details in this paragraph do you find most effective?
6. In paragraph 3, Mailer writes that Paret had "started to take some bad maulings." Is "maulings" a more effective noun than "beatings"? In paragraph 4, he tells us that Paret began "to wilt." Is this verb better than "to weaken"? What other effective nouns and verbs does Mailer use?
7. This selection begins with an anecdote (brief story) about what passed between Griffith and Paret before the fight. Does this anecdote make for a good introduction? How does it help prepare us for what is to follow?

Suggestions for Journal Entries

1. Think about a serious or significant event you recently witnessed: a car accident, a natural disaster, or perhaps an important ceremony. Use one of the strategies for prewriting discussed in Getting Started to gather details that will help you to describe this incident and to discuss its impact on you or on anyone else who may have seen it. Include figures of speech in your list of details.
2. Whether physical or verbal, violence always leaves us shaken and disturbed. Think about a fight you saw or were involved in recently. Do some focused freewriting for about five or ten minutes in which you explain how you felt during or after the incident. Include figures of speech that *show* what you were feeling at the time.

Pain for a Daughter

Anne Sexton

Born in Newton, Massachusetts, in 1924, Anne Sexton began writing poetry as psychological therapy prescribed by her doctor. By 1967 she had published several volumes of verse and had won the Pulitzer prize, one of many important awards for literature she received.

Like "Pain for a Daughter," most of her poetry is autobiographical. It focuses on important emotional concerns, and it often reveals Sexton's feelings about herself and about those she loved most.

Her ability to deal with language, especially figurative language, made Sexton one of the most widely read poets of the last two decades. America lost one of its brightest literary stars when Anne Sexton committed suicide in 1974.

Looking Ahead

1. Sexton begins each stanza (verse paragraph) by writing that her daughter was "Blind with...." This is a metaphor that helps describe the child's emotional state at various times in her life; it does not mean that she could not see. As you read this poem, try to determine what the metaphor "Blind with..." at the beginning of each stanza reveals about Sexton's daughter.
2. In the last stanza, Sexton creates a vivid image to describe her daughter's physical and mental pain. Read this part of the poem very carefully.

Vocabulary

cajoles   Coaxes.
distemper   An infectious disease caused by a virus that can paralyze and kill horses, dogs, and other mammals.
reigning   Controlling, directing.
rites   Ceremonies, rituals.
squeamish   Easily sickened or frightened.

Blind with love, my daughter
has cried nightly for horses,
those long-necked marchers and churners
that she has mastered, any and all,
reigning them in like a circus hand—
the excitable muscles and the ripe neck—
tending, this summer, a pony and a foal.
She who is too squeamish to pull

5

a thorn from the dog's paw
watched her pony blossom with distemper,   10
the underside of the jaw swelling
like an enormous grape.
Gritting her teeth with love,
she drained the boil and scoured it
with hydrogen peroxide until pus   15
ran like milk on the barn floor.

Blind with loss all winter,
in dungarees, a ski jacket, and a hard hat,
she visits the neighbors' stable,
our acreage not zoned for barns,   20
they who own the flaming horses
and the swan-whipped thoroughbred
that she tugs at and cajoles,
thinking it will burn like a furnace
under her small-hipped English seat.
                                                           25
Blind with pain, she limps home.
The thoroughbred has stood on her foot.
He rested there like a building.
He grew into her foot until they were one.
The marks of the horseshoe printed   30
into her flesh, the tips of her toes
ripped off like pieces of leather,
three toenails swirled like shells
and left to float in blood in her riding boot.

Blind with fear, she sits on the toilet,   35
her foot balanced over the washbasin,
her father, hydrogen peroxide in hand,
performing the rites of the cleansing.
She bites on a towel, sucked in breath,
sucked in and arched against the pain,   40
her eyes glancing off me where
I stand at the door, eyes locked
on the ceiling, eyes of a stranger,
and then she cries...
Oh, my God, help me!   45
Where a child would have cried *Mama!*
Where a child would have believed *Mama!*
She bit the towel and called on God,
and I saw her life stretch out...

I saw her torn in childbirth,   50
and I saw her, at that moment,
in her own death, and I knew that she
knew.

Questions for Discussion

1. Stanza 1 contains a number of vivid similes that help Sexton explain the love and anguish her daughter felt for horses. What are these similes?
2. What other similes do you find in this poem? What do they show us about Sexton's daughter or about her experiences with horses?
3. What does the metaphor "Blind with...," which begins each stanza of this poem, reveal about Sexton's daughter?
4. What does Sexton mean in line 10, when she tells us that her daughter watched her pony "blossom with distemper"? What other effective metaphors do you find in this poem?
5. In Looking Ahead you were asked to pay particular attention to the image Sexton creates in the last stanza. How would you describe this image? Pay particular attention to lines 35 to 45. Which of the five senses does Sexton use to create this verbal picture?
6. Like Mailer in "The Death of Benny Paret," Sexton makes sure to use nouns that will draw a strong response from her readers. In line 3, for example, she calls the horses "marchers and churners," not simply "horses." What other specific nouns in this poem are particularly effective?
7. In line 28, Sexton writes that a thoroughbred "rested" on her daughter's foot. Is this verb more effective than something like "stayed there for a while"? Why? Find other words in this poem that cause a strong emotional response in you.

Suggestions for Journal Entries

1. Have you ever felt severe emotional or physical pain like the kind described in this poem? For instance, have you ever suffered the death of a loved one, whether human or animal? Or have you ever been, like Sexton's daughter, in such physical pain that you thought you might die? Do some focused freewriting in your journal, showing what you went through at the time. If possible, include some figures of speech to describe your anguish.
2. Sexton's daughter obviously had a love for horses. Do you love animals? If so, use your journal to begin describing an animal or species of animal you have grown attached to. List details describing how this particular animal or species of animal looks and acts, and explain why you are so fond of it. Once again, use as many figures of speech as you can to make your writing colorful and emphatic.

A Farewell to Arms

Richard B. Elsberry

Richard Elsberry, a contemporary American writer, wrote the following essay as a feature article for *The New York Times Magazine*. It was published in the fall of 1987.

Looking Ahead

1. The title of this essay is borrowed from Hemingway's *A Farewell to Arms*, a famous novel about an American ambulance driver in World War I. In this case, however, the title is ironic because the war Elsberry describes can be compared to real combat only as a joke.
2. Like di Pasquale, Elsberry uses an extended metaphor. He compares his attempts to get rid of a garden mole to full-scale warfare *throughout* the essay. Again, however, his intention is to make us smile. In paragraph 8, for instance, he mimics what ancient gladiators used to shout before going into mortal combat during the Roman games. In paragraph 11, he talks about the "scorched-earth policy" of the Union Army during General Sherman's infamous march through Georgia at the end of the Civil War.
3. Elsberry also alludes to popular movies and books in this essay. Among them is Rachel Carson's *Silent Spring*, an important book about the harmful effects of pesticides.

Vocabulary

armistice   A peace treaty.
bunkers   Fortified shelters.
genetically   Through birth.
leach   Dissolve.
Lilliputian   Tiny, miniature.
nemesis   Unbeatable opponent or enemy.
ramparts   Barricades, walls used for defense.
reconnaissance   Inspection.
recurring   Happening again.
rogue   Outlaw, villain.
slights   Insults.
sonic   Relating to sound.

The war started with a sneak attack. I was cutting my grass in the summer of 1986 when the mower made a strange sound. Looking down, I saw the 1 blade had cut into and exposed brown soil. It had ripped open the top of a burrow, which snaked across my yard like the path of some drunken sailor.

There was no doubt about it. I had been invaded by a member of the 2 family *Talpidae*—a mole.

Switching from Nikes to boots, I proceeded to stomp the maze of sur- 3 face runs so that I could finish cutting the grass without creating an unsightly gash across the yard.

The mole had completed a reconnaissance of my yard, staking out my 4 turf. And I had retaliated by putting my foot down.

The battle was joined.   5

The nearly blind burrower struck by night, tunneling his way through 6 my bluegrass with the speed of a Japanese bullet train. By day, I flattened his ramparts and flooded his bunkers with a garden hose. The mole learned to do the backstroke.

Reluctantly, I resorted to chemical warfare. Poison gas. Sulfurous- 7 looking chemicals were placed in the runs, the fuse lighted, and the top of the burrow replaced. Then I stood back to watch blue fumes rise slowly through the leaves of grass.

"Mole who is about to die, I salute you."   8

A few days later, I stepped on another burrow and twisted an ankle. 9 Like a demon from *Poltergeist*, he was back. The campaign dragged on into the fall. The mole ranged farther afield—an unstoppable six-inch-long bundle of fur and claws. Finally, winter arrived, and the mole hibernated. I schemed.

As soon as the grass started turning green last spring, I visited my friendly 10 hardware-store manager. He explained that the mole was harvesting cutworms, grubs and other insects that make up his diet. Eliminate the food supply, he said, and you eliminate the problem.

I got out my spreader and put down a double coating of insecticide over 11 all the areas the mole had invaded last year. It was my scorched-earth policy. Any mole operating in this area—like a crow flying over the path of William Tecumseh Sherman's army as it marched through Georgia—was going to have to carry his own rations.

In late April, while planting onions in the garden, I caught sight of an 12 exploratory burrow leading up from a clump of bushes. A combat patrol probing into what I had come to refer to as No Mole Land.

As the weeks passed, the mole kept coming, seemingly living on stored 13 fat. "What's the matter with you, you dumb animal," I raged as I flattened burrows. "Why don't you move on to greener pastures? There's nothing here to eat."

Then a thought occurred to me. I bought a can of mole bait—poison 14 pellets—and scattered them throughout the tunnels.

"Bon appétit," I murmured.   15

I waited a few days and then flattened all the burrows. They stayed flat. 16

Maybe, just maybe, I'd done it. I kept my fingers crossed. But, perhaps, like a depth-charged submarine, he was simply playing possum back in his nest. Like U-boats, moles can run silent, run deep.

After a week, I figured either the poison pills or the grubless wasteland 17 I had created had done the trick. But as I went out to check the garden, my roving eye spied a ripple moving across the turf, a rogue wave on a sea of green tranquillity.

My god, he was at it in midday!   18

But now I had him pinpointed. I rushed back to the garage and grabbed 19 two shovels. One I rammed into the burrow to block any retreat. Then, gleefully, I began to dig. After a time, I had created a small foxhole, surrounded by sod, rocks and loose dirt. But there was no sign of the mole.

Had he heard my original footfalls—or my little cry of "Aha, gotcha!"— 20 and quickly beat a retreat? Was he able to adopt the camouflage of a clump of dirt? Could he read my mind?

Slowly, I repaired the damage as best I could, tamping the raped earth 21 into place, putting down new grass seed and watering it in. I had given it my best shot, but the mole had countered every move I made. Sightless, defenseless, starved, poisoned, gassed—yet my Lilliputian enemy survived.

There were expensive battery-operated sonic devices I could buy—like 22 the thumpers that called the big sandworms in *Dune*. I was told these would drive the mole away, at least while the batteries lasted. And there were costly chemicals that were said to do the trick, assuring not just a silent spring, but a silent summer and a silent fall as well. But I feared they would eventually leach into the ground water and make their way to our well. As I reviewed my options, it seemed this was a war I was never going to win. And, it suddenly struck me, I no longer really cared about winning it.

This was a devastating thought, considering that American males are 23 brought up with the idea that winning is the only thing that counts. Winning is our national obsession. It's what makes our day. And yet my preoccupation with besting an unseen mole was gnawing at me day and night.

As I've gotten older and have witnessed endlessly recurring shoving 24 matches and fistfights over imagined slights, I've noticed that my genetically inherited combativeness seems to be melting away. I've become more inclined to walk away from human conflict—to hang it up and get on with my life. Why not do that with this animal, as well?

It was time, I decided firmly, to reach an accommodation with my nem- 25 esis. To sign an armistice.

I went out and bought a lawn roller.   26

Questions for Discussion

1. As you learned in Looking Ahead, Elsberry uses an extended metaphor throughout this essay to compare his fight with the mole to a war. He

introduces this metaphor in the very first line of the essay. What other metaphor does he use in that line?

2. How do the historical references to combat help Elsberry develop this extended metaphor?

3. What other metaphors relating to war did you come across in this essay?

4. In paragraph 9, the author explains that the mole was like a demon from the movie *Poltergeist*. What other similes did you find in this essay?

5. In paragraph 23, Elsberry tells us that realizing he was never going to win this war was "devastating." What does he mean by this?

6. Unlike the other selections in this chapter, Elsberry's essay seems to have been written as much to entertain us as to explain an idea. What parts of "A Farewell to Arms" did you find humorous?

Suggestions for Journal Entries

1. Think of a major problem you've recently tried to solve at school, at home, or at work. Did you, like Elsberry, feel as if you were engaged in a kind of battle? Were your attempts to solve this problem as difficult as rolling a stone up a mountain or as running a twenty-mile marathon in tight shoes? Or is there some other kind of extended metaphor you might use to describe this experience?

   Begin listing details about your problem and about your attempts to solve it. Then determine what kind of extended metaphor you might use to discuss this experience later on in a longer piece of writing. Begin developing this metaphor in a brief paragraph or two in your journal.

2. Elsberry compares the mole to figures from two popular movies: *Poltergeist* and *Dune*. Think of a particular animal or person you know well. Can he or she be compared to someone or something you have seen in a current movie or television show or have read about in a book, newspaper, or magazine recently? If so, begin listing similarities in your journal, and include as many figures of speech as you can in the process.

SUGGESTIONS FOR WRITING

1. After reading di Pasquale's "Joy of an Immigrant," you might have made journal notes to explain how a dramatic change in your life affected you. Expand your notes into a short essay filled with concrete details and figurative language that will help your readers understand the full effect of this change. Make sure that your introduction contains a formal thesis statement and that your essay is unified and coherent.

2. One of the suggestions for journal writing following "Old Man Timochenko" asks that you gather details and figures of speech to help you create a portrait of an interesting person you know well. Develop this ma-

terial into a full-length essay. Don't be afraid to show your readers how you feel about your subject.

3. After completing Mailer's "The Death of Benny Paret," you might have used one of the prewriting strategies explained in Getting Started to gather details in your journal about a serious or significant event you witnessed recently.

   Look over your notes, and add to them. Next, write a brief essay that discusses how this incident affected you and anyone else who witnessed it. Use concrete details and figures of speech to make your writing more emphatic and more interesting. Again, express your central idea in a thesis statement.

4. If you have ever seen a fight close up, you know how frightening physical or verbal violence can be. Think about a fight you saw or were involved in recently. Then, in a well-developed essay, describe your feelings during and after the fight.

   Before you begin, review the notes you made after reading "The Death of Benny Paret," especially those in response to item 2 of Suggestions for Journal Entries. Make sure to put the concrete details and figures of speech you have already collected into your essay.

5. In "Pain for a Daughter," Sexton shows us her child's intense love for horses. Reread the journal notes you made after reading this poem; they might contain several details and figures of speech about a favorite animal or species of animal. Add to this information, and write a short essay that describes the animal and explains how deeply you feel about it. Finally, include a clear thesis statement early in the essay, and keep your writing unified and coherent.

6. The extended metaphor Elsberry uses in "A Farewell to Arms" helps him show how hard it is to get rid of a garden mole. Item 1 of Suggestions for Journal Entries following this essay asks you to create an "extended metaphor" to explain how *you* tried to solve an important problem. Develop this metaphor fully in an essay of four or five paragraphs. Like Elsberry, include concrete details and figures of speech to demonstrate how important your problem was and/or how difficult it was to solve.

7. If you responded to item 2 of the Suggestions for Journal Entries after "A Farewell to Arms," you have begun listing similarities between an animal or person you know well and someone or something you have read about or have seen in a movie or on television.

   Focus on the three or four similarities that you find most striking, and discuss each of them fully in an essay that compares your subjects. Devote at least one well-developed paragraph to each similarity, and include as many concrete details and figures of speech as you can. As always, state your thesis clearly in your introduction, and make sure your essay is unified and coherent.

Chapter 7

Sentence Structure: Creating Emphasis and Variety

In Chapters 5 and 6 you learned to express your ideas more effectively by using language that is concrete, specific, and vivid. In this chapter you will learn how to use sentence structure to give your writing emphasis and variety, making it even more interesting and effective.

EMPHASIS

Communicating ideas clearly and effectively often depends on the ability to emphasize (or stress) one idea over another. By structuring (arranging) the words in a sentence carefully, you can emphasize certain ideas and direct your readers' attention to the heart of your message.

A good way to emphasize an idea is to express it in a simple sentence of its own. Often, however, you will find it necessary to write sentences containing two or more ideas. In some cases, these ideas will be equally important and should receive the same emphasis; in others, one idea will be the most important and should be emphasized over the others.

Create Emphasis through Coordination

Ideas that are equally important can be expressed in the same sentence by using coordination, as in this example:

We found a clearing, pitched the tent, and started a small fire.

This sentence coordinates (makes equal) three words in a series ("found," "pitched," and "started"), placing equal emphasis on each.

140

You can also use coordination to join two or more main clauses. A _main clause_ is a group of words that contains a subject and verb and that expresses a complete idea. One way to join main clauses is to use both a comma and a coordinating conjunction, such as "and," "but," "or," "nor," "for," or "so." Here are some examples, with the main clauses shown underlined:

We found a clearing, we pitched our tent, and we built a camp fire.
Uncle Harry is not the richest person in the world, but he is one of the most generous.
The neighborhood raccoon has not been near our house for three days, nor has he been missed.
Mullens will return on the midnight train, or she will have to spend another day in the city.
Arnold wants to get all A's, so he is studying very hard this semester.
I am going to ask Professor Garcia if I can rewrite my paper, for I just found some important new information about my topic.

Another way to coordinate main clauses within a sentence is to join them with a semicolon:

We danced all night long; in the morning we soaked our feet in the cool stream.
Alice's car is an antique; it was built in 1927.

Create Emphasis through Subordination

The sentences above contain complete ideas—main clauses—that are equal in emphasis. However, let's assume that one of the ideas in each of these sentences is more important than the other(s) and that you want to emphasize it. You can do this through a process called _subordination_. Subordination enables you to express the most important of these ideas in a main clause and to put the less important idea(s) in one or more subordinate clauses. A _subordinate clause_ is a group of words that contains a subject and a verb. However, unlike a main clause, it does not express a complete idea; therefore, it cannot stand alone as a complete sentence.

For example, let's rewrite the sentence "Uncle Harry is not the richest person in the world, but he is one of the most generous," making one of its two main clauses into a subordinate clause. If we want to subordinate the first clause in order to emphasize Uncle Harry's generosity, we could write:

Although Uncle Harry isn't the richest person in the world, he is certainly one of the most generous.

The word "Although" makes the first clause subordinate by changing it from a complete thought to an incomplete one (in other words, "Although he isn't the richest person" makes no sense all by itself). This subordination thus puts the emphasis on the complete idea in the main clause: "he is certainly one of the most generous" people.

Subordination can be used to rewrite some of the other sentences above in order to emphasize one idea over another. In each example below, the main clause has been underlined.

We built a camp fire after we found a clearing and pitched our tent.
Although the neighborhood raccoon has not been near our house for the last
three days, he has not been missed.
If Mullens doesn't return on the midnight train, she will have to spend another day in the city.
Because he wants to get all A's, Arnold is studying very hard this semester.
As result of having found some important new information about my topic,
I am going to ask Professor Garcia if I can rewrite my paper.

Create Emphasis by Using the Active or Passive Voice

Sentences that use the *active voice* contain subjects—persons, places, or things—that perform an action. Sentences that use the *passive voice* contain subjects that are acted upon. Notice how the structure of a sentence changes when it is put into the passive voice:

Active: The enthusiastic listeners applauded the young guitarist.
Passive: The young guitarist was applauded by the enthusiastic listeners.

Generally, using the active voice makes it easier to stress the subject of a sentence than using the passive voice. For instance, if you wanted to report that the president of your college announced her decision to resign, it wouldn't make much sense to write, "Her decision to resign was announced by President Greenspan." A clearer and more emphatic version would be "President Greenspan announced her decision to resign."

Create Emphasis by Repeating Key Words and Phrases

Repeating important words and phrases, if done sparingly and carefully, can help you stress important ideas over those which deserve less emphasis. Examples of this technique can be found in the speeches of President John F. Kennedy and of Reverend Martin Luther King, Jr.

In his "Inaugural Address," Kennedy gave a special meaning to his plans for the nation when he said:

> All this will not be finished in the first one hundred days. Nor will it
> be finished in the first one thousand days, nor in the life of this
> administration, nor even perhaps in our lifetime on this planet. But let
> us begin.

Dr. King used repetition to communicate a sense of urgency about civil rights to a massive audience at the Lincoln Memorial when he delivered the speech now known as "I Have a Dream":

> Now is the time to make real the promises of democracy. Now is the time to rise from the dark and desolate valley of segregation to the sunlit path of racial justice. Now is the time to lift our nation from the quicksands of racial injustice to the solid rock of brotherhood. Now is the time to make justice a reality for all of God's children.

Create Emphasis through Parallelism

Parallelism is a way to connect facts and ideas of equal importance in the same sentence and thereby give them added emphasis. Sentences that are parallel list items by expressing each of them in the same grammatical form. For instance, Adlai Stevenson's eulogy of Winston Churchill, the great British prime minister, contains several examples of parallelism:

> The voice that led nations, raised armies, inspired victories and blew fresh courage into the hearts of men is silenced. We shall hear no longer the remembered eloquence and wit, the old courage and defiance, the robust serenity of indomitable faith. Our world is thus poorer, our political dialogue is diminished and the sources of public inspiration run more thinly in all of us. There is a lonesome place against the sky.

In the first sentence, Stevenson places equal emphasis on Churchill's accomplishments by expressing each of them in a verb phrase, a verb followed by an object: "led nations," "raised armies," "inspired victories," and "blew fresh courage into the hearts of men." In the second sentence, he creates parallelism by using a list of noun phrases, nouns modified by adjectives, to describe Churchill's best qualities: "the remembered eloquence and wit," "the old courage and defiance," "the robust serenity of indomitable faith." In the third, Stevenson explains the effects of Churchill's loss in a series of independent clauses: "Our world is thus poorer," "our political dialogue is diminished," and "the sources of public inspiration run more thinly in all of us."

Whether you use independent clauses, prepositional phrases, infinitives, or other grammatical structures to create parallelism, remember to be consistent. In other words, make sure that each and every idea in a sentence is expressed in the *same* grammatical form. For instance, Stevenson's eulogy would have been less emphatic and would have sounded awkward had he written that Churchill's voice "led nations, raised armies, inspired victories, and it blew fresh courage into the hearts of men." The first three of these items are verb phrases; the fourth is an independent clause.

VARIETY

One sure way to make your readers lose interest in what you have to say—no matter how important—is to ignore the need for variety. Good writers try not to repeat vocabulary monotonously, and they vary the length and structure of their sentences whenever possible.

Create Variety by Changing Sentence Length

A steady diet of long, complicated sentences is sure to put your readers to sleep. On the other hand, relying solely on short, choppy sentences can make your writing seem disconnected and even childish. Therefore, one of the most important things to remember about the sentences you write is to vary their length. You can do this by combining some of them into longer, more complex units and by leaving others short and to the point.

Reread the passage from President Kennedy's "Inaugural Address" in the previous section. One reason that it holds our interest so well is that it contains sentences of three different lengths. Notice that the last and shortest of these carries a special kind of punch and leaves us with a strong and lasting impression. This would not have been the case if all the sentences in the paragraph were of the same length, for they would have seemed equally important.

You can combine two or three short sentences into a longer unit in three ways: subordination, coordination, or compounding.

Coordination This is useful if you want to write a longer sentence in which all the main ideas receive equal emphasis. The easiest way to do this is to combine sentences with a comma and the appropriate coordinating conjunction or to use a semicolon, as explained in the previous section.

Subordination As you know, subordination is useful if you want to combine two or more sentences and to emphasize one idea over another. It's also a good way to make your sentences more interesting. Say that you've just written the following:

> I had been standing at the bus stop for about five minutes. It was a hot and sultry afternoon. I began to perspire almost immediately. I was anxious to get home as soon as I could. I wanted only to shower, cool off, and relax. I had had a hard day at work. A huge truck rumbled by and covered me with exhaust fumes. Suddenly, I wondered how long it would take the bus to get there.

As you reread this paragraph, you realize that you haven't emphasized your most important ideas and that your style is choppy and monotonous.

Therefore, you decide to rewrite it by combining sentences through subordination:

> I had been standing at the bus stop for about five minutes. It was such a hot and sultry afternoon that I began to perspire almost immediately. I was anxious to get home as soon as I could because I desperately needed to shower, cool off, and relax. I had had a hard day. Suddenly, as a huge truck rumbled by and covered me with exhaust, I wondered how long it would take the bus to get there.

In combining some sentences, you've made your writing smoother and more interesting because you've created sentences of different lengths. What's more, some ideas have gained emphasis.

Compounding This involves putting subjects, verbs, adjectives, and adverbs together in the same sentence as long as they modify or relate to one another logically.

Sometimes, ideas that are very similar seem awkward and boring if expressed in separate sentences. For example: "Egbert has been transferred to Minneapolis. Rowena has also been transferred to that city." Notice how much more interesting these short sentences become when you combine their subjects to make a compound sentence: "Egbert and Rowena have been transferred to Minneapolis." Here are a few more examples:

Original	The blue jay flew through the open window. It nearly crashed into my computer.
Compound verb	The blue jay flew through the open window and nearly crashed into my computer.
Original	The weather around here is sometimes unpredictable. Sometimes it becomes treacherous.
Compound adjective	The weather around here is sometimes unpredictable and treacherous.
Original	Steven called to his brother loudly. He called repeatedly.
Compound adverb	Steven called to his brother loudly and repeatedly.

Create Variety by Changing Sentence Structure

As you know, all complete sentences contain a subject, a verb, and a complete idea; some also contain modifiers (adjectives, adverbs, prepositional phrases, etc.). However, there is no rule that all sentences must begin with a subject, that a verb must follow the subject immediately, or that everything else must be placed at the end of a sentence. Depending on their purpose, good writers create as many patterns as they need to make their writing interesting and effective. Here are a few ways you can vary the basic patterns of your sentences.

Begin with an Adverb   Adverbs modify verbs, adjectives, or other adverbs. They help explain *how, when, where,* or *why.* The following examples begin with adverbs or with groups of words that serve as adverbs (shown in italics):

As she stepped off the train, she remembered that she had forgotten her book.
Suddenly the lights went out.
Near the wreck of an old freighter the divers found two large chests.
Since she hadn't eaten in nearly seven hours Samina stopped at a roadside restaurant.

Begin with an Infinitive   An infinitive is the simple form of a verb with the word "to" in front of it:

To get the best deal on a car Debbie looked at over twenty-five different models and visited ten automobile dealerships.
To learn more about word processing Professor Malinowski has enrolled in a special weekend seminar on computers.

Begin with a Preposition or Prepositional Phrase   Prepositions connect, or show the relationship between, a particular noun or pronoun and the rest of the sentence. A prepositional phrase is made up of a preposition, a noun or pronoun (also known as the object of the preposition), and any modifiers:

Near the edge of the river stood a large willow.
Without love, life is empty.
At the romantic dinner he had been planning for weeks, Ari finally convinced Felicia to marry him.

Use Participles and Participial Phrases at the Beginning and End of Sentences   A participle is a verb that acts as an adjective; participles end in "-ed" or "-ing." A participial phrase is a group of words that contains a participle and its modifiers:

Screeching, the infant birds told their mother they were hungry.
Exhausted, I fell asleep as soon as my head touched the pillow.
I stayed home that night, *having nowhere else to go.*
Suddenly, the old bicycle broke apart, *scattering spokes and bits of chain everywhere.*
Jamie wept openly, *his dream destroyed.*

Use a Rhetorical Question   This is the kind of question to which the answer is obvious. If used sparingly, rhetorical questions are good ways to introduce information or emphasize important points, as in the following examples:

> *Will it ever stop raining?* We have been deluged for the last five days,
> and the forecast is not encouraging. Two small streams have become
> raging torrents and flooded the downtown area. The mayor's office
> estimates that the weather has caused over $1 million in damages.

> Many large companies employ high-paid lobbyists to influence our
> government representatives in Washington and in the state capitals.
> The same is true of powerful special-interest groups, which often seek
> support for causes that are not best for the nation as a whole.
> Individual voters, however, can't afford such "special" representation.
> *Shouldn't we limit the ability of lobbyists to influence our lawmakers?*

Reverse the Position of the Subject and the Verb Say that you write, "Two
small pines grew at the crest of the hill." When you read your rough draft,
you realize that this is the kind of pattern you've used in many other sentences. To vary the pattern, simply reverse the position of your subject and
verb: "At the crest of the hill grew two small pines."

The following selections will help you develop the ability to create sentences
that are both varied and emphatic. As you read on, try to apply the techniques
you're learning in this chapter to your own writing. Don't hesitate to reread
important sections in the introduction to this chapter when you need to.

Gettysburg Address

Abraham Lincoln

Abraham Lincoln is one of the best-loved U.S. Presidents. His "Second Inaugural Address" and the "Gettysburg Address" are landmarks in American public speaking.

In November 1863, Lincoln came to Gettysburg, Pennsylvania, to dedicate a cemetery at the site of the Civil War's bloodiest contest. The Battle of Gettysburg, which proved to be the turning point of the war, had raged for four days and killed 50,000 Americans before Confederate forces under General Robert E. Lee withdrew.

Lincoln's "Gettysburg Address" is an eloquent and powerful statement of his grief over the death of his countrymen on both sides and of his belief "that government of the people, by the people, for the people, shall not perish from the earth."

Looking Ahead

1. In his concluding sentence, Lincoln describes a "great task remaining before us." Read this important section of the speech a few times to make sure you understand it fully.
2. "Four score and seven years" equals eighty-seven years. A "score" is twenty.
3. Throughout this speech, and especially in paragraph 3, Lincoln uses parallelism, a technique that makes his sentences more forceful, more emphatic, and memorable.

Vocabulary

conceived   Created.

consecrate   Bless, sanctify.

detract   Take away from, lessen.

hallow   Make holy or sacred.

in vain   For no reason or purpose.

measure   Amount.

proposition   Idea, principle.

resolve   Decide, determine.

Four score and seven years ago our fathers brought forth on this con-   1
tinent a new nation, conceived in Liberty, and dedicated to the proposition
that all men are created equal.

Now we are engaged in a great civil war, testing whether that nation, or ₂ any nation so conceived and so dedicated, can long endure. We are met on a great battle-field of that war. We have come to dedicate a portion of that field, as a final resting place for those who here gave their lives that that nation might live. It is altogether fitting and proper that we should do this.

But, in a larger sense, we can not dedicate—we can not consecrate—we ₃ can not hallow—this ground. The brave men, living and dead, who struggled here, have consecrated it, far above our poor power to add or detract. The world will little note, nor long remember what we say here, but it can never forget what they did here. It is for us the living, rather, to be dedicated here to the unfinished work which they who fought here have thus far so nobly advanced. It is rather for us to be here dedicated to the great task remaining before us—that from these honored dead we take increased devotion to that cause for which they gave the last full measure of devotion—that we here highly resolve that these dead shall not have died in vain—that this nation, under God, shall have a new birth of freedom—and that government of the people, by the people, for the people, shall not perish from the earth.

Questions for Discussion

1. What words and ideas are repeated in paragraph 3? What ideas does this repetition emphasize?
2. What examples of parallelism do you find in the "Gettysburg Address"?
3. Most of the sentences in this speech are rather long and involved. However, Lincoln does seem to vary the length of his sentences. Identify sections of the speech in which he does so.
4. What two participial phrases does Lincoln use at the end of his first sentence? Do they help make this sentence more interesting than if he had put the information they convey into another sentence?
5. Does Lincoln include a participial phrase in paragraph 2? Where?
6. What is Lincoln's central idea? What devices or techniques does he use to maintain coherence?

Suggestions for Journal Entries

1. Many speeches in American history have served as sources of inspiration from decade to decade, from generation to generation. With the help of your instructor or your college librarian, locate a speech that you'd like to read or reread. Then analyze this speech. Pick out examples of parallelism, repetition, and other techniques the writer has used to create emphasis. Here are a few speeches you might choose from:

Abraham Lincoln, "Second Inaugural Address"
Franklin Delano Roosevelt, "First Inaugural Address"

Adlai Stevenson, "Eulogy to Eleanor Roosevelt"
Martin Luther King, Jr., "I Have a Dream"

2. Using as many paragraphs as you like, rewrite Lincoln's speech in your own words. Make sure that you express his central idea clearly and that you emphasize his other important ideas through parallelism, repetition, or any of the other techniques you've learned for creating emphasis.

A Longing

Alice Wnorowski

"A Longing" is a tender, almost dreamlike recollection of a beautiful childhood experience that continues to haunt the author. Wnorowski wrote this short essay in response to a freshman English assignment designed to help students learn to use concrete detail. However, it also illustrates several important principles about sentence structure discussed earlier in this chapter.

Looking Ahead

1. You've learned that coordination can be used to create sentences in which two or more ideas receive equal emphasis and that subordination can be used to create sentences in which one idea is stressed over others. Look for examples of coordination and subordination in this essay.
2. The author puts variety into her writing by using techniques discussed earlier in this chapter. They include beginning sentences with an adverb and a prepositional phrase and using participles to vary sentence structure and length.
3. Remember what you learned about using details in Chapter 5, especially those that appeal to the five senses. Identify such details in "A Longing."

Vocabulary

acknowledge Recognize.
conceived Understood.
yearn Desire, long for.

An easy breeze pushed through the screen door, blowing into my open   1
face and filling my nostrils with the first breath of morning. The sun beamed

warm rays of white light onto my lids, demanding they lift and acknowledge the day's arrival.

Perched in the nearby woods, a bobwhite proudly shrieked to the world that he knew who he was. His song stirred deep feelings within me, and I was overcome by an urge to run barefoot through his woods. I jumped up so abruptly I startled the dog lying peacefully beside me. His sleepy eyes looked into mine questioningly, but I could give him no answer. I only left him bewildered, pushing through the front door and trotting down the grassy decline of the front lawn.

The morning dew chilled my naked feet, and I stopped on the sandy lane. From out of the corner of my eye, I suddenly caught a movement in the wide, open hay field that lay before me. Five deer, three does and two fawns, were grazing in the mist-filled dips of the roller-coaster landscape. I sat down in the damp earth to watch them and got my white nightdress all brown and wet.

They casually strolled along through the thigh-high grass, stopping every other step to dip their heads into the growth and pop them back up again, with the long, tender timothy stems dangling from the sides of their mouths.

The fawns were never more than two or three yards behind their mothers, and I knew a buck must not be far off in the woods, keeping lookout for enemies. Suddenly, a car sped along the adjacent road, disrupting the peace of the moment. The deer jumped up in terror and darted towards the trees. They took leaps, clearing eight to ten feet in a single bound. I watched their erect, white puffs of tails bounce up and down, until the darkness of the woods swallowed them up and I could see them no more.

I don't think that at the simple age of eleven I quite conceived what a rare and beautiful sight I had witnessed. Now, eight years later, I yearn to awaken to the call of a bobwhite and to run barefoot through wet grass in search of him.

Questions for Discussion

1. Find a few examples of both coordination and subordination in this essay.
2. Identify some of the adverbs, prepositional phrases, and participles that Wnorowski uses to give her writing variety.
3. In paragraph 5, she varies the length of her sentences in order to make her writing more exciting and interesting. Explain how she does this.
4. Wnorowski concludes this short essay by using parallelism. Reread the last sentence, and explain in what way it illustrates parallel structure.
5. To which of our five senses do the details in this essay appeal?
6. What is the meaning of Wnorowski's title? Why is it appropriate?
7. What techniques does the writer use to maintain coherence in and between her paragraphs?

Suggestions for Journal Entries

1. Think back to an experience you would like to relive. Make a list of the things that made this experience memorable and that will explain why you have such "a longing" to relive it.
2. Use the brainstorming technique discussed in Getting Started to list details about a natural setting (meadow, mountain, seashore, etc.) that you experienced recently or remember vividly.

Inaugural Address

John Fitzgerald Kennedy

One of the most popular leaders in American history, JFK took the oath of office as our thirty-fifth President on January 20, 1961. Through more than a quarter of a century, his speeches have served to inspire and to instruct new generations of Americans.

The best-remembered and most frequently quoted of Kennedy's speeches, his "Inaugural Address," seems fresh and new even after three decades. Perhaps this has to do with his ability to speak to what is deepest and most universal in the human spirit—the real hopes and problems that all generations and all peoples share.

Looking Ahead

1. Like most Presidents, Kennedy relied on a professional speech writer. Ted Sorenson composed his "Inaugural Address."
2. Kennedy begins by recognizing several dignitaries on the platform. Among them are Dwight D. Eisenhower, the thirty-fourth President; Richard Nixon, the outgoing Vice President and later the thirty-seventh President; and the new Vice President, Lyndon B. Johnson, who became President upon Kennedy's death in 1963.
3. Paragraphs 19 and 23 make reference to the Old Testament and especially to the prophet Isaiah, who wrote that someday the armies of the world would "beat their swords into plowshares and their spears into pruning hooks."
4. This selection makes especially good use of parallel structure and repetition. Look for examples of these techniques.
5. One reason this speech is so spellbinding is that its language and sentence structure are both powerful and varied. The writer was especially successful at changing the length of its sentences at just the right times. As you

read JFK's "Inaugural Address," identify some of the other methods you've learned for maintaining variety.

Vocabulary

abolish   Eliminate, do away with.

asunder   Apart.

belaboring   Talking about for an unreasonable length of time.

formulate   Create, make.

invective   Verbal abuse, insult.

invoke   Call upon, use.

prescribed   Recommended, directed, dictated.

symbolizing   Representing.

tribulation   Suffering, trouble.

writ   Authority.

Vice President Johnson, Mr. Speaker, Mr. Chief Justice, President Eisen-   1
hower, Vice President Nixon, President Truman, Reverend Clergy, Fellow Cit-
izens: We observe today not a victory of party but a celebration of freedom—
symbolizing an end as well as a beginning—signifying renewal as well as change.
For I have sworn before you and Almighty God the same solemn oath our
forebears prescribed nearly a century and three quarters ago.

The world is very different now. For man holds in his mortal hands the   2
power to abolish all forms of human poverty and all forms of human life. And
yet the same revolutionary beliefs for which our forebears fought are still at
issue around the globe—the belief that the rights of man come not from the
generosity of the state but from the hand of God.

We dare not forget today that we are the heirs of that first revolution.   3
Let the word go forth from this time and place, to friend and foe alike, that
the torch has been passed to a new generation of Americans—born in this
century, tempered by war, disciplined by a hard and bitter peace, proud of
our ancient heritage—and unwilling to witness or permit the slow undoing of
those human rights to which this nation has always been committed, and to
which we are committed today, at home and around the world.

Let every nation know, whether it wishes us well or ill, that we shall pay   4
any price, bear any burden, meet any hardship, support any friend or oppose
any foe to assure the survival and the success of liberty.

This much we pledge—and more.   5

To those old allies whose cultural and spiritual origins we share, we   6
pledge the loyalty of faithful friends. United, there is little we cannot do in
a host of cooperative ventures. Divided, there is little we can do—for we dare
not meet a powerful challenge at odds and split asunder.

To those new states whom we welcome to the ranks of the free, we 7
pledge our word that one form of colonial control shall not have passed away
merely to be replaced by a far more iron tyranny. We shall not always expect
to find them supporting our view.

But we shall always hope to find them strongly supporting their own 8
freedom—and to remember that, in the past, those who foolishly sought power
by riding the back of the tiger ended up inside.

To those people in the huts and villages of half the globe struggling to 9
break the bonds of mass misery, we pledge our best efforts to help them help
themselves, for whatever period is required—not because the Communists
may be doing it, not because we seek their votes, but because it is right. If a
free society cannot help the many who are poor, it cannot save the few who
are rich.

To our sister republics south of our border, we offer a special pledge—to 10
convert our good words into good deeds—in a new alliance for progress—to
assist free men and free governments in casting off the chains of poverty. But
this peaceful revolution of hope cannot become the prey of hostile powers. Let
all our neighbors know that we shall join with them to oppose aggression or
subversion anywhere in the Americas. And let every other power know that
this hemisphere intends to remain the master of its own house.

To that world assembly of sovereign states, the United Nations, our last 11
best hope in an age where the instruments of war have far outpaced the instruments of peace, we renew our pledge of support—to prevent it from becoming merely a forum for invective—to strengthen its shield of the new and
the weak—and to enlarge the area in which its writ may run.

Finally, to those nations who would make themselves our adversary, we 12
offer not a pledge but a request: That both sides begin anew the quest for
peace, before the dark powers of destruction unleashed by science engulf all
humanity in planned or accidental self-destruction.

We dare not tempt them with weakness. For only when our arms are 13
sufficient beyond doubt can we be certain beyond doubt that they will never
be employed.

But neither can two great and powerful groups of nations take comfort 14
from our present course—both sides overburdened by the cost of modern
weapons, both rightly alarmed by the steady spread of the deadly atom, yet
both racing to alter that uncertain balance of terror that stays the hand of
mankind's final war.

So let us begin anew—remembering on both sides that civility is not a 15
sign of weakness, and sincerity is always subject to proof. Let us never negotiate out of fear. But let us never fear to negotiate.

Let both sides explore what problems unite us instead of belaboring 16
those problems which divide us.

Let both sides, for the first time, formulate serious and precise pro- 17 posals for the inspection and control of arms—and bring the absolute power to destroy other nations under the absolute control of all nations.

Let both sides seek to invoke the wonders of science instead of its ter- 18 rors. Together let us explore the stars, conquer the deserts, eradicate disease, tap the ocean depths and encourage the arts and commerce.

Let both sides unite to heed in all corners of the earth the command of 19 Isaiah—to "undo the heavy burdens...[and] let the oppressed go free."

And if a beachhead of cooperation may push back the jungle of suspi- 20 cion, let both sides join in creating a new endeavor: not a new balance of power, but a new world of law, where the strong are just and the weak secure and the peace preserved.

All this will not be finished in the first one hundred days. Nor will it be 21 finished in the first one thousand days, nor in the life of this administration, nor even perhaps in our lifetime on this planet. But let us begin.

In your hands, my fellow citizens, more than mine, will rest the final 22 success or failure of our course. Since this country was founded, each generation of Americans has been summoned to give testimony to its national loyalty. The graves of young Americans who answered the call to service surround the globe.

Now the trumpet summons us again—not as a call to bear arms, though 23 arms we need—not as a call to battle, though embattled we are—but a call to bear the burden of a long twilight struggle, year in and year out, "rejoicing in hope, patient in tribulation"—a struggle against the common enemies of man: Tyranny, poverty, disease and war itself.

Can we forge against these enemies a grand and global alliance, North 24 and South, East and West, that can assure a more fruitful life for all mankind? Will you join in that historic effort?

In the long history of the world, only a few generations have been granted 25 the role of defending freedom in its hour of maximum danger.

I do not shrink from this responsibility—I welcome it. I do not believe 26 that any of us would exchange places with any other people or any other generation. The energy, the faith, the devotion which we bring to this endeavor will light our country and all who serve it—and the glow from that fire can truly light the world.

And so, my fellow Americans: Ask not what your country can do for 27 you—ask what you can do for your country.

My fellow citizens of the world: Ask not what America will do for you, 28 but what together we can do for the freedom of man.

Finally, whether you are citizens of America or citizens of the world, ask 29 of us here the same high standards of strength and sacrifice which we ask of you. With a good conscience our only sure reward, with history the final judge of our deeds, let us go forth to lead the land we love, asking His blessing and His help, but knowing that here on earth God's work must truly be our own.

Questions for Discussion

1. Reread any three or four paragraphs in this selection, and identify examples of parallel structure that are used to create emphasis.
2. Reread paragraph 21, which illustrates repetition. Then, elsewhere in this speech, find other passages where Kennedy repeats key words and phrases to create emphasis.
3. Paragraphs 6, 7, 9, 10, and 11 are introduced by phrases that begin with the preposition "to." This repetition helps the speaker draw connections between and emphasize important ideas in each of these paragraphs. In what other section of this speech does he use repetition to begin a series of paragraphs?
4. The speech writer's ability to vary sentence length is evident throughout this selection. In what paragraphs is this skill most apparent?
5. Near the conclusion, JFK asks two rhetorical questions that add variety and interest to his presentation. What are they?
6. The speech writer often creates coherence between sentences and paragraphs by beginning with a coordinating conjunction: "And," "But," and "For." Find places in which he does so.

Suggestions for Journal Entries

1. Pick out one or two paragraphs in Kennedy's "Inaugural Address" that you find particularly moving and effective. Put the ideas he expresses into your own words. Vary sentence lengths and structures by using the techniques for creating variety explained earlier in this chapter and found in this selection.
2. Kennedy's speech seems fresh and current because it touches something universal in the human spirit, the hopes and the problems of all generations and all peoples. In your journal, list the issues (or problems) mentioned in Kennedy's "Inaugural Address" that you believe are still important today. Begin discussing details which, in a later assignment, might help show your readers how current these problems still are. Draw these details from your own experiences and/or from what you know about current events.

The Measure of Eratosthenes

Carl Sagan

A professor of astronomy at Cornell University, Carl Sagan has worked on a number of NASA projects and has completed extensive research on the possibility of life on other planets. He has done much to popularize the study of science and is especially well known as a result of having hosted the public-television series *Cosmos*. Among his most widely read books are *The Dragons of Eden*, for which he won the Pulitzer prize in 1977, *Broca's Brain*, and *Cosmos*.

Sagan published "The Measure of Eratosthenes" (era-TOSS-the-neez) to honor an ancient Greek thinker who, seventeen centuries before Columbus, accurately measured the Earth and proved that it was round.

Looking Ahead

1. In paragraph 4, Sagan claims that "in almost everything, Eratosthenes was 'alpha.'" Alpha is the first letter of the Greek alphabet.
2. Papyrus, mentioned in paragraph 5, is a plant from which paper was made in ancient times.
3. One reason that this selection holds our interest so well is that Sagan succeeds in varying the structure and length of his sentences. Find places where he does this.

Vocabulary

cataract A large waterfall.
circumference The distance around a circle or globe.
compelling Difficult to ignore.
inclined Slanted.
intergalactic Between galaxies.
intersect Cross.
musings Thoughts.
pronounced Significant.
randomly By chance.

The earth is a place. It is by no means the only place. It is not even a   1
typical place. No planet or star or galaxy can be typical, because the cosmos is mostly empty. The only typical place is within the vast, cold, universal vacuum, the everlasting night of intergalactic space, a place so strange and desolate that, by comparison, planets and stars and galaxies seem achingly rare and lovely.

If we were randomly inserted into the cosmos, the chance that we would   2
find ourselves on or near a planet would be less than one in a billion trillion trillion (10^{33}, a one followed by 33 zeros). In everyday life, such odds are called compelling. Worlds are precious.

The discovery that the earth is a *little* world was made, as so many im-   3
portant human discoveries were, in the ancient Near East, in a time some

humans call the third century B.C., in the greatest metropolis of the age, the Egyptian city of Alexandria.

Here there lived a man named Eratosthenes. One of his envious contemporaries called him "beta," the second letter of the Greek alphabet, because, he said, Eratosthenes was the world's second best in everything. But it seems clear that, in almost everything, Eratosthenes was "alpha." 4

He was an astronomer, historian, geographer, philosopher, poet, theater critic, and mathematician. His writings ranged from "Astronomy" to "On Freedom from Pain." He was also the director of the great library of Alexandria, where one day he read, in a papyrus book, that in the southern frontier outpost of Syene (now Aswan), near the first cataract of the Nile, at noon on June 21 vertical sticks cast no shadows. On the summer solstice, the longest day of the year, as the hours crept toward midday, the shadows of the temple columns grew shorter. At noon, they were gone. A reflection of the sun could then be seen in the water at the bottom of a deep well. The sun was directly overhead. 5

It was an observation that someone else might easily have ignored. Sticks, shadows, reflections in wells, the position of the sun—of what possible importance could such simple, everyday matters be? But Eratosthenes was a scientist, and his musings on these commonplaces changed the world: in a way, they made the world. 6

Eratosthenes had the presence of mind to do an experiment—actually to observe whether *in Alexandria* vertical sticks cast shadows near noon on June 21. And, he discovered, sticks do. 7

Eratosthenes asked himself how, at the same moment, a stick in Syene could cast no shadow and a stick in Alexandria, far to the north, could cast a pronounced shadow. 8

Consider a map of ancient Egypt with two vertical sticks of equal length, one stuck in Alexandria, the other in Syene. Suppose that, at a certain moment, neither stick casts any shadow at all. This is perfectly easy to understand—provided the earth is flat. The sun would then be directly overhead. If the two sticks cast shadows of equal length, that also would make sense on a flat earth: the sun's rays would then be inclined at the same angle to the two sticks. But how could it be that at the same instant there was no shadow at Syene and a substantial shadow at Alexandria? 9

The only possible answer, he saw, was that the surface of the earth is curved. Not only that: the greater the curvature, the greater the difference in the shadow lengths. The sun is so far away that its rays are parallel when they reach the earth. Sticks placed at different angles to the sun's rays cast shadows of different lengths. For the observed difference in the shadow lengths, the distance between Alexandria and Syene had to be about seven degrees along the surface of the earth; that is, if you imagine the sticks extending down to the center of the earth, they would intersect there at an angle of seven degrees. 10

Seven degrees is something like one-fiftieth of 360 degrees, the full cir- 11
cumference of the earth. Eratosthenes knew that the distance between Alexandria and Syene was approximately 800 kilometers, because he had hired a
man to pace it out.

Eight hundred kilometers times 50 is 40,000 kilometers; so that must be 12
the circumference of the earth. (Or, if you like to measure things in miles, the
distance between Alexandria and Syene is about 500 miles, and 500 miles
times 50 is 25,000 miles.)

This is the right answer.   13

Eratosthenes' only tools were sticks, eyes, feet, and brains, plus a taste 14
for experiment. With them he deduced the circumference of the earth with
an error of only a few percent, a remarkable achievement for 2,200 years ago.
He was the first person accurately to measure the size of a planet.

Questions for Discussion

1. Analyze any of the longer paragraphs in this essay: 1, 5, 9, or 10, for example. Explain how Sagan varies the length and structure of the sentences
   in that paragraph. If necessary, review the techniques for creating variety
   discussed earlier.
2. Does Sagan make use of rhetorical questions in this selection? What do
   such questions help him accomplish?
3. Like Kennedy, Sagan sometimes begins a sentence with a coordinating
   conjunction to create coherence and emphasis. Where in this essay does he
   do so?
4. Paragraph 3 contains a good example of parallel structure. Identify it.
5. Another way Sagan emphasizes important ideas and creates interest is repetition. Find an example of this practice.

Suggestions for Journal Entries

1. In your own words, summarize the accomplishments of Eratosthenes that
   Sagan discusses in this selection. Vary your sentence structure as much as
   you can. If you need to, begin by listing short, simple sentences; then
   create variety by combining some of these sentences through coordination,
   subordination, and compounding.
2. Sagan obviously has a great deal of respect for Eratosthenes and what he
   accomplished. Think about someone you greatly admire. This person need
   not be an important public servant, artist, athlete, or scientist, and he or
   she need not hold a prominent place in history. In fact, your grandmother,
   neighbor, high school chemistry teacher, or close friend might make the
   best subject. In any case, use your journal to list the qualities or accomplishments that make this person worthy of admiration.

SUGGESTIONS FOR WRITING

1. One of the Suggestions for Journal Entries after Alice Wnorowski's "A Longing" asks you to think about an experience you would like to relive. If you responded to this suggestion, you've made a list of effective details that will help explain why you have such "a longing" to repeat this experience.

   Add to your notes, and expand them into a short essay that shows your reader what made the experience so memorable. Develop your thesis in concrete detail, and don't forget to make your writing unified and coherent by using techniques discussed in Chapter 2.

   After you've written your first draft, read your essay carefully. Should you do more to emphasize important ideas or to maintain your readers' interest? If so, revise your paper by using some of the techniques for creating emphasis and variety explained in the introduction to this chapter.

2. The second item in the Suggestions for Journal Entries after "A Longing" invites you to begin listing details about a natural setting—a forest, meadow, seashore, mountain, river, etc.—that you visited recently or remember vividly.

   Follow the advice in item 1 of Suggestions for Writing, and turn these notes into a short essay. Don't forget to review your rough draft carefully. If parts of it need greater emphasis and variety, make use of the techniques discussed earlier in this chapter.

3. If you read President Kennedy's "Inaugural Address" and responded to item 2 in the Suggestions for Journal Entries that follow it, you have probably collected details to show that many of the serious problems mentioned in that speech are still with us today. Identify the *one* problem you know most about, either through personal experience or through your knowledge of current events, and continue to add details about this problem in your journal.

   Turn your notes into an essay that states the problem clearly and describes its effects as you know them. Your thesis might be something like: "Three decades after President John F. Kennedy delivered his 'Inaugural Address,' extreme poverty still plagues even our richest cities."

   As always, take time to revise your rough draft and to give your sentences both variety and emphasis. Finally, don't forget to make your writing unified, coherent, and well developed.

4. Item 2 in the Suggestions for Journal Entries after Sagan's "The Measure of Eratosthenes" asks that you begin gathering information about someone you admire. If you responded to this item, read your journal notes carefully and add to them.

   Next, organize what you've written into the paragraphs of an essay. In your thesis, which should appear in the introduction, explain that you respect this person as a result of what he or she has accomplished in life. Then, in *each* of the paragraphs that follows, describe one of these important accomplishments fully.

Try to make use of one or more techniques for creating emphasis and variety discussed earlier in this chapter. As with all assignments, make sure your writing is well developed, unified, and coherent.

Section III

Description

This section's two chapters show how to develop verbal portraits—pictures in words—of people, places, and things you know well. The more specific you make any piece of writing, the more interesting, exciting, and effective it will be. And this is especially true of descriptive writing. Successful descriptions require a lot of specific details.

KNOWING YOUR SUBJECT

Gathering descriptive details becomes easier when you know the person, place, or thing you're describing. If you need to learn more about your subject, spend some time observing it. Use your five senses—sight, hearing, touch, taste, and smell—to gather important information. And don't be afraid to take notes. Write your observations, reactions, and impressions in your journal, on note cards, or at least on scratch paper. They will come in handy as you sit down to put together your verbal portrait.

USING LANGUAGE THAT SHOWS

As you learned in Chapter 5, using language that shows makes any writing you do far more *concrete*, *specific*, and *vivid* than simply telling your readers what you mean. Such language is vital to description.

For instance, it's one thing to say that your mother "came home from work looking very tired." It's quite another to describe "the dark shadows under her eyes and the slowness of her walk as she entered the house."

In the first version, the writer uses a weak abstraction to get the point across. But, "looking very tired" can mean different things to different people. It doesn't show the reader exactly what the writer sees. It doesn't point to things about the subject—the dark shadows under her eyes, the slowness of her walk—that *show* she is tired.

163

Use Concrete Nouns and Adjectives

The next thing to remember is to make your details as concrete as possible. For example, if you're describing a friend, don't just say that "He's not a neat dresser" or that his "wardrobe could be improved." Include concrete nouns and adjectives that will enable your readers to come to the same conclusion. Talk about "the red dirt along the sides of his scuffed, torn shoes, the large rips in the knees of his faded bluejeans, and the many jelly spots on his shirt."

The same is true when describing objects and places. It's not enough to claim that your 1959 convertible is "a real eyesore." You've got to *show* it! Describe the scrapes, scratches, dents, and rust spots; mention the cracked headlights, the corroded bumpers, and the bald tires; talk about the fact that the top is faded.

Use Specific Details

After you've chosen a number of important details that are concrete—details that show rather than tell something about your subject—make your description more specific. For instance, revise the description of your friend's attire to: "Red clay was caked along the sides of his scuffed, torn loafers, his knees bulged from the large rips in his faded Levi's, and strawberry jelly was smeared on the collar of his white Oxford shirt."

When describing that 1959 convertible, don't be content simply to mention "the scratches and scrapes on the paint job." Go on to specify that "some of them are more than an inch wide and a half-inch deep." Make sure your readers know that those "corroded bumpers" are made of "chrome" and "are scarred with thousands of tiny pockmarks and rusty blemishes." Finally, don't say that the top is "faded"; explain that "the canvas top, which was once sparkling white, has turned dirty gray with age."

Use Figures of Speech

In Chapter 6 you learned that one of the best ways to make your writing clear and vivid is to use figures of speech, expressions that convey a meaning beyond their literal sense. Writers rely heavily on figures of speech when they need to explain or clarify abstract, complex, or unfamiliar ideas. Metaphors and similes are the most useful figures of speech for description because they can be used to compare an aspect of the person, place, or thing being described to something else with which the reader may already be familiar. Gilbert Highet makes excellent use of a simile when, in "Subway Station" (Chapter 8), he tells us that the paint is peeling off the station walls "like scabs from an old wound."

In addition, figures of speech make it possible for writers to dramatize or make vivid feelings, concepts, or ideas that would otherwise have remained abstract and difficult to understand. If you read Emanuel di Pasquale's "Joy of an Immigrant" (Chapter 6), you might remember that the poet compares his journey to America with the flight of a bird to a land where he "can build a dry nest" and where his "song can echo."

BEING OBJECTIVE OR SUBJECTIVE

Describing something objectively requires the writer to report what he or she sees, hears, etc. as accurately and as thoroughly as possible. Subjective description allows the writer to communicate his or her personal feelings or reactions to the subject as well. Both types of description serve important purposes.

Most journalists and historians try to remain objective by communicating facts, not opinions about those facts. In other words, they try to give us the kind of information we'll need to make up our own minds about the subject.

Notice how objective student Meg Potter remains as she describes a "shopping bag lady," one of the thousands of homeless people living on the streets of our major cities:

> This particular [shopping bag lady] had no shoes on, but her feet were bound in plastic bags that were tied with filthy rags. It was hard to tell exactly what she was wearing. She had on such a conglomeration of tattered material that I can only say they were rags. I couldn't say how old she was, but I'd guess in her late fifties. The woman's hair was grey and silver, and she was beginning to go bald.

> As I watched for a while, I realized she was sorting out her bags. She had six of them, each stuffed and overflowing with God knows what! I caught a glimpse of ancient magazines, empty bottles, filthy pieces of clothing, an inside-out umbrella, and several mismatched shoes. The lady seemed to be taking things out of one bag and putting them into another. All the time she was muttering to herself.... ["The Shopping Bag Ladies"]

Sometimes, however, writers reveal their feelings about the person, place or thing they're describing. Doing so often adds interest and depth to their work. This is the case with "Dawn Watch," a selection in Chapter 8 in which John Ciardi begins his moving description of sunrise by explaining that "Unless a man is up for the dawn and for the half hour or so of first light, he has missed the best of the day."

Watch for examples of objective and subjective description as you read the poems and essays in Chapters 8 and 9. At the same time, try to identify concrete and specific details and figures of speech, which will help you better appreciate and understand what goes into the writing of a vivid, interesting, and well-written piece of description.

Chapter 8

Describing Places and Things

The introduction to Section III explained several ways to increase your powers of description regardless of the subject. This chapter presents several selections that describe places and things. It also explains two new techniques that will help you make your subjects as interesting and as vivid to your readers as they are to you: using proper nouns and effective verbs.

USING PROPER NOUNS

In addition to filling your writing with concrete details and figures of speech, you might also want to include a number of *proper nouns*, the names of particular persons, places, and things. Here are some examples of proper nouns: the state of Arizona, the University of Tennessee, Lake Michigan, the Farmers' and Merchants' Savings and Loan, the First Baptist Church, Spanish, Chinese, Belmont Avenue, the Singer Sewing Machine Company, Harold Smith, the San Francisco Opera House, *Business Week* magazine, and the Minnesota Vikings.

Such nouns should be easily recognized by your readers and might help make what you're describing more familiar to them. At the very least, mentioning proper nouns makes your writing more believable.

Notice how Alfred Kazin's recollection of his childhood home is enriched by his use of the names of places and things (shown in italics) in this passage from "The Kitchen":

> In the corner next to the toilet was the sink at which we washed, and the square tub in which my mother did our clothes. Above it, tacked to the shelf on which were pleasantly arranged square, blue-bordered white sugar and spice jars, hung calendars from the *Public National Bank* on *Pitkin Avenue* and the *Minsker Progressive Branch* of the

Workman's Circle; receipts for the payment of insurance premiums and household bills on a spindle; two little boxes engraved with *Hebrew* letters. One of these was for the poor, the other to buy back the *Land of Israel.*

USING EFFECTIVE VERBS

We know how important verbs are to narration, but effective verbs can also add much to a piece of description. Writers use verbs to make descriptions more specific, accurate, and interesting. For instance, "the wind had chiseled deep grooves into the sides of the cliffs" is more specific than "the wind had made deep grooves." The verb *chiseled* also gives the reader a more accurate picture of the wind's action than *made* does.

Earlier you learned how to enrich the description of a friend's clothing by adding specific details. Notice that lively verbs (in italics) make as much of a difference in that sentence as do concrete nouns and adjectives:

> Red clay *was caked* along the sides of scuffed, torn loafers, his knees *bulged* from the large rips in his faded Levi's, and strawberry jelly *was smeared* on the collar of his white Oxford shirt."

As you can see, these verbs are not just specific and accurate. They are also interesting!

In all three ways, verbs (shown in italics) add to Robert K. Massie's description of Moscow, found at the very beginning of his *Peter the Great:*

> Around Moscow, the country *rolls* gently up from the rivers *winding* in silvery loops across the pleasant landscape. Small lakes and patches of woods are *sprinkled* among the meadowlands. Here and there, a village *appears, topped* by the onion dome of its church. People *are walking* through the fields on dirt paths *lined* with weeds. Along the riverbanks they *are fishing, swimming* and *lying* in the sun. It is a familiar Russian scene, *rooted* in centuries.

Before you go on to read the essays and poems in this chapter, have one more look at an example of the effective use of verbs, this time in Annie Dillard's "In the Jungle," which appears later in this chapter:

> Green fireflies *spattered* lights across the air and *illumined* for seconds now here, now there, the pale trunks of enormous, solitary trees. Beneath us the brown Napo River *was rising,* in all silence; it *coiled* up the sandy bank and *tangled* its foam in vines that *trailed* from the forest and roots that *looped* the shore.

The Eagle

Alfred Lord Tennyson

One of the most famous poets in English, Tennyson (1809–1892) is remembered chiefly as a spokesperson for the Victorian age. In 1850 he was named poet laureate of Great Britain, a position of great distinction, and in this capacity he wrote numerous poems commemorating state occasions and special events. His most famous works include "The Lady of Shalott," "The Lotus-Eaters," and "Ulysses."

In "The Eagle," Tennyson captures the majesty and strength of this magnificent bird in six short but very powerful verses (lines). Like many of his poems, it shows his masterful use of concrete details and figurative language in creating a lifelike portrait.

Looking Ahead

1. As you read the poem, don't expect much descriptive detail about the eagle itself; instead, Tennyson tells us more about the "lonely" world it inhabits. To learn more about the eagle, ask yourself how it interacts with that world.
2. The verbs in the first three lines seem appropriate to a still life; the ones in the second stanza convey action. This two-part view of the eagle helps Tennyson give us a far more complete portrait than if he had simply relied only on physical description and talked about size, shape, color, etc.
3. Tennyson uses three figures of speech (personification, metaphor, and simile) to make his description more concrete and easier to visualize. (To review what you've learned about figurative language, see Chapter 6.)

Vocabulary

azure   Deep blue.
crag   Rocky cliff.

He clasps the crag with crooked hands;
Close to the sun in lonely lands,
Ring'd with the azure world, he stands.

The wrinkled sea beneath him crawls;
He watches from his mountain walls,
And like a thunderbolt he falls.

5

Questions for Discussion

1. Tennyson makes excellent use of adjectives in this poem. What are they? What nouns does he use to describe the eagle?
2. The poem includes more detail about the eagle's world than about the eagle itself. What kind of land is it? What does it tell us about the eagle?
3. Tennyson divides his poem into two three-line sections, called triplets. How does *each* of these triplets picture the eagle for the reader?
4. Most readers see the eagle as courageous, majestic, and powerful. What details in the poem support this view?
5. What figures of speech does Tennyson use in this poem?

Suggestions for Journal Entries

1. Continue Tennyson's description of the eagle's environment by writing down several of your own impressions that might help other readers see this world even more clearly. Then make your description more concrete by putting it into paragraph form and including as many effective adjectives and nouns as you can.
2. Write your own short description of an animal (perhaps a family pet) about which you have strong feelings (negative or positive). Start by listing characteristics you have come to associate with this animal. Is it beautiful, swift, and elegant? Is it ferocious and menacing? Is it clumsy, awkward, or humorous to watch? Then focus sharply on *one* of these characteristics (such as its strength, its beauty, *or* its ferocity). Use concrete nouns and adjectives to develop your description and, if possible, include some figures of speech to make your writing more vivid and exciting.

The Wood-Pile

Robert Frost

Robert Frost (1874–1963) is perhaps the best known of all modern American poets. Because his poems use familiar language and deal with themes that seem simple, they are almost always included in collections of popular literature and are read the world over.

Frost spent most of his life in rural New Hampshire, where he gathered many of the natural images found in his work. Among his best-rememberd poems are "Mending Wall," "Home Burial," "The Road Not Taken," "Birches," and "Stopping by Woods on a Snowy Evening," all of which were inspired by his life in the New England countryside.

Frost won the Pulitzer prize for poetry in 1924, 1931, 1937, and again in 1943. But it wasn't until he read "The Gift Outright" at President Kennedy's inauguration in 1961 that he assumed the role of America's unofficial poet laureate.

Looking Ahead

1. As you read the poem, ask yourself if it reminds you of a walk you might have taken through a swamp, garden, wood, or other natural setting. Then pick out details in the poem that caused you to recollect that experience.
2. At first, Frost seems to be describing the "frozen swamp" as a lonely, lifeless place. After only a few lines, however, we learn that even in the dead of winter the wilderness shows signs of life. The most obvious of these is the small bird that the speaker stops to watch. Look for other signs as well.
3. In line 13, the speaker begins to wonder what the bird is thinking. He assumes that this little creature believes he wants to pluck a feather from its tail. At first, you might think the speaker is a bit eccentric. Then again, don't we all have a tendency to speculate about how others (whether human or animal) see us when they cross our path?
4. Although the poem is entitled "The Wood-Pile," it describes a great deal more than a cord of firewood. The wood pile itself is pictured against the larger, natural setting of the "frozen swamp" and all it contains. Unlike the swamp, the wood pile is a human creation, a product of civilization, even though it was cut from and has remained in nature. As such, it contrasts nicely with the wilderness and becomes the focus, or centerpiece, of the poem.
5. When wood burns, it mixes with oxygen in the air through a process called oxidation. The same thing occurs when wood goes through the natural process of decay, only much more slowly. This may help explain what Frost means in line 40, where he mentions the "slow smokeless burning of decay."

Vocabulary

clematis   A climbing vine found throughout eastern North America.
cord   A stack of firewood that measures $4 \times 4 \times 8$ feet.
lighted   Landed.
undeceived   Revealed the truth to.

Out walking in the frozen swamp one gray day,
I paused and said, "I will turn back from here.
No, I will go on farther—and we shall see."
The hard snow held me, save where now and then
One foot went through. The view was all in lines   5
Straight up and down of tall slim trees
Too much alike to mark or name a place by

So as to say for certain I was here
Or somewhere else: I was just far from home.
A small bird flew before me. He was careful   10
To put a tree between us when he lighted,
And say no word to tell me who he was
Who was so foolish as to think what *he* thought.
He thought that I was after him for a feather—
The white one in his tail; like one who takes   15
Everything said as personal to himself.
One flight out sideways would have undeceived him.
And then there was a pile of wood for which
I forgot him and let his little fear
Carry him off the way I might have gone,   20
Without so much as wishing him good-night.
He went behind it to make his last stand.
It was a cord of maple, cut and split
And piled—and measured, four by four by eight.
And not another like it could I see.   25
No runner tracks in this year's snow looped near it.
And it was older sure than this year's cutting,
Or even last year's or the year's before.
The wood was gray and the bark warping off it
And the pile somewhat sunken. Clematis   30
Had wound strings round and round it like a bundle.
What held it, though, on one side was a tree
Still growing, and on one a stake and prop,
These latter about to fall. I thought that only
Someone who lived in turning to fresh tasks   35
Could so forget his handiwork on which
He spent himself, the labor of his ax,
And leave it there far from a useful fireplace
To warm the frozen swamp as best it could
With the slow smokeless burning of decay.   40

Questions for Discussion

1. What are your impressions of the setting against which Frost describes the
   wood pile? What kind of day is it when the speaker enters the swamp?
   How would you describe the swamp?
2. In Looking Ahead you learned that the setting of the poem is the natural
   world, but the wood pile itself is a product of civilization. What details
   show that the wood pile is different from the natural environment?

3. Most authors rely on what they can see, smell, hear, feel or taste in order to describe a scene. In other words, they tell us about what's there. In "The Wood-Pile," however, Frost also relies on *what's not there* to tell us something; in line 26, he explains that "No runner tracks in this year's snow looped near" the wood pile. What does this statement add to his description of the scene?

4. A master of observation, Frost could look at a scene or object and draw important inferences (conclusions) about it that might have escaped other observers. In line 27, for instance, he explains that the wood pile was "older sure than this year's cutting." What details in the poem have led him to this conclusion?

5. Frost also assumes something about the person who cut and stacked the wood. What does he mean when he says in line 35 that the woodcutter "lived in turning to fresh tasks"?

Suggestions for Journal Entries

1. Jot down some details about an interesting object, plant, or animal you may have come upon on a walk through the woods, on a beach, in a park, or just along the street. Describe both the subject itself and the setting in which you found it.

2. As discussed above, Frost was able to infer something about the wood-cutter from his observation of the wood pile. Choose someone you know well and begin to jot down details about the home he lives in, the pets she owns, the clothes he wears, the car she drives, etc. Then draw an inference (or conclusion) from these details about your subject's personality, habits, or lifestyle. Explain this conclusion in a few short sentences in your journal.

Subway Station

Gilbert Highet

Gilbert Highet (1906–1978) came to the United States from Scotland in 1937 to teach Greek and Latin at Columbia University in New York City. A witty and urbane writer and speaker, he served as editor of the Book-of-the-Month Club and was chief book reviewer for *Harper's Magazine*. He also hosted *People, Places, and Books,* a weekly radio talk show, and published hundreds of essays on life in New York City.

What Highet describes in "Subway Station" is typical of the thousands of stations in New York's vast underground rail system. Another selection by Highet appears in Chapter 9.

Looking Ahead

1. The most important thing "Subway Station" shows us is Highet's ability to create a photograph in words by piling detail upon detail. For instance, he makes it a point to tell us that the "electric bulbs" were "meager"; then he adds that they were "unscreened, yellow, and coated with filth." Look for other examples of his ability to do this.
2. Highet is also famous for using figurative language, especially metaphors and similes. As you learned in the introduction to Section III, one of the most startling of these comes about midway in this selection, when he describes the "gloomy vaulting from which dingy paint was peeling off like scabs from an old wound." Look for and mark other examples of figurative language as you read this piece.
3. "Subway Station" mixes objective with subjective description. When Highet recalls various "advertisement posters on the walls," he remains objective. He does not explain whether he approves or disapproves of them, whether he finds them attractive or distasteful. When he tells us that "the floor was a nauseating dark brown," on the other hand, he is being subjective. Look for other places in which Highet is particularly subjective or objective.

Vocabulary

abominable   Disgusting, abhorrent.
congealed   Clotted.
defilement   Filth, dirt, object of disgust.
dubious   Unknown.
encrusted   Covered over, encased with a crusty layer.
laden   Covered with.
leprous   Relating to leprosy, a disease in which parts of the body begin to decay and the skin exhibits sores and severe scaling.
meager   Sparse, skimpy.
nauseating   Sickening.
obscenities   Indecent or offensive language.
perfunctory   Apathetic, without care.
relish   Enjoy.
vaulting   Arched or rounded ceiling.

Standing in a subway station, I began to appreciate the place—almost   1
to enjoy it. First of all, I looked at the lighting: a row of meager electric bulbs,

unscreened, yellow, and coated with filth, stretched toward the black mouth of the tunnel, as though it were a bolt hole in an abandoned coal mine. Then I lingered, with zest, on the walls and ceiling: lavatory tiles which had been white about fifty years ago, and were now encrusted with soot, coated with the remains of a dirty liquid which might be either atmospheric humidity mingled with smog or the result of a perfunctory attempt to clean them with cold water; and, above them, gloomy vaulting from which dingy paint was peeling off like scabs from an old wound, sick black paint leaving a leprous white undersurface. Beneath my feet, the floor was a nauseating dark brown with black stains upon it which might be stale oil or dry chewing gum or some worse defilement; it looked like the hallway of a condemned slum building. Then my eye traveled to the tracks, where two lines of glittering steel—the only positively clean object in the whole place—ran out of darkness into darkness about an unspeakable mass of congealed oil, puddles of dubious liquid, and a mishmash of old cigarette packets, mutilated and filthy newspapers, and the debris that filtered down from the street above through a barred grating in the roof. As I looked up toward the sunlight, I could see more debris sifting slowly downward, and making an abominable pattern in the slanting beam of dirt-laden sunlight. I was going on to relish more features of this unique scene: such as the advertisement posters on the walls—here a text from the Bible, there a half-naked girl, here a woman wearing a hat consisting of a hen sitting on a nest full of eggs, and there a pair of girl's legs walking up the keys of a cash register—all scribbled over with unknown names and well-known obscenities in black crayon and red lipstick; but then my train came in at last, I boarded it, and began to read. The experience was over for the time.

Questions for Discussion

1. In Looking Ahead you were asked to find examples of Highet's ability to pile detail upon detail to create a kind of verbal picture—a photograph in words—of the scene. What examples did you find?
2. What examples of figurative language, other than those mentioned in Looking Ahead, did you find?
3. Do you believe that Highet succeeded in conveying an accurate picture of what he saw? What overall feeling or impression of the station does he communicate to us?
4. Which of his concrete details contribute to this impression the most? Which nouns and adjectives have the strongest effect on you?
5. As you know, "Subway Station" contains both subjective and objective description. Where does Highet use subjective description (showing his personal feelings or emotional reactions)?

Suggestions for Journal Entries

1. Review your responses to item 1 of the Questions for Discussion. Then write a one-sentence description of a familiar object or place by gathering details (adjectives and nouns) that give the reader a verbal portrait of your subject. For instance, start with an ordinary piece of furniture—perhaps the desk or table you're working on right now—and then begin adding details until you have a list that looks something like this:

> The desk
> The wooden desk
> The large wooden desk
> The large, brown, wooden desk
> The large, brown, wooden desk covered with junk
> The large, brown, wooden desk covered with junk, which squats in the corner of my room
> The large, brown, wooden desk covered with junk, books and papers, which squats in the corner of my room

> Repeat this process, adding as many items as you can, until you've exhausted your mind's supply of nouns and adjectives. Then review your list. Can you make your descriptions even more specific and concrete? For instance, the above example might be revised to read:

> The four-foot-long, dark-brown, oak desk covered with my math book, an old dictionary with the cover ripped off, two chemistry test papers, today's French notes, a half-eaten bologna sandwich, and a can of diet cola.

2. Choose an object or place you know quite well and can describe easily. Start with a totally objective description; then write down your subjective reactions to it in a sentence or two. Repeat the process with three or four other places or things.

   Whenever possible, use a simile, metaphor, or other figure of speech to get your feelings across. For instance, describe the bedroom your brother has failed to clean out in two years as "his private garbage scow," or compare your home computer to an "electronic maze."

In the Jungle

Annie Dillard

Born in Pittsburgh in 1945, Annie Dillard worked at *Harper's Magazine* from 1973 to 1981 as a contributing editor. Before she was thirty, she won a Pulitzer prize for *Pilgrim at Tinker Creek*, a narrative about the Roanoke Valley of Virginia, where she once lived. She has also written a book of poetry entitled *Tickets for a Prayer Wheel*.

In 1982 she published *Teaching a Stone to Talk*, an anthology of essays, which includes "In the Jungle." In this essay, Dillard describes a jungle village she visited while traveling in Ecuador, South America.

Looking Ahead

1. While describing the jungle, the village, and the people, Dillard also takes time to tell us about several events that occurred during and even before her visit. In other words, she combines description with narration, two kinds of writing that work together naturally.
2. In addition to nouns, adjectives, and figures of speech, Dillard uses verbs to make her writing concrete and vivid. In paragraph 3, for instance, she writes that "the brown Napo River was rising, in all silence; it *coiled* up the sandy bank and *tangled* its foam in vines that *trailed* from the forest and roots that *looped* the shore." Keep a sharp lookout for other interesting, descriptive verbs as you read "In the Jungle."
3. In the previous selections, Frost, Highet, and Tennyson have appealed to our sense of sight when describing their subjects. Dillard includes other senses as well. Find places in this essay where she appeals to hearing, taste, and smell.
4. Ecuador is located on the western coast of South America between Colombia and Peru. The Andes Mountains dominate the landscape of Ecuador, but in the eastern portion are jungles through which flow tributaries of the Amazon, the world's second-longest river. The Napo is one of these tributaries, or "headwaters."
5. The official language of Ecuador is Spanish, but the Indians speak Quechua or Jarva. The predominant religion is Roman Catholic.
6. In paragraph 3, Dillard writes: "It was February, the middle of summer." That's not a misprint. When North America is experiencing winter, it's summer in South America.

Vocabulary

canopies   Coverings or kinds of roofs.

goiters   Swellings of the thyroid, a gland found in the neck.

Jesuit   An order of Roman Catholic priests.

illumined   Lit up.

impaled   Stuck upon.

muted   Quieted, muffled.

nightjar   A jungle bird that is active at night.

opaque   Not reflecting light, dull.

Orion   A constellation.

recorder   A musical instrument resembling a flute.

roil   To stir and become muddy.

swath   A patch.

thatch   Leaves, grasses, reeds, or other natural building materials used as roofing and
sometimes as siding.

uncanny   Strange, unexplainable.

wistful   Sweetly sad, melancholic.

Like any out-of-the-way place, the Napo River in the Ecuadorian jungle   1
seems real enough when you are there, even central. Out of the way of *what?*
I was sitting on a stump at the edge of a bankside palm-thatch village, in the
middle of the night, on the headwaters of the Amazon. Out of the way of
human life, tenderness, or the glance of heaven?

A nightjar in deep-leaved shadow called three long notes, and hushed.   2
The men with me talked softly in clumps: three North Americans, four Ec-
uadorians who were showing us the jungle. We were holding cool drinks and
idly watching a hand-sized tarantula seize moths that came to the lone bulb
on the generator shed beside us.

It was February, the middle of summer. Green fireflies spattered lights   3
across the air and illumined for seconds, now here, now there, the pale trunks
of enormous, solitary trees. Beneath us the brown Napo River was rising, in
all silence; it coiled up the sandy bank and tangled its foam in vines that
trailed from the forest and roots that looped the shore.

Each breath of night smelled sweet, more moistened and sweet than any   4
kitchen, or garden, or cradle. Each star in Orion seemed to tremble and stir
with my breath. All at once, in the thatch house across the clearing behind us,
one of the village's Jesuit priests began playing an alto recorder, playing a
wordless song, lyric, in a minor key, that twined over the village clearing, that
caught in the big trees' canopies, muted our talk on the bankside, and wandered over the river, dissolving downstream.

This will do, I thought. This will do, for a weekend, or a season, or a   5
home.

Later that night I loosed my hair from its braids and combed it 6
smooth—not for myself, but so the village girls could play with it in the
morning.

We had disembarked at the village that afternoon, and I had slumped 7
on some shaded steps, wishing I knew some Spanish or some Quechua so
I could speak with the ring of little girls who were alternately staring at me
and smiling at their toes. I spoke anyway, and fooled with my hair, which
they were obviously dying to get their hands on, and laughed, and soon
they were all braiding my hair, all five of them, all fifty fingers, all my hair,
even my bangs. And then they took it apart and did it again, laughing, and
teaching me Spanish nouns, and meeting my eyes and each other's with
open delight, while their small brothers in blue jeans climbed down from
the trees and began kicking a volleyball around with one of the North
American men.

Now, as I combed my hair in the little tent, another of the men, a free- 8
lance writer from Manhattan, was talking quietly. He was telling us the tale
of his life, describing his work in Hollywood, his apartment in Manhattan, his
house in Paris. . . . "It makes me wonder," he said, "what I'm doing in a tent
under a tree in the village of Pompeya, on the Napo River, in the jungle of
Ecuador." After a pause he added, "It makes me wonder why I'm going *back*."

The point of going somewhere like the Napo River in Ecuador is not to 9
see the most spectacular anything. It is simply to see what is there.

What is there is interesting. The Napo River itself is wide (I mean wider 10
than the Mississippi at Davenport) and brown, opaque and smeared with floating foam and logs and branches from the jungle. White egrets hunch on shoreline deadfalls and parrots in flocks dart in and out of the light. Under the
water in the river, unseen, are anacondas—which are reputed to take a few
village toddlers every year—and water boas, stingrays, crocodiles, manatees,
and sweet-meated fish.

Low water bares gray strips of sandbar on which the natives build tiny 11
palm-thatch shelters, arched, the size of pup tents, for overnight fishing trips.
You see these extraordinarily clean people (who bathe twice a day in the river,
and whose straight black hair is always freshly washed) paddling down the
river in dugout canoes, hugging the banks.

Some of the Indians of this region, earlier in the century, used to sleep 12
naked in hammocks. The nights are cold. Gordon MacCreach, an American
explorer in these Amazon tributaries, reported that he was startled to hear the
Indians get up at three in the morning. He was even more startled, night after
night, to hear them walk down to the river slowly, half asleep, and bathe in
the water. Only later did he learn what they were doing: they were getting
warm. The cold woke them; they warmed their skins in the river, which was
always ninety degrees; then they returned to their hammocks and slept through
the rest of the night.

The riverbanks are low, and from the river you see an unbroken wall 13 of dark forest in every direction, from the Andes to the Atlantic. You get a taste for looking at trees: trees hung with the swinging nests of yellow troupials, trees from which ant nests the size of grain sacks hang like black goiters, trees from which seven-colored tanagers flutter, coral trees, teak, balsa and breadfruit, enormous emergent silk-cotton trees, and the pale-barked *samona* palms.

When you are inside the jungle, away from the river, the trees vault out 14 of sight. It is hard to remember to look up the long trunks and see the fans, strips, fronds, and sprays of glossy leaves....Butterflies, iridescent blue, striped, or clear-winged, thread the jungle paths at eye level. And at your feet is a swath of ants bearing triangular bits of green leaf. The ants with their leaves look like a wide fleet of sailing dinghies—but they don't quit. In either direction they wobble over the jungle floor as far as the eye can see.

Long lakes shine in the jungle. We traveled one of these in dugout ca- 15 noes, canoes with two inches of freeboard, canoes paddled with machete-hewn oars chopped from buttresses of silk-cotton trees, or poled in the shallows with peeled cane or bamboo. Our part-Indian guide had cleared the path to the lake the day before; when we walked the path we saw where he had impaled the lopped head of a boa, open-mouthed, on a pointed stick by the canoes, for decoration.

The lake and river waters are as opaque as rain-forest leaves; they are 16 veils, blinds, painted screens. You see things only by their effects. I saw the shoreline water roil and the sawgrass heave above a thrashing *paichi*, an enormous black fish of these waters; one had been caught the previous week weighing 430 pounds. Piranha fish live in the lakes, and electric eels. I dangled my fingers in the water, figuring it would be worth it.

We would eat chicken that night in the village, and rice, yucca, onions, 17 beets and heaps of fruit. The sun would ring down, pulling darkness after it like a curtain. Twilight is short, and the unseen birds of twilight wistful, uncanny, catching the heart. The two nuns in their dazzling white habits— the beautiful-boned young nun and the warm-faced old—would glide to the open cane-and-thatch schoolroom in darkness, and start the children singing. The children would sing in piping Spanish, high-pitched and pure; they would sing "Nearer My God to Thee" in Quechua, very fast. (To reciprocate, we sang for them "Old MacDonald Had a Farm"; I thought they might recognize the animal sounds. Of course they thought we were out of our minds.) As the children became excited by their own singing, they left their log benches and swarmed around the nuns, hopping, smiling at us, everyone smiling, the nuns' faces bursting in their cowls, and the clear-voiced children still singing, and the palm-leafed roofing stirred.

The Napo River: it is not out of the way. It is in the way, catching 18 sunlight the way a cup catches poured water; it is a bowl of sweet air, a basin of greenness, and of grace, and, it would seem, of peace.

Questions for Discussion

1. Dillard mentions some terms that may be unfamiliar to you. From the way she uses them, take a guess at the meaning of "egrets," "anacondas," "manatees," "troupials," "tanagers," and "machete."
2. The author says little about how the Indians looked, but she does explain what they did. In what paragraphs does she tell us about the natives of Pompeya, and what do these anecdotes reveal about them?
3. Why does Dillard bother to mention in paragraph 12 that "the Indians get up at three in the morning" to bathe in the river? Does this help her describe the jungle?
4. Besides the Indians, what inhabitants of the village does Dillard mention? What is her opinion of these other people?
5. Which paragraph in this selection do you find most descriptive? Identify nouns, adjectives, and figures of speech that make it work so well.
6. Where in the essay does Dillard use proper nouns? Pick out a few examples of such words and explain why their inclusion makes "In the Jungle" more effective.
7. As noted earlier, Dillard makes excellent use of descriptive verbs in paragraph 3. Another example is in paragraph 14, where she writes that "inside the jungle...the trees *vault* out of sight." Where else in her essay have you found such descriptive verbs?
8. Overall, Dillard sees the jungle as a very beautiful and pleasant place, but she also includes details that might lead us to the opposite conclusion. Identify such details, and explain what they reveal.
9. Dillard relies heavily on objective description, but she uses subjective description as well. In what paragraphs are her feelings about the jungle and its people most apparent?

Suggestions for Journal Entries

1. Think of a natural setting (a park, forest, garden, seashore, etc.) that you visited recently, and list its most pleasant (or unpleasant) aspects. Then, in one or two sentences, sum up your overall reaction to (or impression of) the place.
2. Dillard isn't very specific about what the Indians of Pompeya look like, but she gives us enough details to infer certain things about them. Given the climate, for instance, they probably wear little clothing. Try to describe what these people look like from what the author tells us about them. If you run into trouble, use your imagination and make up details that you think might apply.

Dawn Watch

John Ciardi

A splendid poet, critic, scholar, and translator of Dante's *Divine Comedy*, John Ciardi (1916–1986) was one of the warmest and most personable of all contemporary American writers. Ciardi's subjects are taken from everyday life, and his works, like their author, are down to earth and easy to approach. His poems and essays are rich with the kinds of detail we see around us all the time, but they give us a clearer, deeper, and more beautiful vision of the world than we had before we read them.

"Dawn Watch" is a richly detailed account of one of the most common events we know: sunrise.

Looking Ahead

1. One reason why dawn is so special to Ciardi is that certain sights and sounds can be seen and heard only at this time of the day. One such sound comes from the brook he mentions in paragraph 2. Identify others.
2. Like Dillard, Ciardi makes use of narration to describe his subject. That is, besides describing the sights and sounds of dawn, he also shows what typically happens during this time.
3. Ciardi's thesis appears at the very beginning: "Unless a man is up for the dawn and for the half hour or so of first light, he has missed the best of the day." As you read "Dawn Watch," notice how almost every detail helps prove this statement.

Vocabulary

bedraggled   Limp, tired.
braggarts   People who enjoy boasting about themselves.
exhalation   Breath, vapor, exhaling.
foliage   The leaves of a plant.
grackles   A kind of blackbird.
inured   Hardened.
pincer   Pinch.
thickets   Thick bushes or shrubs.
wire services   Organizations that provide national and local news stories to newspapers across the country.

Unless a man is up for the dawn and for the half hour or so of first light, he has missed the best of the day.

1

The traffic has just started, not yet a roar and a stink. One car at a time 2
goes by, the tires humming almost like the sound of a brook a half mile down
in the crease of a mountain I know—a sound that carries not because it is loud
but because everything else is still.

It isn't exactly a mist that hangs in the thickets but more nearly the 3
ghost of a mist—a phenomenon like side vision. Look hard and it isn't there,
but glance without focusing and something registers, an exhalation that will
be gone three minutes after the sun comes over the treetops.

The lawns shine with a dew not exactly dew. There is a rabbit bobbing 4
about on the lawn and then freezing. If it were truly a dew, his tracks would
shine black on the grass, and he leaves no visible track. Yet, there is something on the grass that makes it glow a depth of green it will not show again
all day. Or is that something in the dawn air?

Our cardinals know what time it is. They drop pure tones from the 5
hemlock tops. The black gang of grackles that makes a slum of the pine oak
also knows the time but can only grate at it. They sound like a convention of
broken universal joints grating uphill. The grackles creak and squeak, and the
cardinals form tones that only occasionally sound through the noise. I scatter
sunflower seeds by the birdbath for the cardinals and hope the grackles won't
find them.

My neighbor's tomcat comes across the lawn, probably on his way home 6
from passion, or only acting as if he had had a big night. I suspect him of being
one of those poolroom braggarts who can't get next to a girl but who likes to
let on that he is a hot stud. This one is too can-fed and too lazy to hunt for
anything. Here he comes now, ignoring the rabbit. And there he goes.

As soon as he has hopped the fence, I let my dog out. The dog charges 7
the rabbit, watches it jump the fence, shakes himself in a self-satisfied way,
then trots dutifully into the thicket for his morning service, stopping to sniff
everything on the way back.

There is an old mountain laurel on the island of the driveway turn- 8
around. From somewhere on the wind a white morning-glory rooted next to
it and has climbed it. Now the laurel is woven full of white bells tinged pink
by the first rays through the not quite mist. Only in earliest morning can they
be seen. Come out two hours from now and there will be no morning-glories.

Dawn, too, is the hour of a weed I know only as day flower—a bright 9
blue button that closes in full sunlight. I have weeded bales of it out of my
flower beds, its one daytime virtue being the shallowness of its root system
that allows it to be pulled out effortlessly in great handfuls. Yet, now it shines.
Had it a few more hours of such shining in its cycle, I would cultivate it as
a ground cover, but dawn is its one hour, and a garden is for whole days.

There is another blue morning weed whose name I do not know. This 10
one grows from a bulb to pulpy stems and a bedraggled daytime sprawl. Only
a shovel will dig it out. Try weeding it by hand and the stems will break off

to be replaced by new ones and to sprawl over the chosen plants in the flower bed. Yet, now and for another hour it outshines its betters, its flowers about the size of a quarter and paler than those of the day flower but somehow more brilliant, perhaps because of the contrast of its paler foliage.

And now the sun is slanting in full. It is bright enough to make the 11 leaves of the Japanese red maple seem a transparent red bronze when the tree is between me and the light. There must be others, but this is the only tree I know whose leaves let the sun through in this way—except, that is, when the fall colors start. Aspen leaves, when they first yellow and before they dry, are transparent in this way. I tell myself it must have something to do with the red-yellow range of the spectrum. Green takes sunlight and holds it, but red and yellow let it through.

The damned crabgrass is wrestling with the zinnias, and I stop to weed 12 it out. The stuff weaves too close to the zinnias to make the iron claw usable. And it won't do to pull at the stalks. Crabgrass (at least in a mulched bed) can be weeded only with dirty fingers. Thumb and forefinger have to pincer into the dirt and grab the root-center. Weeding, of course, is an illusion of hope. Pulling out the root only stirs the soil and brings new crabgrass seeds into germinating position. Take a walk around the block and a new clump will have sprouted by the time you get back. But I am not ready to walk around the block. I fill a small basket with the plucked clumps, and for the instant I look at them, the zinnias are weedless.

Don't look back. I dump the weeds in the thicket where they will be 13 smothered by the grass clippings I will pile on at the next cutting. On the way back I see the cardinals come down for the sunflower seeds, and the jays join them, and then the grackles start ganging in, gate-crashing the buffet and clattering all over it. The dog stops chewing his rawhide and makes a dash into the puddle of birds, which splashes away from him.

I hear a brake-squeak I have been waiting for and know the paper has 14 arrived. As usual, the news turns out to be another disaster count. The function of the wire services is to bring us tragedies faster than we can pity. In the end we shall all be inured, numb, and ready for emotionless programming. I sit on the patio and read until the sun grows too bright on the page. The cardinals have stopped singing, and the grackles have flown off. It's the end of birdsong again.

Then suddenly—better than song for its instant—a hummingbird the 15 color of green crushed velvet hovers in the throat of my favorite lily, a lovely high-bloomer I got the bulbs for but not the name. The lily is a crest of white horns with red dots and red velvet tongues along the insides of the petals and with an odor that drowns the patio. The hummingbird darts in and out of each horn in turn, then hovers an instant, and disappears.

Even without the sun, I have had enough of the paper. I'll take that 16 hummingbird as my news for this dawn. It is over now. I smoke one more cigarette too many and decide that, if I go to bed now, no one in the family need know I have stayed up for it again. Why do they insist on shaking their heads when they find me still up for breakfast, after having scribbled through the dark hours? They always do. They seem compelled to express pity for an old loony who can't find his own way to bed. Why won't they understand that this is the one hour of any day that must not be missed, as it is the one hour I couldn't imagine getting up for, though I can still get to it by staying up? It makes sense to me. There comes a time when the windows lighten and the twittering starts. I look up and know it's time to leave the papers in their mess. I could slip quietly into bed and avoid the family's headshakes, but this stroll-around first hour is too good to miss. Even my dog, still sniffing and circling, knows what hour this is.

Come on, boy. It's time to go in. The rabbit won't come back till to- 17 morrow, and the birds have work to do. The dawn's over. It's time to call it a day.

Questions for Discussion

1. Ciardi makes it a point to record the sounds as well as the sights of dawn. What are some of these sounds?
2. What does Ciardi mean by "There is a rabbit bobbing about on the lawn and then *freezing*"?
3. "Weeding is an illusion of hope," the author tells us. What details does he use to explain this remark?
4. Ciardi is a master at using nouns and adjectives that are concrete and specific. Which paragraph(s) in this essay contain(s) the most descriptive details?
5. In paragraph 15, Ciardi creates a snapshot in words when he writes that "better than song for its instant—a hummingbird the color of green crushed velvet hovers in the throat of my favorite lily." What is he describing here?
6. What is his family's attitude toward his staying up to meet the dawn? Explain what he means when he suggests that he and his dog "call it a day."

Suggestions for Journal Entries

1. Describe the sounds of morning, afternoon, or evening in a park, on campus, in your backyard, in your kitchen, or anywhere else you choose. Focus on three or four of the sounds you like best and re-create them for your reader. In doing so, you might want to use figures of speech—metaphors and similes. An excellent example of a simile can be found in paragraph 5, where the grackles "sound like a convention of broken universal joints grating uphill."
2. What is the best part of the day for you—dawn, sundown, late afternoon? Jot down a few details about the things that make it special. Then put these

details into a short paragraph describing this time and explaining why it is your favorite part of the day.

3. As mentioned in Questions for Discussion, Ciardi creates a snapshot in words when he describes a hummingbird hovering in his favorite lily. Look around you. Wherever you are, at whatever time of day, you will come upon brief but beautiful moments like that one. Remember these scenes, and create your own verbal snapshot by writing one or two sentences about each in your journal.

SUGGESTIONS FOR WRITING

1. In this chapter, you read a very vivid description of an animal, Tennyson's "Eagle." If you completed a journal entry for this selection, you've probably already gathered detail that you can use in a longer piece.

   Write an essay in which you continue to describe the animal you began writing about in your journal. Provide the reader with as many details as you can to describe its physical appearance, but don't be afraid to reveal your feelings (subjective description) about this creature. Appeal to as many of the reader's senses as you can, and use figures of speech whenever possible.

2. Like Robert Frost, you've probably come upon an interesting sight during a walk through the woods, or you may have seen a strange house, building, or storefront as you strolled along the streets of your hometown. Describe this place or thing in a full-length essay. Reveal your subjective reactions to it if you feel that they're appropriate.

3. Robert Frost, Annie Dillard, and John Ciardi draw upon nature for inspiration. Look over the journal entries you made in response to the works of these writers. You've probably already begun jotting down details and ideas that might serve as the start of a longer essay describing a wood, beach, park, garden or backyard, desert, mountainside, or even a jungle. Expand your notes into a full-length essay. Provide many more concrete details, and describe more natural objects or features than you did in your journal.

4. In "Subway Station," Highet describes a public place both subjectively and objectively. Think about a public place you visit often, such as a bus or train station, the post office, your church, or your school gymnasium. Following Highet's lead, describe the place with specific, concrete details that show your readers what it looks, sounds, smells, and, if possible, feels like. Then explain the emotions you feel when you visit this place—your emotional or subjective response to it.

5. Ciardi's essay is unique among those found in this chapter because it describes a time as well as a place or object. In response to Suggestions for

Journal Entries following "Dawn Watch," you may have already begun to describe the "sounds" of a place during a particular time of day or night. Continue by describing the sounds one might hear at other times of the day as well. Another suggestion is to focus on only one time and describe the sights, smells *and sounds* one might experience during that part of the day.

Chapter 9

Describing People

What makes describing people different from describing places and things? The writer's purpose. Writers describe wood piles, gardens at dawn, snow-covered hillsides, skyscrapers, or dirty subway stations because they are impressed or moved by what they see, hear, etc. They describe human beings because they are interested in their behavior and values as well as their looks and the sounds of their voices. Of course, many writers start by describing physical appearance—what's on the outside. But they usually wind up talking about their subjects' personalities—what's on the inside.

All of the authors represented in this chapter use concrete and specific details (nouns and adjectives) to describe the physical characteristics of their subjects. This is always a good way to begin. You can start off by explaining something about your subjects' physical appearance, the clothes they wear, the sound of their voices, the language they use, or simply the way they walk. Such description might also help you introduce your subjects' personalities to your readers, for someone's physical appearance can reveal a great deal about what he or she is like inside.

You can also communicate a great deal about the people you're describing by telling your reader what you've heard about them from others and even what you've heard them say about themselves; such information is usually conveyed through dialogue (quoted material). Recalling anecdotes about your subjects is still another good way to convey important information about them. Finally, some authors comment directly on their subjects' personalities or use figurative language to make their descriptions more lively and appealing. Remember such techniques when you gather and communicate important information about your subjects.

DESCRIBING WHAT YOUR SUBJECT LOOKS LIKE

Physical appearance can show a great deal about a person's character, and writers don't hesitate to use outward details as signs or symbols of what's

188

inside. For instance, how often have you heard people mention deep-set, shifty eyes or a sinister smile when describing a villain? Aren't heavy people often described as jolly? And often, aren't the clothes people wear or the way the comb their hair seen (fairly or unfairly) as a sign of their character?

Russell Baker makes use of physical appearance as a sign of character when, in the first chapter of *Growing Up* (a selection in this chapter), he describes the inner determination and spiritual fierceness that he saw in his mother's face:

> She had always been a small woman—short, light-boned, delicately structured—but now, under the white hospital sheet, she was becoming tiny. I thought of a doll with huge, fierce eyes. There had always been a fierceness in her. It showed in that angry, challenging thrust of the chin when she issued an opinion, and a great one she had always been for issuing opinions.

EXPLAINING WHAT OTHERS SAY ABOUT YOUR SUBJECT

One of the quickest ways to learn about someone is to ask people who know this individual to tell you about his or her personality, lifestyle, morals, disposition, etc. Often, authors use dialogue or quotes from other people to reveal something important about their subject's character. In "Crazy Mary," student Sharon Robertson combines physical description (concrete details) with information she learned from other people (dialogue) to create a memorable and disturbing portrait of an unfortunate woman she once knew:

> She was a middle-aged woman, short and slightly heavy, with jet-black hair and solemn blue eyes that were bloodshot and glassy. She always looked distant, as if her mind were in another place and time, and her face lonely and sad. We called her "Crazy Mary."
>
> Mary came to the diner that I worked in twice a week. She would sit at the counter with a scowl on her face and drink her coffee and smoke cigarettes. The only time she looked happy was when an old song would come on the radio. Then Mary would close her eyes, shine a big tobacco-stained smile, and sway back and forth to the music.
>
> One day an elderly couple came in for dinner. They were watching Mary over their menus and whispering. I went over to their table and asked if they knew who she was. The old man replied, "Aw, dat's just old Mary. She's loonier than a June bug, but she ain't nutten to be afraid of. A few years back, her house caught fire and her old man and her kids got kilt. She ain't been right since."
>
> After hearing this, it was easy to understand her odd behavior.

Other people can make good sources of information. We know from experience, however, that what others say about a person is often inaccurate, and how they react to special kinds of people is sometimes very unfair. For example, consider two of the selections in this chapter: At the end of Edwin Arlington Robinson's "Richard Cory" we learn that Cory was certainly not as happy a man as the townspeople believed, a revelation that is important to understanding his character *and* theirs. And in Gilbert Highet's "Diogenes" the townspeople call the philosopher Diogenes a madman, but the author is quick to point out that his approach to life is far more sane than theirs.

INCLUDING ANECDOTES ABOUT YOUR SUBJECT

An anecdote can help you highlight and illustrate one or more important characteristics of the person you're describing. For instance, in Sandburg's essay (a selection in this chapter), Lincoln's sensitivity and "natural grace" are demonstrated in the story of his expression of grief at a friend's funeral.

Enjoy reading the poem and essays that follow. Each contains examples of the practices discussed above, and each provides additional hints about how to make your writing stronger and more interesting.

Richard Cory

Edwin Arlington Robinson

Born in Gardiner, Maine, Edwin Arlington Robinson (1869–1935) wrote a number of poems that are psychological portraits of people who in some respects resemble characters found in a typical New England, if not typical American, town of his time. Many of his works reveal a pessimistic outlook on life, the result of a troubled family environment.

In 1922 his *Collected Poems* won him a Pulitzer prize, but it is for his earlier work, like "Richard Cory," that Robinson has remained popular. In this poem he created one of the saddest and most memorable characters in literature. The same is true of "Miniver Cheevy," a companion piece with a similar theme. Both poems first appeared in a collection called *Children of the Night* (1897).

Looking Ahead

Robinson makes sure to draw a distinction between Richard Cory and everyone else in town. Look for this distinction as you read the poem.

Vocabulary

arrayed   Adorned, dressed elegantly.
fluttered   Ruffled.
grace   A pleasing quality, charm, refinement.

Whenever Richard Cory went down town,
We people on the pavement looked at him:
He was a gentleman from sole to crown,
Clean favored, and imperially slim.

And he was always quietly arrayed,   5
And he was always human when he talked;
But still he fluttered pulses when he said,
"Good-morning," and he glittered when he walked.

And he was rich—yes, richer than a king—
And admirably schooled in every grace: 10
In fine, we thought that he was everything
To make us wish that we were in his place.

So on we worked, and waited for the light,
And went without the meat, and cursed the bread;

And Richard Cory, one calm summer night,   15
Went home and put a bullet through his head.

Questions for Discussion

1. The details used to describe Richard Cory have been chosen carefully. What do words like "crown," "imperially," "arrayed," "glittered," and "grace" tell us about him?
2. What do the townspeople think of Cory? Why do their pulses flutter every time they see him? What do we learn about the townspeople in lines 13 and 14?
3. The townspeople were obviously wrong about Cory. He wasn't "everything / To make us wish that we were in his place." What was he missing?
4. We can learn a lot about someone from his or her behavior. What do Richard Cory's actions tell us about his personality?
5. One of the themes (or main ideas) in this poem is that appearances are deceiving. How does Robinson make this clear?

Suggestions for Journal Entries

1. Robinson doesn't give us a great deal of detail about Cory's physical appearance, except to say that he was well dressed and thin. Using your imagination, make up some details that describe how you think Cory looked.
2. Have you ever met anyone you'd consider a tragic figure? Describe this person briefly, and explain why you find the person tragic.

From *Growing Up*

Russell Baker

Born in a small town in the Virginia countryside, Russell Baker spent most of his boyhood in a suburb of Newark, New Jersey. Later, his family moved to Baltimore, where he attended Johns Hopkins University and began his career as a reporter for the *Baltimore Sun*. For years, he wrote a world-famous syndicated column called the "Observer," for which he won his first Pulitzer prize in 1979. He received a second Pulitzer prize in 1983 for *Growing Up*, his best-selling autobiography.

Looking Ahead

1. While reading this description of the author's mother, ask yourself if she reminds you of any older person, male or female, you know well—perhaps a grandparent or elderly neighbor. If so, what are the similarities? Make notes in the margins; they'll come in handy when you write your journal entries.
2. Baker provides little physical description of his mother; rather, he portrays her soul—her internal, emotional characteristics. So don't expect a lot of details about the color of her eyes or the way she combed her hair.
3. Baker *does* tell us about events in his mother's life that reveal the kind of person she was and the kind of life she led. Earlier in this chapter, we discussed the fact that writers often describe people's personalities by recalling anecdotes—brief, interesting stories from their lives. Try to pick out such stories and determine what they reveal about the author's mother as you read this selection.
4. Guy Fawkes, to whom Mrs. Baker refers, was one of the leaders of the Gunpowder Plot, a conspiracy in 1605 to blow up the Houses of Parliament and bring back a Catholic king to Protestant England. The plot failed, and the conspirators were executed. The English now celebrate Guy Fawkes Day every November 5.

Vocabulary

catastrophically Completely and tragically, disastrously.
debris Remains, rubble.
formidable Strong, difficult to overcome or defeat.
inconceivable Not able to be thought of, unbelievable.
interrogators Questioners.
libertine Someone without morals, interested only in his or her own physical pleasure.
slugabed Lazy person, someone who likes to oversleep.
wrest To pull.

At the age of eighty my mother had her last bad fall, and after that her mind wandered free through time. Some days she went to weddings and funerals that had taken place half a century earlier. On others she presided over family dinners cooked on Sunday afternoons for children who were now gray with age. Through all this she lay in bed but moved across time, traveling among the dead decades with a speed and ease beyond the gift of physical science.   1

"Where's Russell?" she asked one day when I came to visit at the nursing home.   2

"I'm Russell," I said.   3

She gazed at this improbably overgrown figure out of an inconceivable   4
future and promptly dismissed it.

"Russell's only this big," she said, holding her hand, palm down, two   5
feet from the floor. That day she was a young country wife with chickens in
the backyard and a view of hazy blue Virginia mountains behind the apple
orchard, and I was a stranger old enough to be her father.

Early one morning she phoned me in New York. "Are you coming to   6
my funeral today?" she asked.

It was an awkward question with which to be awakened. "What are you   7
talking about, for God's sake?" was the best reply I could manage.

"I'm being buried today," she declared briskly, as though announcing   8
an important social event.

"I'll phone you back," I said and hung up, and when I did phone back she   9
was all right, although she wasn't all right, of course, and we all knew she wasn't.

She had always been a small woman—short, light-boned, delicately struc-   10
tured—but now, under the white hospital sheet, she was becoming tiny. I
thought of a doll with huge, fierce eyes. There had always been a fierceness
in her. It showed in that angry, challenging thrust of the chin when she issued
an opinion, and a great one she had always been for issuing opinions.

"I tell people exactly what's on my mind," she had been fond of boast-   11
ing. "I tell them what I think, whether they like it or not." Often they had
not liked it. She could be sarcastic to people in whom she detected evidence
of the ignoramus or the fool.

"It's not always good policy to tell people exactly what's on your mind,"   12
I used to caution her.

"If they don't like it, that's too bad," was her customary reply, "because   13
that's the way I am."

And so she was. A formidable woman. Determined to speak her mind,   14
determined to have her way, determined to bend those who opposed her. In
that time when I had known her best, my mother had hurled herself at life
with chin thrust forward, eyes blazing, and an energy that made her seem
always on the run.

She ran after squawking chickens, an axe in her hand, determined on   15
a beheading that would put dinner in the pot. She ran when she made the
beds, ran when she set the table. One Thanksgiving she burned herself badly
when, running up from the cellar oven with the ceremonial turkey, she tripped
on the stairs and tumbled back down, ending at the bottom in the debris of
giblets, hot gravy, and battered turkey. Life was combat, and victory was not
to the lazy, the timid, the slugabed, the drugstore cowboy, the libertine, the
mushmouth afraid to tell people exactly what was on his mind whether people
liked it or not. She ran.

But now the running was over. For a time I could not accept the in-   16 evitable. As I sat by her bed, my impulse was to argue her back to reality. On my first visit to the hospital in Baltimore, she asked who I was.

"Russell," I said.   17

"Russell's way out west," she advised me.   18

"No, I'm right here."   19

"Guess where I came from today?" was her response.   20

"Where?"   21

"All the way from New Jersey."   22

"When?"   23

"Tonight."   24

"No, you've been in the hospital for three days," I insisted.   25

"I suggest the thing to do is calm down a little bit," she replied. "Go 26 over to the house and shut the door."

Now she was years deep into the past, living in the neighborhood where 27 she had settled forty years earlier, and she had just been talking with Mrs. Hoffman, a neighbor across the street.

"It's like Mrs. Hoffman said today: The children always wander back 28 to where they came from," she remarked.

"Mrs. Hoffman has been dead for fifteen years."   29

"Russ got married today," she replied.   30

"I got married in 1950," I said, which was the fact.   31

"The house is unlocked," she said.   32

So it went until a doctor came by to give one of those oral quizzes that 33 medical men apply in such cases. She failed catastrophically, giving wrong answers or none at all to "What day is this?" "Do you know where you are?" "How old are you?" and so on. Then, a surprise.

"When is your birthday?" he asked.   34

"November 5, 1897," she said. Correct. Absolutely correct.   35

"How do you remember that?" the doctor asked.   36

"Because I was born on Guy Fawkes Day," she said.   37

"Guy Fawkes?" asked the doctor. "Who is Guy Fawkes?"   38

She replied with a rhyme I had heard her recite time and again over the 39 years when the subject of her birth date arose:

"Please to remember the Fifth of November,
Gunpowder treason and plot.
I see no reason why gunpowder treason
Should ever be forgot."

Then she glared at this young doctor so ill informed about Guy Fawkes' 40 failed scheme to blow King James off his throne with barrels of gunpowder in 1605. She had been a schoolteacher, after all, and knew how to glare at a dolt. "You may know a lot about medicine, but you obviously don't know any history," she said. Having told him exactly what was on her mind, she left us again.

The doctors diagnosed a hopeless senility. Not unusual, they said. "Hard- 41 ening of the arteries" was the explanation for laymen. I thought it was more complicated than that. For ten years or more the ferocity with which she had once attacked life had been turning to a rage against the weakness, the boredom, and the absence of love that too much age had brought her. Now, after the last bad fall, she seemed to have broken chains that imprisoned her in a life she had come to hate and to return to a time inhabited by people who loved her, a time in which she was needed. Gradually I understood. It was the first time in years I had seen her happy.

She had written a letter three years earlier which explained more than 42 "hardening of the arteries." I had gone down from New York to Baltimore, where she lived, for one of my infrequent visits and, afterwards, had written her with some banal advice to look for the silver lining, to count her blessings instead of burdening others with her miseries.

She wrote back in an unusually cheery vein intended to demonstrate, I 43 suppose, that she was mending her ways. She was never a woman to apologize, but for one moment with the pen in her hand she came very close. Referring to my visit, she wrote: "If I seemed unhappy to you at times—" Here she drew back, reconsidered, and said something quite different:

"If I seemed unhappy to you at times, I am, but there's really nothing 44 anyone can do about it, because I'm just so very tired and lonely that I'll just go to sleep and forget it." She was then seventy-eight.

Now, three years later, after the last bad fall, she had managed to forget 45 the fatigue and loneliness and, in these free-wheeling excursions back through time, to recapture happiness. I soon stopped trying to wrest her back to what I considered the real world and tried to travel along with her on those fantastic swoops into the past. One day when I arrived at her bedside she was radiant.

"Feeling good today," I said.   46

"Why shouldn't I feel good?" she asked. "Papa's going to take me up 47 to Baltimore on the boat today."

At that moment she was a young girl standing on a wharf at Merry 48 Point, Virginia, waiting for the Chesapeake Bay steamer with her father, who had been dead sixty-one years. William Howard Taft was in the White House, Europe still drowsed in the dusk of the great century of peace, America was a young country, and the future stretched before it in beams of crystal sunlight. "The greatest country on God's green earth," her father might have said, if I had been able to step into my mother's time machine and join him on the wharf with the satchels packed for Baltimore.

I could imagine her there quite clearly. She was wearing a blue dress 49 with big puffy sleeves and long black stockings. There was a ribbon in her hair and a big bow tied on the side of her head. There had been a childhood photograph in her bedroom which showed all this, although the colors of course had been added years later by a restorer who tinted the picture.

After her father, my grandfather, I could only guess, and indeed, about 50 the girl on the wharf with the bow in her hair, I was merely sentimentalizing. Of my mother's childhood and her people, of their time and place, I knew very little. A world had lived and died, and though it was part of my blood and bone I knew little more about it than I knew of the world of the pharaohs. It was useless now to ask for help from my mother. The orbits of her mind rarely touched present interrogators for more than a moment.

Questions for Discussion

1. What does Baker mean in paragraph 1 when he tells us that his mother's mind "wandered free through time"? What examples of such wanderings does he provide later in this selection?
2. Explain what Baker means in paragraph 41 by the "ferocity" with which his mother "had once attacked life."
3. Baker gives us only a few brief details about his mother's physical appearance. What are they?
4. How does Baker's use of conversation help him describe his mother? What characteristics do her own words reveal about her?
5. In what ways does Baker's recollection of his mother's past add to the description?
6. Why does Baker include sections of a letter that his mother wrote him shortly before she died? What does this letter tell us about her?

Suggestions for Journal Entries

1. Would you describe yourself as a "formidable" person? Or are you a gentler, quieter type? Think back to an important, emotion-filled event in your life that revealed something very basic about your personality. Write a few paragraphs in your journal about what happened—but instead of just telling a story, *describe* the kind of person you are. Therefore, make sure to show and explain what your involvement in the event revealed about you.
2. Look over the notes you made in response to item 1 of Looking Ahead. Does Baker's description of his mother bring to mind someone you know well? If so, jot down some general comments about this individual's appearance and personality. In what way is she (or he) like Baker's mother?
3. Besides describing the author's mother, this selection tells us a great deal about his feelings for her and about the relationship they shared. Briefly, how would you describe the relationship you have with an older member of your family? What goes through your head when you think about his or her growing older?

Abraham Lincoln

Carl Sandburg

One of America's best-loved poets and biographers, Carl Sandburg (1878–1967) had a deep respect for common folk, and he filled his work with images from their simple and sometimes tragic lives. He is remembered chiefly for *Corn Huskers* (1918) and for *The People, Yes* (1936), a collection of poems published during the great depression. He is also known for his six-volume biography of Abraham Lincoln, for which he won one of his three Pulitzer prizes.

The following excerpt describes Lincoln at age thirty-seven, about the time he left New Salem, Illinois, and his job as postmaster, lawyer, and storekeeper to enter the U.S. Congress (1847–1849). For a time, Lincoln had served in the Illinois legislature in Springfield, where he certainly would not have won the "best-dressed" award. For Sandburg, however, there's more to a person than his clothing; therefore, he goes well beyond appearances to reveal the inner strength and nobility of our sixteenth President.

Another selection by Sandburg appears in Chapter 11.

Looking Ahead

1. Sandburg uses a number of interesting anecdotes (brief, sometimes humorous stories) from Lincoln's life to illustrate something about his personality. Look for such anecdotes as you read through this piece.
2. The author also uses specific and concrete details in this early portrait of Lincoln. Many have to do with his physical appearance—his height, the way his eyes looked, the shape of his nose and cheeks, etc. Ask yourself what Lincoln's physical appearance tells you about his character.
3. Sandburg explains in paragraph 1 that by the time Lincoln was thirty-seven, he "had changed with a changing western world." In the 1840s Illinois and Kentucky were still considered the "west" (although this concept was changing fast as the United States pushed its borders toward the Pacific).

   Nonetheless, as the author tells us, there was still a great deal of the simple frontiersman in Lincoln, the "central" idea that ties this essay together and gives it focus. You can review what you've already learned about central ideas by rereading the introduction to Chapter 1.

Vocabulary

angular   Thin and bony.
broadcloth   Plain, tightly woven wool cloth.

buckskin breeches Pants made of deer hide.

cravat Necktie.

dejection Emotional depression.

falsetto A tone much higher than the normal range of men's voices.

granitic Hard as granite.

gravity Seriousness.

melancholy Sadness.

modulations Variations.

niche Nook, place.

pretenses False show.

resolve Steadfastness, determination.

shambled Shuffled, walked lazily.

The thirty-seven-year-old son of Thomas Lincoln and Nancy Hanks 1
Lincoln had changed with a changing western world. His feet had worn deer-
skin moccasins as a boy; they were put into rawhide boots when he was full-
grown; now he had them in dressed calf leather. His head-cover was a coon-
skin cap when he was a boy, and all men and boys wore the raccoon tail as
a high headpiece; floating down the Mississippi to New Orleans he wore a
black felt hat from an eastern factory and it held the post-office mail of New
Salem; now he was a prominent politician and lawyer wearing a tall, stiff, silk
hat known as a "stovepipe," also called a "plug hat."

In this "stovepipe" hat he carried letters, newspaper clippings, deeds, 2
mortgages, checks, receipts. Once he apologized to a client for not replying
to a letter; he had bought a new hat and in cleaning out the old hat he missed
this particular letter. The silk stovepipe hat was nearly a foot high, with a
brim only an inch or so in width; it was a high, lean, longish hat and it made
Lincoln look higher, leaner, more longish.

And though Lincoln had begun wearing broadcloth and white shirts 3
with a white collar and black silk cravat, and a suggestion of sideburns coming
down three-fourths the length of his ears, he was still known as one of the
carelessly dressed men of Springfield....

The loose bones of Lincoln were hard to fit with neat clothes; and, once on, 4
they were hard to keep neat; trousers go baggy at the knees of a story-teller who
has the habit, at the end of a story, where the main laugh comes in, of putting
his arms around his knees, raising his knees to his chin, and rocking to and fro.
Those who spoke of his looks often mentioned his trousers creeping to the ankles
and higher; his rumpled hair, his wrinkled vest. When he wasn't away making
speeches, electioneering or practicing law on the circuit, he cut kindling wood,
tended to the cordwood for the stoves in the house, milked the cow, gave her a
few forks of hay, and changed her straw bedding every day.

He looked like a farmer, it was often said; he seemed to have come from 5 prairies and barns rather than city streets and barber shops; and in his own way he admitted and acknowledged it; he told voters from the stump that it was only a few years since he had worn buckskin breeches and they shrank in the rain and crept to his knees leaving the skin blue and bare. The very words that came off his lips in tangled important discussions among lawyers had a wilderness air and a log-cabin smack. The way he pronounced the word "idea" was more like "idee,"the word "really" more like a drawled Kentucky "ra-a-ly."

As he strode or shambled into a gathering of men, he stood out as a   6
special figure for men to look at; it was a little as though he had come farther on harder roads and therefore had longer legs for the traveling; and a little as though he had been where life is stripped to its naked facts and it would be useless for him to try to put on certain pretenses of civilization.

The manners of a gentleman and a scholar dropped off him sometimes like   7
a cloak, and his speech was that of a farmer who works his own farm, or a lawyer who pails a cow morning and evening and might refer to it incidentally in polite company or in a public address. He was not embarrassed, and nobody else was embarrassed, when at the Bowling Green funeral he had stood up and, instead of delivering a formal funeral address on the character of the deceased, had shaken with grief and put a handkerchief to his face and wept tears, and motioned to the body-bearers to take his dead friend away. There was a natural grace to it; funerals should be so conducted; a man who loves a dead man should stand up and try to speak and find himself overwhelmed with grief so that instead of speaking he smothers his face in a handkerchief and weeps. This was the eloquence of naked fact beyond which there is no eloquence.

Standing, Lincoln loomed tall with his six feet, four inches of height; sit-   8
ting in a chair he looked no taller than other men, except that his knees rose higher than the level of the seat of the chair. Seated on a low chair or bench he seemed to be crouching. The shoulders were stooped and rounded, the head bent forward and turned downward; shirt-collars were a loose fit; an Adam's apple stood out on a scrawny neck; his voice was a tenor that carried song-tunes poorly but had clear and appealing modulations in his speeches; in rare moments of excitement it rose to a startling and unforgettable falsetto tone that carried every syllable with unmistakable meaning. In the stoop of his shoulders and the for-ward bend of his head there was a grace and familiarity so that it was easy for shorter people to look up into his face and talk with him.

The mouth and eyes, and the facial muscles running back from the mouth   9
and eyes, masked a thousand shades of meaning. In hours of melancholy, when poisons of dejection dragged him, the underlip and its muscles drooped.... [However,] across the mask of his dark gravity could come a light-ray of the quizzical, the puzzled. This could spread into the beginning of a smile and then spread farther into wrinkles and wreaths of laughter that lit the whole face into a glow; and it was of the quality of his highest laughter that it traveled through his whole frame, currents of it vitalizing his toes.

A fine chiseling of lines on the upper lip seemed to be some continuation 10 of the bridge of the nose, forming a feature that ended in a dimple at the point of the chin. The nose was large; if it had been a trifle larger he would have been called big-nosed; it was a nose for breathing deep sustained breaths of air, a strong shapely nose, granitic with resolve and patience. Two deepening wrinkles started from the sides of the right and left nostrils and ran down the outer rims of the upper lip; farther out on the two cheeks were deepening wrinkles that had been long crude dimples when he was a boy; hours of toil, pain, and laughter were deepening these wrinkles. From the sides of the nose, angular cheek-bones branched right and left toward the large ears, forming a base for magnificently constructed eye-sockets. Bushy black eyebrows shaded the sockets where the eyeballs rested. . . . In his eyes as nowhere else was registered the shifting light of his moods; their language ran from rapid twinkles of darting hazel that won the hearts of children on to a fixed baffling gray that the shrewdest lawyers and politicians could not read, to find there an intention he wanted to hide.

The thatch of coarse hair on the head was black when seen from a dis- 11 tance, but close up it had a brownish, rough, sandy tint. He had been known to comb it, parting it far on the right side, and slicking it down so that it looked groomed by a somewhat particular man; but most of the time it was loose and rumpled. The comb might have parted it either on the far right or on the far left side; he wasn't particular.

It was natural that Abraham Lincoln was many things to many people; 12 some believed him a cunning, designing lawyer and politician who coldly figured all his moves in advance; some believed him a sad, odd, awkward man trying to find a niche in life where his hacked-out frame could have peace and comfort; some believed him a superb human struggler with solemn and comic echoes and values far off and beyond the leashes and bones that held him to earth and law and politics.

Questions for Discussion

1. As noted in Looking Ahead, Sandburg's central idea is that Lincoln had a great deal of the simple frontiersman in him. In any one paragraph, which details develop this central idea?
2. In paragraph 1, Sandburg gives a brief history of Lincoln's footwear. What do his shoes reveal about him?
3. From the physical details Sandburg provides, what do you think Lincoln looked like?
4. Lincoln's trousers were "baggy at the knees." Look back to paragraph 4. What does this physical description reveal about his character?
5. What other details about Lincoln's appearance help us understand his personality?

umber of anecdotes in this selection show us things about Lincoln's
onality. What does his sobbing at a friend's funeral reveal about him?
out two or three other anecdotes that you find especially revealing.

7. In paragraphs 9 and 10, Sandburg indicates that Lincoln could experience
a variety of moods. Describe these moods.

8. The public held differing views of Lincoln. What were they?

Suggestions for Journal Entries

1. Use your journal to list details you found in this selection that build a full
portrait of Lincoln's physical appearance.

2. How would you describe Lincoln's personality? Use details from Sandburg to write a paragraph about the kind of person he was. Start by listing
words that might help you define his character. For instance, you might
include "simple," "straightforward," "honest," or "humorous."

3. Lincoln's inner nobility, simplicity, and lack of pretense were reflected in
the way he dressed. Do you know people whose outward appearance provides clues to what they are inside? Write a short description of one such
person, concentrating on only one or two outward features that reveal what
he or she is like inside.

Diogenes

Gilbert Highet

In the introduction to "Subway Station" (Chapter 8), you learned that
Highet taught Greek and Latin at Columbia University. His studies of Greek
and Roman literature, history, and mythology made him one of the best-
known classical scholars of our time. The following selection originally appeared as part of "Diogenes and Alexander," a larger essay in which Highet
compared Diogenes with Alexander the Great.

Looking Ahead

1. Diogenes was a Greek philosopher in the fourth century B.C. who believed
that living simply was the way to virtue. It was Diogenes who walked
about holding a lantern, searching for an honest man.

2. The followers of the philosophy of Cynicism, which Highet mentions in
paragraph 2, believed that virtue can be achieved only by those who lead
a simple life.

3. Paragraph 3 mentions Sparta and Athens, city-states that fought each other during the Peloponnesian Wars (431–404 B.C.). The wars were so named because Athens and Sparta are in the Peloponnesus, a peninsula that makes up the southern half of Greece. The Spartans eventually won.

4. Plato, mentioned in paragraph 6, founded the Academy, a school in which he created a system of thought that influenced the development of western thought. His most famous work is *The Republic*, a treatise on government. Plato's most celebrated student, Aristotle, was just as influential. He founded the Lyceum, where he taught his own philosophy, and he was the tutor of Alexander the Great.

5. Highet concludes with a series of anecdotes that will add to your understanding of Diogenes. Pay particular attention to them as you approach the end of this selection.

Vocabulary

anxiously   Nervously.

conventions   Rules, customs, principles.

converting   Changing one's belief or opinion.

creed   Belief.

degenerate   A moral deviant.

mischievous   Troublesome, irritating, annoying.

recluse   A hermit.

sanctuaries   Holy places, safe hideaways.

satirizing   Criticizing, poking fun at.

scant   Few, little.

stylite   A member of an early Christian group who lived on the tops of high columns exposed to the weather.

superfluities   Excess, overabundance.

Lying on the bare earth, shoeless, bearded, half-naked, he looked like 1
a beggar or a lunatic. He was one, but not the other. He had opened his eyes
with the sun at dawn, scratched, done his business like a dog at the roadside,
washed at the public fountain, begged a piece of breakfast bread and a few
olives, eaten them squatting on the ground, and washed them down with a
few handfuls of water scooped from the spring. (Long ago he had owned a
rough wooden cup, but he threw it away when he saw a boy drinking out of
his hollowed hands.) Having no work to go to and no family to provide for,
he was free. As the market place filled up with shoppers and merchants and
gossipers and sharpers and slaves and foreigners, he had strolled through it
for an hour or two. Everybody knew him, or knew of him. They would throw
sharp questions at him and get sharper answers. Sometimes they threw jeers,
and got jibes; sometimes bits of food, and got scant thanks; sometimes a mis-

chievous pebble, and got a shower of stones and abuse. They were not quite sure whether he was mad or not. He knew they were mad, each in a different way; they amused him. Now he was back at his home.

It was not a house, not even a squatter's hut. He thought everybody lived   2 far too elaborately, expensively, anxiously. What good is a house? No one needs privacy; natural acts are not shameful; we all do the same things, and need not hide them. No one needs beds and chairs and such furniture: the animals live healthy lives and sleep on the ground. All we require, since nature did not dress us properly, is one garment to keep us warm, and some shelter from rain and wind. So he had one blanket—to dress him in the daytime and cover him at night—and he slept in a cask. His name was Diogenes. He was the founder of the creed called Cynicism (the word means "doggishness"); he spent much of his life in the rich, lazy, corrupt Greek city of Corinth, mocking and satirizing its people, and occasionally converting one of them.

His home was not a barrel made of wood: too expensive. It was a storage   3 jar made of earthenware, something like a modern fuel tank—no doubt discarded because a break had made it useless. He was not the first to inhabit such a thing: the refugees driven into Athens by the Spartan invasion had been forced to sleep in casks. But he was the first who ever did so by choice, out of principle.

Diogenes was not a degenerate or a maniac. He was a philosopher who   4 wrote plays and poems and essays expounding his doctrine; he talked to those who cared to listen; he had pupils who admired him. But he taught chiefly by example. All should live naturally, he said, for what is natural is normal and cannot possibly be evil or shameful. Live without conventions, which are artificial and false; escape complexities and superfluities and extravagances: only so you can live a free life. The rich man believes he possesses his big house with its many rooms and its elaborate furniture, his pictures and his expensive clothes, his horses and his servants and his bank accounts. He does not. He depends on them, he worries about them, he spends most of his life's energy looking after them; the thought of losing them makes him sick with anxiety. They possess him. He is their slave. In order to procure a quantity of false, perishable goods he has sold the only true, lasting good, his own independence.

There have been many men who grew tired of human society with its   5 complications, and went away to live simply—on a small farm, in a quiet village, in a hermit's cave, or in the darkness of anonymity. Not so Diogenes. He was not a recluse, or a stylite or a beatnik. He was a missionary. His life's aim was clear to him: it was "to restamp the currency." (He and his father had once been convicted for counterfeiting, long before he turned to philosophy, and this phrase was Diogenes' bold, unembarrassed joke on the subject.) To restamp the currency: to take the clean metal of human life, to erase the old false conventional markings, and to imprint it with its true values.

The other great philosophers of the fourth century before Christ taught   6 mainly their own private pupils. In the shady groves and cool sanctuaries of the Academy, Plato discoursed to a chosen few on the unreality of this contingent existence. Aristotle, among the books and instruments and specimens and archives and research-workers of his Lyceum, pursued investigations and gave lectures that were rightly named *esoteric:* "for those within the walls." But for Diogenes, laboratory and specimens and lecture halls and pupils were all to be found in a crowd of ordinary people. Therefore he chose to live in Athens or in the rich city of Corinth, where travelers from all over the Mediterranean world constantly came and went.

He thought most people were only half-alive, most men only half-men. At bright noonday he walked through the market place carrying a lighted lamp and inspecting the face of everyone he met. They asked him why. Diogenes answered, "I am trying to find a *man.*" 7

To a gentleman whose servant was putting on his shoes for him, Diogenes said, "You won't be really happy until he wipes your nose for you: that will come after you lose the use of your hands." 8

Once there was a war scare so serious that it stirred even the lazy, profit-happy Corinthians. They began to drill, clean their weapons, and rebuild their neglected fortifications. Diogenes took his old cask and began to roll it up and down, back and forward. "When you are all so busy," he said, "I felt I ought to do *something!*" 9

And so he lived—like a dog, some said, because he cared nothing for privacy and other human conventions, and because he showed his teeth and barked at those whom he disliked. 10

Questions for Discussion

1. In paragraph 1, Highet says that Diogenes threw away his drinking cup. Why did Diogenes do this, and what does it reveal about him?
2. Which of Diogenes's personal beliefs does Highet emphasize? Taken all together, what do these beliefs reveal about Diogenes's character?
3. Explain how the people in the market place reacted to Diogenes. What do these reactions show us about him?
4. How does Highet describe Diogenes's outward appearance?
5. Why does Highet bother to tell us that the word "cynicism" means "doggishness"? Does this help us understand Diogenes better? What other sections of the essay compare Diogenes's life to that of a dog?
6. Why did Diogenes believe the rich are slaves?
7. From the information that Highet presents, in what ways was Diogenes different from the other philosophers of his time?
8. What do the anecdotes at the end of the essay reveal about Diogenes?
9. Summarize Highet's personal opinion of Diogenes. See paragraph 4 especially.

Suggestions for Journal Entries

1. Do you believe Diogenes was a lunatic? Describe those things about him that make him seem odd or insane. Then list those qualities in him that you find admirable.

2. Some might say that Diogenes was a benevolent eccentric, a friendly oddball. Write a short character sketch in your journal about a "friendly oddball" you have known.

SUGGESTIONS FOR WRITING

1. In "Richard Cory" you read about a tragic figure. If you responded to this poem in your journal, you might have already begun gathering details about a "tragic figure" you know from personal experience. Use these details to describe this person in a full-length essay.

   Make sure to provide a good introduction, which will explain what *you* mean by "tragic" and why the person you are describing fits that definition. Then, develop each of the paragraphs in the body of your essay with the details you've already recorded in your journal. Add more details to your essay as needed.

2. One of the Suggestions of Journal Entries that follows the essay from Russell Baker's *Growing Up* asks that you write a few paragraphs in which you tell an anecdote that illustrates or reveals something about your personality. Develop this piece of writing further by adding anecdotes from your life that tell your readers even more about you.

   Make sure to begin your essay with an effective thesis statement that clearly indicates those aspects or qualities of your personality that the anecdotes reveal.

3. If you responded to item 3 of Suggestions of Journal Entries after Sandburg's "Abraham Lincoln," you have already begun to write a description of a person whose outward appearance might provide some clues or insights to his or her character. Develop this character sketch further.

   Try to describe as many of this individual's physical characteristics as you can and explain what they reveal. Don't be afraid to include any strange mannerisms you've noticed, perhaps the odd gestures she uses while speaking or the curious way he shuffles down the street.

4. Look over your journal entries in response to the Suggestions for Journal Entries following Highet's "Diogenes." You have probably accumulated good notes and might even have begun to write an effective character sketch about a "friendly oddball" you once knew. If so, add details to this character sketch and expand it into a full-length essay.

Section IV

Narration

The selections in the three chapters of this section have a great deal in common. Their most basic and most obvious similarity is that they tell stories. They do this through narration, a process by which events or incidents are presented to the reader in a particular order. Usually, this is done in chronological order, or order of time.

The logical arrangement of events in a story is called its plot. Often, writers begin by telling us about the first event in this series, the event that sets the whole plot in motion. And they usually end their stories with the last bit of action that takes place.

But this is not always the case. Where a writer begins or ends really depends upon the kind of story he or she is telling and the reason or purpose for telling it. Some stories begin in the middle; some even start at the end and use flashbacks to narrate things that happened earlier. Finally, some are preceded or concluded with information or commentary that the author thinks might be important to his or her readers. For instance, in "38 Who Saw Murder..." (Chapter 11), Martin Gansberg tells us about the police investigation of the murder before narrating the events that took place during the crime itself.

More than 2300 years ago, the Greek philosopher Aristotle taught that a narrative must have a beginning, a middle, and an end. In other words, a successful story must be complete; it must contain all the information a reader will need to learn what has happened and to follow along easily.

That's the single most important idea to remember about writing effective narratives. However, there are a number of others that you should keep in mind.

DISTINGUISHING FICTION FROM NONFICTION

Narration can be divided into two types: fiction and nonfiction. Works of nonfiction recount events that actually occurred. Works of fiction, though

207

sometimes based on real-life experiences, are born of the author's imagination and do not re-create events exactly as they happened. The short stories that appear in Chapter 12 are examples of fiction.

DETERMINING PURPOSE AND THEME

Many pieces of nonfiction are written to keep people informed about events or developments that affect or interest them. Newspaper stories are perfect examples. Fiction, on the other hand, is written to entertain people, though good fiction almost always enriches the emotional, spiritual, and/or intellectual lives of its readers as well.

However, many stories (whether fiction or nonfiction) are written because they dramatize or present an important (central) idea, often called a "theme." They portray life in such a way as to tell us something important about ourselves, about human nature, about society, or about life itself. At times, this theme is stated in a "moral," as in the fables of Aesop, the ancient Greek stories intended to teach lessons about life. More often than not, however, the theme or idea behind a story will be unstated or implied. It will be revealed only as the plot unfolds. In other words, the story will speak for itself.

As a developing writer, one of the most important things to remember as you sit down to write a narrative is to ask yourself if the story you're about to tell is important to you in some way. That *doesn't mean* that you should limit yourself to narrating events from personal experience only, though personal experience can often provide just the kind of information you'll need to spin a good yarn. It *does mean* that the more you know about the people, places, and events you're writing about and the more those people, places, and events mean to you, the better able you'll be to make your writing interesting and meaningful to your readers.

FINDING THE MEANING IN YOUR STORY

As explained above, you won't always have to reveal why you've written your story or what theme it is supposed to present. You can allow the events you're narrating to speak for themselves. Often, in fact, you won't know what the theme of your story is or why you thought it important until you're well into the writing process. Sometimes, you won't know that until after you've finished.

But that's just fine! One of the best things about writing is that it will help you discover important things about your subject (and yourself) that you would never have known had you not begun the process in the first place. *Just make sure that you choose to write about something you believe is important or at least interesting to you.* That is the first step in telling a successful story. You can always begin to figure out why your story is important or what theme you want it to demonstrate later in the process, when you write your second or third draft.

DECIDING WHAT TO INCLUDE

In most cases, you won't have much trouble deciding what details to include. You'll be able to put down events as they happened or at least as you remember them. However, in some cases—especially when you are trying to present a particular theme or idea—you'll have to decide which events, people, etc. should be emphasized or talked about in great detail, which should be mentioned only briefly, and which should be excluded from the story altogether.

In "Back Home" (Chapter 11), for example, Langston Hughes's purpose is to explain the racism he encountered on his trip home from Mexico. He could have talked about many of the events on the journey that had nothing to do with racial prejudice. However, he chose to exclude them and to focus on the only two incidents that illustrate his theme.

MAKING YOUR STORIES LIVELY AND INTERESTING

Once again, good stories dramatize ideas or themes. They do this through actions and characters that seem vivid and interesting, as if they were alive or real.

One of the best ways to keep your readers' interest and to make your writing vivid is to use verbs effectively. More than any part of speech, verbs convey action! They tell *what happened.* It's important to be accurate when reporting an incident you've experienced or witnessed. You ought to recapture it exactly as you remember and without exaggeration. However, good writing can be both accurate and interesting, both truthful and colorful. You can achieve this balance by choosing verbs carefully.

For instance, in "Exile and Return" (Chapter 10), Jim Keller prefers to say that he "galloped" through the hallways and over the playing fields of his old high school, rather than that he "ran" through them. Of course, "galloping" *is* a form of running, but it is much more descriptive of what Keller actually did, and it is far more interesting than "ran"!

Similarly, notice how Edgar Lee Masters' use of verbs in "Lucinda Matlock" (Chapter 10) reveals his subject as an energetic, vivacious, and agreeable person. In the middle of the poem, he tells us that she "*Rambled* over the fields" and that she could be heard "*Shouting* to the wooded hills, *singing* to the green valleys." How less interesting she would have seemed had he shown her "walking" through the fields and "talking" to the hills.

SHOWING THE PASSAGE OF TIME

Of course, the most important thing in a story is the plot, a series of events occurring in time. Writers must make sure that their plots make sense, that they are easy to follow, and that each event or incident flows into the next logically.

One of the best ways to show time order is to indicate the actual time that an event took place. In "38 Who Saw Murder...," for instance, Martin Gansberg introduces the story of Kitty Genovese's murder with: "This is what the police say happened beginning at 3:20 a.m." Later on, he tells us that a bus passed the scene at "3:35 a.m." and that an ambulance finally took the body away at "4:25 a.m."

Another way of indicating the passage of time is by using transitions or connectives, the kinds of words and expressions used to create coherence within and between paragraphs. In his popular essay about future trips to outer space, Kenneth Jon Rose uses a number of such transitional devices (in italics) as he explains what it might be like to leave the earth on a tourist shuttle to the stars. Notice how they keep the story moving and make it easy to follow:

> [While] looking out your window, you'll see the earth rapidly falling
> away, and the light blue sky progressively turning blue-black. You'll
> now be about 30 miles up, traveling at about 3000 mph. Within
> minutes, the sky will appear jet black, and only the fuzzy curve of the
> earth will be visible. Then, at perhaps 130 miles above the surface of
> the earth and traveling at 17,000 mph, engines will shut down
> and...you'll become weightless. ["2001: Space Shuttle"]

If you want to refresh your memory about other effective transitional devices to use in your writing, turn back to Chapter 2.

DESCRIBING SETTING AND DEVELOPING CHARACTERS

Establishing the setting of your story involves describing the time and place in which it occurs. You've probably done some of that in response to the assignments in Chapter 8, Describing Places and Things. Developing characters involves many of the skills you practiced in Chapter 9, Describing People.

In general, the more you say about the people in your narrative and about the time and place in which it is set, the more realistic and convincing it will seem to your readers. And the more they will appreciate what it has to say! Remember that your purpose in writing a narrative is to tell a story. But the kind of characters who inhabit that story and the kind of world in which it takes place can be as interesting and as important to your readers as the events themselves.

An important element of many stories is dialogue, which you can use to help develop characters and to describe setting as well as to reveal important events that move the plot along. In fact, many of the authors in the selections that follow allow their characters to explain what happened or to comment upon the action of the story in their own words. Usually, their comments are quoted exactly—complete with grammatical errors, slang expressions, and all. So, whether you're writing fiction or nonfiction, don't hesitate to let your characters speak for themselves. They may be able to tell your readers much about themselves and about the settings and plots of the stories in which they appear.

Chapter 10

Personal Reflection and Autobiography

Though different in style and content, the selections in this chapter are similar because they are written in the "first person." This is the "point of view" the authors have chosen to tell their stories. In first-person narration, the storyteller, also known as the narrator, participates in the action and recalls the events from his or her personal perspective.

When writers reveal things about other people's lives or talk about events in which they were not involved, they often rely on third-person narration and use the pronouns "he," "she," "it," and "they" to explain who did what in the story. Examples of this kind of writing can be found in Chapter 11, Reporting Events. However, all of the selections in Chapter 10 are intended to reveal something important about the lives or personalities of their storytellers. That's why they can be classified as "personal reflection" or "autobiography" and are written from the first-person point of view, using the pronouns "I" or "we."

This is even true of the two poems from *Spoon River Anthology*. To make his poems more believable, Edgar Lee Masters lets his title characters speak for themselves and tell us about their lives in their own words. As such, Lucinda Matlock and Margaret Fuller Slack become the narrators of the poems that bear their names.

Incident

Countee Cullen

    Countee Cullen (1903–1946) played a significant role in the Harlem Renaissance, one of the most influential artistic movements in modern America. As a member of this important group of black poets, novelists, and playwrights in New York's Harlem during the 1920s, he helped create an authentic voice for American blacks and contributed to a tradition that is among the finest in American literature.

    During his brief lifetime he authored several volumes of poetry, was the editor of two important black journals, and at age thirty published *Caroling Dusk*, a collection of poetry by important black writers.

Looking Ahead

Although brief, "Incident" contains the basic narrative elements: plot, setting, character, and dialogue.

Vocabulary

whit   A bit, a small amount.

Once riding in old Baltimore,
Heart-filled, head-filled with glee,
I saw a Baltimorean
Keep looking straight at me.

Now I was eight and very small,   5
And he was no whit bigger,
And so I smiled, but he poked out
His tongue, and called me, "Nigger."

I saw the whole of Baltimore
From May until December,   10
Of all the things that happened there
That's all that I remember.

Questions for Discussion

1. What is the narrator's mood as he rides in "old Baltimore"?
2. What three events make up the plot of "Incident"?
3. What example of dialogue do we find in this selection? How is it important to the poem?

4. Why does the speaker tell us that the "Baltimorean" he met was about his age and size?
5. Cullen does not provide many details about the setting, but he does give us a clue. Where does the poem take place?

Suggestions for Journal Entries

1. Think of an incident from your childhood in which someone insulted you, called you names, or tried to degrade you in some way. Briefly recall what happened and explain your reaction to this incident.
2. In your journal, explain your emotional reaction to "he poked out / His tongue, and called me, 'Nigger.'"

Exile and Return

James Keller

As managing editor and feature writer for the student newspaper at the college he attended, James Keller wrote numerous outstanding articles, essays, and stories. In "Exile and Return" he recalls a visit to his high school several years after graduation. Notice how much he reveals about himself in describing this visit.

Looking Ahead

1. Keller makes excellent use of descriptive passages (setting) to help explain how different his high school is from how he remembered it. Look for such passages.
2. The visions Keller sees in the halls and playing fields of his old school are expressed sometimes with humor and sometimes with sadness. Pick out examples of humor and sadness as you read this autobiographical narrative; they'll increase your enjoyment of it.
3. Keller creates a number of startling images (verbal pictures) in describing what happens as he roams around his high school. Many reveal as much about the author himself as about the events he's relating. Perhaps the most vivid of these begins, "The empty stands play sentinel" (paragraph 6).
4. "Had forked no lightning" (paragraph 5) is from "Do Not Go Gentle into That Good Night," a poem by Dylan Thomas.

Vocabulary

arcane   Secret, known only by a few.
asbestos   An insulating material, now prohibited because it is a health hazard.
banality   Boring quality, boring appearance.
predicting   Giving signs of, foretelling.
stifling   Suffocating.

It's all different, quiet and grey now. Like the sun reflecting on the 1
previous night's darkness, or predicting the afternoon's storm. On this stifling summer morning, I scarcely recognize the school I had attended for four
years. The life and laughter have died. It is another world now.

I walk down the hollow vacant halls, and what light there is shines a 2
path on the mirrored beige floors, leading me past imposing grey lockers that
stand erect in columns. Lockers that at one time woke the dead in closing, but
now remain closed in silence. I remember the faces that would stand and
sometimes slump before them, after the classes—friendly faces that would
look up and nod, and say "Hello" as I galloped past. Now there are other faces
of different people I no longer know.

The lockers soon give way to the classrooms, cement cells we once lived 3
in, learned in, and often slept in. The steel I-beams hang like doom over the
cracked and peeling walls. The architect left them exposed, for want of talent,
I assume. From the color scheme of putrid green to the neutral asbestos ceiling and steel rafters, the overall banality of the rooms is extraordinary.

The rooms are empty now, empty save the ancient desks. They are yel- 4
low clay and steel and much smaller than I remember them. I can still read
the arcane graffiti on their dull surfaces. The handwriting is my own. I recognize the doodles drawn as every minute ran past like a turtle climbing up
a glass wall. They killed the time. They didn't do much for the furniture
either.

Eventually my eyes come to rest on the chalkboards. Old habits die 5
hard. I remember staring at them through teachers whose words "had forked
no lightning." The teachers are gone, but many faces remain. They turn and
stare from seats in front and to my side. They are shadows of the past, blood-
less visions, returned from long exile to mock my exile and return. They're
looking for me, and through me. But they're only memories. They've left,
you know—some gone to school, some gone to the world, others gone quite
literally to hell, not soon to return. Faces that laughed, young and innocent,
and now cry, worn and haggard. Expressions hiding lives that were true and
alive, but are now neither.

Out of the building I walk on grassy playing fields that were greener in 6
another spring. Places where so many of us found brief, insignificant glory.
The empty stands play sentinel over the lonely track and football field, and

a thousand ghosts applaud a hundred athletes only I can see. So much happiness and so much pain. I no longer remember who won and lost. Only that somehow we all walked away winners and losers to the same heart.

It is more than I can bear. I leave now, maybe forever. I wonder if I ever   7 existed and was ever here at all. To say good-bye is to die a little. And so I do.

Questions for Discussion

1. In paragraph 1, Keller writes that the high school he returns to "is another world now." This might very well serve as the central idea of his essay. What details does he present to support (or dramatize) this idea?
2. Keller uses the first-person point of view ("I"). His purpose might be defined as an attempt to look back and examine the world he knew as a high school student. Is he also able to look back at himself in the process? In what way? Think about the "arcane graffiti" he mentions in paragraph 4.
3. In paragraph 2, Keller says that he often "galloped" along the hallways. What does this show about his disposition? What else does the story reveal about him?
4. What verb tense (past, present, or future) is "Exile and Return" written in? How is it appropriate to Keller's purposes?
5. What examples of humor do you find in the story? What parts seem especially sad or touching to you?

Suggestions for Journal Entries

1. Take a mental stroll through the hallways, classrooms, or athletic fields of your old high school. What do you remember most about it? What do you remember about yourself? List these memories in your journal.
2. "To say good-bye is to die a little," Keller writes at the end. Recall an incident in which you had to say good-bye to someone, something, or some place. Write a brief story about the event, clearly revealing why saying good-bye was so hard.

From *Spoon River Anthology*

Edgar Lee Masters

Spoon River Anthology is a collection of poems spoken by people buried in the cemetery of a fictional nineteenth-century village that Masters based

upon recollections of his hometown. One by one, Spoon River's citizens are
made to address us from the grave and to reveal important secrets about their
relatives and friends, and, most of all, about themselves.

Born in Kansas in 1869, Masters eventually settled in Chicago, where
he practiced law for several years before taking up writing as a career. When
Spoon River Anthology was published, it became a literary sensation. The idea
of unraveling the story of a town through the recollections of people lying in
its cemetery was unique, and it attracted the attention of thousands of readers
and many imitators. "Lucinda Matlock" and "Margaret Fuller Slack," the
two poems in this selection, are taken from *Spoon River Anthology*.

Looking Ahead

1. Lucinda's and Margaret's very different outlooks on life reveal a great deal
   about their personalities. Ask yourself what their attitudes tell you about
   them.
2. Chandlerville and Winchester, which Lucinda mentions, are towns near
   Spoon River. By including these place names, Masters makes the poem
   and Lucinda seem more realistic and believable.
3. Margaret claims that she could have been as good a writer as George Eliot.
   "George Eliot" was the pen name of the nineteenth-century English nov-
   elist Mary Ann Evans, who wrote *The Mill on the Floss*, *Silas Marner*, and
   Middlemarch.

Vocabulary

celibacy   Life without sex.

degenerate   Not strong in spirit.

ere   Before.

holiday   Vacation.

ironical   Ironic, exactly the opposite of what is expected. Margaret's death as a result
   of tetanus was "ironical" because one of the disease's first symptoms is lockjaw.

luring   Attracting.

repose   Rest.

unchastity   Sex outside of marriage.

untoward   Unhappy, unlucky.

Lucinda Matlock

I went to the dances at Chandlerville,
And played snap-out at Winchester.
One time we changed partners,
Driving home in the moonlight of middle June,

And then I found Davis.   5
We were married and lived together for seventy years,
Enjoying, working, raising the twelve children,
Eight of whom we lost
Ere I had reached the age of sixty.
I spun, I wove, I kept the house, I nursed the sick,   10
I made the garden, and for holiday
Rambled over the fields where sang the larks,
And by Spoon River gathering many a shell,
And many a flower and medicinal weed—
Shouting to the wooded hills, singing to the green valleys.   15
At ninety-six I had lived enough, that is all,
And passed to a sweet repose.
What is this I hear of sorrow and weariness,
Anger, discontent and drooping hopes?
Degenerate sons and daughters,   20
Life is too strong for you—
It takes life to love Life.

Margaret Fuller Slack

I would have been as great as George Eliot
But for an untoward fate.
For look at the photograph of me made by Penniwit,
Chin resting on hand, and deep-set eyes—
Gray, too, and far-searching.   5
But there was the old, old problem:
Should it be celibacy, matrimony or unchastity?
Then John Slack, the rich druggist, wooed me,
Luring me with the promise of leisure for my novel,
And I married him, giving birth to eight children,   10
And had no time to write.
It was all over with me, anyway,
When I ran the needle in my hand
While washing the baby's things,
And died from lock-jaw, an ironical death.   15
Hear me, ambitious souls,
Sex is the curse of life!

Questions for Discussion

1. Lucinda seems to have had a very active and productive life. What events
   in her poem make this clear?

2. Masters uses a number of interesting verbs to describe Lucinda's life. Identify these verbs in the poem. What do they reveal about her?
3. Lucinda's life hasn't been all joy. Which events in the poem reveal that she has experienced great sorrow too?
4. Why does Lucinda call her sons and daughters "degenerate"?
5. What does Lucinda mean when she says that "It takes life to love Life"? What does this tell us about her personality?
6. Margaret Fuller Slack says that she was lured into her marriage "with the promise of leisure for [her] novel." What does this reveal about her attitude toward marriage? How does her attitude differ from Lucinda's, and what does this difference tell us about Margaret's character?
7. What does Margaret mean by "Sex is the curse of life!"?
8. What verbs does Masters use in "Margaret Fuller Slack" to keep the story moving and to maintain the reader's interest?

Suggestions for Journal Entries

1. In a paragraph or two, describe Lucinda's rather healthy attitude toward life and contrast it to Margaret's view.
2. Do you know someone like Lucinda Matlock, who has kept smiling and maintained a courageous attitude even though he or she has had a difficult life? Make a list of the difficulties this person has experienced, and explain how he or she manages to remain hopeful and happy.
3. Do you know someone like Margaret, who is resentful about the way his or her life has unfolded? What events in this person's life have caused him or her to adopt this attitude?

The Boys

Maya Angelou

Born Marguerita Johnson in 1928, Maya Angelou has had a magnificent career as a writer, dancer, and actress. She has appeared in musical and dramatic productions the world over, including the TV miniseries *Roots*.

Angelou grew up in Stamps, Arkansas, where her grandmother (known as "Sister Henderson" to the neighbors and "Momma" to her grandchildren) owned the general store, which was Angelou's home and which serves as the setting for "The Boys." She published the first volume of her autobiography, *I Know Why the Caged Bird Sings*, in 1970. Taken from this book, "The

Boys" recalls a moving childhood experience that both angered and demoralized her.

Looking Ahead

1. Uncle Willie, who is really the central character in this story, walked with a severe limp. This is the "affliction" Angelou mentions in paragraph 4. Bailey, whom Angelou first mentions in paragraph 2, is her younger brother.
2. Angelou introduces the story by providing a very complete description of the setting. This comes in the first several paragraphs, which describe the "Store" at various times of the day. Read these paragraphs carefully, picking out the various ways in which Angelou indicates the passage of time.
3. The story contains several examples of personification, simile, and metaphor. (To review figurative language, see Chapter 6.)

Vocabulary

abominations   Hateful, disgusting things.

astraddle   Across.

concoctions   Mixtures.

condoned   Excused.

covenant   Agreement, contract.

heinous   Horrible, evil.

nonchalance   Carelessness, ease.

obsession   A preoccupation, a constant desire for.

rakishly   In a sexy or suggestive way.

squire   Rich landowner, country gentleman.

tedious   Boring, tiresome.

testimony   A witnessing or swearing to.

twang   A nasal sound.

Weighing the half-pounds of flour, excluding the scoop, and depositing   1
them dust-free into the thin paper sacks held a simple kind of adventure for me. I developed an eye for measuring how full a silver-looking ladle of flour, mash, meal, sugar or corn had to be to push the scale indicator over to eight ounces or one pound. When I was absolutely accurate our appreciative customers used to admire: "Sister Henderson sure got some smart grandchildrens." If I was off in the Store's favor, the eagle-eyed women would say, "Put some more in that sack, child. Don't you try to make your profit offa me."

Then I would quietly but persistently punish myself. For every bad   2
judgment, the fine was no silver-wrapped Kisses, the sweet chocolate drops that I loved more than anything in the world, except Bailey. And maybe canned

pineapples. My obsession with pineapples nearly drove me mad. I dreamt of the days when I would be grown and able to buy a whole carton for myself alone.

Until I was thirteen and left Arkansas for good, the Store was my fa-   3
vorite place to be. Alone and empty in the mornings, it looked like an un-
opened present from a stranger. Opening the front doors was pulling the ribbon off the unexpected gift. The light would come in softly (we faced north),
easing itself over the shelves of mackerel, salmon, tobacco, thread. It fell flat
on the big vat of lard and by noontime during the summer the grease had
softened to a thick soup. Whenever I walked into the Store in the afternoon,
I sensed that it was tired. I alone could hear the slow pulse of its job half done.
But just before bedtime, after numerous people had walked in and out, had
argued over their bills, or joked about their neighbors, or just dropped in "to
give Sister Henderson a 'Hi y'all,'" the promise of magic mornings returned
to the Store and spread itself over the family in washed life waves.

Momma opened boxes of crispy crackers and we sat around the meat   4
block at the rear of the Store. I sliced onions, and Bailey opened two or even
three cans of sardines and allowed their juice of oil and fishing boats to ooze
down and around the sides. That was supper. In the evening, when we were
alone like that, Uncle Willie didn't stutter or shake or give any indication that
he had an "affliction." It seemed that the peace of a day's ending was an
assurance that the covenant God made with children, Negroes and the crip-
pled was still in effect.

Throwing scoops of corn to the chickens and mixing sour dry mash with   5
leftover food and oily dish water for the hogs were among our evening chores.
Bailey and I sloshed down twilight trails to the pig pens, and standing on the
first fence rungs we poured down the unappealing concoctions to our grateful
hogs. They mashed their tender pink snouts down into the slop, and rooted
and grunted their satisfaction. We always grunted a reply only half in jest. We
were also grateful that we had concluded the dirtiest of chores and had only
gotten the evil-smelling swill on our shoes, stockings, feet and hands.

Late one day, as we were attending to the pigs, I heard a horse in the   6
front yard (it really should have been called a driveway, except that there was
nothing to drive into it), and ran to find out who had come riding up on a
Thursday evening when even Mr. Steward, the quiet, bitter man who owned
a riding horse, would be resting by his warm fire until the morning called him
out to turn over his field.

The used-to-be sheriff sat rakishly astraddle his horse. His nonchalance   7
was meant to convey his authority and power over even dumb animals. How
much more capable he would be with Negroes. It went without saying.

His twang jogged in the brittle air. From the side of the Store, Bailey   8
and I heard him say to Momma, "Annie, tell Willie he better lay low tonight.
A crazy nigger messed with a white lady today. Some of the boys'll be coming

over here later." Even after the slow drag of years, I remember the sense of fear which filled my mouth with hot, dry air, and made my body light.

The "boys"? Those cement faces and eyes of hate that burned the clothes 9 off you if they happened to see you lounging on the main street downtown on Saturday. Boys? It seemed that youth had never happened to them. Boys? No, rather men who were covered with graves' dust and age without beauty or learning. The ugliness and rottenness of old abominations.

If on Judgment Day I were summoned by St. Peter to give testimony 10 to the used-to-be sheriff's act of kindness, I would be unable to say anything in his behalf. His confidence that my uncle and every other Black man who heard of the Klan's coming ride would scurry under their houses to hide in chicken droppings was too humiliating to hear. Without waiting for Momma's thanks, he rode out of the yard, sure that things were as they should be and that he was a gentle squire, saving those deserving serfs from the laws of the land, which he condoned.

Immediately, while his horse's hoofs were still loudly thudding the 11 ground, Momma blew out the coal-oil lamps. She had a quiet, hard talk with Uncle Willie and called Bailey and me into the Store.

We were told to take the potatoes and onions out of their bins and knock 12 out the dividing walls that kept them apart. Then with a tedious and fearful slowness Uncle Willie gave me his rubber-tipped cane and bent down to get into the now-enlarged empty bin. It took forever before he lay down flat, and then we covered him with potatoes and onions, layer upon layer, like a casserole. Grandmother knelt praying in the darkened Store.

It was fortunate that the "boys" didn't ride into our yard that evening 13 and insist that Momma open the Store. They would have surely found Uncle Willie and just as surely lynched him. He moaned the whole night through as if he had, in fact, been guilty of some heinous crime. The heavy sounds pushed their way up out of the blanket of vegetables and I pictured his mouth pulling down on the right side and his saliva flowing into the eyes of new potatoes and waiting there like dew drops for the warmth of morning.

Questions for Discussion

1. What is the story's central idea, or theme?
2. What point of view does Angelou use?
3. The author establishes the setting of her story by mentioning a number of events or incidents that tell us what a typical day at the "Store" was like. What are they?
4. "Whenever I walked into the Store in the afternoon," Angelou writes in paragraph 3, "I sensed that it was tired." What does this personification suggest about her attitude toward this place?
5. What is Angelou's reaction to Uncle Willie's having to hide in the vege-

table bin? What does this reaction and her description of his suffering reveal about her?

6. Who are the "boys," and what is Angelou's attitude toward them?

Suggestions for Journal Entries

1. Angelou begins by describing the "Store" in detail at different times of the day. Think of a setting you spend a lot of time in, such as the place where you work. Jot down your impressions of this place at different times of the day or night.
2. Recall an incident in which you were forced to do something that demoralized or offended you. Briefly describe what happened, and explain in a sentence or two why you felt demoralized or offended.
3. Angelou's indignation at Uncle Willie's having to hide in the vegetable bin reveals her pride in her family and her race as well as her belief in the dignity of all people. Recall a stressful or emotion-filled incident in your life, and briefly explain what your reaction to this incident says about you.

From *Zen and the Art of Motorcycle Maintenance*

Robert Pirsig

A native of Minneapolis–St. Paul, Robert Pirsig taught composition and rhetoric at the University of Chicago and has worked as a technical writer for several years.

Zen and the Art of Motorcycle Maintenance is one of the most celebrated books of the 1970s. It re-creates Pirsig's experiences on cross-country motorcycle trips, through which he learned how to come to grips with important aspects of his own personality and to care for a highly technical piece of machinery. According to Pirsig: "The real cycle you're working on is a cycle called 'yourself.' Working on a motorcycle, working well, caring, is to become part of a process, to achieve an inner peace of mind."

In the following selection from *Zen*, we meet Pirsig as he and his young son, Chris, encounter some very bad weather while cycling to Canada.

Looking Ahead

1. The word "Zen" comes from "Zen Buddhism," an ancient sect of Buddhism still followed by millions in Japan, China, and other parts of Asia.

It stresses personal meditation and individual thinking over a blind adherence to rules. Thinking problems out thoroughly and independently is also an important aspect of Pirsig's work.

2. Pirsig writes that "The whole experience was kind of dumb and sad." As you read the story of his journey through the storm and the events that follow, ask yourself what was "sad" about the experience and what was "dumb" about it.

3. The author makes excellent use of transitions to indicate the passage of time. In paragraph 4, for instance, he says: "The cycle slowed down to twenty-five, *then* twenty. *Then* it started missing..." Look for several other transitional words or expressions in this narrative.

4. Each paragraph in this selection covers only one incident in the long series of events. Notice how Pirsig provides only those details necessary to keep the story moving steadily and to maintain the reader's interest.

5. Pirsig waits until the last paragraph to reveal the theme of his story. It tells us what he learned from his experiences, both about motorcycle maintenance and about himself.

Vocabulary

ponchos   Large waterproof cloaks used as raincoats.

stopcock   The valve that controls the flow of gasoline.

I remember Chris and I were on a trip to Canada a few years ago, got 1 about 130 miles and were caught in a warm front of which we had plenty of warning but which we didn't understand. The whole experience was kind of dumb and sad.

We were on a little six-and-one-half-horsepower cycle, way overloaded 2 with luggage and way underloaded with common sense. The machine could do only about forty-five miles per hour wide open against a moderate head wind. It was no touring bike. We reached a large lake in the North Woods the first night and tented amid rainstorms that lasted all night long. I forgot to dig a trench around the tent and at about two in the morning a stream of water came in and soaked both sleeping bags. The next morning we were soggy and depressed and hadn't had much sleep, but I thought that if we just got riding the rain would let up after a while. No such luck. By ten o'clock the sky was so dark all the cars had their headlights on. And then it really came down.

We were wearing the ponchos which had served as a tent the night be- 3 fore. Now they spread out like sails and slowed our speed to thirty miles an hour wide open. The water on the road became two inches deep. Lightning bolts came crashing down all around us. I remember a woman's face looking astonished at us from the window of a passing car, wondering what in earth we were doing on a motorcycle in this weather. I'm sure I couldn't have told her.

The cycle slowed down to twenty-five, then twenty. Then it started 4 missing, coughing and popping and sputtering until, barely moving at five or six miles an hour, we found an old run-down filling station by some cutover timberland and pulled in.

At the time... I hadn't bothered to learn much about motorcycle main- 5 tenance. I remember holding my poncho over my head to keep the rain from the tank and rocking the cycle between my legs. Gas seemed to be sloshing around inside. I looked at the plugs, and looked at the points, and looked at the carburetor, and pumped the kick starter until I was exhausted.

We went into the filling station, which was also a combination beer joint 6 and restaurant, and had a meal of burned-up steak. Then I went back out and tried it again. Chris kept asking questions that started to anger me because he didn't see how serious it was. Finally I saw it was no use, gave it up, and my anger at him disappeared. I explained to him as carefully as I could that it was all over. We weren't going anywhere by cycle on this vacation. Chris suggested things to do like check the gas, which I had done, and find a mechanic. But there weren't any mechanics. Just cutover pine trees and brush and rain.

I sat in the grass with him at the shoulder of the road, defeated, staring 7 into the trees and underbrush. I answered all of Chris's questions patiently and in time they became fewer and fewer. And then Chris finally understood that our cycle trip was really over and began to cry. He was eight then, I think.

We hitchhiked back to our own city and rented a trailer and put it on 8 our car and came up and got the cycle, and hauled it back to our own city and then started out all over again by car. But it wasn't the same. And we didn't really enjoy ourselves much.

Two weeks after the vacation was over, one evening after work, I re- 9 moved the carburetor to see what was wrong but still couldn't find anything. To clean off the grease before replacing it, I turned the stopcock on the tank for a little gas. Nothing came out. The tank was out of gas. I couldn't believe it. I can still hardly believe it.

I have kicked myself mentally a hundred times for that stupidity and 10 don't think I'll ever really, finally get over it. Evidently what I saw sloshing around was gas in the reserve tank which I had never turned on. I didn't check it carefully because I assumed the rain had caused the engine failure. I didn't understand then how foolish quick assumptions like that are. Now we are on a twenty-eight-horse machine and I take the maintenance of it very seriously.

Questions for Discussion

1. As Pirsig finally reveals, he didn't check the gas carefully enough because of a "quick" assumption about the engine. What was this assumption?

2. In what way was Pirsig's experience "dumb"? In what way was it "sad"?
3. What transitional words or expressions did you find in this essay?
4. As discussed in Looking Ahead, Zen Buddhism stresses the importance of thinking for oneself. How do Pirsig's problems with the cycle relate to this idea?
5. Pirsig includes only those details that relate to the story's central idea, or theme. What is this central idea, or theme, of his story? What has Pirsig learned from his experiences?
6. Do Chris's many questions in paragraphs 6 and 7 relate to the central idea? Why does Pirsig bother to include them?
7. What does the author's relationship with his son reveal about him?

Suggestions for Journal Entries

1. Did you ever make a very wrong assumption about someone or something? What happened as a result? In a paragraph or two, sketch out a short narrative about this incident and explain what you learned from it.
2. Have you ever traveled through a heavy or dangerous storm? In your journal, list the details that come to mind about this incident. Then write a short paragraph describing what happened and explaining how you felt as you endured this journey.
3. Recall a long trip you took with someone you are or were close to. In your journal, list the things that the trip revealed about you and/or about your relationship with this person.

SUGGESTIONS FOR WRITING

1. Several of the selections in this chapter reveal a great deal about the narrator's personality. Write the story of an important event in your life that you recall vividly. What did your actions reveal about you? Before you begin this assignment, reread your journal entries for Angelou's "The Boys" and Keller's "Exile and Return"; they might provide you with useful details.
2. A few of the authors in this chapter talk about adolescent or childhood experiences that had a significant effect on their lives. Look over your journal entries for "Incident," "The Boys," and other appropriate selections. You've probably begun gathering details about an important incident in your life. Write this story in as much detail as possible, and don't forget to explain what kind of impact the event has had on you.
3. How we face life's problems and hardships says a lot about the people we are. This is especially true of Masters' "Lucinda Matlock." Narrate the story of how a close friend, neighbor, or relative dealt with or is dealing with a significant hardship. Make sure that the events of the story reveal something important about this individual's character. Begin by re-reading

any journal entries you made after reading the two poems by Edgar Lee
Masters earlier in this chapter.

4. In the selection from *Zen and the Art of Motorcycle Maintenance*, Pirsig
   recounts a time in his life when he learned things that were helpful to his
   emotional and intellectual growth. Write the story of an event that helped
   you grow in some way. Once again, check your journal for appropriate
   details before you start writing.

5. Like Pirsig, tell the story of a long trip you took with someone you love
   or loved. Make sure to explain what the events of the trip revealed about
   your relationship with this person. If you made a journal entry in response
   to Pirsig's essay, you may have already gotten a good jump on this assignment.

Chapter 11

Reporting Events

The preceding chapter contains poems and essays that reveal a great deal about their narrators. They are autobiographical and, as such, are told from the first-person point of view. The selections you are about to read explain more about the narrator's world, its people, and its problems than about the narrator him/herself.

However, some of them re-create incidents from their storytellers' lives and, so, show them involved in the action of the story in some way. Because of this, they too, are written in first person. A good example is Schwartz's "Colossus in the Kitchen," a story of racism in South Africa, told from the perspective of its young narrator.

However, this is not the case with Gansberg's "38 Who Saw Murder. . . ." In that essay, the narrator was not involved in the action and, as such, he tells the story from the third-person point of view, using "he," "she," and "they" to explain who did what. As you can see, then, the point of view from which a story is told depends upon whether the narrator is a participant or is an outsider—someone actually involved in the action or someone who has only observed it or learned about it secondhand.

Whatever point of view the selections in this chapter use, each provides a sometimes touching, sometimes terrifying, but always interesting account of the author's world. Reporting events that you've heard about, witnessed, or even been part of can be an excellent way to develop your writing skills. It can also help you discover a clearer and more perceptive vision of the world, at least the world you're writing about.

Child of the Romans

Carl Sandburg

In the introduction to "Abraham Lincoln" (Chapter 9), you learned that Sandburg is one of America's best-loved poets and biographers. His respect for the common people and his support for labor are evident in "Child of the Romans," a sketch of an Italian immigrant railroad worker. For Sandburg, this "dago shovelman" was typical of the immigrant laborers who built America's factories and railroads.

Looking Ahead

1. "Dago" is an insulting term for an Italian. The poem's title refers to the fact that 2000 years ago Italy was the center of the powerful Roman Empire.
2. Sandburg compares the life of the shovelman to those of the people on the train. It is this comparison that serves as the theme of the poem.
3. Verbs and adjectives create a sense of reality in this poem and keep it interesting. Look for them as you read "Child of the Romans."

Vocabulary

eclairs   Rich, custard-filled pastries topped with chocolate.
jonquils   Garden plants of the narcissus family with lovely yellow or white flowers.

The dago shovelman sits by the railroad track
Eating a noon meal of bread and bologna.
A train whirls by, and men and women at tables
Alive with red roses and yellow jonquils,
Eat steaks running with brown gravy,   5
Strawberries and cream, eclairs and coffee.
The dago shovelman finishes the dry bread and bologna,
Washes it down with a dipper from the water-boy,
And goes back to the second half of a ten-hour day's work
Keeping the road-bed so the roses and jonquils   10
Shake hardly at all in the cut glass vases
Standing slender on the tables in the dining cars.

Questions for Discussion

1. The poem's plot is very simple. What events take place during the shovelman's lunch?

2. Sandburg gets very detailed in listing the various items that the railroad passengers are dining on. How do these contrast with what the shovelman is eating?
3. Why does Sandburg make sure to tell us that the train "whirls" by as the man eats his lunch? How does his description of the movement of the train contrast with what you read in the last three lines of this poem?
4. How long is the shovelman's day? In what way does his work, "keeping the road-bed," affect the passengers?
5. The poem has two very different settings. What are they, and how does the contrast between the two help Sandburg get his point across?

Suggestions for Journal Entries

1. If you know a hard-working immigrant who has come here in search of a better life, write a story about this person's typical workday.
2. If you have ever had a job in which you provided a service for other people (perhaps as a housepainter, waitress, or salesclerk), narrate one or two events from a typical workday.
3. After reading Sandburg's story of the shovelman's difficult life, many readers are inclined to count their blessings. List some things in your life that make it easier and more hopeful than that of the shovelman.

Twins

E. B. White

E. B. White was born in 1899 in Mount Vernon, a suburb of New York City just above the Bronx, where "Twins" takes place. A regular contributor to *The New Yorker* magazine and to *Harper's Magazine,* he remains one of the best-known and most highly respected of American essayists of this century. White also wrote several children's books, including *Charlotte's Web* and *Stuart Little,* and, with William Strunk, Jr., he co-authored *Elements of Style,* a classic little book on language usage.

Looking Ahead

1. The Bronx Zoo, in New York City, is one of the largest municipal animal parks in the world.
2. The setting of "Twins" is very important. Look for the details that describe it.

Vocabulary

captious   Complaining, hard to please.

fastnesses   Enclosed areas.

ingenuity   Skill, cleverness.

Mittel Bronx   The middle of the Bronx.

primate   A member of the family of mammals that includes monkeys, apes, and human beings.

primly   Stiffly.

reducing glass   A lens that makes things look smaller.

resentful   Displeased.

sullenly   With a gloomy or dull expression.

sylvan   Forestlike.

trinket   A tiny ornament or toy.

twinning   Giving birth to twins.

withered   Dried out, dead.

On a warm, miserable morning last week we went up to the Bronx Zoo   1
to see the moose calf and to break in a new pair of black shoes. We encountered better luck than we had bargained for. The cow moose and her young one were standing near the wall of the deer park below the monkey house, and in order to get a better view we strolled down to the lower end of the park, by the brook. The path there is not much travelled. As we approached the corner where the brook trickles under the wire fence, we noticed a red deer getting to her feet. Beside her, on legs that were just learning their business, was a spotted fawn, as small and perfect as a trinket seen through a reducing glass. They stood there, mother and child, under a gray beech whose trunk was engraved with dozens of hearts and initials. Stretched on the ground was another fawn, and we realized that the doe had just finished twinning. The second fawn was still wet, still unrisen. Here was a scene of rare sylvan splendor, in one of our five favorite boroughs, and we couldn't have asked for more. Even our new shoes seemed to be working out all right and weren't hurting much.

The doe was only a couple of feet from the wire, and we sat down on   2
a rock at the edge of the footpath to see what sort of start young fawns get in the deep fastnesses of Mittel Bronx. The mother, mildly resentful of our presence and dazed from her labor, raised one forefoot and stamped primly. Then she lowered her head, picked up the afterbirth, and began dutifully to eat it, allowing it to swing crazily from her mouth, as though it were a bunch of withered beet greens. From the monkey house came the loud, insane hooting of some captious primate, filling the whole woodland with a wild hooroar. As we watched, the sun broke weakly through, brightened the rich red of the fawns, and kindled their white spots. Occasionally a sightseer would appear

and wander aimlessly by, but of all who passed none was aware that anything extraordinary had occurred. "Looka the kangaroos!" a child cried. And he and his mother stared sullenly at the deer and then walked on.

In a few moments the second twin gathered all his legs and all his in- 3 genuity and arose, to stand for the first time sniffing the mysteries of a park for captive deer. The doe, in recognition of his achievement, quit her other work and began to dry him, running her tongue against the grain and paying particular attention to the key points. Meanwhile the first fawn tiptoed toward the shallow brook, in little stops and goes, and started across. He paused midstream to make a slight contribution, as a child does in bathing. Then, while his mother watched, he continued across, gained the other side, selected a hiding place, and lay down under a skunk-cabbage leaf next to the fence, in perfect concealment, his legs folded neatly under him. Without actually going out of sight, he had managed to disappear completely in the shifting light and shade. From somewhere a long way off a twelve-o'clock whistle sounded. We hung around awhile, but he never budged. Before we left, we crossed the brook ourself, just outside the fence, knelt, reached through the wire, and tested the truth of what we had once heard: that you can scratch a new fawn between the ears without starting him. You can indeed.

Questions for Discussion

1. How has White described the setting of "Twins"? Why is it important for us to know about the surroundings into which the two deer have been born?
2. The story's plot is rather simple. What are its most significant events?
3. Some of the natural processes that White reports, such as the doe's disposing of the afterbirth, might startle some readers. Should he have left such details out?
4. The author mentions the "insane hooting of some captious primate." What do such details add to the story?
5. White has captured the beauty of the fawns and doe by describing their movements. What verbs, adjectives, and adverbs communicate this beauty to us? Look especially at paragraph 3.
6. Compared to the monkeys and kangaroos in paragraph 2, deer are not very exotic animals. What qualities in the deer have evidently moved White to write this simple, lovely story about them? Perhaps the title is a clue.

Suggestions for Journal Entries

1. If you've ever been present at the birth of any creature, list in your journal the event's most important and startling details. How did the birth you witnessed compare with what is described in "Twins"?
2. List details that capture your memories of a recent trip through a park,

zoo, or other natural place. Then, in a paragraph or two, describe the most memorable of the sights and events you observed.

The Colossus in the Kitchen

Adrienne Schwartz

Adrienne Schwartz was born in Johannesburg in the Republic of South Africa, where she lived until 1978. Now a U.S. citizen, she is completing her studies in English to become a professional writer.

"The Colossus in the Kitchen" is about the tragedy of apartheid, the political system in South Africa that denies civil and human rights to blacks. Tandi, the black woman Schwartz makes the centerpiece of her story, was her nursemaid for several years and occupied a special place in her home and her heart.

Looking Ahead

1. The "Group Areas Act," which Schwartz refers to in paragraph 7, requires blacks to seek work *only* in those areas of the country for which the government has granted them a permit. Unfortunately, Tandi's legal husband was not allowed to work in the same region as she.
2. The "Colossus" was the giant bronze statue of a male figure straddling the inlet to the ancient Greek city of Rhodes. It was known as one of the seven wonders of the ancient world. More generally, this term refers to anything that is very large, impressive, and very powerful. As you read this essay, ask yourself what made Tandi a colossus in the eyes of young Schwartz.

Vocabulary

apoplectic Characterized by a sudden loss of muscle control or ability to move.
ashen Gray.
cavernous Like a cave or cavern.
confections Sweets.
cowered Lowered in defeat.
dauntless Fearless.
deviants Moral degenerates.
disenfranchised Without rights or power.
entailed Involved.

flaying   Whipping.

gangrenous   Characterized by decay of the flesh.

nebulous   Without a definite shape or form.

prerogative   Privilege.

sage   Wise.

I remember when I first discovered the extraordinary harshness of daily   1
life for black South Africans. It was in the carefree, tumbling days of childhood that I first sensed apartheid was not merely the impoverishing of the
landless and all that that entailed, but a flaying of the innermost spirit.

The house seemed so huge in those days, and the adults were giants   2
bestriding the world with surety and purpose. Tandi, the cook, reigned with
the authoritarian discipline of a Caesar. She held audience in the kitchen, an
enormous room filled with half-lights and well-scrubbed tiles, cool stone floors
and a cavernous black stove. Its ceilings were high, and during the heat of
midday I would often drowse in the corner, listening to Tandi sing, in a lilting
voice, of the hardships of black women as aliens in their own country. From
half-closed eyes I would watch her broad hands coax, from a nebulous lump
of dough, a bounty of confections, filled with yellow cream and new-picked
apricots.

She was a peasant woman and almost illiterate, yet she spoke five lan-   3
guages quite competently; moreover, she was always there, sturdy, domi-
neering and quick to laugh.

Our neighbors, in conformity with established thinking, had long branded   4
my mother, and therefore all of us, as deviants, agitators, and no less than
second cousins to Satan himself. The cause of this dishonorable labeling was
founded in the fact that we had been taught to believe in the equality and
dignity of man.

"Never take a person's dignity away from him," my mother had said,   5
"no matter how angry or hurt you might be because in the end you only
diminish your own worth."

That was why I could not understand the apoplectic reaction of the   6
neighbors to my excited news that Tandi was going to have a baby. After all,
this was not politics; this was new life.

Tandi's common-law husband lived illegally with her in the quarters   7
assigned to them; complying with the law on this and many other petty issues
was not considered appropriate in our household. It was the Group Areas Act
that had been responsible for the breakup of Tandi's marriage in the first
place. Her lawful husband, who was not born in the same area as she, had
been refused a permit to work in the Transvaal, and like others placed in such
a burdensome situation, suffered the continuous degradation of being dragged
from his wife's bed in the middle of the night and of being jobless more often

than he could tolerate. Eventually, he simply melted away, wordlessly, never to be seen or heard from again, making legal divorce impossible.

The paradox of South Africa is complex in the extreme. It is like a rare 8 and precious stone, set amid the barren wastes, and yet close up it is a gangrenous growth that feeds off its own flesh.

The days passed and Tandi's waist swelled, and pride glowed in her 9 dauntless eyes.

And then the child was born, and he lived for a day, and then he died. 10

I could not look at Tandi. I did not know that the young could die. I 11 thought death was the prerogative of the elderly. I could not bear to see her cowered shoulders or ashen face.

I fled to the farthest corner of the yard. One of the neighbors was out picking 12 off dead buds from the rose bushes. She looked over the hedge in concern.

"Why! You look terrible...are you ill, dear?" she said.   13

"It's Tandi, Mrs. Green. She lost her baby last night," I replied.   14

Mrs. Green sighed thoughtfully and pulled off her gardening gloves. 15 "It's really not surprising," she said, not unkindly, but as if she were imparting as sage a piece of advice as she could. "These people (a term reserved for the disenfranchised) have to learn that the punishment always fits the crime."

Questions for Discussion

1. Schwartz's reference to Tandi as a colossus is obviously complimentary. What details does she use to show that Tandi is impressive and powerful?
2. The author uses dialogue to emphasize major ideas. What does the quote from Mrs. Green reveal about the world Schwartz grew up in?
3. What was the Schwartz family's attitude toward apartheid, and what did their neighbors think of them because of their political opinions?
4. Why did Tandi's lawful husband leave her? Is it important for Schwartz to explain the reasons for his departure?
5. Schwartz describes the kind of life that Tandi is forced to live by recounting several events about her (in paragraphs 2, 7, 9, and 10). Which event made the greatest impression on you?
6. The death of Tandi's baby and the reactions of her neighbors convinced Schwartz of how harsh a life black South Africans have to endure. She writes in paragraph 1 that apartheid is not "merely the impoverishing of the landless" but also "a flaying of the innermost spirit." What does she mean by this? In what way do the events at the end of the story dramatize this "flaying"?

Suggestions for Journal Entries

1. Have you or anyone you know well ever witnessed or been involved in a case of intolerance based on race, color, creed, or sex? List the important

events that made up this incident and, if appropriate, use the focused-freewriting method (explained in Getting Started) to write short descriptions of the characters involved.

2. Schwartz's essay is a startling account of her learning some new and very painful things about life. Using any of the prewriting methods discussed in Getting Started, make notes about an incident from your childhood that opened your eyes to some new and perhaps unpleasant reality.

3. Were you ever as close to an older person as Schwartz was to Tandi? Examine your relationship with the individual by briefly narrating one or two experiences you shared with him or her.

Back Home

Langston Hughes

In Chapter 10 you met Countee Cullen, a member of the Harlem Renaissance. Another important figure of this 1920s literary movement was Langston Hughes (1902–1967). One of the best-known black American writers, Hughes used his personal experiences as the basis for many of his works.

"Back Home" first appeared in *The Big Sea* (1940), an autobiography covering his early years. In this selection Hughes narrates two disturbing and disheartening events in which he suffered racial discrimination during his return to the United States after a long stay in Mexico.

Looking Ahead

1. Until the Civil Rights Act of 1964, "Jim Crow" laws prevented blacks from using waiting rooms, restaurants, and other public facilities reserved for whites.

2. Hughes includes excellent examples of dialogue in this essay. Ask yourself how they help make his writing more interesting and realistic.

Vocabulary

pomade   A perfumed hairdressing.

pullman berth   A small sleeping compartment on a train.

On the way back to Cleveland an amusing thing happened. During the   1
trip to the border, several American whites on the train mistook me for a

Mexican, and some of them even spoke to me in Spanish, since I am of a
copper-brown complexion, with black hair that can be made quite slick and
shiny if it has enough pomade on it in the Mexican fashion. But I made no
pretense of passing for a Mexican, or anything else, since there was no need
for it—except in changing trains at San Antonio in Texas, where colored people had to use Jim Crow waiting rooms, and could not purchase a Pullman
berth. There, I simply went in the main waiting room, as any Mexican would
do, and made my sleeping-car reservations in Spanish.

But that evening, crossing Texas, I was sitting alone at a small table in   2
the diner, when a white man came in and took the seat just across the table
from mine. Shortly, I noticed him staring at me intently, as if trying to puzzle
out something. He stared at me a long time. Then, suddenly, with a loud cry,
the white man jumped up and shouted: "You're a nigger, ain't you?" And
rushed out of the car as if pursued by a plague.

I grinned. I had heard before that white Southerners never sat down to   3
table with a Negro, but I didn't know until then that we frightened them that
badly.

Something rather less amusing happened at St. Louis. The train pulled   4
into the station on a blazing-hot September afternoon, after a sticky, dusty
trip, for there were no air-cooled coaches in those days. I had a short wait
between trains. In the center of the station platform there was a news stand
and soda fountain where cool drinks were being served. I went up to the
counter and asked for an ice cream soda.

The clerk said: "Are you a Mexican or a Negro?"   5
I said: "Why?"   6
"Because if you're a Mexican, I'll serve you," he said. "If you're col-   7
ored, I won't."

"I'm colored," I replied. The clerk turned to wait on some one else. I   8
knew I was home in the U.S.A.

Questions for Discussion

1. What similarities are there between the two episodes (or stories within a
   story) in "Back Home"? What is the point Hughes is trying to make in
   them?
2. Why does he bother to say that he could have passed for a Mexican if he
   had wanted to?
3. In Looking Ahead, you read that Hughes makes excellent use of dialogue.
   In what way does the dialogue in "Back Home" make it more interesting
   and more realistic?
4. Hughes uses transitional words and phrases to show the passage of time
   and maintain coherence. What are some of these words and phrases?

Suggestion for a Journal Entry

Hughes says that he "made no pretense of passing for a Mexican, or anything else, since there was no need for it" (paragraph 1). If you've ever been insulted or looked down upon because of who or what you are, write a summary of this incident and explain how you felt.

Tragedy in Toluca

Langston Hughes

Also from *The Big Sea*, "Tragedy in Toluca" is a story of human jealousy in which Hughes narrowly escaped death.

Looking Ahead

1. To make "Tragedy in Toluca" more realistic, the author sprinkles information about the setting throughout the story. He also provides a great many details about his characters and about the circumstances that brought them together. Look for such details as you read this selection.
2. As in "Back Home," Hughes uses transitional words and expressions to keep the story moving. Mark such transitions as you read this selection.
3. The "war" mentioned in paragraph 7 is World War I. "Frau" means "Mrs." in German.

Vocabulary

amiable Friendly.
awkward Not graceful, a little clumsy.
sober Serious.

Our German housekeeper, Frau Schultz, had an old friend from Berlin 1
in Mexico City, whose husband was not well and whose income was therefore reduced. This friend had several children, the oldest, a daughter of seventeen or eighteen in need of work.

That winter in Toluca, the wife of the German brewery-master died, 2
and so he began looking about for a housekeeper. The brewery-master was sixty-five years old, and merely wanted someone to manage his Mexican servants and see that he got something to eat, German-style, once in a while. Frau Schultz immediately thought of her friend's daughter for the job. Al-

though a young girl, she was nevertheless sober and industrious in her habits, and a very good cook, to boot.

She sent for the girl. Her name was Gerta Kraus. She was a very plain 3 girl, awkward, shy and silent, with stringy ashen hair and a long face. She spoke no Spanish beyond *Buenos Dias,* so that was all we ever said to each other as long as I knew her. The old German gave her the job as his house-keeper. And as the winter went on, Frau Schultz reported that the girl was doing very well, that she kept the brewery-master's home spotless, and sent her wages to her parents in Mexico City.

Perhaps twice a week, Gerta would come down to our house and spend 4 a few hours in the afternoon with Frau Schultz. Occasionally, I would come home from my various English classes and find them chattering away in German at a great rate, over a big pot of coffee and a platter of cakes. But I seldom joined them. My pupils' parents gave me chocolate, or sweetmeats, or something to eat or drink almost every time I taught a class, so I was seldom hungry until dinner time.

In the spring, Frau Kraus came up from Mexico City to spend a week 5 with Frau Schultz and see her daughter, whom she hadn't seen all winter. That week the outdoor brick oven in our corral was always full of long loaves of bread and yellow cakes. All the German friends of Frau Schultz in Toluca came to call on Frau Kraus from Mexico City—that is all the Germans in *their* circle—for the wealthier Germans, like the brewery-master, did not move in such poor society.

My father had gone to the ranch, so the women had the house to them-6 selves. Because I found Frau Schultz very kind and amiable, I was glad she was having a holiday week with her friends. Every day, Gerta came down to our house to be with her mother, and things were very lively and the patio was filled with feminine voices speaking German. Most of the time, I kept out of the way, since we couldn't understand one another, the Germans and I.

Then Friday came. The week was almost over and Frau Kraus would 7 return to Mexico City on Sunday. But on Friday the terrible thing happened. Fortunately, there were no guests in the house that afternoon. Only Frau Schultz and her little girl, Lotte, Frau Kraus and her daughter, Gerta. It was a chilly, dismal afternoon, so they were all seated at the table in the dining room just off the warm kitchen. The coffee was hot, and the apple-cakes almost like the cakes at home in Germany, where the ovens were not built of adobe brick in dusty corrals. They were having a good time, the two women talking of days before the war in their suburb of Berlin, and of their children, and how ten-year-old Lotte was learning Spanish and becoming Catholic al-ready in that Catholic school, and of how well Gerta had done with her job under the tall, cranky old brewery-master.

Just then someone knocked commandingly at the street entrance. Ten-8 year-old Lotte went down the corridor and across the patio to answer the door. There stood the brewery-master, tall with iron-white hair and a big white mustache. He did not say a word to Lotte. He came in and strode slowly along the corridor that skirted the patio, looking into each room as he passed. He came to the dining-room, which was at the end of the corridor. Hearing voices, he pushed open the door and walked in.

No one had time to say a word, to rise to greet him, or to offer him a 9 chair. For the brewery-master took a pistol from his pocket and, without warning, began to fire on the women. First he fired on Gerta point-blank, sending a bullet through her head, another through her jaw, another through her shoulder, before she slumped unconscious to the floor beneath the table. In panic, the two women tried to run, but the old man, blocking the door, fired again, striking Frau Schultz in the right arm and breaking it. Then he went all through the patio looking for me, looking, looking, out into the corral and through the stables.

Lotte, wild-eyed, reached the street and called the neighbors. Frau Kraus 10 lay in a dead faint in the kitchen. Frau Schultz crouched, stunned, in a corner against the wall, afraid to move. A crowd of Indians assembled, but were wary of entering the house.

Finally the old German walked past the men on the sidewalk, with his 11 pistol still in hand, and no one stopped him. He went directly to the police station and gave himself up. He had two bullets left in his gun, and he told the police he had intended them for me. He said he thought Gerta had been coming to our house to be with me. He said he was in love with Gerta and he wanted to kill her and to kill me.

When I got home a half-hour after the shooting, the ambulance had just 12 taken every one to the hospital. The police would not let me in until they had completed their inspection. When I finally did get into the house, I found the dining room floor a pool of blood, a chair splintered by a bullet, and the tiles of the corridor spotted with red.

Since my father was at the ranch, I went in search of a German friend 13 of his, a buyer of mines, who saw to it that proper hospitalization was provided for the women. Then we went to visit the jail. The old brewery-master sat in his cell, not saying a word, except that he was glad he had killed the girl. He was glad, he mumbled, glad!

But strangely enough, Gerta did not die! She was unconscious for six 14 weeks, and remained in the hospital almost a year—but she didn't die. She finally got well again, with the marks of three bullets on her face and body. The court gave the old man twenty years in prison.

Had I arrived at home that afternoon a half-hour earlier, I probably 15 would not be here today.

Questions for Discussion

1. What do we know of Frau Schultz and Gerta? What about the brewery

master? Why do you think Hughes gives us so much information about
these people in particular?

2. What transitional words and expressions does Hughes include in this story
   to keep the plot moving?
3. There are a great many details in this essay to describe the setting and to
   make the story more realistic. In what kind of place does the story take
   place? What does Hughes's house look like after the shooting?
4. The author takes us through the shooting of Gerta and Frau Schultz quite
   slowly, describing the action in great detail. Reread this part of the essay,
   and identify the adjectives and verbs that make it particularly exciting.

Suggestion for a Journal Entry

If you've ever seen an automobile accident, mugging, house fire, raging flood,
or other example of human or natural violence, briefly report on the events
you witnessed.

---

38 Who Saw Murder Didn't Call the Police

Martin Gansberg

Martin Gansberg was a reporter and editor at *The New York Times* when
he wrote "38 Who Saw Murder..." for that newspaper in 1964. This story
about the murder of a young woman is doubly terrifying, for the thirty-eight
witnesses to the crime might very well have saved her life if only they had had
the courage to become involved.

Looking Ahead

1. The setting is Kew Gardens, a well-to-do neighborhood in Queens, New
   York. One reason Gansberg describes it in great detail is to make his story
   realistic. Another is to show his readers that the neighbors had a clear view
   of the crime from their windows. But there are other reasons as well. Pay
   close attention to the details used to describe the setting.
2. Gansberg begins the story by using dialogue to report an interview he had
   with the police. He ends it similarly, including dialogue from interviews
   with several witnesses. Read these two parts of the narrative as carefully
   as the story of the murder itself. They contain important information about
   Gansberg's reaction to the incident and his purpose in writing this piece.
3. The story of Kitty Genovese is a comment about the fact that people some-

times ignore their responsibilities to neighbors and lose that important sense of community which binds us together. Identify this central idea, or theme, as you read "38 Who Saw Murder...."

Vocabulary

deliberation   Thinking.
distraught   Very upset, nervous.
punctuated   Were clearly heard (literally "made a mark in").
recitation   Speech, lecture.
Tudor   A type of architecture in which the beams are exposed.

For more than half an hour 38 respectable, law-abiding citizens in Queens 1 watched a killer stalk and stab a woman in three separate attacks in Kew Gardens.

Twice their chatter and the sudden glow of their bedroom lights inter- 2 rupted him and frightened him off. Each time he returned, sought her out, and stabbed her again. Not one person telephoned the police during the assault; one witness called after the woman was dead.

That was two weeks ago today.   3

Still shocked is Assistant Chief Inspector Frederick M. Lussen, in charge 4 of the borough's detectives and a veteran of 25 years of homicide investigations. He can give a matter-of-fact recitation on many murders. But the Kew Gardens slaying baffles him—not because it is a murder, but because the "good people" failed to call the police.

"As we have reconstructed the crime," he said, "the assailant had three 5 chances to kill this woman during a 35-minute period. He returned twice to complete the job. If we had been called when he first attacked, the woman might not be dead now."

This is what the police say happened beginning at 3:20 A.M. in the staid, 6 middle-class, tree-lined Austin Street area:

Twenty-eight-year-old Catherine Genovese, who was called Kitty by al- 7 most everyone in the neighborhood, was returning home from her job as manager of a bar in Hollis. She parked her red Fiat in a lot adjacent to the Kew Gardens Long Island Rail Road Station, facing Mowbray Place. Like many residents of the neighborhood, she had parked there day after day since her arrival from Connecticut a year ago, although the railroad frowns on the practice.

She turned off the lights of her car, locked the door, and started to walk 8 the 100 feet to the entrance of her apartment at 82-70 Austin Street, which is in a Tudor building, with stores in the first floor and apartments on the second.

The entrance to the apartment is in the rear of the building because the 9 front is rented to retail stores. At night the quiet neighborhood is shrouded in the slumbering darkness that marks most residential areas.

Miss Genovese noticed a man at the far end of the lot, near a seven-story 10
apartment house at 82-40 Austin Street. She halted. Then, nervously, she
headed up Austin Street toward Lefferts Boulevard, where there is a call box
to the 102nd Police Precinct in nearby Richmond Hill.

She got as far as a street light in front of a bookstore before the man 11
grabbed her. She screamed. Lights went on in the 10-story apartment house
at 82-67 Austin Street, which faces the bookstore. Windows slid open and
voices punctuated the early-morning stillness.

Miss Genovese screamed: "Oh, my God, he stabbed me! Please help 12
me! Please help me!"

From one of the upper windows in the apartment house, a man called 13
down: "Let that girl alone!"

The assailant looked up at him, shrugged and walked down Austin Street 14
toward a white sedan parked a short distance away. Miss Genovese struggled
to her feet.

Lights went out. The killer returned to Miss Genovese, now trying to 15
make her way around the side of the building by the parking lot to get to her
apartment. The assailant stabbed her again.

"I'm dying!" she shrieked. "I'm dying!"   16

Windows were opened again, and lights went on in many apartments. 17
The assailant got into his car and drove away. Miss Genovese staggered to her
feet. A city bus, Q-10, the Lefferts Boulevard line to Kennedy International
Airport, passed. It was 3:35 A.M.

The assailant returned. By then, Miss Genovese had crawled to the back 18
of the building, where the freshly painted brown doors to the apartment house
held out hope for safety. The killer tried the first door; she wasn't there. At
the second door, 82-62 Austin Street, he saw her slumped on the floor at the
foot of the stairs. He stabbed her a third time—fatally.

It was 3:50 by the time the police received their first call, from a man 19
who was a neighbor of Miss Genovese. In two minutes they were at the scene.
The neighbor, a 70-year-old woman, and another woman were the only persons on the street. Nobody else came forward.

The man explained that he had called the police after much delibera- 20
tion. He had phoned a friend in Nassau County for advice and then he had
crossed the roof of the building to the apartment of the elderly woman to get
her to make the call.

"I didn't want to get involved," he sheepishly told the police.   21

Six days later, the police arrested Winston Moseley, a 29-year-old 22
business-machine operator, and charged him with homicide. Moseley had no
previous record. He is married, has two children and owns a home at 133-19
Sutter Avenue, South Ozone Park, Queens. On Wednesday, a court committed him to Kings County Hospital for psychiatric observation.

When questioned by the police, Moseley also said that he had slain Mrs. 23

Annie May Johnson, 24, of 146-12 133rd Avenue, Jamaica, on Feb. 29 and Barbara Kralik, 15, of 174-17 140th Avenue, Springfield Gardens, last July. In the Kralik case, the police are holding Alvin L. Mitchell, who is said to have confessed to that slaying.

The police stressed how simple it would have been to have gotten in 24 touch with them. "A phone call," said one of the detectives, "would have done it." The police may be reached by dialing "O" for operator or SPring 7-3100.

Today witnesses from the neighborhood, which is made up of one-family 25 homes in the $35,000 to $60,000 range with the exception of the two apartment houses near the railroad station, find it difficult to explain why they didn't call the police.

A housewife, knowingly if quite casually, said, "We thought it was a 26 lover's quarrel." A husband and wife both said, "Frankly, we were afraid." They seemed aware of the fact that events might have been different. A distraught woman, wiping her hands on her apron, said, "I didn't want my husband to get involved."

One couple, now willing to talk about that night, said they heard the 27 first screams. The husband looked thoughtfully at the bookstore where the killer first grabbed Miss Genovese.

"We went to the window to see what was happening," he said, "but the 28 light from our bedroom made it difficult to see the street." The wife, still apprehensive, added: "I put out the light and we were able to see better."

Asked why they hadn't called the police, she shrugged and replied: "I 29 don't know."

A man peeked out from the slight opening in the doorway to his apart- 30 ment and rattled off an account of the killer's second attack. Why hadn't he called the police at the time? "I was tired," he said without emotion. "I went back to bed."

It was 4:25 A.M. when the ambulance arrived to take the body of Miss 31 Genovese. It drove off. "Then," a solemn police detective said, "the people came out."

Questions for Discussion

1. Catherine Genovese "was called Kitty by almost everyone in the neighborhood" (paragraph 7). What does this fact reveal about her relationship with her neighbors?
2. In Looking Ahead, you learned that there are several reasons for Gansberg's including details to describe the setting of this story. In what kind of neighborhood does the murder take place? What kind of people live in it?
3. The story's theme might be that people seem to be losing their sense of

community for fear of "getting involved." Using details from the story, explain this idea more fully.

4. In reporting several interviews he had with the police and with witnesses, Gansberg frames the story with dialogue at the beginning and end. What do we learn from this dialogue?
5. The author keeps the story moving by mentioning the times at which various episodes in the attack took place. Where does he mention these times?
6. In addition, what transitional words or expressions does Gansberg use to show the passage of time?
7. The story's verbs demonstrate how brutal and terrifying the murder of Kitty Genovese actually was. Identify a few of these verbs.

Suggestions for Journal Entries

1. Make a list of things you might have done to help Kitty Genovese had you been an eyewitness.
2. This story illustrates what can happen when people lose their sense of community and refuse to "get involved." Use focused freewriting to make notes about one or two incidents from your own experiences that might very well illustrate this idea too.
3. Recall a time when you thought you were in some danger. Briefly describe what it was like. What did you do to try to avoid or escape physical harm?

SUGGESTIONS FOR WRITING

1. Sandburg's "Child of the Romans" tells a touching story with which you might be able to relate. In the same way that Sandburg contrasts the shovelman's difficult life with the easy life of the railroad passengers, write a narrative that shows how difficult or how easy your life is when contrasted to the life of someone you know well.

    If you responded to items 1 or 3 in Suggestions for Journal Entries following "Child of the Romans," read your notes carefully. They might help you get started.
2. Have you ever been present at the birth of an animal—or human being for that matter? Write an essay in which you narrate the birth you witnessed. If you can, include details about the newborn's (or newborns') first few minutes of life. Before you begin, however, read the journal notes you recorded after reading E.B. White's "Twins."
3. Like other selections in this chapter, Schwartz's "Colossus in the Kitchen" explains how its author learned about one of the more painful realities of life. Write an essay recalling an event that taught you something distressing about life. If appropriate, base your essay on the journal notes you made after reading "Colossus in the Kitchen," Hughes's "Back Home," or Gansberg's "38 Who Saw Murder...."

4. Several selections in this chapter speak of the unfair treatment of people because of their race or nationality. If you've ever been the object of some sort of prejudice, tell your story as vividly as you can and include some indication of how it made you feel. Most important, explain what you learned from it. Incidentally, you may already have recorded some notes about this incident in your journal in response to the suggestions that follow the selections by Schwartz, Sandburg, and Hughes.

5. If you've ever seen an automobile accident, mugging, house fire, raging flood or other example of human or natural violence, report on the events you witnessed. What did the incident tell you about human nature or about the world we live in? Once again, refer to the journal entries you've made to give you a head start. Look most closely at what you wrote after reading "38 Who Saw Murder. . . ."

Chapter 12

The Short Story

In the introduction to Section III, you learned the major difference between nonfiction and fiction. The former is based upon fact. The latter is, for the most part, a product of the author's imagination and, as such, does not recreate events as they actually happened.

Whether fiction or nonfiction, the selections in Section III use important narrative tools like character, setting, dialogue, point of view, and, of course, plot to develop a central idea or theme. In some cases, especially in works of nonfiction, this idea or theme is stated plainly, in a thesis. In fact, writers of nonfiction often use their stories as concrete illustrations or examples of an important principle or idea about themselves, other people, or life in general.

However, in works of fiction, like the selections you will read in this chapter, the theme is rarely stated openly. What the writer wishes to tell his or her readers about life is revealed through plot, character development, and other narrative elements. In most cases, in fact, it is up to the reader to try to identify the theme for him/herself after having read and analyzed the story carefully. This process, known as interpretation, can make reading fiction both challenging and exciting for you, and it is sure to make it more enjoyable.

Charles

Shirley Jackson

Shirley Jackson (1919–1965) launched her writing career in the 1940s, when she began to publish short stories in important periodicals like *The American Mercury, The New Republic,* and *The New Yorker.* Her single most important story is "The Lottery." Like many of her other stories, it uses a common and realistic setting—in this case a typical American farming town—to reveal something strange and terrifying about the human character.

The setting of "Charles," the short story that follows, is also quite recognizable, and it, too, prods us into realizing something peculiar if not downright disturbing about human nature. But Jackson's intent here is to poke us with gentle humor rather than to scare the wits out of us.

Looking Ahead

1. There seem to be two main characters in this selection, Laurie and Charles. See if you can pick out similarities in their personalities. Compare what one says and does with what you learn about the other.
2. To make the story realistic, Jackson has Laurie's mother tell it in her own words. She is the narrator.
3. Pay close attention to the dialogue that Jackson uses to re-create family discussions in which Laurie reveals things about Charles and about himself.

Vocabulary

cynically   Distrustfully, skeptically.
incredulously   Doubtfully, without believing.
insolently   Disrespectfully.
renounced   Rejected.
unsettling   Disturbing.

The day my son Laurie started kindergarten he renounced corduroy 1
overalls with bibs and began wearing blue jeans with a belt; I watched him go off the first morning with the older girl next door, seeing clearly that an era of my life was ended, my sweet-voiced nursery-school tot replaced by a long-trousered, swaggering character who forgot to stop at the corner and wave good-bye to me.

He came home the same way, the front door slamming open, his cap on 2
the floor, and the voice suddenly become raucous shouting, "Isn't anybody *here?*"

At lunch he spoke insolently to his father, spilled his baby sister's milk,   3
and remarked that his teacher said we were not to take the name of the Lord
in vain.

"How *was* school today?" I asked, elaborately casual.   4

"All right," he said.   5

"Did you learn anything?" his father asked.   6

Laurie regarded his father coldly. "I didn't learn nothing," he said.   7

"Anything," I said. "Didn't learn anything."   8

"The teacher spanked a boy, though," Laurie said, addressing his bread   9
and butter. "For being fresh," he added, with his mouth full.

"What did he do?" I asked. "Who was it?"   10

Laurie thought. "It was Charles," he said. "He was fresh. The teacher   11
spanked him and made him stand in a corner. He was awfully fresh."

"What did he do?" I asked again, but Laurie slid off his chair, took a   12
cookie, and left, while his father was still saying, "See here, young man."

The next day Laurie remarked at lunch, as soon as he sat down, "Well,   13
Charles was bad again today." He grinned enormously and said, "Today
Charles hit the teacher."

"Good heavens," I said, mindful of the Lord's name, "I suppose he got   14
spanked again?"

"He sure did," Laurie said. "Look up," he said to his father.   15

"What?" his father said, looking up.   16

"Look down," Laurie said. "Look at my thumb. Gee, you're dumb."   17
He began to laugh insanely.

"Why did Charles hit the teacher?" I asked quickly.   18

"Because she tried to make him color with red crayons," Laurie said.   19
"Charles wanted to color with green crayons so he hit the teacher and she
spanked him and said nobody play with Charles but everybody did."

The third day—it was Wednesday of the first week—Charles bounced   20
a see-saw on to the head of a little girl and made her bleed, and the teacher
made him stay inside all during recess. Thursday Charles had to stand in a
corner during story-time because he kept pounding his feet on the floor. Friday Charles was deprived of blackboard privileges because he threw chalk.

On Saturday I remarked to my husband, "Do you think kindergarten   21
is too unsettling for Laurie? All this toughness, and bad grammar, and this
Charles boy sounds like such a bad influence."

"It'll be all right," my husband said reassuringly. "Bound to be people   22
like Charles in the world. Might as well meet them now as later."

On Monday Laurie came home late, full of news. "Charles," he shouted   23
as he came up the hill; I was waiting anxiously on the front steps. "Charles,"
Laurie yelled all the way up the hill, "Charles was bad again."

"Come right in," I said, as soon as he came close enough. "Lunch is   24
waiting."

"You know what Charles did?" he demanded, following me through the 25
door. "Charles yelled so in school they sent a boy in from first grade to tell
the teacher she had to make Charles keep quiet, and so Charles had to stay
after school. And so all the children stayed to watch him."

"What did he do?" I asked.   26

"He just sat there," Laurie said, climbing into his chair at the table. 27
"Hi, Pop, y'old dust mop."

"Charles had to stay after school today," I told my husband. "Everyone 28
stayed with him."

"What does this Charles look like?" my husband asked Laurie. "What's 29
his other name?"

"He's bigger than me," Laurie said. "And he doesn't have any rubbers 30
and he doesn't ever wear a jacket."

Monday night was the first Parent-Teachers meeting, and only the fact 31
that the baby had a cold kept me from going; I wanted passionately to meet
Charles's mother. On Tuesday Laurie remarked suddenly, "Our teacher had
a friend come to see her in school today."

"Charles's mother?" my husband and I asked simultaneously.   32

"Naaah," Laurie said scornfully. "It was a man who came and made us 33
do exercises, we had to touch our toes. Look." He climbed down from his
chair and squatted down and touched his toes. "Like this," he said. He got
solemnly back into his chair and said, picking up his fork, "Charles didn't
even *do* exercises."

"That's fine," I said heartily. "Didn't Charles want to do exercises?" 34

"Naaah," Laurie said. "Charles was so fresh to the teacher's friend he 35
wasn't *let* do exercises."

"Fresh again?" I said.   36

"He kicked the teacher's friend," Laurie said. "The teacher's friend 37
told Charles to touch his toes like I just did and Charles kicked him."

"What are they going to do about Charles, do you suppose?" Laurie's 38
father asked him.

Laurie shrugged elaborately. "Throw him out of school, I guess," he 39
said.

Wednesday and Thursday were routine; Charles yelled during story hour 40
and hit a boy in the stomach and made him cry. On Friday Charles stayed
after school again and so did all the other children.

With the third week of kindergarten Charles was an institution in our 41
family; the baby was being a Charles when she cried all afternoon; Laurie did
a Charles when he filled his wagon full of mud and pulled it through the
kitchen; even my husband, when he caught his elbow in the telephone cord
and pulled telephone, ashtray, and a bowl of flowers off the table, said, after
the first minute, "Looks like Charles."

During the third and fourth weeks it looked like a reformation in Charles; 42

Laurie reported grimly at lunch on Thursday of the third week, "Charles was
so good today the teacher gave him an apple."

"What?" I said, and my husband added warily, "You mean Charles?"   43

"Charles," Laurie said. "He gave the crayons around and he picked up   44
the books afterward and the teacher said he was her helper."

"What happened?" I asked incredulously.   45

"He was her helper, that's all," Laurie said, and shrugged.   46

"Can this be true, about Charles?" I asked my husband that night. "Can   47
something like this happen?"

"Wait and see," my husband said cynically. "When you've got a Charles   48
to deal with, this may mean he's only plotting."

He seemed to be wrong. For over a week Charles was the teacher's helper;   49
each day he handed things out and he picked things up; no one had to stay
after school.

"The P.T.A. meeting's next week again," I told my husband one evening.   50
"I'm going to find Charles's mother there."

"Ask her what happened to Charles," my husband said. "I'd like to   51
know."

"I'd like to know myself," I said.   52

On Friday of that week things were back to normal. "You know what   53
Charles did today?" Laurie demanded at the lunch table, in a voice slightly
awed. "He told a little girl to say a word and she said it and the teacher washed
her mouth out with soap and Charles laughed."

"What word?" his father asked unwisely, and Laurie said, "I'll have to   54
whisper it to you, it's so bad." He got down off his chair and went around to
his father. His father bent his head down and Laurie whispered joyfully. His
father's eyes widened.

"Did Charles tell the little girl to say *that?*" he asked respectfully.   55

"She said it *twice*," Laurie said. "Charles told her to say it *twice*."   56

"What happened to Charles?" my husband asked.   57

"Nothing," Laurie said. "He was passing out the crayons."   58

Monday morning Charles abandoned the little girl and said the evil word   59
himself three or four times, getting his mouth washed out with soap each
time. He also threw chalk.

My husband came to the door with me that evening as I set out for the   60
P.T.A. meeting. "Invite her over for a cup of tea after the meeting," he said.
"I want to get a look at her."

"If only she's there," I said prayerfully.   61

"She'll be there," my husband said. "I don't see how they could hold   62
a P.T.A. meeting without Charles's mother."

At the meeting I sat restlessly, scanning each comfortable matronly face,   63
trying to determine which one hid the secret of Charles. None of them looked

to me haggard enough. No one stood up in the meeting and apologized for the way her son had been acting. No one mentioned Charles.

After the meeting I identified and sought out Laurie's kindergarten 64 teacher. She had a plate with a cup of tea and a piece of chocolate cake; I had a plate with a cup of tea and a piece of marshmallow cake. We maneuvered up to one another cautiously, and smiled.

"I've been so anxious to meet you," I said. "I'm Laurie's mother."   65

"We're all so interested in Laurie," she said.   66

"Well, he certainly likes kindergarten," I said. "He talks about it all the 67 time."

"We had a little trouble adjusting, the first week or so," she said primly, 68 "but now he's a fine little helper. With occasional lapses, of course."

"Laurie usually adjusts very quickly," I said. "I suppose this time it's 69 Charles's influence."

"Charles?"   70

"Yes," I said, laughing, "you must have your hands full in that kin- 71 dergarten, with Charles."

"Charles?" she said. "We don't have any Charles in the kindergarten." 72

Questions for Discussion

1. Although the truth may come as a shock, there are indications throughout the story that Charles is none other than Laurie. What things does Laurie do at home that are similar to what Charles does in school?
2. How would you describe Laurie's personality? Is the fact that he has created an imaginary friend unusual?
3. What changes do we see in Laurie's personality as the story progresses?
4. There are many things about Laurie's family life that seem quite ordinary. Are there others that strike you as strange?
5. What kind of parents are Laurie's mother and father? Does the fact that they can't see through Laurie's lies seem believable to you? Would you have been able to see through Laurie's lies if you were his parents?
6. Think about your answer to question 5. What is the theme of this story? What does it tell us about human nature?
7. Much of what we know about Laurie and Charles comes to us directly from Laurie. Why didn't Jackson have Laurie's mother, the narrator, tell us what he said?

Suggestions for Journal Entries

1. Write a short character sketch of Laurie. Compare him to children you've known who like to pretend a lot.
2. Sometimes we have difficulty recognizing the truth even when it is right

under our noses. Recall an incident from your own experience or from something you've read recently (Pirsig's essay in Chapter 10 might be an excellent choice) that illustrates this theme. In a brief journal entry, explain in what ways the incident is similar to Shirley Jackson's "Charles."

3. Did you ever have an imaginary friend or classmate as a child? Use the focused-freewriting method (explained in Getting Started) to recall one or two experiences you had with this companion. If you can, explain why you created this person in the first place.

The Son from America

Isaac Bashevis Singer

One of the most popular living American writers of short stories, Singer continues to compose his works in Yiddish, his first language, and then to translate them into English. Born in Poland, the country in which the following selection takes place, Singer immigrated to the United States in 1935. He writes regularly for the *Jewish Daily Forward*, a Yiddish publication, and for *The New Yorker* magazine.

In 1978, Singer won the Nobel prize for literature, the most prestigious honor that can be bestowed upon any writer. "The Son from America" appears in *A Crown of Feathers*, the collection of short stories for which he won The National Book Award.

Looking Ahead

1. The story takes place at about the turn of the century, a time when Russia controlled part of Poland. The characters in this story were driven out of their homes in Russia and forced to settle in Poland as a result of the "pogroms," the severe persecution of Jews by the government of the czar (the Russian emperor). Warsaw, mentioned in paragraph 5, is Poland's capital.

2. The story's setting reveals a great deal about its characters and theme. Keep a sharp lookout for details about Lentshin, the town in which the story takes place, and about the home of Berl and Berlcha, the main characters.

3. The story's theme can be seen most clearly in the differences between the two worlds: the old world of Europe and the new world of America.

Vocabulary

circumcision   A religious ceremony in which the foreskin of a male infant's penis is surgically removed.

contours   Outline.

Gentile   A non-Jewish person.

hinterland   A remote region.

Kaddish   Prayers for the dead.

Messiah   The deliverer or savior of the Jewish people sent by God as promised in the scriptures.

squiresses   Women squires or wealthy landowners.

synagogue   A temple, a house of worship.

Talmud   A collection of sacred writings.

Torah   The body of Jewish literature, both written and oral, that contains the sacred laws and teachings of the religion.

Yiddish   The language spoken by Jews in eastern Europe.

The village of Lentshin was tiny—a sandy marketplace where the peas- 1
ants of the area met once a week. It was surrounded by little huts with thatched roofs or shingles green with moss. The chimneys looked like pots. Between the huts there were fields, where the owners planted vegetables or pastured their goats.

In the smallest of these huts lived old Berl, a man in his eighties, and 2
his wife, who was called Berlcha (wife of Berl). Old Berl was one of the Jews who had been driven from their villages in Russia and had settled in Poland. In Lentshin, they mocked the mistakes he made while praying aloud. He spoke with a sharp "r." He was short, broad-shouldered, and had a small white beard, and summer and winter he wore a sheepskin hat, a padded cotton jacket, and stout boots. He walked slowly, shuffling his feet. He had a half acre of field, a cow, a goat, and chickens.

The couple had a son, Samuel, who had gone to America forty years 3
ago. It was said in Lentshin that he became a millionaire there. Every month, the Lentshin letter carrier brought old Berl a money order and a letter that no one could read because many of the words were English. How much money Samuel sent his parents remained a secret. Three times a year, Berl and his wife went on foot to Zakroczym and cashed the money orders there. But they never seemed to use the money. What for? The garden, the cow, and the goat provided most of their needs. Besides, Berlcha sold chickens and eggs, and from these there was enough to buy flour for bread.

No one cared to know where Berl kept the money that his son sent him. 4
There were no thieves in Lentshin. The hut consisted of one room, which contained all their belongings: the table, the shelf for meat, the shelf for milk foods, the two beds, and the clay oven. Sometimes the chickens roosted in the

woodshed and sometimes, when it was cold, in a coop near the oven. The goat, too, found shelter inside when the weather was bad. The more prosperous villagers had kerosene lamps, but Berl and his wife did not believe in newfangled gadgets. What was wrong with a wick in a dish of oil? Only for the Sabbath would Berlcha buy three tallow candles at the store. In summer, the couple got up at sunrise and retired with the chickens. In the long winter evenings, Berlcha spun flax at her spinning wheel and Berl sat beside her in the silence of those who enjoy their rest.

Once in a while when Berl came home from the synagogue after evening 5 prayers, he brought news to his wife. In Warsaw there were strikers who demanded that the czar abdicate. A heretic by the name of Dr. Herzl had come up with the idea that Jews should settle again in Palestine. Berlcha listened and shook her bonneted head. Her face was yellowish and wrinkled like a cabbage leaf. There were bluish sacks under her eyes. She was half deaf. Berl had to repeat each word he said to her. She would say, "The things that happen in the big cities!"

Here in Lentshin nothing happened except usual events: a cow gave 6 birth to a calf, a young couple had a circumcision party, or a girl was born and there was no party. Occasionally, someone died. Lentshin had no cemetery, and the corpse had to be taken to Zakroczym. Actually, Lentshin had become a village with few young people. The young men left for Zakroczym, for Nowy Dwor, for Warsaw, and sometimes for the United States. Like Samuel's, their letters were illegible, the Yiddish mixed with the languages of the countries where they now living. They sent photographs in which the men wore top hats and the women fancy dresses like squiresses.

Berl and Berlcha also received such photographs. But their eyes were 7 failing and neither he nor she had glasses. They could barely make out the pictures. Samuel had sons and daughters with Gentile names—and grandchildren who had married and had their own offspring. Their names were so strange that Berl and Berlcha could never remember them. But what difference do names make? America was far, far away on the other side of the ocean, at the edge of the world. A Talmud teacher who came to Lentshin had said that Americans walk with their heads down and their feet up. Berl and Berlcha could not grasp this. How was it possible? But since the teacher said so it must be true. Berlcha pondered for some time and then she said, "One can get accustomed to everything."

And so it remained. From too much thinking—God forbid—one may 8 lose one's wits.

One Friday morning, when Berlcha was kneading the dough for the 9 Sabbath loaves, the door opened and a nobleman entered. He was so tall that he had to bend down to get through the door. He wore a beaver hat and a cloak bordered with fur. He was followed by Chazkel, the coachman from Zakroczym, who carried two leather valises with brass locks. In astonishment Berlcha raised her eyes.

The nobleman looked around and said to the coachman in Yiddish, "Here 10 it is." He took out a silver ruble and paid him. The coachman tried to hand him change but he said, "You can go now."

When the coachman closed the door, the nobleman said, "Mother, it's 11 me, your son Samuel—Sam."

Berlcha heard the words and her legs grew numb. Her hands, to which 12 pieces of dough were sticking, lost their power. The nobleman hugged her, kissed her forehead, both her cheeks. Berlcha began to cackle like a hen, "My son!" At that moment Berl came in from the woodshed, his arms piled with logs. The goat followed him. When he saw a nobleman kissing his wife, Berl dropped the wood and exclaimed, "What is this?"

The nobleman let go of Berlcha and embraced Berl. "Father!" 13

For a long time Berl was unable to utter a sound. He wanted to recite 14 holy words that he had read in the Yiddish Bible, but he could remember nothing. Then he asked, "Are you Samuel?"

"Yes, Father, I am Samuel." 15

"Well, peace be with you." Berl grasped his son's hand. He was still not 16 sure that he was not being fooled. Samuel wasn't as tall and heavy as this man, but then Berl reminded himself that Samuel was only fifteen years old when he had left home. He must have grown in that faraway country. Berl asked, "Why didn't you let us know you were coming?"

"Didn't you receive my cable?" Samuel asked. 17

Berl did not know what a cable was. 18

Berlcha had scraped the dough from her hands and enfolded her son. He 19 kissed her again and asked, "Mother, didn't you receive a cable?"

"What? If I lived to see this, I am happy to die," Berlcha said, amazed 20 by her own words. Berl, too, was amazed. These were just the words he would have said earlier if he had been able to remember. After a while Berl came to himself and said, "Pescha, you will have to make a double Sabbath pudding in addition to the stew."

It was years since Berl had called Berlcha by her given name. When 21 he wanted to address her, he would say, "Listen," or "Say." It is the young or those from the big cities who call a wife by her name. Only now did Berlcha begin to cry. Yellow tears ran from her eyes, and everything became dim. Then she called out, "It's Friday—I have to prepare for the Sabbath." Yes, she had to knead the dough and braid the loaves. With such a guest, she had to make a larger Sabbath stew. The winter day is short and she must hurry.

Her son understood what was worrying her, because he said, "Mother, 22 I will help you."

Berlcha wanted to laugh, but a choked sob came out. "What are you 23 saying? God forbid."

The nobleman took off his cloak and jacket and remained in his vest, on 24 which hung a solid-gold watch chain. He rolled up his sleeves and came to the

trough. "Mother, I was a baker for many years in New York," he said, and
he began to knead the dough.

"What! You are my darling son who will say Kaddish for me." She wept   25
raspingly. Her strength left her, and she slumped onto the bed.

Berl said, "Women will always be women." And he went to the shed to   26
get more wood. The goat sat down near the oven; she gazed with surprise at
this strange man—his height and his bizarre clothes.

The neighbors had heard the good news that Berl's son had arrived from   27
America and they came to greet him. The women began to help Berlcha prepare for the Sabbath. Some laughed, some cried. The room was full of people,
as at a wedding. They asked Berl's son, "What is new in America?" And
Berl's son answered, "America is all right."

"Do Jews make a living?"   28

"One eats white bread there on weekdays."   29

"Do they remain Jews?"   30

"I am not a Gentile."   31

After Berlcha blessed the candles, father and son went to the little syn-   32
agogue across the street. A new snow had fallen. The son took large steps, but
Berl warned him, "Slow down."

In the synagogue the Jews recited "Let Us Exult" and "Come, My   33
Groom." All the time, the snow outside kept falling. After prayers, when Berl
and Samuel left the Holy Place, the village was unrecognizable. Everything
was covered with snow. One could see only the contours of the roofs and the
candles in the windows. Samuel said, "Nothing has changed here."

Berlcha had prepared gefilte fish, chicken soup with rice, meat, carrot   34
stew. Berl recited the benediction over a glass of ritual wine. The family ate
and drank, and when it grew quiet for a while one could hear the chirping of
the house cricket. The son talked a lot, but Berl and Berlcha understood little.
His Yiddish was different and contained foreign words.

After the final blessing Samuel asked, "Father, what did you do with all   35
the money I sent you?"

Berl raised his white brows. "It's here."   36

"Didn't you put it in a bank?"   37

"There is no bank in Lentshin."   38

"Where do you keep it?"   39

Berl hesitated. "One is not allowed to touch money on the Sabbath, but   40
I will show you." He crouched beside the bed and began to shove something
heavy. A boot appeared. Its top was stuffed with straw. Berl removed the
straw and the son saw that the boot was full of gold coins. He lifted it.

"Father, this is a treasure!" he called out.   41

"Well."   42

"Why didn't you spend it?"   43

"On what? Thank God, we have everything."   44

"Why didn't you travel somewhere?"   45

"Where to? This is our home."   46

The son asked one question after the other, but Berl's answer was al- 47
ways the same: they wanted for nothing. The garden, the cow, the goat, the
chickens provided them with all they needed. The son said, "If thieves knew
about this, your lives wouldn't be safe."

"There are no thieves here."   48

"What will happen to the money?"   49

"You take it."   50

Slowly, Berl and Berlcha grew accustomed to their son and his Amer- 51
ican Yiddish. Berlcha could hear him better now. She even recognized his
voice. He was saying, "Perhaps we should build a larger synagogue."

"The synagogue is big enough," Berl replied.   52

"Perhaps a home for old people."   53

"No one sleeps in the street."   54

The next day after the Sabbath meal was eaten, a Gentile from Zak- 55
roczym brought a paper—it was the cable. Berl and Berlcha lay down for a
nap. They soon began to snore. The goat, too, dozed off. The son put on his
cloak and his hat and went for a walk. He strode with his long legs across the
marketplace. He stretched out a hand and touched a roof. He wanted to smoke
a cigar, but he remembered it was forbidden on the Sabbath. He had a desire
to talk to someone, but it seemed that the whole of Lentshin was asleep. He
entered the synagogue. An old man was sitting there, reciting psalms. Samuel
asked, "Are you praying?"

"What else is there to do when one gets old?"   56

"Do you make a living?"   57

The old man did not understand the meaning of these words. He smiled, 58
showing his empty gums, and then he said, "If God gives health, one keeps
on living."

Samuel returned home. Dusk had fallen. Berl went to the synagogue for 59
the evening prayers and the son remained with his mother. The room was
filled with shadows.

Berlcha began to recite in a solemn singsong, "God of Abraham, Isaac, 60
and Jacob, defend the poor people of Israel and Thy name. The Holy Sabbath
is departing; the welcome week is coming to us. Let it be one of health, wealth
and good deeds."

"Mother, you don't need to pray for wealth," Samuel said. "You are 61
wealthy already."

Berlcha did not hear—or pretended not to. Her face had turned into a 62
cluster of shadows.

In the twilight Samuel put his hand into his jacket pocket and touched 63
his passport, his checkbook, his letters of credit. He had come here with big
plans. He had a valise filled with presents for his parents. He wanted to be-

stow gifts on the village. He brought not only his own money but funds from the Lentshin Society in New York, which had organized a ball for the benefit of the village. But this village in the hinterland needed nothing. From the synagogue one could hear hoarse chanting. The cricket, silent all day, started again its chirping. Berlcha began to sway and utter holy rhymes inherited from mothers and grandmothers:

> Thy holy sheep
> In mercy keep,
> In Torah and good deeds;
> Provide for all their needs,
> Shoes, clothes, and bread
> And the Messiah's tread.

Questions for Discussion

1. What does the story's setting reveal about Berl and Berlcha and about their standard of living?
2. Why didn't they learn about the coming of their son until after he arrived? What does this tell you about their village?
3. Singer includes details about the kind of life the son leads in America. What are these details, and what do they show us about the son?
4. There are indications that Berl and Berlcha have led very hard lives. What are some of these indications?
5. Despite all his wealth, the son from America worries about certain things. What is the source of his worry?
6. Despite their problems, Berl and Berlcha seem content; in fact, they refuse to spend the money their son has sent them over the years. What is the source of their contentment?
7. What is the theme of this story?

Suggestions for Journal Entries

1. Berl and Berlcha are set on finding happiness (or contentment) despite the hardships of life. In Chapter 10, Edgar Lee Masters' Lucinda Matlock also possessed this positive attitude. If you've ever known or read about anyone else like this, write a brief journal entry about a memorable event in this person's life that illustrates how courageous he or she is.
2. The story's setting reveals a lot about its major characters. Do you know someone whose home, office, or backyard shows something about the kind of life that he or she has lived? Describe this setting in as much detail as you can.

3. Explain your personal reaction to the characters in Singer's story. How do you feel about Berl, Berlcha, and their son?
4. This is a story in which religious principles and a belief in God are extremely important. Recall an incident in which your belief in a moral, ethical, or religious principle had a significant effect on you or on someone you know well. Sketch out a few details about the story and explain why the principle in question was important.

Indian Camp

Ernest Hemingway

Ernest Hemingway (1899–1961) is perhaps the most widely read American author of this century. Born in Oak Park, Illinois, he spent many of his early years as a reporter. It was in this capacity that he learned to write in the simple, direct style for which he is famous.

No other American writer seems to have combined a love of adventure and a love of literature so intensely as Hemingway. He is probably the only person who has received both the Nobel prize for literature (1954) and the Bronze Star for valor, which he was awarded in World War II.

Among his best-known novels are *A Farewell to Arms*, *For Whom the Bell Tolls*, and *The Old Man and the Sea*. "Indian Camp," part of a collection entitled *In Our Time*, is one of the many stories about Nick Adams, a character who many readers believe is based on the young Hemingway.

Looking Ahead

1. Many of Hemingway's stories are told almost exclusively through what their characters say and little through what the narrator says. Read the dialogue in this selection very carefully.
2. The story's setting is described in great detail. In addition to making "Indian Camp" realistic, these details help explain why some of the events in the story take place.
3. Many works of fiction portray painful human realities for which there are no acceptable solutions or explanations. Facing such realities and recognizing their significance, however, often causes a character to learn something important about life and to grow emotionally. Keep this in mind as you read about Nick Adams in "Indian Camp."

Vocabulary

Caesarian   A type of delivery in which the baby has to be taken through surgery.

exhilaration   Elation, enthusiasm.

leaders   Lengths of animal gut or nylon that connect hooks to the fishing line.

reminiscently   Knowingly, remembering what occurred.

stern   Rear.

At the lake shore there was another rowboat drawn up. The two Indians   1
stood waiting.

Nick and his father got in the stern of the boat and the Indians shoved   2
it off and one of them got in to row. Uncle George sat in the stern of the camp
rowboat. The young Indian shoved the camp boat off and got in to row Uncle
George.

The two boats started off in the dark. Nick heard the oarlocks of the   3
other boat quite a way ahead of them in the mist. The Indians rowed with
quick choppy strokes. Nick lay back with his father's arm around him. It was
cold on the water. The Indian who was rowing them was working very hard,
but the other boat moved further ahead in the mist all the time.

"Where are we going, Dad?" Nick asked.   4

"Over to the Indian camp. There is an Indian lady very sick."   5

"Oh," said Nick.   6

Across the bay they found the other boat beached. Uncle George was   7
smoking a cigar in the dark. The young Indian pulled the boat way up on the
beach. Uncle George gave both the Indians cigars.

They walked up from the beach through a meadow that was soaking wet   8
with dew, following the young Indian who carried a lantern. Then they went
into the woods and followed a trail that led to the logging road that ran back
into the hills. It was much lighter on the logging road as the timber was cut
away on both sides. The young Indian stopped and blew out his lantern and
they all walked on along the road.

They came around a bend and a dog came out barking. Ahead were the   9
lights of the shanties where the Indian bark-peelers lived. More dogs rushed
out at them. The two Indians sent them back to the shanties. In the shanty
nearest the road there was a light in the window. An old woman stood in the
doorway holding a lamp.

Inside on a wooden bunk lay a young Indian woman. She had been   10
trying to have her baby for two days. All the old women in the camp had been
helping her. The men had moved off up the road to sit in the dark and smoke
out of range of the noise she made. She screamed just as Nick and the two
Indians followed his father and Uncle George into the shanty. She lay in the
lower bunk, very big under a quilt. Her head was turned to one side. In the

upper bunk was her husband. He had cut his foot very badly with an ax three days before. He was smoking a pipe. The room smelled very bad.

Nick's father ordered some water to be put on the stove, and while it 11 was heating he spoke to Nick.

"This lady is going to have a baby, Nick," he said.   12

"I know," said Nick.   13

"You don't know," said his father. "Listen to me. What she is going 14 through is called being in labor. The baby wants to be born and she wants it to be born. All her muscles are trying to get the baby born. That is what is happening when she screams."

"I see," Nick said.   15

Just then the woman cried out.   16

"Oh, Daddy, can't you give her something to make her stop scream- 17 ing?" asked Nick.

"No. I haven't any anaesthetic," his father said. "But her screams are 18 not important. I don't hear them because they are not important."

The husband in the upper bunk rolled over against the wall.   19

The woman in the kitchen motioned to the doctor that the water was 20 hot. Nick's father went into the kitchen and poured about half of the water out of the big kettle into a basin. Into the water left in the kettle he put several things he unwrapped from a handkerchief.

"Those must boil," he said, and began to scrub his hands in the basin 21 of hot water with a cake of soap he had brought from the camp. Nick watched his father's hands scrubbing each other with the soap. While his father washed his hands very carefully and thoroughly, he talked.

"You see, Nick, babies are supposed to be born head first but some- 22 times they're not. When they're not they make a lot of trouble for everybody. Maybe I'll have to operate on this lady. We'll know in a little while."

When he was satisfied with his hands he went in and went to work.   23

"Pull back that quilt, will you George?" he said. "I'd rather not touch 24 it."

Later when he started to operate Uncle George and three Indian men 25 held the woman still. She bit Uncle George on the arm and Uncle George said, "Damn squaw bitch!" and the young Indian who had rowed Uncle George over laughed at him. Nick held the basin for his father. It all took a long time.

His father picked the baby up and slapped it to make it breathe and 26 handed it to the old woman.

"See, it's a boy, Nick," he said. "How do you like being an intern?" 27

Nick said, "All right." He was looking away so as not to see what his 28 father was doing.

"There. That gets it," said his father and put something into the basin. 29

Nick didn't look at it.   30

"Now," his father said, "there's some stitches to put in. You can watch 31
this or not, Nick, just as you like. I'm going to sew up the incision I made."

Nick did not watch. His curiosity had been gone for a long time.   32

His father finished and stood up. Uncle George and the three Indian 33
men stood up. Nick put the basin out in the kitchen.

Uncle George looked at his arm. The young Indian smiled reminiscently. 34

"I'll put some peroxide on that, George," the doctor said.   35

He bent over the Indian woman. She was quiet now and her eyes were 36
closed. She looked very pale. She did not know what had become of the baby
or anything.

"I'll be back in the morning," the doctor said, standing up. "The nurse 37
should be here from St. Ignace by noon and she'll bring everything we need."

He was feeling exalted and talkative as football players are in the dress- 38
ing room after a game.

"That's one for the medical journal, George," he said. "Doing a Cae- 39
sarian with a jack-knife and sewing it up with nine-foot, tapered gut leaders."

Uncle George was standing against the wall, looking at his arm.   40

"Oh, you're a great man, all right," he said.   41

"Ought to have a look at the proud father. They're usually the worst 42
sufferers in these little affairs," the doctor said. "I must say he took it all
pretty quietly."

He pulled back the blanket from the Indian's head. His hand came away 43
wet. He mounted on the edge of the lower bunk with the lamp in one hand
and looked in. The Indian lay with his face toward the wall. His throat had
been cut from ear to ear. The blood had flowed down into a pool where his
body sagged the bunk. His head rested on his left arm. The open razor lay,
edge up, in the blankets.

"Take Nick out of the shanty, George," the doctor said.   44

There was no need of that. Nick, standing in the door of the kitchen, 45
had a good view of the upper bunk when his father, the lamp in one hand,
tipped the Indian's head back.

It was just beginning to be daylight when they walked along the logging 46
road back toward the lake.

"I'm terribly sorry I brought you along, Nickie," said his father, all his 47
post-operative exhilaration gone. "It was an awful mess to put you through."

"Do ladies always have such a hard time having babies?" Nick asked.   48

"No, that was very, very exceptional."   49

"Why did he kill himself, Daddy?"   50

"I don't know, Nick. He couldn't stand things, I guess."   51

"Do many men kill themselves, Daddy?"   52

"Not very many, Nick."   53

"Do many women?"   54

"Hardly ever."   55

"Don't they ever?"   56
"Oh, yes. They do sometimes."   57
"Daddy?"   58
"Yes."   59
"Where did Uncle George go?"   60
"He'll turn up all right."   61
"Is dying hard, Daddy?"   62
"No, I think it's pretty easy, Nick. It all depends."   63

They were seated in the boat, Nick in the stern, his father rowing. The 64
sun was coming up over the hills. A bass jumped, making a circle in the water.
Nick trailed his hand in the water. It felt warm in the sharp chill of the morning.

In the early morning on the lake sitting in the stern of the boat with his 65
father rowing, he felt quite sure that he would never die.

Questions for Discussion

1. This story consists of two major events. What are they? What painful realities of life do they reveal to Nick?
2. How does young Nick's reaction to the birth differ from his reaction to the suicide? How do we know that he has grown up a little after witnessing the death of the baby's father?
3. The Indian's suicide is horrible and bloody. Nevertheless, Nick does not turn away when the body is uncovered. What does this fact reveal about his character?
4. As noted in Looking Ahead, Hemingway reveals a great deal about his plots through dialogue. For instance, we learn only from Nick's father's own words that he did the "Caesarian with a jack-knife" (Paragraph 39). What other important facts about the story come through dialogue?
5. Hemingway's description of the setting helps make the story realistic, but it may also help shed some light on the reasons behind the story's events. In what kind of place is the story set? How does the setting help prepare us for the difficult delivery and even for the suicide of the baby's father?
6. What do you think the story's theme is? What does it tell you about life?

Suggestions for Journal Entries

1. Uncle George claims (perhaps ironically) that Nick's father is "a great man." Do you know someone who is "great"? Write a brief definition of greatness, and explain how the person you're thinking about fits your definition. To demonstrate your point, include an anecdote or two about this individual.
2. How does his visit to the Indian camp affect Nick? Use focused freewriting

(explained in Getting Started) to develop one or two paragraphs that describe the changes you see in his personality.
3. Have you ever witnessed a birth, death, or other traumatic human event?
Use freewriting to recall this incident in a brief journal entry. Remember
to describe your emotional reactions. If appropriate, explain what you
learned from this event or how it changed you in some way.

A Worn Path

Eudora Welty

Like many great authors, Pulitzer-prize winner Eudora Welty relies on
her powers of observation to write about the people and things she knows
best. That's why many of her stories are set in the rural south, where she has
lived most of her life. She was born in Jackson, Mississippi, in 1909.

Welty's strength lies in her ability to create clear portraits of characters
who remain stuck in our minds and hearts long after we've read their stories.
Many of these people might seem eccentric, even bizarre. Often their stories
are comical, disturbing, and touching all at the same time. And sometimes the
nobility of the human character, which Welty is also fond of portraying, shines
through them so brightly that we cannot help being uplifted by the experience.

Looking Ahead

1. The major character in this story, Phoenix Jackson, gets her first name
from a mythical bird that became a symbol of rebirth. According to myth,
the phoenix would live for 500 years and then burn itself into a pile of ashes
from which another phoenix would arise.
2. We learn a great deal about Phoenix Jackson by what she does in this story.
Try to analyze each of her actions as you make your way through the plot.
3. Look closely at the dialogue that old Phoenix uses when she talks to herself, to the animals, and to the other natural objects along the way. Incidentally, you'll notice that Welty has realistically captured the natural
rhythm and sound of her speech, complete with regional pronunciation
and grammatical errors.
4. As you've learned in Chapter 9, what we come to know about a character
from other people in the story may be just as important as what the nar-

rator says. Phoenix meets a few people during the story, each of whom reveals something important about her.

Vocabulary

appointed   Assigned.
enduring   Lasting.
frailest   Most delicate.
grave   Somber, sad.
illuminated   Lit up.
limber   Agile, flexible.
meditative   Thoughtful, prayerful.
pullets   Young hens.
ravine   A gorge.
rouse   Awaken, stir up.
severe   Sharp, hard, grim.

It was December—a bright frozen day in the early morning. Far out in 1 the country there was an old Negro woman with her head tied in a red rag, coming along a path through the pinewoods. Her name was Phoenix Jackson. She was very old and small and she walked slowly in the dark pine shadows, moving a little from side to side in her steps, with the balanced heaviness and lightness of a pendulum in a grandfather clock. She carried a thin, small cane made from an umbrella, and with this she kept tapping the frozen earth in front of her. This made a grave and persistent noise in the still air, that seemed meditative like the chirping of a solitary little bird.

She wore a dark striped dress reaching down to her shoe tops, and an 2 equally long apron of bleached sugar sacks, with a full pocket: all neat and tidy, but every time she took a step she might have fallen over her shoe-laces, which dragged from her unlaced shoes. She looked straight ahead. Her eyes were blue with age. Her skin had a pattern all its own of numberless branching wrinkles and as though a whole little tree stood in the middle of her forehead, but a golden color ran underneath, and the two knobs of her cheeks were illuminated by a yellow burning under the dark. Under the red rag her hair came down on her neck in the frailest of ringlets, still black, and with an odor like copper.

Now and then there was a quivering in the thicket. Old Phoenix said, 3 "Out of my way, all you foxes, owls, beetles, jack rabbits, coons, and wild animals!... Keep out from under these feet, little bob-whites.... Keep the big wild hogs out of my path. Don't let none of those come running my direction. I got a long way." Under her small black-freckled hand her cane, limber as a buggy whip, would switch at the brush as if to rouse up any hiding things.

On she went. The woods were deep and still. The sun made the pine 4
needles almost too bright to look at, up where the wind rocked. The cones
dropped as light as feathers. Down in the hollow was the mourning dove—it
was not too late for him.

The path ran up a hill. "Seem like there is chains about my feet, time 5
I get this far," she said, in the voice of argument old people keep to use with
themselves. "Something always take a hold of me on this hill—pleads I should
stay."

After she got to the top she turned and gave a full, severe look behind 6
her where she had come. "Up through pines," she said at length. "Now down
through oaks."

Her eyes opened their widest, and she started down gently. But before 7
she got to the bottom of the hill a bush caught her dress.

Her fingers were busy and intent, but her skirts were full and long, so 8
that before she could pull them free in one place they were caught in another.
It was not possible to allow the dress to tear. "I in the thorny bush," she said.
"Thorns, you doing your appointed work. Never want to let folks pass—no
sir. Old eyes thought you was a pretty little *green* bush."

Finally, trembling all over, she stood free, and after a moment dared to 9
stoop for her cane.

"Sun so high!" she cried, leaning back and looking, while the thick tears 10
went over her eyes. "The time getting all gone here."

At the foot of this hill was a place where a log was laid across the creek. 11

"Now comes the trial," said Phoenix. 12

Putting her right foot out, she mounted the log and shut her eyes. Lift- 13
ing her skirt, levelling her cane fiercely before her, like a festival figure in
some parade, she began to march across. Then she opened her eyes and she
was safe on the other side.

"I wasn't as old as I thought," she said. 14

But she sat down to rest. She spread her skirts on the bank around her 15
and folded her hands over her knees. Up above her was a tree in a pearly cloud
of mistletoe. She did not dare to close her eyes, and when a little boy brought
her a little plate with a slice of marble-cake on it she spoke to him. "That
would be acceptable," she said. But when she went to take it there was just
her own hand in the air.

So she left that tree, and had to go through a barbed-wire fence. There 16
she had to creep and crawl, spreading her knees and stretching her fingers like
a baby trying to climb the steps. But she talked loudly to herself: she could
not let her dress be torn now, so late in the day, and she could not pay for
having her arm or her leg sawed off if she got caught fast where she was.

At last she was safe through the fence and risen up out in the clearing. 17
Big dead trees, like black men with one arm, were standing in the purple
stalks of the withered cotton field. There sat a buzzard.

"Who you watching?"   18

In the furrow she made her way along.   19

"Glad this not the season for bulls," she said, looking sideways, "and 20
the good Lord made his snakes to curl up and sleep in the winter. A pleasure
I don't see no two-headed snake coming around that tree, where it come once.
It took a while to get by him, back in the summer."

She passed through the old cotton and went into a field of dead corn. 21
It whispered and shook and was taller than her head. "Through the maze
now," she said, for there was no path.

Then there was something tall, black, and skinny there, moving before 22
her.

At first she took it for a man. It could have been a man dancing in the 23
field. But she stood still and listened, and it did not make a sound. It was as
silent as a ghost.

"Ghost," she said sharply, "who be you the ghost of? For I have heard 24
of nary death close by."

But there was no answer—only the ragged dancing in the wind. 25

She shut her eyes, reached out her hand, and touched a sleeve. She 26
found a coat and inside that an emptiness, cold as ice.

"You scarecrow," she said. Her face lighted. "I ought to be shut up for 27
good," she said with laughter. "My senses is gone. I too old. I the oldest
people I ever know. Dance, old scarecrow," she said, "while I dancing with
you."

She kicked her foot over the furrow, and with mouth drawn down, shook 28
her head once or twice in a little strutting way. Some husks blew down and
whirled in streamers about her skirts.

Then she went on, parting her way from side to side with the cane, 29
through the whispering field. At last she came to the end, to a wagon track
where the silver grass blew between the red ruts. The quail were walking
around like pullets, seeming all dainty and unseen.

"Walk pretty," she said. "This the easy place. This the easy going." 30

She followed the track, swaying through the quiet bare fields, through 31
the little strings of trees silver in their dead leaves, past cabins silver from
weather, with the doors and windows boarded shut, all like old women under
a spell sitting there. "I walking in their sleep," she said, nodding her head
vigorously.

In a ravine she went where a spring was silently flowing through a hol- 32
low log. Old Phoenix bent and drank. "Sweet-gum makes the water sweet,"
she said, and drank more. "Nobody know who made this well, for it was here
when I was born."

The track crossed a swampy part where the moss hung as white as lace 33
from every limb. "Sleep on, alligators, and blow you bubbles." Then the
track went into the road.

Deep, deep the road went down between the high green-colored banks. 34
Overhead the live-oaks met, and it was as dark as a cave.

A black dog with a lolling tongue came up out of the weeds by the ditch. 35
She was meditating, and not ready, and when he came at her she only hit him
a little with her cane. Over she went in the ditch, like a little puff of milk-
weed.

Down there, her senses drifted away. A dream visited her, and she 36
reached her hand up, but nothing reached down and gave her a pull. So she
lay there and presently went to talking. "Old woman," she said to herself,
"that black dog come up out of the weeds to stall you off, and now there he
sitting on his fine tail, smiling at you."

A white man finally came along and found her—a hunter, a young man, 37
with his dog on a chain.

"Well, Granny!" he laughed. "What are you doing there?"   38

"Lying on my back like a June-bug waiting to be turned over, mister," 39
she said, reaching up her hand.

He lifted her up, gave her a swing in the air, and set her down, "Any- 40
thing broken, Granny?"

"No sir, them old dead weeds is springy enough," said Phoenix, when 41
she had got her breath. "I thank you for your trouble."

"Where do you live, Granny?" he asked, while the two dogs were growl- 42
ing at each other.

"Away back yonder, sir, behind the ridge. You can't even see it from 43
here."

"On your way home?"   44

"No, sir, I going to town."   45

"Why, that's too far! That's as far as I walk when I come out myself, 46
and I get something for my trouble." He patted the stuffed bag he carried,
and there hung down a little closed claw. It was one of the bob-whites, with
its beak hooked bitterly to show it was dead. "Now you go on home, Granny!"

"I bound to go to town, mister," said Phoenix. "The time come around." 47

He gave another laugh, filling the whole landscape. "I know you old 48
colored people! Wouldn't miss going to town to see Santa Claus!"

But something held Old Phoenix very still. The deep lines in her face 49
went into a fierce and different radiation. Without warning, she had seen with
her own eyes a flashing nickel fall out of the man's pocket onto the ground.

"How old are you, Granny?" he was saying.   50

"There is no telling, mister," she said, "no telling."   51

Then she gave a little cry and clapped her hands and said, "Git on away 52
from here, dog! Look! Look at that dog!" She laughed as if in admiration.
"He ain't scared of nobody. He a big black dog." She whispered, "Sic him!"

"Watch me get rid of that cur," said the man. "Sic him, Pete! Sic him!" 53

Phoenix heard the dogs fighting, and heard the man running and throw- 54
ing sticks. She even heard a gunshot. But she was slowly bending forward by

that time, further and further forward, the lids stretched down over her eyes, as if she were doing this in her sleep. Her chin was lowered almost to her knees. The yellow palm of her hand came out from the fold of her apron. Her fingers slid down and along the ground under the piece of money with the grace and care they would have in lifting an egg from under a sitting hen. Then she slowly straightened up, she stood erect, and the nickel was in her apron pocket. A bird flew by. Her lips moved. "God watching me the whole time. I come to stealing."

The man came back, and his own dog panted about them. "Well, I 55 scared him off that time," he said, and then he laughed and lifted his gun and pointed it at Phoenix.

She stood straight and faced him. 56

"Doesn't the gun scare you?" he said, still pointing it. 57

"No, sir, I seen plenty go off closer by, in my day, and for less than what 58 I done," she said, holding utterly still.

He smiled, and shouldered the gun. "Well, Granny," he said, "you 59 must be a hundred years old, and scared of nothing. I'd give you a dime if I had any money with me. But you take my advice and stay home, and nothing will happen to you."

"I bound to go on my way, mister," said Phoenix. She inclined her head 60 in the red rag. Then they went in different directions, but she could hear the gun shooting again and again over the hill.

She walked on. The shadows hung from the oak trees to the road like 61 curtains. Then she smelled wood-smoke, and smelled the river, and she saw a steeple and the cabins on their steep steps. Dozens of little black children whirled around her. There ahead was Natchez shining. Bells were ringing. She walked on.

In the paved city it was Christmas time. There were red and green elec- 62 tric lights strung and crisscrossed everywhere, and all turned on in the day-time. Old Phoenix would have been lost if she had not distrusted her eyesight and depended on her feet to know where to take her.

She paused quietly on the sidewalk where people were passing by. A 63 lady came along in the crowd, carrying an armful of red-, green-, and silver-wrapped presents; she gave off perfume like the red roses in hot summer, and Phoenix stopped her.

"Please, missy, will you lace up my shoe?" She held up her foot. 64

"What do you want, Grandma?" 65

"See my shoe," said Phoenix. "Do all right for out in the country, but 66 wouldn't look right to go in a big building."

"Stand still then, Grandma," said the lady. She put her packages down 67 on the sidewalk beside her and laced and tied both shoes tightly.

"Can't lace 'em with a cane," said Phoenix. "Thank you, missy. I 68 doesn't mind asking a nice lady to tie up my shoe, when I gets out on the street."

Moving slowly and from side to side, she went into the big building and   69
into a tower of steps, where she walked up and around and around until her
feet knew to stop.

She entered a door, and there she saw nailed up on the wall the doc-   70
ument that had been stamped with the gold seal and framed in the gold frame,
which matched the dream that was hung up in her head.

"Here I be," she said. There was a fixed and ceremonial stiffness over   71
her body.

"A charity case, I suppose," said an attendant who sat at the desk before   72
her.

But Phoenix only looked above her head. There was sweat on her face,   73
the wrinkles in her skin shone like a bright net.

"Speak up, Grandma," the woman said. "What's your name? We must   74
have your history, you know. Have you been here before? What seems to be
the trouble with you?"

Old Phoenix only gave a twitch to her face as if a fly were bothering her.   75

"Are you deaf?" cried the attendant.   76

But then the nurse came in.   77

"Oh, that's just old Aunt Phoenix," she said. "She doesn't come for   78
herself—she has a little grandson. She makes these trips just as regular as
clockwork. She lives away back off the Old Natchez Trace." She bent down.
"Well, Aunt Phoenix, why don't you just take a seat? We won't keep you
standing after your long trip." She pointed.

The old woman sat down, bolt upright in the chair.   79

"Now, how is the boy?" asked the nurse.   80

Old Phoenix did not speak.   81

"I said, how is the boy?"   82

But Phoenix only waited and stared straight ahead, her face very solemn   83
and withdrawn into rigidity.

"Is his throat any better?" asked the nurse. "Aunt Phoenix, don't you   84
hear me? Is your grandson's throat any better since the last time you came for
the medicine?"

With her hands on her knees, the old woman waited, silent, erect and   85
motionless, just as if she were in armour.

"You mustn't take up our time this way, Aunt Phoenix," the nurse said.   86
"Tell us quickly about your grandson, and get it over. He isn't dead, is he?"

At last there came a flicker and then a flame of comprehension across   87
her face, and she spoke.

"My grandson. It was my memory had left me. There I sat and forgot   88
why I made my long trip."

"Forgot?" The nurse frowned. "After you came so far?"   89

Then Phoenix was like an old woman begging a dignified forgiveness for   90
waking up frightened in the night. "I never did go to school, I was too old at

the Surrender," she said in a soft voice. "I'm an old woman without an education. It was my memory fail me. My little grandson, he is just the same, and I forgot it in the coming."

"Throat never heals, does it?" said the nurse, speaking in a loud, sure 91
voice to Old Phoenix. By now she had a card with something written on it,
a little list. "Yes. Swallowed lye. When was it—January—two-three years
ago—"

Phoenix spoke unasked now. "No, missy, he not dead, he just the same. 92
Every little while his throat begin to close up again, and he not able to swallow. He not get his breath. He not able to help himself. So the time come
around, and I go on another trip for the soothing medicine."

"All right. The doctor said as long as you came to get it, you could have 93
it," said the nurse. "But it's an obstinate case."

"My little grandson, he sit up there in the house all wrapped up, waiting 94
by himself," Phoenix went on. "We is the only two left in the world. He suffer
and it don't seem to put him back at all. He got a sweet look. He going to last.
He wear a little patch quilt and peep out holding his mouth open like a little
bird. I remembers so plain now. I not going to forget him again, no, the whole
enduring time. I could tell him from all the others in creation."

"All right." The nurse was trying to hush her now. She brought her a 95
bottle of medicine. "Charity," she said, making a check mark in a book.

Old Phoenix held the bottle close to her eyes and then carefully put it 96
into her pocket.

"I thank you," she said.   97

"It's Christmas time, Grandma," said the attendant. "Could I give you 98
a few pennies out of my purse?"

"Five pennies is a nickel," said Phoenix stiffly.   99

"Here's a nickel," said the attendant.   100

Phoenix rose carefully and held out her hand. She received the nickel 101
and then fished the other nickel out of her pocket and laid it beside the new
one. She stared at her palm closely, with her head on one side.

Then she gave a tap with her cane on the floor.   102

"This is what come to me to do," she said. "I going to the store and buy 103
my child a little windmill they sells, made out of paper. He going to find it
hard to believe there such a thing in the world. I'll march myself back where
he waiting, holding it straight up in this hand."

She lifted her free hand, gave a little nod, turned round, and walked out 104
of the doctor's office. Then her slow step began on the stairs, going down.

Questions for Discussion

1. Welty provides numerous vivid and exciting details to establish the story's setting. Why does she spend so much time describing the country through which Phoenix has to travel?

2. Phoenix's comments to the animals, trees, and other natural objects on her journey might be an indication that she is going mad or that she is a very colorful character with a vivid imagination. What do you think?

3. One thing is for sure: Phoenix is a survivor. What in the story shows us that she is persistent? What signs are there that Phoenix is, in fact, quite clever?

4. What do the people whom she encounters reveal about Phoenix through their conversations with her?

5. Is "Phoenix" appropriately named? Are there times in the story when she seems to be defeated, only to rise again?

6. What events in the story demonstrate the nobility of Phoenix Jackson? How does the story's title contribute to this idea?

Suggestions for Journal Entries

1. "A Worn Path" dramatizes the strength, courage, and selflessness of Phoenix Jackson. Do you know someone who displays similar qualities? Use the focused-freewriting method to recall an incident from his or her life that illustrates nobility of character.

2. Discuss the emotions you felt when you learned the reason for Phoenix's long journey.

3. If you saw Phoenix on the street corner, you might take her for a poor, lonely eccentric to be pitied by those who lead more fortunate lives. In what ways would "A Worn Path" disprove your theory?

SUGGESTIONS FOR WRITING

1. Shirley Jackson's "Charles" is about a young boy who creates an imaginary classmate to explain his behavior during his first weeks in school. If you've ever had an imaginary companion, tell the story of your "adventures" with this individual and try to explain why you created him or her. Don't hesitate to use dialogue whenever you think it will make your story more interesting and believable.

   Before you begin, check your journal. You may have already jotted down some useful notes, ideas and insights if you read this short story and responded to one or more of the Suggestions for Journal Entries that follow it.

2. Write a short story or narrative essay about a person or group of people you know whose outlook on life is positive or even courageous. If possible, expand upon the journal notes you made after reading Singer's "The Son from America." Include at least one important event that demonstrates how courageous or positive your character(s) really is (are).

3. At important times in our lives we all experience conflicts, problems, or very stressful events that change us, causing us to mature in some way or teaching us something very important about life. (Such is the case with Nick, an eyewitness to the pain of birth and the horror of death in Hemingway's "Indian Camp.") Write the story of an event, whether fictional or real, that had an impact on your main character. Review your journal notes for details that may help you develop this story.

4. In "A Worn Path," Welty tells the moving story of a woman she might have seen in her hometown. However, whether the story of Phoenix Jackson is true isn't important. What matters is the fact that Welty relies on a knowledge of her native Mississippi and its people for the details of her narrative.

   Write a story set in your county, town, or neighborhood or in any locality you know well. Like Welty, rely on your knowledge of the place and its inhabitants, and make your story as realistic as you can by using concrete details to describe its setting and its people.

5. Several selections in this chapter describe people who are admirable in some way. Write your own story, whether fictional or real, of a person who possesses one or more characteristics you admire. You may wish to narrate the story yourself. As much as possible, however, allow the plot, characters, setting, and/or dialogue to portray, or dramatize, those characteristics for you.

   As with other assignments, consult your journal first. Review the entries you've made for "The Son from America," "Indian Camp," and "A Worn Path." They may provide you with ideas and details you can use in your story.

Section V
Exposition

Many new writers begin to develop their skills by practicing the kinds of writing in Sections III and IV, description and narration. As you learned in previous chapters, description and narration usually involve writing about subjects that are concrete and, often, very specific—people, places, events, or objects that the reader can picture or understand easily. The primary purpose of description, of course, is to explain what someone or something looked like, sounded like, etc. The primary purpose of narration is simply to tell what happened, although many short stories and narrative essays do a great deal more.

However, new writers are often faced with the problem of writing with a very different purpose: to discuss abstract ideas that can't be explained through narration and description alone. In such cases, a writer must rely on a variety of methods and techniques associated with exposition, also called "writing that explains." Among these are illustration, comparison/ contrast, and process analysis, which can be used alone or in combination with other types of writing to explain important ideas.

The reading selections in the three chapters that follow rely on illustration, comparison/contrast, or process analysis as the *primary* way to develop an idea. However, they also use other methods of development that you've read about earlier. In fact, writers often use a combination of techniques to develop ideas. That's why comparison/contrast essays frequently contain anecdotes (brief stories) and why many process analysis papers include a lot of descriptive detail. Essays that use illustration as the primary method of development sometimes rely heavily on anecdotes, comparisons or contrasts, and description, for these techniques often serve as good sources of concrete examples through which to explain an idea.

Whether an expository writer relies on only one method of development or combines that method with others, one thing is for sure. His or her purpose will be to explain or develop ideas clearly, concretely, and effectively.

ILLUSTRATION

One of the most important and popular methods for focusing on and developing an idea is illustration, the method of development you first read about in Chapter 3. Illustration involves the use of examples to help make an otherwise abstract and general idea more specific, more concrete, and easier to understand. As the word implies, in fact, an illustration provides the reader with a clear "picture" of an idea that would otherwise have remained vague and undefined.

For instance, if you wanted a clearer and more definitive notion of what your friend meant when she claimed to have met several "interesting characters" since coming to school, you might ask her to describe a few of those "characters" specifically and to show you in what ways they were "interesting." Each of the people she discussed would then serve as an illustration or picture of what she meant by the abstract word "interesting."

COMPARISON/CONTRAST

Comparison/contrast, another effective way to develop an idea, involves pointing out similarities or differences between two people, objects, experiences, ways of doing something, etc. More often than not, writers compare things (point out similarities between them) to make one or both more recognizable or understandable to the reader. For instance, if you wanted to explain what a computer monitor was to someone who had never seen one, you might start by comparing it to a television set. Of course, contrast can also be used for this purpose. In the example above, it might also help to follow up with an explanation of how a computer monitor differs from a typical television.

In many instances, however, writers point out differences between things (contrast) in order to explain why one is better than the other. Such is the case in "Watch the Cart!" (Chapter 14), which explains why the author thinks women are more adept at grocery shopping than men.

There are many reasons for comparing or contrasting the subjects you wish to write about. Whatever your purpose, you may find that comparing or contrasting will help you bring abstract ideas into sharper focus and make them more concrete than if you had simply tried to discuss each of your subjects separately.

PROCESS ANALYSIS

Process analysis is often used in scientific and technical writing to help readers understand the workings of both natural and humanly made processes like the formation of rain clouds, the circulation of blood within the human body, or the workings of an automobile engine. However, it can be used to explain non-scientific processes as well. For instance, you might want to use this technique to explain how U.S. Presidents are elected, how money is transferred from one bank to another electronically, or even how your Aunt Millie manages to turn the most solemn occasion into a party!

Process analysis is also useful when you need to provide the reader with directions or instructions to complete a specific task. Subjects for such essays include "how to change the brakes on a Ford Mustang," "how to bake lasagna," or even "how to get to school from the center of town."

In each of these examples, the writer is assigning him/herself the task of explaining, as specifically and as clearly as possible, an idea that might be very new and unfamiliar to the reader. And, in each case, the essay will focus on "how to do something" or "how something is done."

Though it may often seem deceptively simple, writing a process paper is often a painstaking task and must be approached carefully. Remember that your readers might be totally unfamiliar with what you're explaining and will need a great deal of information to follow the process easily and to understand it thoroughly.

As a matter of fact, the need to be clear and concrete often causes writers of process analysis to rely on other methods of development as well. Among them are narration, description, illustration, and comparison/contrast. Of these, writers of process analysis rely most heavily on narration. After all, a process is, in fact, a story. Like narratives, process papers are often organized in chronological order and explain a series of events. Unlike narratives, however, process essays don't simply tell *what* happens; they also explain *how* and *why* something happens or *how* and *why* something should be done.

Illustration, comparision/contrast, and process analysis are only a few of the types of expository writing you will learn about and use as you continue your education. However, they represent important skills of development and organization that will help you build a foundation for success as you grow as a writer.

Chapter 13

Illustration

You've learned that the most interesting and effective writing uses specific and concrete details to *show* rather than to *tell* the reader something. One of the best ways to show your readers what you mean is to provide them with clear, relevant examples, or illustrations. Illustrations will help you turn an otherwise abstract and general idea into one that is concrete, specific, and easily recognized by your readers. In fact, illustration can be used as the primary method to develop a thesis.

Effective illustrations can help you make reference to specific people, places, and things—concrete realities that your readers will recognize or understand easily. Say that you want to convince them that your 1988 "Wizbang" is an economical car. Instead of being content to rely on their understanding of a vague word like "economical," you decide to provide examples that show exactly what you think this term means. Therefore, you explain that the Wizbang gets about 65 miles per gallon around town, that its purchase price is $4000 less than its least-expensive competitor's, and that it needs only one $50 tune-up every 40,000 miles. Now that's economical!

Several types of examples are discussed below. The important thing to remember is that the examples you choose must relate to and be appropriate to the idea you're illustrating. For instance, you probably wouldn't cite statistics about the Wizbang's safety record if you wanted to impress your readers with how inexpensive it is to own and operate that car.

SPECIFIC INSTANCES OR OCCURRENCES

One of the best ways to get examples into your writing is to use specific instances of the idea you're explaining. For instance, if you want to prove that the Wizbang doesn't perform very well in bad weather, you might explain that it stalled twice during a recent rainstorm or that it didn't start when the temperature fell below freezing last week. Or if you want to show that the people

281

in your town are community-minded, you might specify that they recently opened a shelter for the homeless or that they organized a meals-on-wheels program for the elderly.

A number of selections in this chapter use specific instances to develop important ideas. Among the best is "A Fable for Tomorrow," in which Rachel Carson predicts the devastating effect that chemical pesticides will have on our environment.

STATISTICS

Mathematical figures, or statistics, can also be included to strengthen your readers' understanding of an abstract idea. If you want to prove that the cost of living in your hometown has increased dramatically over the last five years, you might explain that the price of a three-bedroom home has increased by about 30 percent, from $75,000 to $98,000, that real estate taxes have doubled from an average of $1000 per family to $2000 per family, and that the cost of utilities has nearly tripled, with each household now spending about $120 per month on heat and electricity.

SPECIFIC PEOPLE, EVENTS, OR OBJECTS

Mentioning specific people, events, and objects familiar to your readers can also help illustrate ideas. If you're demonstrating that the American South is famous for the many Presidents and statespeople it has produced, you might mention George Washington, Thomas Jefferson, Henry Clay, Lyndon Johnson, Martin Luther King, and Jimmy Carter. If you're explaining that the 1960s were years of turmoil in America, you could refer to the assassinations of John and Robert Kennedy and of Martin Luther King, the urban riots, and the antiwar marches. And if you're discussing how fascinated people in this country have become with gadgets, you might specify various labor-saving devices found in the typical American home, just as in Carol Biederstadt's "Electrical Appliances," which follows.

ANECDOTES

As you probably know, anecdotes are brief, informative stories that are used to develop an idea or to prove a point. John Naisbitt's "Needed: High-Tech Skills" relies heavily on anecdotes to illustrate the importance of technological know-how in a complex industrial society. His very factual accounts of real emergencies at nuclear power-plants and of the widespread breakdowns in city bus lines show how important technology and technical training are to every one of us.

You'll find effective anecdotes combined with other examples in Benjamin Duke's "The Truth Will Come Out in the Wash." Like those in this chapter's other selections, they serve to make the abstract ideas they illustrate more interesting, more believable and, most important of all, more easily understood. Keep this in mind as you read and enjoy the following essays and especially as you begin your own writing projects.

The Truth Will Come Out in the Wash

Benjamin C. Duke

Benjamin Duke is an American professor at the International Christian University in Tokyo, Japan. In "The Truth Will Come Out in the Wash," which he wrote in 1986, Duke tells us why he and his family believe Japanese products are superior to those made in the United States. He also explains what we must do to improve the competitiveness of American products so that they will sell better in other countries.

This essay was first published in *The New York Times* as a companion piece to two other articles on America's large foreign-trade deficit. Also known as a "trade imbalance," the trade deficit is our huge debt to other countries that has resulted from the fact that we import (or buy) many more goods from these countries than we export (or sell) to them.

Looking Ahead

1. Considering his essay's title, what American and Japanese products do you think Duke will be comparing in this essay? In other words, what examples do you think he'll use to illustrate his ideas?
2. In paragraph 5, Duke mentions "the exchange rate," the ratio at which one country's currency is exchanged (or cashed in) for another's. In the eleven months before this article was published, the American dollar dropped in value against the Japanese yen. As a result, the Japanese could get more dollars for their yen, and the prices of American goods sold in Japan decreased. Unfortunately, this did not convince Japanese consumers to "buy American."
3. In paragraph 5, Duke also refers to "exhortations by Prime Minister Yasuhiro Nakasone," then the head of the Japanese government. In order to help the United States increase its exports to his country, Nakasone and other leaders agreed to appeal to their fellow citizens to buy more American goods.

Vocabulary

controversy   Dispute.
exhortations   Appeals, pleadings.
immersed   Submerged in, totally involved in.
minuscule   Very small, tiny.
nub   The central or most important point.
saturated   Completely filled, soaked.
versatile   Capable of being put to many different uses.

As an American who has spent half his life in Japan, I am constantly 1
struck dumb by the way we conveniently ignore the most critical factor in our
trade relations with Japan. What is the missing ingredient? Surely it is the
product itself. We never confront the issue of why so many American and
Japanese consumers prefer Japanese products.

Let's look at a real situation in Japan. Our old G.E. washer finally gave 2
out last year. With a family of five, including three teenagers, we have always
felt that the small Japanese washers designed for small homes and minuscule
apartments were not for us. However, while browsing through the famous
Akihabara electronic bargain area of Tokyo, we spotted a new and larger Hitachi model. Simply designed, compact and lightweight, it contained all the
automatic features we had grown accustomed to, and more. And the price was
reasonable.

After 16 months of heavy use, we have had to call in the repairman on 3
only one occasion, when the washer failed to fill up quickly. The Hitachi man
arrived within a day, discovered that the in-take sift was clogged with tiny
stones, showed us how to keep it clear and departed with a bow and no bill.
"Service," he said.

Why would we buy another G.E. washer in Japan? Why would any 4
Japanese buy an American washer? Indeed, when our large and cumbersome
American drier dries no longer, we will search for a Japanese replacement.
After this experience, one wonders why Japanese washers and driers have not
yet hit the American market. If and when they do, we predict they will be well
received.

Name any manufactured product and we will choose the Japanese ver- 5
sion—from our versatile Sharp VCR to our attractive Hitachi refrigerator to
our Kawai grand piano. Few Japanese consumers would do otherwise, regardless of the exchange rate or exhortations from Prime Minister Yasuhiro
Nakasone.

Americans involved in the trade controversy—especially economists, fi- 6
nancial experts and politicians—often ignore the most difficult and basic issue. Japanese companies, immersed in a cutthroat competition to supply a
saturated domestic market, must achieve a high standard of reliability, design
and appearance in their products. Also, the Japanese take for granted follow-
up service that would make a typical American manufacturer choke.

This, then, brings us to the nub of our trading problems. We can fiddle 7
with currency rates, pressure the Japanese to open up their markets to our
goods, or whatever. But as long as so many Japanese and Americans believe
that Japanese products are superior to American, the trade imbalances will
persist in favor of Japan.

Simply put, American companies must produce better quality products 8
more cheaply so that both American and Japanese consumers believe that
American and Japanese products are similar in quality, performance and re-

liability; or better yet, that American products are superior to Japanese products. Until we face the issue of the productivity and reliability of our industrial base, we cannot meet the challenge from Japan.

Questions for Discussion

1. What does Duke mean by "struck dumb" in the first paragraph?
2. What specific products and brand names does Duke mention to illustrate his belief that Japanese products are superior to American products?
3. Duke places a great deal of emphasis on service, an idea he explains in an anecdote, which serves as a specific and concrete example. What is this anecdote? How is it effective in helping him make his point?
4. Why do Japanese consumers prefer goods made in their own country to those shipped in from the United States?
5. According to Duke, how can Americans make their products more competitive in Japan?

Suggestions for Journal Entries

1. Do you agree with Duke? Are the foreign products you know about better than American products? List a few examples of foreign-made products (cars, TV sets, VCRs, appliances, watches, etc.) that you or your friends own or have used. Are they better-made, more reliable, and more durable than similar American-made products?
2. Take an inventory of your possessions or those of your family. What examples do you find of foreign-made goods in your home? List them. Does the number of imported goods you own surprise you? What country do most of these goods come from?

A Fable for Tomorrow

Rachel Carson

One of America's best-known conservationists, Rachel Carson (1907–1964) was educated as a marine biologist and worked for the U.S. Fish and Wildlife Service for several years. An eloquent and powerful writer, Carson produced a number of popular scientific works that helped increase public concern about the effects of pollution on the natural environment. In 1951 she won the National Book Award for one of her most widely read works, *The Sea Around Us;* a short excerpt from this book appears in Chapter 1.

Carson is best remembered for *Silent Spring* (1962), a very early and very remarkable study of the destructiveness of pesticides and other chemicals. "A Fable for Tomorrow" is the introduction to *Silent Spring*.

Looking Ahead

1. "A Fable for Tomorrow" is a "fable" because it communicates an important lesson, or moral. The title of the book itself refers to the "silencing" of the natural sounds of animals and insects, which we are most aware of in springtime.
2. Carson has organized "A Fable for Tomorrow" by contrasting what a typical American town might be like before and after the pollution of the natural environment. Notice how each half of this contrast is developed with concrete illustrations. Incidentally, Carson's use of contrast to organize this essay shows once again that professional writers often combine various types of writing to develop their ideas effectively.
3. Carson waits until the last sentence to state her thesis: "A grim specter has crept upon us almost unnoticed, and this imagined tragedy may easily become a stark reality we all shall know." This grim specter (or terrifying ghost) has to do with the deadly effects of environmental pollution.

Vocabulary

anglers People who fish with hooks.
blight A disease that kills plants and animals.
brooded Nested, sat on their eggs.
counterparts Others of the same type.
droned Made a low, humming sound.
maladies Illnesses.
migrants Birds that travel north and south with the change of the seasons.
moribund Approaching death.
pollination The process by which bees carry pollen from one flower to another.
stricken Struck down.

There was once a town in the heart of America where all life seemed to 1 live in harmony with its surroundings. The town lay in the midst of a checkerboard of prosperous farms, with fields of grain and hillsides of orchards where, in spring, white clouds of bloom drifted above the green fields. In autumn, oak and maple and birch set up a blaze of color that flamed and flickered across a backdrop of pines. Then foxes barked in the hills and deer silently crossed the fields, half hidden in the mists of the fall mornings.

Along the roads, laurel, viburnum and alder, great ferns and wildflow- 2 ers delighted the traveler's eye through much of the year. Even in winter the roadsides were places of beauty, where countless birds came to feed on the berries and on the seed heads of the dried weeds rising above the snow. The countryside was, in fact, famous for the abundance and variety of its bird life, and when the flood of migrants was pouring through in spring and fall people traveled from great distances to observe them. Others came to fish the streams, which flowed clear and cold out of the hills and contained shady pools where trout lay. So it had been from the days many years ago when the first settlers raised their houses, sank their wells, and built their barns.

Then a strange blight crept over the area and everything began to change.   3
Some evil spell had settled on the community: mysterious maladies swept the flocks of chickens; the cattle and sheep sickened and died. Everywhere was a shadow of death. The farmers spoke of much illness among their families. In the town the doctors had become more and more puzzled by new kinds of sickness appearing among their patients. There had been several sudden and unexplained deaths, not only among adults but even among children, who would be stricken suddenly while at play and die within a few hours.

There was a strange stillness. The birds, for example—where had they   4
gone? Many people spoke of them, puzzled and disturbed. The feeding stations in the backyards were deserted. The few birds seen anywhere were moribund; they trembled violently and could not fly. It was a spring without voices. On the mornings that had once throbbed with the dawn chorus of robins, catbirds, doves, jays, wrens, and scores of other bird voices there was now no sound; only silence lay over the fields and woods and marsh.

On the farms the hens brooded, but no chicks hatched. The farmers   5
complained that they were unable to raise any pigs—the litters were small and the young survived only a few days. The apple trees were coming into bloom but no bees droned among the blossoms, so there was no pollination and there would be no fruit.

The roadsides, once so attractive, were now lined with browned and   6
withered vegetation as though swept by fire. These, too, were silent, deserted by all living things. Even the streams were now lifeless. Anglers no longer visited them, for all the fish had died.

In the gutters under the eaves and between the shingles of the roofs, a   7
white granular powder still showed a few patches; some weeks before it had fallen like snow upon the roofs and the lawns, the fields and streams.

No witchcraft, no enemy action had silenced the rebirth of new life in   8
this stricken world. The people had done it themselves.

This town does not actually exist, but it might easily have a thousand   9
counterparts in America or elsewhere in the world. I know of no community that has experienced all the misfortunes I describe. Yet every one of these disasters has actually happened somewhere, and many real communities have already suffered a substantial number of them. A grim specter has crept upon us almost unnoticed, and this imagined tragedy may easily become a stark reality we all shall know.

Questions for Discussion

1. What are some of the examples Carson uses to describe what her imaginary American town was like before a "strange blight" attacked it?
2. What illustrations does she use in paragraph 3 to describe the effects of this blight?
3. What examples does Carson include to develop the idea that in the future we might experience "silent" springs? What are some of the natural sounds that might be lost?
4. In paragraphs 2 and 4, Carson mentions the names of several kinds of plants and birds. Would these paragraphs have been as effective had she not specified these names and simply let us imagine the kinds of plants and animals she is referring to?
5. In addition to silencing the beautiful sounds of spring, environmental pollution will result in a number of other tragic consequences. Which ones does Carson mention in this selection?
6. What do you think the "white granular powder" mentioned in paragraph 7 might be? Should Carson have given it a name?

Suggestions for Journal Entries

1. What other sounds might we not hear if we allowed pollution to destroy our natural environment? Name and describe a few of these.
2. We experience environmental pollution every day of our lives, and we often see its devastating results quite plainly. Pick a form of environmental pollution (air, ground, water, noise) that you find most offensive, and list a few examples of its destructive effects.
3. What has your community done to fight pollution, and what should be done to continue the fight? List a few examples.

Electrical Appliances

Carol Biederstadt

Carol Biederstadt majored in history at Middlesex County College and Rutgers University in central New Jersey. "Electrical Appliances," which she wrote for a freshman composition class, discusses a number of gadgets that were familiar, if unnecessary, items in the Biederstadt household. Her essay reminds us of the importance of relying on our own experiences and observations as sources of information for all types of writing, including illustration.

Looking Ahead

1. In many respects this selection is organized like a descriptive essay, for Biederstadt tells us a great deal about her home as she points out examples of useless gadgets her family has accumulated over the years.
2. One reason this essay is so interesting and effective is that Biederstadt makes a point of including numerous concrete and specific details. Another is that she uses irony to poke fun at herself. As you probably know, irony is an often humorous device that allows you to communicate an idea by saying or writing the very opposite of what you mean.

Vocabulary

capitalizing on Taking advantage of, making money from.
excessive Too many.

Lately I have been noticing how many electrical appliances there are on 1
the market. It seems to me that there are more now than there were a few years ago. I'm not really sure why this is so but I do have a few ideas. The first reason is that Americans are just too lazy to do things manually anymore. For every little odd job we once had to do, there is now a mechanical "gadget" to do the job for us. The second reason is that appliance companies like General Electric, Norelco, Whirlpool and Toro are capitalizing on the people's laziness and are just trying to make more money.

With all of these electrical appliances around for me to use, I wonder 2
how I would have survived fifty years ago. How would I have cleaned my floor, for example? I guess I could have used one of those things called a "broom," which I rarely see any more. We have one for sweeping the driveway, but I can't remember ever seeing it used anywhere else. And how would I have gotten the dirt out of my car without my "car-vac"? A whisk brush? What's that?

The kitchen is just one of the rooms in our house that has an excessive 3
number of unnecessary electrical appliances. Take the electric can opener, for example. Personally, I think it's easier to use a hand can opener, but the rest of my family seems to like it. I often see them use it, unlike the blender that sits next to it on the counter. I can't remember the last time I saw anyone use that gadget. It's been there for years and collects dust. Luckily for me, we do not own a food processor, yogurt maker, or milkshake machine. Hopefully, we never will own any of them. They would just be more things for me to dust. We do have an electric popcorn popper, but that's a necessity, isn't it?

The garage certainly has the greatest number of unnecessary appliances. 4
There's something in there for every kind of outdoor job I can think of: roto-tiller, snow blower, car vacuum, hedge clipper, and probably more that I have

forgotten. It seems almost ridiculous to have all of those tools, and I think that I would probably feel embarrassed to use most of them. I'd rather rake leaves than hold that leaf blower. I'd also rather get down on my hands and knees to clip weeds than use the electric weed trimmer. However, it is obvious that my father doesn't feel the same way that I do about these things. Maybe he thinks it's fun to buy a new gadget and then come home and try it out.

I'm not trying to say that I don't depend on electrical appliances; I cer-   5
tainly do. I don't know what I would do without my hair dryer! However, I do think that a lot of modern appliances aren't needed and that people may becoming even lazier by using them. Maybe we'll have a catastrophic electric failure some day and find out just how much we really have been depending on our appliances!

Questions for Discussion

1. What is Biederstadt's central idea?
2. Why, according to Biederstadt, are we becoming more and more dependent on electrical gadgets? Why does she mention such companies as General Electric and Norelco by name?
3. What examples of "unnecessary" appliances has the author found in her kitchen? In her garage?
4. What does Biederstadt have against electric leaf blowers and weed trimmers? Why does she prefer their manual versions?
5. What appliances does Biederstadt use regularly?
6. Where does she use irony and humor to help make her writing more interesting?

Suggestions for Journal Entries

1. Look around your bedroom, kitchen, garage, attic, basement, or storage closet. Do you find examples of the kinds of gadgets that Biederstadt is talking about in this essay? Describe a few of these.
2. The author suggests that her father "thinks it's fun to buy a new gadget and then come home and try it out." Do you feel the same way? If so, list some of the "gadgets" you've bought recently, and determine whether you've been able to make good use of them.
3. Are Americans "just too lazy to do things manually anymore," as Biederstadt explains in paragraph 1, or can you cite examples that might disprove this idea? Think of times when you or someone you know well did something the "old-fashioned way" instead of relying on a more modern tool or appliance to do the job.

malfunctioning treatment plants to cut back the flow of sewage. And when the Environmental Protection Agency checked 100 new sewage plants, it found 20 operating poorly at times. "It takes a lot of judgment to run these plants, but finding good operators is a nationwide problem," said Laurence D. Bory of the American Consulting Engineers Council. In an increasingly complicated area, one with the potential for causing massive pollution, the level of salaries is incredibly low, in some parts of the country falling under $10,000 a year. It's not surprising that a study conducted for the Water Pollution Control Federation shows operators often lack the experience and training to understand how the plants operate. "Operators are no longer people who should be thought of as coming to work in T-shirts," says Bill Parish of Maryland's sewage plant compliance section. "They need mechanical engineering and biological backgrounds."

Even the family automobile is becoming too complicated for most of us   8 to fix. "There is already a competency crunch among the nation's 525,000 automechanics," says the president of the National Institute for Automotive Service Excellence, which certifies mechanics. "We may already have passed the day when an individual could work on his own car," asserts John Betti, a Ford vice president.

What's going to happen when we get artificial hearts? Unless we begin   9 to fill the need for skilled technicians, we will be forced to abandon much of our technological infrastructure and return to older, simpler methods.

The high-tech repair problems we already face are testimony to the need 10 for mechanically skilled engineers, technicians, and repair people. All of these are good occupational bets for the next twenty years. But better incentives will have to be created to attract and develop the skills needed to keep our technology viable.

Questions for Discussion

1. What is the major reason behind our inability to maintain our buses, airplanes, power plants, and other high-tech machinery today?
2. Why has the number of qualified workers in the nuclear power industry not kept pace with the demand?
3. What does Naisbitt believe we must do to attract qualified people "to keep our technology viable" (paragraph 10)?
4. What is he driving at when he suggests that we might "be forced to abandon much of our technological infrastructure" (paragraph 9)?
5. As you know, many of Naisbitt's illustrations come in the form of anecdotes. Identify two or three that you find especially interesting or startling.
6. What other illustrations do you find in this selection?

Suggestions for Journal Entries

1. Naisbitt talks about the need for special training in order to operate and maintain much of the high-tech equipment now in use. What special training courses in the technologies do colleges and universities offer today that they didn't offer ten or fifteen years ago? A quick glance at your college catalog might provide a few examples.
2. Pretend that, like Rip Van Winkle, you just woke up from a long sleep. Say that you've slept for about twenty years. What examples of the new technology do you see in the home, in factories, in stores, on the college campus, or elsewhere? Make a list of four or five, and describe them briefly.
3. Many of us lack important training in one or more high-tech skills that we would like to know more about, such as operating computers. Using examples, discuss how mastering a computer or any other type of high-tech equipment would benefit you. Would this skill help you at work, at home, or in school?

SUGGESTIONS FOR WRITING

1. Review the journal notes you made after reading Benjamin Duke's "The Truth Will Come Out in the Wash." Overall, do you prefer foreign-made goods to American-made goods?

    Support your opinion by writing an essay in which you discuss specific examples of American-made *or* foreign-made products. Explain why the foreign products you've decided to discuss are better designed, more reliable, and more durable than their American counterparts or vice versa. Remember that your essay won't be convincing unless it is based on facts, so use examples you know a great deal about (three or four should do it) and develop each of them in detail!

    Finally, don't forget what you've learned about writing good introductions and thesis statements, and make sure your essay is both unified and coherent.
2. In "The Truth Will Come Out in the Wash," Duke also illustrates the concept of "good service" by telling us the story of the "Hitachi man." Think about the times you've had someone repair your car, TV set, typewriter, or such. Use one of these positive or negative experiences to illustrate what you mean by "good service" or "poor service."
3. "A Fable for Tomorrow" provides a number of illustrations to describe what life will be like if we allow environmental pollution to get out of control. Create your own "Fable for Tomorrow" by using illustrations like those in Carson's essay to show how horrible life in your home town or on your campus might become if we continue to pollute our land, air, and water. Make this the central idea (thesis) of your essay.

Overall, your essay should be fictitious because you're going to describe something that *might* happen. However, your illustrations ought to be based on your own very real observations of the destructive effects of pollution. For instance, just recall the last time you stood behind a city bus that was spewing black diesel smoke into the atmosphere or the time you went to your favorite beach only to find that a sewage leak or an oil spill had turned it into an environmental nightmare.

If you responded to any of the suggestions for journal writing at the end of Carson's essay, you've probably gathered many details for this essay already.

4. In "Electrical Appliances," Carol Biederstadt suggests that Americans may be "just too lazy to do things manually anymore." What do you think? Are the modern tools and appliances we have at our disposal causing us to become lazy, or are they making life easier, more efficient, and more productive? Whatever your opinion, support it by describing a few of the modern conveniences you use around the house or on the job to save on manual labor. The journal entries you made after reading "Electrical Appliances" may provide a number of useful illustrations for this paper.

Remember that you're setting out to prove a specific opinion, which you should state in your thesis. Therefore, make sure that all the illustrations you use relate directly and appropriately to this thesis.

5. In the second item of the Suggestions for Journal Entries after Naisbitt's "Needed: High-Tech Skills," you were asked to pretend that, like Rip Van Winkle, you have just awakened from a long sleep and are amazed at how greatly technology has changed since you started your long snooze.

Extend this journal entry into an essay that explains at least three of these changes in detail. For the purposes of this assignment, pretend you were asleep for 20 years. Discuss examples of new technology you've seen in the home, in factories, in stores, on the campus, or elsewhere!

6. Take any *simple* idea (or statement of fact) that you know a great deal about. Then, in a well-developed essay of about four or five paragraphs, try to prove the idea to your readers by using examples. In your thesis, state the idea clearly; for instance:

Winters in _____ can be *treacherous*.
The hurricane that smashed into our town at the end of last summer *devastated* our community.
A student's life is *hectic*.
Doing your own *sewing* (or *carpentry, plumbing, car maintenance, painting, typing*, etc.) can save you a lot of money.
Casual sex can be *quite harmful* to your health.

Notice that the important words above are shown in italics. Make sure to identify the important word or phrase in your thesis before you begin choosing examples to illustrate it. Doing so will help you focus your examples on a specific and well-defined idea, thereby making your essay unified and well developed.

Chapter 14

Comparison and Contrast

Comparison and contrast are methods of organizing and developing ideas by pointing out similarities and differences between subjects.

A comparison essay begins by identifying similarities between subjects that on the *surface* appear to be quite different; for instance, Tom Wolfe's "Columbus and the Moon" in this chapter compares Columbus's voyages with the U.S. space program. A contrast essay begins by identifying differences between subjects that on the *surface* appear to be very much alike; usually, these subjects belong to the same general class or are of the same type. Such is the case with the male and female shoppers in James Langley's "Watch the Cart!"

Contrast can also be used to point out the positive and negative aspects of a particular subject, be it a person, place, object, institution, experience, event, or idea. In "The Best of Times," for example, Kathleen Martin Tanskey contrasts the pros and cons of growing up in a family of nine. Other good topics for such papers might be "the pros and cons of studying in the college library" or "the advantages and disadvantages of living in a city."

One of the greatest advantages of using comparison or contrast is the simplicity with which it allows you to organize information. In fact, putting together a successful comparison or contrast essay doesn't have to be difficult if you follow either of the two standard methods of organization: point-by-point or subject-by-subject.

THE POINT-BY-POINT METHOD

Using the point-by-point method, you compare or contrast a particular aspect (or characteristic) of *both* subjects, often in the same paragraph, before moving on to the next point to be discussed in another paragraph. For example,

298

if you were demonstrating how economical your 1988 Wizbang is by contrasting it with another car, you would outline your essay like this:

- Introduction with thesis statement
  The 1988 Wizbang is far more economical to own and operate than its leading competitor.
- First point of comparison or contrast (purchase price)
  Discussion of subject A (Wizbang)
  Discussion of subject B (competitor)
- Second point of comparison or contrast (maintenance costs)
  Discussion of subject A (Wizbang)
  Discussion of subject B (competitor)
- Third point of comparison or contrast (fuel efficiency)
  Discussion of subject A (Wizbang)
  Discussion of subject B (competitor)
- Conclusion

THE SUBJECT-BY-SUBJECT METHOD

Using the subject-by-subject method, you discuss *one* subject completely before going on to compare or contrast it with another subject in the second half of the essay. For example, you would outline the essay about the Wizbang and its competitor like this:

- Introduction with thesis statement
  The 1988 Wizbang is far more economical to own and operate than its leading competitor.
- Discussion of subject A (Wizbang)
  First point of comparison or contrast (purchase price)
  Second point of comparison or contrast (maintenance costs)
  Third point of comparison or contrast (fuel efficiency)
- Discussion of subject B (competitor)
  First point of comparison or contrast (purchase price)
  Second point of comparison or contrast (maintenance costs)
  Third point of comparison or contrast (fuel efficiency)
- Conclusion

The subject-by-subject method of organization works quite well with shorter essays. However, for longer essays or essays in which many different aspects or characteristics are being discussed, the point-by-point method is usually more useful. It allows readers to digest a large body of information bit by bit and to compare or contrast a great many ideas one at a time. As such, it eliminates the risk that readers will forget what you said in the first half of your essay before they finish the second half! Tom Wolfe's "Columbus and the Moon" is a good example of this pattern of development.

Comparing and contrasting are powerful tools for discovering ideas and developing them effectively. In fact, the very act of pointing out similarities and differences may lead to important discoveries about your subjects that will make your writing richer in detail and more interesting.

The Best of Times

Kathleen Martin Tanskey

A New Jersey housewife and mother, Tanskey began college after the youngest of her children entered kindergarten. In addition to pursuing her studies full-time, she works with her husband in an importing business.

The title of this selection is from the opening of Charles Dickens's *A Tale of Two Cities*. Tanskey wrote it in response to an assignment that asked her to describe a stage in her life and to explain why it was both "the best of times" and "the worst of times."

Looking Ahead

1. This is a contrast essay that uses the point-by-point method. After her introduction, Tanskey devotes one paragraph to each of several important aspects (or points) about her childhood. She discusses each aspect in terms of both its advantages and disadvantages.
2. Although she discusses both the pros and cons of growing up in a large family, Tanskey makes it clear from the start that she cherishes her memories of childhood. Look for her thesis in paragraph 1.

Vocabulary

reflect on   Think about.

When I reflect on the phrase "It was the best of times, it was the worst 1 of times," I can only think of my childhood. The thought of nine people, eight of them women, living in a four-room apartment, with one bathroom, is beyond my comprehension at this stage of my life—four people living in a nine room house, two full bathrooms, etc. However, if I sit very still and listen carefully, I can hear the laughter of days gone by, and if I allow my senses their full freedom, I can almost feel the warmth and love and smell the smells that are all so much a part of whom I am today.

I can remember times when I didn't want to kneel in church for fear that 2 someone behind me would see the holes in the bottom of my shoes, yet I can also remember "flapping" the soles of my shoes, which had come loose, to some tune as I walked down the street. Another thing I remember is that my socks were never whole. They always had a heel or a toe sticking out, and sometimes they didn't match exactly, but they were always the same color because we wore only navy blue socks to school.

With seven girls going to the same school, there were plenty of uniforms 3 and blouses to hand down, but they were in very poor condition by the time

they reached me, for I was the youngest. On the brighter side, I escaped the
hand-me-downs of everyday clothes because I was a twin, and we dressed
exactly alike until we were teenagers. Now that I think of it, that was probably
the reason we chose to dress alike for so long.

    Needless to say, space was at a premium at our house. Everyone slept   4
with someone. In fact, that is the reason I give for being so short; I never
had enough room to grow. Each night we would get our clothes ready for
the next day, and each person had a kitchen chair on which to lay her clean,
pressed clothes. This avoided a lot of running around and looking for things
in the morning, and it is the key factor for my being the organized person
I am today.

    I recall an instance when one morning a bra was missing from one of the   5
chairs. Everyone's possessions were checked and cleared, but the lost item did
not turn up. That evening, however, the case was solved by my father. He had
sat on a chair, "the" chair in this case, and the bra had gotten hooked onto
the back of his trousers. He left the house with it dangling from behind.
Luckily someone on the bus told him that he had a woman's undergarment
attached to his trousers; he removed the bra, put it into his pocket, and brought
it home.

    What a wonderful man he was. I tell this story over and over, and I   6
laugh every time, especially at the fact that he brought the bra home!

Questions for Discussion

1. What is Tanskey's thesis? How would you summarize her attitude about
   growing up in a family of nine?
2. Identify a few anecdotes in "The Best of Times." Which of these is the
   most fully developed?
3. According to Tanskey, what are some of the advantages ("pros") of growing up in a large family? In other words, what was "best" about this time
   in her life?
4. What are some of the disadvantages ("cons")?
5. Why do you think Tanskey tells the story of the missing bra? Why does
   she remember this incident so fondly?

Suggestions for Journal Entries

1. "It was the best of times, it was the worst of times" can be applied to many
   stages in our lives. In a paragraph or two, explain why, for you at least, the
   present is "the best of times," "the worst of times," or both.
2. All of us go through difficult times that require us to make sacrifices. Such
   experiences can teach us a great deal about life, and they can help us grow.
   Make a brief journal entry about a particularly difficult time in your life,
   and explain how this experience changed you for the better.

 3. Do you have a close friend whose family is much larger or smaller than yours? List a few of the advantages and disadvantages you see in your family life when contrasted with his or hers.

The Bright Child and the Dull Child

John Holt

John Holt is one of America's most famous educational theorists and critics. Many of his works, including *How Children Fail, How Children Learn,* and *Escape from Childhood,* which were published in the 1960s and 1970s, continue to be very influential today. His theory of education stresses the importance of giving students the opportunity to discover new ideas and to develop new skills by themselves. For Holt, education should be a challenging and exciting process of growth in which the student's own curiosity and desire to learn are encouraged above all else. "The Bright Child and the Dull Child" first appeared in *How Children Fail.*

Looking Ahead

1. *Moby Dick,* the novel by Herman Melville mentioned in paragraph 3, is not usually taught in the fifth grade because it is considered too difficult for young children.
2. Try to keep a record of the various differences between the bright child and the dull child. They can be found in the central ideas of each of the three paragraphs in this selection.

Vocabulary

emerge   Come forth, spring up.
inclined   Likely, liable.
maxim   A saying.
uncharted   Unmapped, unknown.

Years of watching and comparing bright children and the not-bright, or less bright, have shown that they are very different kinds of people. The bright child is curious about life and reality, eager to get in touch with it, embrace it, unite himself with it. There is no wall, no barrier between him and life. The dull child is far less curious, far less interested in what goes on and what is real, more inclined to live in worlds of fantasy. The bright child likes to experiment, to try things out. He lives by the maxim that there is more than one way to skin a cat. If he can't do something one way, he'll try another. The dull child is usually afraid to try at all. It takes a good deal of urging to get him to try even once; if that try fails, he is through.

The bright child is patient. He can tolerate uncertainty and failure, and   2 will keep trying until he gets an answer. When all his experiments fail, he can even admit to himself and others that for the time being he is not going to get an answer. This may annoy him, but he can wait. Very often, he does not want to be told how to do the problem or solve the puzzle he has struggled with, because he does not want to be cheated out of the chance to figure it out for himself in the future. Not so the dull child. He cannot stand uncertainty or failure. To him, an unanswered question is not a challenge or an opportunity, but a threat. If he can't find the answer quickly, it must be given to him, and quickly; and he must have answers for everything. Such are the children of whom a second-grade teacher once said, "But my children *like* to have questions for which there is only one answer." They did; and by a mysterious coincidence, so did she.

The bright child is willing to go ahead on the basis of incomplete understanding and information. He will take risks, sail uncharted seas, explore   3 when the landscape is dim, the landmarks few, the light poor. To give only one example, he will often read books he does not understand in the hope that after a while enough understanding will emerge to make it worthwhile to go on. In this spirit some of my fifth graders tried to read *Moby Dick*. But the dull child will go ahead only when he thinks he knows exactly where he stands and exactly what is ahead of him. If he does not feel he knows exactly what an experience will be like, and if it will not be exactly like other experiences he already knows, he wants no part of it. For while the bright child feels that the universe is, on the whole, a sensible, reasonable, and trustworthy place, the dull child feels that it is senseless, unpredictable, and treacherous. He feels that he can never tell what may happen, particularly in a new situation, except that it will probably be bad.

Questions for Discussion

1. What is Holt's thesis?
2. What are the major differences between the bright child and the dull child?
3. What point is Holt illustrating when he writes in paragraph 2 that the second-grade teacher says that her students "*like* to have questions for which there is only one answer"?
4. In paragraph 3, what does he mean when he claims that the bright child "will take risks, sail uncharted seas"? Incidentally, what figure of speech is "sail uncharted seas"?

5. Holt uses both examples and anecdotes to develop the differences between the bright child and the dull child. Identify one of each.
6. What transitional devices does he use to maintain coherence?

Suggestions for Journal Entries

1. Use the focused-freewriting method (explained in Getting Started) to jot down some notes about your favorite or least-favorite teacher. Did he or she encourage you to explore and to discover, or was he or she the kind of teacher mentioned at the end of paragraph 2?
2. Our schools are filled with many different types of students, some of whom might make good subjects for contrast. For instance, the typical "bookworm" was probably a great deal different from the "social butterfly" in your high school, while the person who ran for election to student government might have differed greatly from the athlete.

   Think of several different types of students in your high school or college, and begin to describe at least one of these pairs in a brief journal entry. Alternatively, you could write about different types of teachers, coaches, janitors, nurses, cafeteria workers, or any other type of school employee.

Watch the Cart!

James Langley

As a student majoring in English, James Langley wrote "Watch the Cart!" after having worked as a supermarket stock clerk and observing the shopping habits of people for several years. The essay contrasts approaches to shopping by discussing a number of interesting and often humorous differences between the ways that men and women buy groceries. "Watch the Cart!" was written while Langley was a college freshman, but it demonstrates a sensitivity for detail usually seen in the work of professional writers.

Looking Ahead

1. This essay uses the point-by-point method. As you read it, write down a list of the differences Langley describes.

2. In the introduction to Section V, you learned that writers often combine
   various methods of development to support important points. Notice how
   often Langley uses illustrations (examples) to develop contrasts between
   the male and female shoppers he discusses in "Watch the Cart!"

Vocabulary

confines Limits, boundaries.
dictate Demand, make it mandatory.
fluidly Smoothly.
havoc Ruin, confusion, wreckage.
invariably Without fail, without exception.
menace Threat, danger.
preponderance Larger number or quantity.
proficient Skillful.

There is nothing similar in the way men and women shop for groceries. 1
Believe me, I know, because I work in a major supermarket. After watching
scores of people shop for food day in and day out, I have become somewhat
of an expert on the habits of American consumers. I have noticed many things
about them, but nothing stands out more clearly than the differences between
men and women when they shop.

First of all, men never know where anything is. Despite the recent trends 2
in equality, which dictate that a man should share the domestic chores, there
is still a preponderance of women shoppers in America's grocery stores. And
these women know what they're doing. Women are exceptional food shoppers, who always know where something is. Nine times out of ten, it will be
a man who asks an employee to find a product for him. I don't know how
many guys come up to me in the course of a night to ask me where something
is, but 50% of those who do invariably return to me in five minutes still un-
aware of the product's location. Men have no sense of direction in a supermarket. It's as if they're locked up within the confines of some life-sized maze
that is impossible to solve. It has always been my contention that men who
shop should be provided with specially trained dogs to sniff out the products
they desire. It would certainly save me valuable time that is too often wasted
as I explain to some idiot for the tenth time that soup is in aisle 9.

Women, on the other hand, rarely ask for an item's location. When they 3
do, it is usually for some obscure product that only they have ever heard of
and whose name only they can pronounce. Whenever a woman asks me where
some such item is, I always tell her to go to aisle 11. Aisle 11 is the dog food
aisle. Send a man there and he'll forget what he was looking for and just buy
the dog food out of desperation. Send a woman there and she'll be back in five
minutes with the product in hand, thanking me for locating it for her. It's

really weird. I think women control supermarkets in a way that men are un-
aware of.

Another difference between men and women is that women shop at speeds   4
that would get them tickets on freeways, while men shop with all the speed
of a dead snail. A woman who's really good can get her shopping done in the
same amount of time every time she goes. A man who shops just as often will
get worse and worse every time.

The biggest difference between the sexes in regard to shopping, how-   5
ever, involves the manipulation of carts. A woman guides a cart through the
store so fluidly and effortlessly that her movements are almost poetic. Men are
an entirely different story. A man with a shopping cart is a menace to anyone
within two aisles of him. Men bounce their carts off display cases, sideswipe
their fellow patrons, and create havoc wherever they go. They have no idea
of how to control the direction of carts. To a man, a shopping cart is some sort
of crazed metal monster designed to embarrass and harass him.

Overall, then, women are far more proficient shoppers than men. Women   6
are safe and graceful, while men are dangerous and clumsy. I know these
things because I work in a supermarket. I also know these things because I
am a man.

Questions for Discussion

1. What is Langley's thesis? What central idea does he convey in contrasting
   the shopping habits of women and men?
2. According to Langley, there are three major differences between the ways
   that men and women shop for groceries. What are they?
3. Langley relies heavily on examples. One of the most effective is "Men
   bounce their carts off display cases, sideswipe their fellow patrons, and
   create havoc wherever they go" (paragraph 5). What other illustrations do
   you find in this essay?
4. One good metaphor is the description of male shoppers "locked up within
   the confines of some life-sized maze" (paragraph 2). What other examples
   of figurative language do you find in the essay? (To review figurative language, see Chapter 6.)

Suggestions for Journal Entries

1. Choose an activity common to women and men. Begin to compare or contrast the ways they go about this activity. You might want to point out
   similarities or differences between the ways they drive, act at parties, study
   for exams, do housework, shop for birthday gifts, keep physically fit, mend
   a broken heart, shop for automobiles, or get ready for a night out on the
   town.

⟨2. Langley contrasts the ways that men and women shop. Pick two other groups—adults and teenagers, for instance, or rich people and poor people—and make a few notes about the ways their shopping habits differ.

Columbus and the Moon

Tom Wolfe

Tom Wolfe is the author of *The Right Stuff* (1979), a book about the U.S. space program that was made into a major motion picture. He is also widely known as a writer of books and articles in which he demonstrates a powerful talent for social criticism. Wolfe is one of the creators of the "new journalism," a style of news reporting in which writers express personal (subjective) reactions to the events they're covering.

"Columbus and the Moon" compares Columbus's voyages with the exploration of space by the National Aeronautics and Space Administration (NASA).

Looking Ahead

1. At the end of paragraph 5, Wolfe writes that some of the spinoffs of the space program were "not a giant step for mankind." This is a humorous reference to what Neil Armstrong said when he set foot on the lunar surface in 1969: "That's one small step for a man, and one giant leap for mankind."
2. Neil Armstrong, Michael Collins, and Buzz Aldrin were on the Apollo 11 mission, which made the first landing on the moon.

Vocabulary

albeit Although, though.
appropriations Financing, money.
awed Amazed.
evangelical Religious fundamentalist.
ignominy Shame, disgrace.
lurid Racy, suggestive, strange.
psychic phenomena Extrasensory objects or events.
quest A search.
testy Irritable.
traumatized Shocked, emotionally confused.

The National Aeronautics and Space Administration's moon landing 10   1
years ago today was a Government project, but then so was Columbus's voyage to America in 1492. The Government, in Columbus's case, was the Spanish Court of Ferdinand and Isabella. Spain was engaged in a sea race with
Portugal in much the same way that the United States would be caught up in
a space race with the Soviet Union four and a half centuries later.

The race in 1492 was to create the first shipping lane to Asia. The Por-   2
tuguese expeditions had always sailed east, around the southern tip of Africa.
Columbus decided to head due west, across open ocean, a scheme that was
feasible only thanks to a recent invention—the magnetic ship's compass. Until then ships had stayed close to the great land masses even for the longest
voyages. Likewise, it was only thanks to an invention of the 1940's and early
1950's, the high-speed electronic computer, that NASA would even consider
propelling astronauts out of the Earth's orbit and toward the moon.

Both NASA and Columbus made not one but a series of voyages. NASA   3
landed men on six different parts of the moon. Columbus made four voyages
to different parts of what he remained convinced was the east coast of Asia.
As a result both NASA and Columbus had to keep coming back to the Government with their hands out, pleading for refinancing. In each case the reply
of the Government became, after a few years: "This is all very impressive, but
what earthly good is it to anyone back home?"

Columbus was reduced to making the most desperate claims. When he   4
first reached land in 1492 at San Salvador, off Cuba, he expected to find gold,
or at least spices. The Arawak Indians were awed by the strangers and their
ships, which they believed had descended from the sky, and they presented
them with their most prized possessions, live parrots and balls of cotton. Columbus soon set them digging for gold, which didn't exist. So he brought
back reports of fabulous riches in the form of manpower; which is to say,
slaves. He was not speaking of the Arawaks, however. With the exception of
criminals and prisoners of war, he was supposed to civilize all natives and
convert them to Christianity. He was talking about the Carib Indians, who
were cannibals and therefore qualified as criminals. The Caribs would fight
down to the last unbroken bone rather than endure captivity, and few ever
survived the voyages back to Spain. By the end of Columbus's second voyage,
in 1496, the Government was becoming testy. A great deal of wealth was
going into voyages to Asia, and very little was coming back. Columbus made
his men swear to return to Spain saying that they had not only reached the
Asian mainland, they had heard Japanese spoken.

Likewise by the early 1970's, it was clear that the moon was in economic   5
terms pretty much what it looked like from Earth, a gray rock. NASA, in the
quest for appropriations, was reduced to publicizing the "spinoffs" of the
space program. These included Teflon-coated frying pans, a ballpoint pen
that would write in a weightless environment, and a computerized biosensor

system that would enable doctors to treat heart patients without making house calls. On the whole, not a giant step for mankind.

In 1493, after his first voyage, Columbus had ridden through Barcelona at the side of King Ferdinand in the position once occupied by Ferdinand's late son, Juan. By 1500, the bad-mouthing of Columbus had reached the point where he was put in chains at the conclusion of his third voyage and returned to Spain in disgrace. NASA suffered no such ignominy, of course, but by July 20, 1974, the fifth anniversary of the landing of Apollo 11, things were grim enough. The public had become gloriously bored by space exploration. The fifth anniversary celebration consisted mainly of about 200 souls, mostly NASA people, sitting on folding chairs underneath a camp meeting canopy on the marble prairie outside the old Smithsonian Air Museum in Washington listening to speeches by Neil Armstrong, Michael Collins, and Buzz Aldrin and watching the caloric waves ripple. 6

Extraordinary rumors had begun to circulate about the astronauts. The most lurid said that trips to the moon, and even into earth orbit, had so traumatized the men, they had fallen victim to religious and spiritualist manias or plain madness. (Of the total 73 astronauts chosen, one, Aldrin, is known to have suffered from depression, rooted, as his own memoir makes clear, in matters that had nothing to do with space flight. Two teamed up in an evangelical organization, and one set up a foundation for the scientific study of psychic phenomena—interests the three of them had developed long before they flew in space.) The NASA budget, meanwhile, had been reduced to the light-bill level. 7

Columbus died in 1509, nearly broke and stripped of most of his honors as Spain's Admiral of the Ocean, a title he preferred. It was only later that history began to look upon him not as an adventurer who had tried and failed to bring home gold—but as a man with a supernatural sense of destiny, whose true glory was his willingness to plunge into the unknown, including the remotest parts of the universe he could hope to reach. 8

NASA still lives, albeit in reduced circumstances, and whether or not history will treat NASA like the admiral is hard to say. 9

The idea that the exploration of the rest of the universe is its own reward is not very popular, and NASA is forced to keep talking about things such as bigger communications satellites that will enable live television transmission of European soccer games at a fraction of the current cost. Such notions as "building a bridge to the stars for mankind" do not light up the sky today—but may yet. 10

Questions for Discussion

1. What is the central idea of this essay?
2. What are some of the similarities between Columbus's voyages and NASA's space program that Wolfe identifies?

3. Wolfe uses anecdotes about Columbus and about the space program to help explain the similarities between the two. Which anecdotes show that both Columbus and NASA had trouble with finances? Which explain the loss of popularity that both suffered?
4. In what way were Columbus's "desperate claims" about the new world (paragraph 4) like NASA's publicizing the "'spinoffs' of the space program" (paragraph 5)? What were some of these spinoffs?
5. How did Columbus's career end? What does Wolfe predict for NASA?
6. What transitional words and expressions does Wolfe use to keep his essay coherent and easy to read?

Suggestions for Journal Entries

1. One important use of comparison is to let readers discover startling new things about familiar subjects. List a few facts and ideas that this essay taught you about the space program. Then mention a few things it taught you about Columbus.
2. Wolfe's essay compares two great programs of exploration from two very different time periods. Jot down some notes about how people from different centuries have coped with the same problems or accomplished the same tasks.

     For example, list similarities between the ways you celebrate a traditional holiday (Thanksgiving, Christmas, Chanukah, the Fourth of July) and the way your grandparents did. Or consider how people now and long ago have coped with the same type of misfortune (the death of a loved one, the loss of a job) or have marked important events in their lives such as marriage, the birth of a child, or the purchase of a home.

SUGGESTIONS FOR WRITING

1. Review the journal entries you made after reading Kathleen Tanskey's "The Best of Times," earlier in this chapter. Then pick a period in your life that you can call both "the best of times" and "the worst of times." Write an essay that explains what was positive and what was negative about this period. Like Tanskey, consider using the first line of *A Tale of Two Cities* in your introduction; you might even want to make it your thesis.
2. Item 2 of the Suggestions for Journal Entries following Holt's "The Bright Child and the Dull Child" mentions that many of the people you have met in high school and college might make good subjects for contrast. If you responded to this item, you've probably begun describing two very different types of students or school employees in your journal.

     Continue listing characteristics that will help contrast these two types in detail. Then, turn your journal entry into a full-length essay. Start with a thesis statement that sums up the differences you see in these kinds of individuals. You might write:

> While the "dedicated scholar" works late into the night and on weekends, does extra reading in the library, and compares notes with her classmates, the "partier" spends most of her time talking on the phone with friends, watching television, and getting ready for her next date!

Organize the information you have collected according to the subject-by-subject method, which is explained in the introduction to this chapter.

3. If you responded to item 1 in the Suggestions for Journal Entries after "Watch the Cart!" by James Langley, you have probably listed a number of similarities or differences between the ways that women and men pursue a specific activity. Expand your notes into a fully developed essay.

   If you did not respond to this suggestion, consider the following as the kinds of topics you might want to explore in an essay that contrasts the behavior of men and women:

   - How men and women shop for birthday gifts for friends, relatives, and loved ones
   - What men and women do to keep physically fit
   - What men and women do to mend a broken heart
   - How men and women shop for automobiles
   - How men and women get ready for a night out on the town.
   Make sure to start off with a clear thesis statement in your introductory paragraph and to use either the point-by-point or the subject-by-subject method of organization that you read about earlier in this chapter.

4. In "Columbus and the Moon," Tom Wolfe drew similarities between the discovery of the New World and NASA's exploration of outer space. Think about similarities between the way people from different times have:

   - Celebrated an important holiday (Christmas, Chanukah, Thanksgiving);
   - Coped with the same types of misfortune (the death of a loved one, the loss of a job); or
   - Marked the same major events in their lives (marriage, the birth of a child, the purchase of a home).
   Next, write a full-length essay explaining these similarities in detail. Make sure to write an effective thesis for your comparison essay and to arrange your details by using either of the methods of organization discussed in the introduction to this chapter. As with other assignments, you may have already begun gathering details in your journal, so don't forget to review the notes you made after reading "Columbus and the Moon."

5. Think about what your hometown, neighborhood, or street looked like when you were a child and what it looks like now. Decide whether it has changed for the better or the worse, and describe the significant changes in great detail. In your thesis statement, clearly indicate whether you approve or disapprove of these changes; for instance, in your introductory paragraph you might say, "What's happened to the downtown area in the last ten years has convinced me that even the most rundown urban center can be rehabilitated" or "What's happened to Elm Street in recent years has made me a lifelong opponent of urban renewal."

Chapter 15

Process Analysis

Like illustration and comparison/contrast, process analysis is a way to explain or develop an idea. You can use process analysis to show how something works or how it happens. It can also come in handy when you want to give your readers instructions about how to complete a task. Process explanations are organized in chronological order, much like narrative essays and short stories. However, narration explains *what* happened. Process analysis explains *how* something happened (or happens) or *how* something is to be done.

You would be explaining a process if you wrote an essay on how rain clouds form, how an electric light bulb works, how mummies were prepared, or how a mountain range evolved. Examples of such essays in this chapter are Ken Kohler's "How I Came Out to My Parents," and Hendrik Van Loon's "The Setting of the Stage."

Another purpose of process analysis is to show readers how to do something, such as how to change a tire, keep a journal, hang wallpaper, or quit smoking. In this chapter, essays that instruct readers in a specific task are Florence Pettit's "Sharpening Your Jackknife" and Triena Milden's "So You Want to Flunk Out of College."

The thesis in a process-analysis essay is usually a statement of purpose; that is, it explains why the process is important, why it has occurred, or why it should be done. For instance, if you're explaining how to change the oil in a car, you might state that changing oil regularly is the best way to extend the engine's life. In addition to a statement of purpose, writers often begin with a summary or broad overview of the process so that readers can better understand how each detailed step relates to the whole procedure and its end result.

Clarity is essential in process analysis. You must explain the various steps in your process specifically and carefully enough that even readers who are unfamiliar with the subject will be able to follow each step easily. To be clear and to maintain your readers' interest, keep the following in mind:

314

1. *Use clear, simple language* Use words that your readers will have no trouble understanding. If you *must* use terms your readers are not familiar with, provide a brief definition or description. Depending on how much your readers know about how to change a tire, for example, you might have to describe what a lug wrench looks like before you explain how to use it.

2. *Use the clearest, simplest organization* Whenever possible, arrange the steps of your process in chronological order. In addition, use plenty of connective words and phrases between paragraphs (especially to show the passage of time); this will keep your writing coherent and easy to follow.

3. *Discuss simultaneous steps separately* If you need to explain two or more steps that occur at the same time, write about these steps in separate paragraphs. To maintain coherence between paragraphs, use connective elements like "At the same time," "Meanwhile," and "During this stage of the process."

4. *Try not to combine steps* Reserve at least one entire paragraph for each step in the process. Explaining more than one step at a time might confuse your readers and cause you to leave out important information. For instance, imagine how well you'd change a tire for the first time after reading this:

   - After having set the handbrake (and/or put the car in PARK) and jacked up the car, raising the tire about an inch off the ground, use the tapered end of the lug wrench to remove the hubcap, and place the hubcap nearby; it will come in handy.
   - Next, apply the wrench to the lugs and remove them by turning the wrench counterclockwise.

These instructions are much easier to follow and more complete when arranged in separate, detailed steps:

   - First, apply the handbrake. If your car has an automatic transmission, also put it in PARK.
   - Next, jack up the car high enough that the flat tire is about one inch off the ground.
   - Then use the tapered end of the lug wrench to pry off the hubcap (the wheel cover).
   - After you have pried the hubcap off the wheel, place the hubcap nearby on the ground. You will be using it like a bowl to hold the *lugs*, the nuts that are fastened to the bolts and hold the wheel in place.
   - Next, place the socket (the open end) of the lug wrench over any one of the lugs, and loosen the lug slightly by turning the wrench counterclockwise.
   - In the same manner, loosen all the other lugs.
   - Continue turning each lug by hand until you have removed them all. As you remove each one, place it in the hubcap.

X 5. *Give all the necessary information* Always provide enough information to develop each step in the process adequately, and don't forget the small, important details. For instance, if you're explaining how to change the oil in a car, remember to tell your readers to wait for the engine to cool off before loosening the oil-pan nut; otherwise, the oil could severely burn their hands.

6. *Use the right verb tense* If you're explaining a recurring process (one that happens over and over again), use the present tense. In writing about how your student government works, for instance, say that "the representatives *are elected* by fellow students and *meet* together every Friday afternoon." But if you're writing about a process that is over and done with, such as how one individual ran for election, use the past tense.

7. *Use direct commands* When giving instructions, make each step clear and brief by simply telling the reader to do it (that is, by using the imperative mood). For example, don't say, "The first thing to do is to apply the handbrake." Instead, be more direct: "First, apply the handbrake."

Enjoy the four selections that follow. They are well written and should provide you with effective examples of the techniques found in writing that makes good use of process analysis.

Sharpening Your Jackknife or Pocketknife

Florence H. Pettit

Noted for her clear and engaging style, Florence Pettit is the author of a number of books for young readers. "Sharpening Your Jackknife or Pocketknife" is from *How to Make Whirligigs and Whimmy Diddles and Other American Folkcraft Objects.* This fascinating book explains how to make replicas of dolls, toys, blankets, and other objects used by American Indians and Eskimos as well as by early European settlers in this hemisphere.

"Sharpening Your Jackknife or Pocketknife" is typical of the writting found in the best technical or maintenance manuals. It is prose that has a clear and practical purpose and that remains direct and easy to follow throughout.

Looking Ahead

1. In her third sentence, Pettit mentions "gouges and chisels." These are common woodworking tools.
2. When giving instructions, it is important to mention the tools, supplies, and materials the reader will need to complete the process. As you read this essay, make a list (perhaps in your journal) of the things required for sharpening a knife.

Vocabulary

burr   A rough spot that sticks up from the sharpened surface.

oval   An egg shape.

strop   A leather strap used for sharpening.

If you have never done any whittling or wood carving before, the first   1
skill to learn is how to sharpen your knife. You may be surprised to learn that even a brand-new knife needs sharpening. Knives are never sold honed (finely sharpened), although some gouges and chisels are. It is essential to learn the firm stroke on the stone that will keep your blades sharp. The sharpening stone must be fixed in place on the table, so that it will not move around. You can do this by placing a piece of rubber inner tube or a thin piece of foam rubber under it. Or you can tack four strips of wood, if you have a rough worktable, to frame the stone and hold it in place. Put a generous puddle of oil on the stone—this will soon disappear into the surface of a new stone, and you will need to keep adding more oil. Press the knife blade flat against the stone in the puddle of oil, using your index finger. Whichever way the cutting edge of the knife faces is the side of the blade that should get a little more pressure. Move the blade around three or four times in a narrow oval about

the size of your fingernail, going *counterclockwise* when the sharp edge is facing right. Now turn the blade over in the same spot on the stone, press hard, and move it around the small oval *clockwise*, with more pressure on the cutting edge that faces left. Repeat the ovals, flipping the knife blade over six or seven times, and applying lighter pressure to the blade the last two times. Wipe the blade clean with a piece of rag or tissue and rub it flat on the piece of leather strop at least twice on each side. Stroke *away* from the cutting edge to remove the little burr of metal that may be left on the blade.

Questions for Discussion

1. Writers often begin describing a process by explaining its purpose. Why, according to Pettit, is learning how to sharpen a knife important?
2. What tools and materials does Pettit tell us we'll need to sharpen a knife properly?
3. What are the major steps in the process of sharpening your jackknife or pocketknife?
4. Does Pettit use any connective words and phrases (transitions) in this selection? Identify them.
5. Like any good set of instructions, "Sharpening Your Jackknife or Pocketknife" is written in the imperative mood, using direct commands, as discussed earlier in this chapter. Find examples of the such commands in his selection.

Suggestions for Journal Entries

1. Think about a simple process that you've had to complete at home, at work, or at school. For instance, recall the steps you went through the last time you shampooed a rug, painted a wall, cooked macaroni and cheese, cut grass, set the table for dinner, waxed a floor, ironed a load of laundry, or got dressed up for an important date. Make a list of the tools, equipment, utensils, ingredients, and/or materials that you needed to complete this process.
2. Try brainstorming with a friend or two and come up with the steps most people go through to complete a common, everyday activity, such as getting dressed for school or work, preparing for bed, studying for a test, getting a child ready for school, polishing shoes, or shopping for a week's groceries. Briefly list these steps in your journal.

How I Came Out to My Parents

Kenneth Kohler

When his freshman English instructor encouraged the class to "write from the heart," Ken Kohler decided to explain how he accomplished one of the most difficult and meaningful tasks in his life—telling his parents he was gay. Kohler's recollection of the process by which he came to the decision and finally confronted his parents shows how deeply concerned he was about their feelings and about the kind of relationship he would have with them once they knew of his sexual preference.

This selection represents the best of what process writers can achieve, for it combines Kohler's emotional commitment to his subject with clear, logical analysis.

Looking Ahead

1. Like other process essays, "How I Came Out to My Parents" is organized as a narrative. But this is not just another story. What is really important here is not *what* happened, but *how* it happened—the agony Kohler endured to tell his family about his homosexuality.
2. This selection is divided into two sections. The first explains what Kohler went through to decide that "coming out" was the right thing to do. The second describes the revelation itself.

Vocabulary

acknowledged   Admitted.
acutely   Greatly, sharply.
alienation   A state of loneliness, exclusion.

Being a minority within your own family can be a source of conflict. I   1
had always known that I was different from my brother and my sister. My parents, too, may have sensed the difference, but they never acknowledged it to me. For many years, I had struggled with the idea of letting my parents know how different I was from my older brother. I was gay and didn't know how they would react if they ever found out.

My struggle to "come out of the closet" grew out of several needs. First,   2
I had a need to be closer to my parents and to share my life with them. Second, I had a need to be honest with them about who I really was. And third, I needed to let them know that there was someone special in my life. By coming out to my parents, I would risk alienation and rejection for the hope that they would gain a little more understanding of the man whom they called their son.

Rejection by my parents was my greatest fear. Almost every child wants   3
to be loved, and I was no different. At the time, I had friends who had not
spoken to their families for years after telling them that they were gay. Their
parents could not understand how their child could be a "fag" or a "dyke."
Friends also told me stories of the violent reactions that their families had had
to the news. One of them told me that his father chased him around the house
with a butcher knife after hearing that he was gay.

I had no idea how my parents might react when I came out to them. I   4
knew that if my parents reacted violently or negatively it could take years to
heal the damage that would be done by their reaction. It was a chance that I
had to take. I had to risk telling them my deepest secret in an attempt to get
closer to them. It was a risk that my brother would never have to take.

I knew it was possible that none of the negative things that had hap-   5
pened to my friends would happen to me. I also knew that my parents may
have already suspected that I was gay. After all, I had been living with another
man for three years. My lover at the time had told me, "They probably already know about you, the way you swish around!" I knew he might be right,
but I was still afraid. Would my disclosure actually draw me closer to them
as I had hoped, or would it push me away? Would they still accept my lover
as they had accepted him in the past, once they knew about our real relationship? If my parents rejected me, how would I cope with the loss of their
love? These were just a few of the many questions that swept through my
thoughts as I called my mother to ask if I could come over to talk about
something very important.

My heart was racing and my palms were sweating as I stopped the car   6
in front of their house. I turned off the ignition, took a deep breath, and
stepped out of my car. "This is it," I thought. "This is what I've been thinking about doing for years." The walk to the front door had never seemed so
long. I was acutely aware of my heartbeat pounding in my ears. My breath
seemed suspended in the frigid February night air. I swallowed hard and
opened the front door.

My father was sitting in the recliner watching the television. My mother   7
was sitting on the couch folding laundry. "Hi, how are you doing?" I said,
trying to hide my nervousness. They both looked up and smiled at me. I
wondered how my news would change their feelings towards me. I then walked
over and gave each of them a hug.

I took my coat off, sat down next to my mother, and began to help her   8
fold the laundry. We talked a while about my niece and about how fast she
was growing up. While we spoke, I tried to form the words that would either
free me or enslave me. Realizing that there was only one way to say it and that
the time had finally come, I blurted out, "Mom. Dad. I've been thinking
about telling you this for some time now." I swallowed hard. "I'm not telling

you this because I want to hurt you but because I love you. Please try to understand." I paused and took a deep breath and then said those dreaded words. "I'm gay."

There was a moment of silence before my mother spoke. "Are you sure?" 9

"Yes. I've known for a long time, but I was afraid to tell you." 10

There was still no response from my father. I wondered what thoughts 11 were racing through his head. Again my mother spoke. "Are you happy?"

"Yes," I replied with hesitation. I was still not sure what would happen 12 next.

"Well," she paused, "you've always been good to us, and you've never 13 given us any problems."

"Here it comes," I thought, "the guilt trip." 14

"I guess if you're happy," she continued slowly, "then I'll try to un- 15 derstand."

A smile spread across my face as I leaned over and gave her a long, warm 16 hug. It was only then that my father piped up, "I hope you aren't sleeping with someone new every night." I assured him that I wasn't as I gave him a hug. My mother then said, "You know, it's funny. We always thought that your friend was gay, but we didn't know that you were." I tried hard to keep from laughing as I thought of my lover's previous remarks.

I was so relieved. A great burden had finally been lifted from my shoul- 17 ders. I no longer had to hide from my parents. I no longer had to change pronouns or avoid questions about whom I was dating. Although my parents took the news well and seemed to accept me, I knew that they would have to struggle with my gayness as I had done in the past. The important thing was that I knew they still loved me and that they knew I loved them.

Questions for Discussion

1. What were some of the reasons that Kohler felt a need to "come out of the closet"? What purposes would he accomplish by telling his parents that he was gay?
2. What questions and fears did Kohler have before deciding to tell his parents he was gay?
3. What steps did he take to prepare *himself* for the moment that he would tell his parents he was gay?
4. What steps did he take to prepare his *parents* for this moment? Should he have done more to get them ready?
5. In paragraph 5, how does Kohler's conversation with his lover help us understand why he made the decision to reveal his homosexuality?
6. What shows that Kohler accomplished his purpose in coming out to his parents?

Suggestions for Journal Entries

1. Recall a time when you had to tell someone something that he or she might not want to hear, such as confessing that you smashed up the family car, telling a sweetheart that your relationship was over, or informing someone that a relative or close friend died. How did you go about doing so?
2. Kohler's decision to tell his parents that he was gay came out of his need to express some very real and important emotions to them. Write about a time when you needed to express a very sincere and strong emotion to someone, and list a few of the steps that explain how you did it.

So You Want to Flunk Out of College

Triena Milden

This selection is Triena Milden's tongue-in-cheek response to an English assignment that required her to explain various rules or procedures that first-year students might follow to be successful in college. Milden saw this as an opportunity to create a "teaching tool" for herself and her classmates. However, she knew that no one would take her advice if she treated the subject seriously and began "preaching."

That's why she decided on an ironic approach. "I thought about all of the things I'd have to do to get good grades," explained Milden, "and then I simply reversed them."

Looking Ahead

1. Milden isolates each step in the process of flunking out of college in a paragraph of its own. Nonetheless, the essay remains coherent because she uses connective words and phrases to create effective transitions between paragraphs.
2. As you've learned, writers of process analysis use the imperative mood (direct commands) to direct or instruct their readers to do something. For instance, Milden says, "never raise your hand" (paragraph 3). Find other examples of the imperative mood in her essay.

Vocabulary

conveys Communicates.
detrimental Harmful, injurious.
ultimate Final, most important.

Flunking out of college is a relatively easy task. It requires little effort   1
and might even be considered fun. Though it is hard to imagine why anyone
would purposely try to flunk out of college, many people accomplish this task
easily. In fact, whatever the reason one might want to flunk out of college, the
process is quite simple.

First, do not show up for classes very often. It is important, however,   2
to show up occasionally to find out when tests will be scheduled; the importance of this will become apparent later in this essay.

When in class, never raise your hand to ask questions and never vol-   3
unteer any answers to the teacher's questions. If the teacher calls on you,
either answer incorrectly or say "I don't know." Be sure your tone of voice
conveys your lack of interest.

Another thing to avoid is homework. There are two reasons for this.   4
First and most important, completing homework assignments only reinforces
information learned earlier, thereby contributing to higher test scores. Second, although teachers credit homework as only part of the total grade, every
little bit of credit hurts. Therefore, make sure that the teacher is aware that
you are not doing your homework. You can do so by making certain that the
teacher sees you writing down the answers as the homework is discussed in
class.

The next area, tests, can be handled in two ways. They can either not   5
be taken, or they can be failed. If you do not take them, you run the risk of
receiving an "incomplete" rather than a failing grade. In order to flunk out
of college, failing grades are preferable. Therefore, make sure to take and fail
all exams. Incidentally, this is where attendance and homework can really
affect performance. Attending class and doing homework regularly can be
detrimental to obtaining poor test scores.

Since you won't know the correct answers to test questions, make sure   6
to choose those that are as absurd as possible without being obvious. Even if
you guess a few correctly, your overall grade will be an *F* as long as the ma-
jority of your answers are wrong. By the way, one sure way to receive that
cherished zero is to be caught cheating; all teachers promise a zero for this.

The same ideas pertain to any reports or term papers that you are as-   7
signed. If you fail to turn them in, you might get an "incomplete." Therefore,
it is important to hand in all papers, especially if they're poorly written. Make
sure to use poor organization, to present information in a confused manner,
and to write on the wrong topic whenever you can. The paper should be
handwritten, not typed, and barely legible. Misspellings should be plentiful
and as noticeable as possible. Smudged ink or dirty pages add a nice touch to
the finished product. Finally, try to get caught plagiarizing.

By following these few simple suggestions, you will be assured of a fail-   8
ing grade. Try not to make it too obvious that your purpose is to fail. However, if a teacher shows concern and offers help, be sure to exhibit a poor
attitude as you refuse. Should you decide to put extra effort into failing, you

may even finish at the bottom of the class. Someone has to finish last. Why not you?

Questions for Discussion

1. Except for Milden's introduction and conclusion, each paragraph identifies at least one action (or step) that a student should or should not take to flunk out of school. What are these steps?
2. What connective words and phrases does Milden use to maintain coherence between her paragraphs?
3. Each of Milden's steps in the process of flunking out relates to a central idea expressed in the essay's thesis. What is this thesis?
4. What examples of the imperative mood (direct commands) do you find in the essay?
5. What makes her essay especially effective is that Milden takes a tongue-in-cheek (ironic) approach to a serious subject. Which parts of the essay do you find most humorous?

Suggestions for Journal Entries

1. Has Milden covered her topic completely, or can you offer additional advice to those who wish to flunk out of college?
2. Taking a tongue-in-cheek approach, jot down a few suggestions to help a friend *fail* at something important. For instance, offer some advice on one of the following:
   - How to make sure that the person you're dating never wants to go out with you again
   - How to irritate a police officer who has stopped you for a traffic violation
   - How to get fired from a good job
   - How to be the most unpopular person in your neighborhood, class, dormitory, or apartment house
   - How to make sure that the set of tires you just bought will last only 5000 miles.
3. Explain how *not* to do something. For instance, list a few ways not to lose weight, not to ask for a raise, not to stop smoking, not to treat a pet, or not to impress your future in-laws.
4. If you've just made it through a strict diet, gotten a good grade on a test, quit smoking, or completed some other project successfully, list some ways to help a fellow student do the same.

The Setting of the Stage

Hendrik Van Loon

After launching a career as a journalist, Hendrik Van Loon (1882–1944) began to publish full-length studies of history, anthropology, and geography, complete with his own now-famous illustrations. Van Loon sought to make a variety of "scholarly" subjects available to the ordinary reader. His crisp, inviting style earned him a large following among people who had believed that books on history, geography, and the like were written solely for stuffy academics.

"The Setting of the Stage" is the first chapter of his best-remembered work, *The Story of Mankind* (1921).

Looking Ahead

1. Identify connectives, such as "In the beginning," "Finally," and "Then," as you read this selection.
2. Writers often preface explanations of how something occurred or how something works with a brief overview of the process and its purpose. Look for this kind of overview in Van Loon's essay.

Vocabulary

brine   Water that is very salty.
by dint of   Through, because of.
clime   Climate.
dumbly   Without the power of speech.
innumerable   Countless.
myriads   Vast numbers of.
sediments   Soil deposits, residues, settlings.
wherefore   That is why.
whither   Where.

We live under the shadow of a gigantic question mark.   1
Who are we?   2
Where do we come from?   3
Whither are we bound?   4
Slowly, but with persistent courage, we have been pushing this question   5
mark further and further towards that distant line, beyond the horizon, where we hope to find our answer.
We have not gone very far.   6
We still know very little but we have reached the point where (with a   7
fair degree of accuracy) we can guess at many things.

In this chapter I shall tell you how (according to our best belief) the 8
stage was set for the first appearance of man.

If we represent the time during which it has been possible for animal life 9
to exist upon our planet by a line of this length,

--- ⁼

then the tiny line just below indicates the age during which man (or a creature
more or less resembling man) has lived upon this earth.

Man was the last to come but the first to use his brain for the purpose of 10
conquering the forces of nature. That is the reason why we are going to study
him, rather than cats or dogs or horses or any of the other animals, who, all in
their own way, have a very interesting historical development behind them.

In the beginning, the planet upon which we live was (as far as we now 11
know) a large ball of flaming matter, a tiny cloud of smoke in the endless
ocean of space. Gradually, in the course of millions of years, the surface burned
itself out, and was covered with a thin layer of rocks. Upon these lifeless rocks
the rain descended in endless torrents, wearing out the hard granite and carrying the dust to the valleys that lay hidden between the high cliffs of the
steaming earth.

Finally the hour came when the sun broke through the clouds and saw 12
how this little planet was covered with a few small puddles which were to
develop into the mighty oceans of the eastern and western hemispheres.

Then one day the great wonder happened. What had been dead gave 13
birth to life.

The first living cell floated upon the waters of the sea.   14

For millions of years it drifted aimlessly with the currents. But during 15
all that time it was developing certain habits that it might survive more easily
upon the inhospitable earth. Some of these cells were happiest in the dark
depths of the lakes and the pools. They took root in the slimy sediments which
had been carried down from the tops of the hills and they became plants.
Others preferred to move about and they grew strange jointed legs, like scor-
pions, and began to crawl along the bottom of the sea amidst the plants and
the pale green things that looked like jellyfishes. Still others (covered with
scales) depended upon a swimming motion to go from place to place in their
search for food, and gradually they populated the ocean with myriads of fishes.

Meanwhile the plants had increased in number and they had to search 16
for new dwelling places. There was no more room for them at the bottom of
the sea. Reluctantly they left the water and made a new home in the marshes
and on the mudbanks that lay at the foot of the mountains. Twice a day the
tides of the ocean covered them with their brine. For the rest of the time, the
plants made the best of their uncomfortable situation and tried to survive in
the thin air which surrounded the surface of the planet. After centuries of
training, they learned how to live as comfortably in the air as they had done
in the water. They increased in size and became shrubs and trees and at last

they learned how to grow lovely flowers which attracted the attention of the busy big bumble-bees and the birds who carried the seeds far and wide until the whole earth had become covered with green pastures, or lay dark under the shadow of the big trees.

But some of the fishes too had begun to leave the sea, and they had 17 learned how to breathe with lungs as well as with gills. We call such creatures amphibious, which means that they are able to live with equal ease on the land and in the water. The first frog who crosses your path can tell you all about the pleasures of the double existence of the amphibian.

Once outside of the water, these animals gradually adapted themselves 18 more and more to life on land. Some became reptiles (creatures who crawl like lizards) and they shared the silence of the forests with the insects. That they might move faster through the soft soil, they improved upon their legs and their size increased until the world was populated with gigantic forms (which the handbooks of biology list under the names of Ichthyosaurus and Mega-losaurus and Brontosaurus) who grew to be thirty to forty feet long and who could have played with elephants as a full grown cat plays with her kittens.

Some of the members of this reptilian family began to live in the tops 19 of the trees, which were then often more than a hundred feet high. They no longer needed their legs for the purpose of walking, but it was necessary for them to move quickly from branch to branch. And so they changed a part of their skin into a sort of parachute, which stretched between the sides of their bodies and the small toes of their fore-feet, and gradually they covered this skinny parachute with feathers and made their tails into a steering gear and flew from tree to tree and developed into true birds.

Then a strange thing happened. All the gigantic reptiles died within a 20 short time. We do not know the reason. Perhaps it was due to a sudden change in climate. Perhaps they had grown so large that they could neither swim nor walk nor crawl, and they starved to death within sight but not within reach of the big ferns and trees. Whatever the cause, the million year old world-empire of the big reptiles was over.

The world now began to be occupied by very different creatures. They 21 were the descendants of the reptiles but they were quite unlike these because they fed their young from the "mammae" or the breasts of the mother. Where-fore modern science calls these animals "mammals." They had shed the scales of the fish. They did not adopt the feathers of the bird, but they covered their bodies with hair. The mammals however developed other habits which gave their race a great advantage over the other animals. The female of the species carried the eggs of the young inside her body until they were hatched and while all other living beings, up to that time, had left their children exposed to the dangers of cold and heat, and the attacks of wild beasts, the mammals kept their young with them for a long time and sheltered them while they were still too weak to fight their enemies. In this way the young mammals were given a much better chance to survive, because they learned many things from their mothers, as you will know if you have ever watched a cat teaching her kittens to take care of themselves and how to wash their faces and how to catch mice.

But of these mammals I need not tell you much for you know them well. 22 They surround you on all sides. They are your daily companions in the streets and in your home, and you can see your less familiar cousins behind the bars of the zoological garden.

And now we come to the parting of the ways when man suddenly leaves 23 the endless procession of dumbly living and dying creatures and begins to use his reason to shape the destiny of his race.

One mammal in particular seemed to surpass all others in its ability to 24 find food and shelter. It had learned to use its fore-feet for the purpose of holding its prey, and by dint of practice it had developed a hand-like claw. After innumerable attempts it had learned how to balance the whole of the body upon the hind legs. (This is a difficult act, which every child has to learn anew although the human race has been doing it for over a million years.)

This creature, half ape and half monkey but superior to both, became the 25 most successful hunter and could make a living in every clime. For greater safety, it usually moved about in groups. It learned how to make strange grunts to warn its young of approaching danger, and after many hundreds of thousands of years it began to use these throaty noises for the purpose of talking.

This creature, though you may hardly believe it, was your first "man- 26 like" ancestor.

Questions for Discussion

1. In the introductory paragraphs, Van Loon provides a brief overview to explain the purpose this chapter serves in *The Story of Mankind*, the book in which it appears. What is its purpose?
2. What reason does Van Loon give for focusing on man rather than on "any of the other animals" (paragraph 10)?
3. List the major steps of the process that, according to Van Loon, set the stage for the evolution of the human race. Start with the formation of the earth from a "large ball of flaming matter" (paragraph 11).
4. As with most pieces of process analysis, the information in this essay is arranged in chronological order. What verb tense does Van Loon rely on? Is it appropriate to his purpose?
5. What illustrations does Van Loon use to explain how man began "to use his reason to shape the destiny of his race" (paragraph 23)?
6. What transitional elements do you find in this essay?

Suggestions for Journal Entries

1. "The Setting of the Stage" traces the major steps in the process by which our planet evolved before the coming of the human race. Take a few min-

utes to think about the *major* steps we have taken in the last hundred years (or the last thousand years if you prefer) to make our lives more civilized. Mention what you believe are the ten most significant things we have done, invented, or developed to show that the human race is making progress.

2. Think about a natural process repeated day after day that you've observed or read about lately. List and briefly explain the *important* steps in this process. Choose any natural process, such as how the human circulatory system works, how rain clouds form, or how a bird builds its nest, but be sure to write about one you know well.

3. Van Loon identifies a number of characteristics that make humans different from other mammals. Brainstorm for a while and list a few other features or abilities that make us different from other mammals.

SUGGESTIONS FOR WRITING

1. Florence Pettit's "Sharpening Your Jackknife" is a good example of writing that explains how to do a simple but important task. If you read this selection, reread your journal notes, and try to use them as the starting point for writing an essay that explains how to complete a simple but important process.

   Be as thorough and as detailed as you can so that even someone who has no knowledge of the process you're explaining will be able to follow it easily. Like Pettit, begin with a thesis statement that explains why the process is important.

2. Ken Kohler's "How I Came Out to My Parents" explains the painful process of telling people a truth they might not want to learn. Have you ever been in such a situation? For example, have you ever had to confess that you smashed up the family car? Have you ever had to tell a sweetheart that your relationship was over? Have you ever had to inform someone that a relative or close friend died?

   If so, write an essay explaining how you went about doing what had to be done. Make sure your readers know just how difficult a process it was. Once again, try to use your journal as a starting point.

3. Triena Milden takes an ironic (tongue-in-cheek) approach to academic studies in "So You Want to Flunk Out of College." You too may be able to provide advice to help someone *fail* at something important. Write an ironic but fully developed set of instructions to this end. Address your comments to a friend or fellow student.

   Item 2 in the Suggestions for Journal Entries after Milden's essay contains a number of topics you might want to write about. In any event, check your journal for the kinds of details that will help you get started.

4. Similarly, write an essay that explains how *not* to do something, such as how not to study for an important exam, how not to do laundry, or how not to start exercising. You can find more topics in item 3 of the Sugges-

tions for Journal Entries following "So You Want to Flunk Out of College." In fact, you may have already begun gathering details for your essay if you responded to this item in your journal.

5. If you have been able to stick to a strict diet, get a good grade on a test, quit smoking, or achieve some other important personal goal, provide a few suggestions that might give a fellow student encouragement to do the same. A good thesis statement for such an essay might be: "Kicking the nicotine habit requires a great deal of will power and perseverance, but it can be done!"

6. Hendrik Van Loon's "The Setting of the Stage" describes a natural process—the Earth's evolution. One of the suggestions for journal writing that accompanies this selection asks you to think about a natural process that is repeated day after day. Write a full-length essay explaining how this process works. Begin at the beginning, and proceed chronologically (in time) to the end. Choose any natural process, but make sure to write about something you know well.

   Once again, check your journal for facts and ideas that may help you get started. Pretend you're writing to someone who knows very little about the process. As such, use as many details as you can to make your explanation as clear and as easy to follow as possible.

7. Explain a process that human beings have invented to improve their lives. For instance, take the process by which an automobile engine burns fuel to produce power, an incandescent lamp turns electrical energy into light, a washing machine cleans clothes, a lawn mower cuts grass, or a microwave oven cooks food.

GLOSSARY

abstract language   Words that represent ideas rather than things we can see, hear, smell, feel, or taste. The word "love" is abstract, but the word "kiss" is concrete because we can perceive it with one or more of our five senses. (See Chapters 5 and 6.)

allusion   An indirect reference to a person, place, thing, or idea with which the reader is familiar. Such references provide a quick way for a writer to add detail, clarify important points, or set the tone of an essay, poem, or short story. There are several effective allusions in Elsberry's "A Farewell to Arms" (Chapter 6).

analogy   A method by which a writer points out similarities between two things that, on the surface, seem quite different. Analogies are most often used to make abstract or unfamiliar ideas clearer and more concrete. Read Hamer's "The Thick and Thin of It" in Chapter 3 for examples of analogy.

anecdote   A brief, sometimes humorous story used to illustrate or develop a specific point. (See Chapters 9 and 13.)

central idea   The idea that conveys a writer's main point about a subject. It may be either stated explicitly or implied. Also known as the "main idea" or "controlling idea," it determines the kinds and amounts of detail needed in order to develop a piece of writing adequately. (See Chapter 1.)

chronological order   The arrangement of material in order of time.

coherence   The principle that writers observe in making certain that there are logical connections between the ideas and details in one sentence or paragraph and those in the next. (See Chapter 2.)

conclusion   A paragraph or series of paragraphs that ends an essay. Conclusions often restate the writer's central idea or summarize important points used to develop that idea. (See Chapter 4.)

concrete language   Words that represent material things—things we can perceive with our five senses. (See **abstract language** above, and see Chapters 5 and 6.)

coordination   A technique used to express ideas of equal importance in the same sentence. To this end, writers often use compound sentences, which are composed of two independent (main) clauses connected with a coordinating conjunction. "Four students earned scholarships, but only three accepted them" is a compound sentence. (See Chapter 7.)

details   Specific facts or pieces of information that a writer uses to develop ideas.

emphasis   The placing of stress on important ideas by controlling sentence structure through coordination, subordination, and parallelism. (See Chapter 7.)

figurative language (figures of speech)   Words or phrases that explain abstract ideas by comparing them to concrete realities the reader will recognize easily. Analogy, metaphor, simile, and personification are types of figurative language. (See Chapter 6.)

image   A verbal picture made up of sensory details. It expresses a general idea's meaning clearly and concretely. (See Chapter 5.)

introduction   A paragraph or series of paragraphs that begins an essay. It often contains a writer's central idea in the form of a thesis statement. (See Chapter 4.)

irony   A technique used by writers to communicate the very opposite of what their words mean. Irony is often used to create humor. An effective example of irony can be found in Milden's "So You Want to Flunk Out of College" in Chapter 15.

linking pronouns   Pronouns that make reference to nouns that have come before (antecedents). They are one of the ways to maintain coherence in and between paragraphs. (See Chapter 2.)

main point   The point that a writer focuses on in a thesis or topic sentence. (See Chapter 1.)

metaphor   A figure of speech that, like a simile, creates a comparison between two things in order to make the explanation of one of them clearer. Unlike a simile, a metaphor does not use "like" or "as." "The man is a pig" is a metaphor. (See Chapter 6.)

parallelism   A method to express facts and ideas of equal importance in the same sentence and thereby to give them added emphasis. Sentences that are parallel express items of equal importance in the same grammatical form. (See Chapter 7.)

personification   A figure of speech that writers use to discuss animals, plants, and inanimate objects in terms normally associated with human beings: for example, "Our neighborhoods are the *soul* of the city." (See Chapter 6.)

point of view   The perspective from which a narrative is told. Stories that use the first-person point of view are told by a narrator who is involved in the action and who uses words like "I," "me," and "we" to explain what happened. Stories that use the third-person point of view are told by a narrator who may or may not be involved in the action and who uses works like "he," "she," and "they" to explain what happened. (See Chapter 10.)

simile   A figure of speech that, like a metaphor, compares two things for the sake of clarity and emphasis. Unlike a metaphor, however, a simile uses "like" or "as." "Samantha runs like a deer" is a simile. (See Chapter 6.)

subordination   A technique used to emphasize one idea over another by expressing the more important idea in the sentence's main clause and the other in its subordinate clause. (See Chapter 7.)

thesis statement   A clear and explicit statement of an essay's central idea. It often appears in an introductory paragraph but is sometimes found later in the essay. (See Chapter 1.)

topic sentence   A clear and explicit statement of a paragraph's central idea. (See Chapter 1.)

transitions (connectives)   Words or phrases used to make clear and direct connections between sentences and paragraphs, thereby maintaining coherence. (See Chapter 2.)

unity   The principle that writers observe in making certain that all the information in an essay or paragraph relates directly to the central idea, which is often expressed in a thesis statement or topic sentence. (See Chapter 2.)

Acknowledgments

Angelou, Maya, Excerpted "The Boys" from *I Know Why the Caged Bird Sings*. Copyright © 1969. Reprinted by permission of Random House, Inc.

Aronowitz, Paul, "A Brother's Dream." Copyright 1988 by The New York Times Company. Reprinted by permission.

Baker, Russell, from *Growing Up*. Copyright 1982. Reprinted by permission of Contemporary Books, Inc.

Biederstadt, Carol, "Electrical Appliances." Reprinted by permission of the author.

Carson, Rachel, "A Fable for Tomorrow." Reprinted from *Silent Spring* by Rachel Carson. Copyright © 1962 by Rachel L. Carson. Reprinted by permission of Houghton Mifflin Company.

Ciardi, John, "Dawn Watch." Reprinted from *Manner of Speaking*. Copyright © 1972. Published by Rutgers University Press. Reprinted by permission of John Ciardi.

Cirilli, Maria, "Echoes." Reprinted by permission of the author.

Cousins, Norman, "Pain is not the Ultimate Enemy." Reprinted from *Anatomy of an Illness as Perceived by the Patient: Reflections on Healing and Regeneration*, by permission of W. W. Norton & Company, Inc. Copyright © 1979 by W. W. Norton & Company, Inc.

Cullen, Countee, "Incident," from *On These I Stand*. Copyright © 1925 by Harper & Brothers; copyright renewed 1953 by Ida M. Cullen. Reprinted by permission of GRM Associates, Inc., Agents for the Estate of Ida M. Cullen.

DeVoe, Allan, "Hibernations of the Woodchuck." Selection from "The Animals Sleep," from *Lives around Us*, by Allan DeVoe. Copyright © 1942 by Alan DeVoe. Copyright renewed © 1970 by Mary DeVoe Guinn. Reprinted by permission of Farrar, Straus and Giroux, Inc.

Dillard, Annie, "In the Jungle," from *Teaching a Stone to Talk*. Copyright 1982. Reprinted by permission of Harper & Row Publishers, Inc.

Duke, Benjamin, C., "The Truth Will Come Out in the Wash." Copyright 1986 by The New York Times Company. Reprinted by permission.

Elsberry, Richard, B., "A Farewell to Arms." Copyright 1987 by The New York Times Company. Reprinted by permission.

Frost, Robert, "The Wood-Pile," from *North of Boston*. Copyright 1930, 1939 by Holt, Rinehart and Winston, Inc. Copyright 1958 by Robert Frost. Copyright 1967 by Lesley Frost Ballantine. Reprinted from *The Poetry of Robert Frost*, edited by Edward Connery Lathem, by permission of Henry Holt and Company, Inc.

Gansberg, Martin, "38 Who Saw Murder Didn't Call the Police." Copyright 1964 by The New York Times Company. Reprinted by permission.

Harris, Sydney J., "How to Keep Air Clean." Reprinted from *For the Time Being*, by Sydney J. Harris. Copyright © 1972 by Sydney J. Harris. Copyright © 1969, 1970, 1971, 1972 by Publishers-Hall Syndicate. Reprinted by Houghton Mifflin Company.

Hayden, Robert, "Those Winter Sundays." Reprinted from *Angel of Ascent, New and Selected Poems*, by Robert Hayden, by permission of Liveright Publishing Corporation. Copyright © 1975, 1972, 1970, 1966 by Robert Hayden.

Hemingway, Ernest, "Indian Camp." Reprinted with permission of Charles Scribner's Sons, and imprint of Macmillan Publishing Company from *In Our Time*, by Ernest Hemingway. Copyright © 1925 by Charles Scribner's Sons, renewed 1953 by Ernest Hemingway.

Highet, Gilbert, "Diogenes," from "Diogenes and Alexander." Reprinted by permission from *Horizon*, Volume 5, number 4. Copyright © 1963 by American Heritage, a division of Forbes Inc. "Station," from *Talents and Geniuses*. Reprinted by permission by Curtis Brown, Ltd. Copyright 1957 by Gilbert Highet.

Hughes, Langston, "Back Home," and "Tragedy in Toluca," excerpted from *The Big Sea*, by Langston Hughes. Copyright © 1940 by Langston Hughes. Copyright renewed © 1968 by Arna Bontemps and George Houston Bass. Reprinted by permission of Farrar, Straus and Giroux, Inc.

Jackson, Shirley, "Charles." Reprinted from *The Lottery and Other Stories*. Copyright © 1948, 1949 by Shirley Jackson. Copyright renewed © 1976, 1977 by Laurence Hyman, Barry Hyman, Mrs. Sarah Webster, and Mrs. Joanne Schnurer. Reprinted by permission of Farrar, Straus and Giroux, Inc.

Jordan, Susan Britt, "Fun, Oh Boy Fun. You Could Die from It." Copyright 1979 by The New York Times Company. Reprinted by permission.

Keller, James, "Exile and Return." Reprinted by permission of the author.

Kohler, Kenneth, "How I Came Out to My Parents." Reprinted by permission of the author.

Langley, James, "Watch that Cart." Reprinted by permission of the author.

Mailer, Norman, "The Death of Benny Paret," from *The Presidential Papers*. Copyright 1963, Putnam. Reprinted by permission of the author and the author's agents, Scott Meredith Literary Agency, Inc.

Masters, Edgar Lee, "Lucinda Matlock," and "Margaret Fuller Slack." Reprinted from *Spoon River Anthology*, copyright © 1943, by permission of Ellen C. Masters.

Milden, Triena, "So You Want to Flunk Out of College." Reprinted by permission of the author.

Naisbitt, John, "Needed: High-Tech Skills." Reprinted by permission of Warner Books/ New York from *Megatrends*. Copyright © 1982 by John Naisbitt.

Osgood, Charles, "'Real' Men and Women." Reprinted from *Nothing Could Be Finer Than a Crisis That Is Minor in the Morning*, by Charles Osgood. Copyright © 1979 by CBS, Inc. Reprinted by permission of Henry Holt and Company, Inc.

Pettit, Florence, "How to Sharpen Your Jackknife or Pocketknife," from *How to Make Whirligigs and Other American Folkcraft Objects*, 1972.

Pirsig, Robert M., a selection from *Zen and the Art of Motorcycle Maintenance*. Copyright 1974 by Robert Pirsig. Reprinted by permission of William Morrow and Co., Inc.

Robinson, Edwin Arlington, "Richard Cory," from *The Children of the Night*. Copyright 1894 by Charles Scribner's Sons.

Rose, Kenneth Jon, "2001 Space Shuttle." *Travel and Leisure*, November 1979. Permission granted by author.

Sandburg, Carl, excerpted selection from *Abraham Lincoln: The Prairie Years*, Volume I, by Carl Sandburg. Copyright © 1926 by Harcourt Brace Jovanovich, Inc., and renewed 1954 by Carl Sandburg. Reprinted by permission of the publisher.

Sandburg, Carl, "Child of the Romans." Reprinted from *Chicago Poems*, by Carl Sandburg. Copyright © 1916 by Holt, Rinehart and Winston, Inc., renewed 1944 by Carl Sandburg, reprinted by permission of Harcourt Brace Jovanovich, Inc.

Schwartz, Adrienne, "The Colossus in the Kitchen." Reprinted by permission of the author.

Scott, Howard, "Vegetable Gardens are for the Birds." Copyright © 1985 by The New York Times Company. Reprinted by permission.

Sexton, Anne, "Pain for a Daughter." Reprinted from *Live or Die*, by Anne Sexton. Copyright © 1966 by Anne Sexton. Reprinted by permission of Houghton Mifflin Company.

Singer, Isaac Bashevis, "The Son from America." Reprinted from *A Crown of Feathers*. Copyright © 1970, 1971, 1972, 1973 by Isaac Bashevis Singer. Reprinted by permission of Farrar, Straus and Giroux, Inc.

Stickell, Henry, N., "Sinnit Cave." Reprinted by permission of the author.

Tanskey, Kathleen Martin, "The Best of Times." Reprinted by permission of the author.

Tierney, John, Linda Wright, and Karen Springer, from "The Search for Adam and Eve," January 11, 1988 issue of *Newsweek*, page 46.

Van Loon, Hendrik Willem, "The Setting of the Stage," is reprinted from *The Story of Mankind* by Hendrik Willem Van Loon, by permission of Liveright Publishing Corporation. Copyright © 1984 by Liveright Publishing Corporation. Copyright © 1972, 1984 by Henry B. Van Loon and Gerald W. Van Loon. Copyright © 1921, 1926 by Boni and Liveright, Inc. Copyright renewed 1948 by Helen C. Van Loon. Copyright renewed 1954 by Liveright Publishing Corporation. Copyright © 1936, 1938, 1951, 1967 by Liveright Publishing Corporation.

Volk, Patricia, "A Family of Firsts." Copyright © 1987, reprinted by permission of Patricia Volk and her agents, Raines & Raines, 71 Park Avenue, New York, NY 10016.

Welty, Eudora, "Worn Path." Copyright © 1941, 1969 by Eudora Welty. Reprinted from her volume *A Curtain of Green and Other Stories*, by permission of Harcourt Brace Jovanovich, Inc.

White, E. B., "Twins." Copyright 1948 by E. B. White, from *Poems and Sketches of E. B. White*, by E. B. White. Originally published in *The New Yorker*. Reprinted by permission of Harper & Row, Publishers, Inc.

Witt, Michael, "Gambling." Reprinted by permission of the author.

Wnorowski, Alice, "A Longing." CINDReprinted by permission of the author.

Index